Trillion
Dollar Economists

Since 1996, Bloomberg Press has published books for financial professionals, as well as books of general interest in investing, economics, current affairs, and policy affecting investors and business people. Titles are written by well-known practitioners, Bloomberg News® reporters and columnists, and other leading authorities and journalists. Bloomberg Press books have been translated into more than 20 languages.

For a list of available titles, please visit our Web site at www.wiley.com/go/bloombergpress.

Trillion Dollar Economists

*How Economists
and Their Ideas
Have Transformed Business*

Robert E. Litan

WILEY | **Bloomberg** PRESS

Published by John Wiley & Sons, Inc., Hoboken, New Jersey.
Published simultaneously in Canada.

For general information on our other products and services or for technical support, please contact our Customer Care Department within the United States at (800) 762-2974, outside the United States at (317) 572-3993 or fax (317) 572-4002.

Wiley publishes in a variety of print and electronic formats and by print-on-demand. Some material included with standard print versions of this book may not be included in e-books or in print-on-demand. If this book refers to media such as a CD or DVD that is not included in the version you purchased, you may download this material at http://booksupport.wiley.com. For more information about Wiley products, visit www.wiley.com.

Library of Congress Cataloging-in-Publication Data:
Litan, Robert E., 1950–
    Trillion dollar economists : how economists and their ideas have transformed
business / Robert E. Litan.
        pages cm
        Includes index.
        ISBN 978-1-118-78180-7 (hardback) — 1. Decision making.   2. Economists.
    3. Economics.   4. Commerce.   I. Title.
    HD30.23.L578   2014
    338.5—dc23
                                                                    2014013664

Printed in the United States of America.
10 9 8 7 6 5 4 3 2 1

Dedicated to
Dr. Michael Boyle
Johns Hopkins Medical School
and
Dr. Steven Stites
Kansas University Medical Center

Contents

Preface

M any, and possibly most, authors have a love–hate relationship with what they do. Writing every day, or trying to, can be a painful experience. Some days you have it and the words flow, and other days, your head is in a fog and you struggle to write a single sentence or paragraph.

I have had numerous jobs throughout my career where writing was not my main function, but in each one of them, writing memos, briefs, and articles was one element of what I was hired to do. I also had the good fortune through most of my working life to be employed by organizations that either paid me to write books or encouraged me to do so. And, to be honest, I have that love–hate attitude toward writing that I just described.

But not for this book; I wrote it while I was 63, at or near the culmination of my career, and every day I spent working on it was a joy. Like the swimming I look forward to each day, I couldn't wait to sit down for however long I was able to do it, and at least write a few paragraphs or, ideally, several pages.

It's not my age that explains this, but the subject matter (or matters), to be more precise. I hope that as you read the book, you can tell that I love economics and I am grateful to have a career in which I have been able to meet and occasionally work with so many outstanding, brilliant individuals. This book is kind of an ode to all of them and to the subject in general.

I got the inspiration to write it from three basic sources. First, I felt after the financial crisis that the economics profession, while somewhat justifiably criticized, was also misunderstood by many in the media and many non-economist friends. Second, for a long time I have felt that many hardheaded people in business give too little credit to economists and their ideas. Many of them, as I argue in what you are about to read, probably are not even aware of where certain ideas originated that have powered businesses quite successfully, maybe even *their* business. This book is an effort to correct these misimpressions, while ideally helping many undergraduate students and perhaps some graduate business students taking their first or intermediate-level economics course to understand why the subject matters and how it has been, and will continue to be, highly useful in the real world. This is true even as the field of economics changes and conceivably morphs into other social sciences, as I will comment on in the last chapter.

Third, although I don't know him, I want to credit Steven Leavitt, the award-winning economist at the University of Chicago, and his coauthor, Stephen Dubner, of the highly successful *Freakonomics* series, with demonstrating that there is a real market, maybe even a hunger, for books about economics in plain English. I was inspired by Leavitt's and Dubner's success and hope that this book will achieve at least some significant fraction of the attention and admiration that their books have.

No book can be completed without a lot of help from a lot of people. This work is no exception. I want to thank Rob Barnett, Barry Bosworth, Will Baumol, Patrick Driessen, George Kaufman, Richard Levine, Bruce Owen, Roger Noll, Chris Payne, Brian Rye, and Hal Varian for reviewing parts of the draft manuscript. I am indebted to my good friend Phil Auerswald for coming up with the title. I pride myself on coming up with titles for my own books and for others, but on this one Phil outdid me and for that I am grateful.

I am also grateful for the excellent initial drafting assistance in Chapters 5, 7, and 15 provided by Miguel Garrido, my close former colleague at Bloomberg Government. I also want to thank several others at Bloomberg: Dan Doctoroff, president and chief executive officer of Bloomberg, L.P., and Don Baptiste, head of Bloomberg Government, for their encouragement and support for this project, and Marialuisa Mendiola for providing research assistance. I also want to specially thank Norman Pearlstine, formerly chief content officer at Bloomberg and currently the chief content officer at Time, Inc., for reading the initial chapters of this book, and giving me his enthusiastic reaction that sustained me through the long months of drafting the rest of the book.

I also owe a deep debt of thanks to all my colleagues, some of whom are no longer with us, at the Brookings Institution, where I spent roughly two decades of my professional life, and where I am now a nonresident senior fellow. Certain of these economics super-stars inspired me to go on to graduate school to get my PhD, along with my law degree (you'll see why I did both at the beginning of the first chapter). Arthur Okun, the great economist who left us far too early, was the first to take a chance on me (on the recommenda-tion of Lawrence Klein at the University of Pennsylvania), by hiring me as his research assistant for two years. While there I was also asked to work with two other great economists who are no longer with us, Ned Gramlich and Joe Pechman, the longtime director of economic research at Brookings. I also was greatly influenced by and privileged even-to-eat-regularly-with the likes of Alice Rivlin (who has been one of my mentors throughout my professional life), George Perry, Tony Downs, Barry Bosworth, and Charles Schultze, and also with (then) young Brookings stars, including Robert Crandall, Bill Gale, Cliff Winston, and Josh Epstein. You will read short biographies of or refer-ences to many of these individuals in the course of this book, and if my long experience at Brookings makes me biased toward emphasiz-ing their influence on the profession, public policy, and indirectly on business (of which many of them may be unaware), then I plead guilty. I couldn't have been more fortunate to work with a more committed, brilliant, and compassionate group of scholars, who became (and still are) like my own family.

Finally, every good book (and I hope readers will agree with me about the adjective) benefits from excellent editing, and here too, this book is no exception. I am grateful to my editors at John Wiley & Sons, Judy Howarth and Tula Batanchiev, and everyone else at Wiley for deciding to publish and market this book.

ROBERT E. LITAN
September 2014

Chapter 1

Introduction: Economists as Innovators

Practical men, who believe themselves to be quite exempt from any intellectual influence, are usually the slaves of some defunct economist.
—John Maynard Keynes

Kids ask the best questions, like the one I am sure most economists who have children get at some point in their lives: Mom or Dad, what do you actually do? Not only have my own children asked that question, but even my mother couldn't understand why I wanted to go on after finishing college to earn a doctorate in economics (she told me to go law school instead because it would enable me to get a real job, so I went to a school that let me earn both degrees, on the theory that at a relatively young age it would be best to diversify). One reason I have written this book is to tell you why my instincts about economics were right, not just for me but many others in the very practical world of business and policy making.

I suspect most everyone who is not an economist thinks economists are trained to be soothsayers, predictors of how the economy will perform over coming months, and perhaps a year or two, or longer:

1

to tell us how much inflation or unemployment will rise or fall, and how fast total output (GDP or gross domestic product) will or will not grow. Perhaps even more important, many non-economists may believe that economists can tell them what's going to happen to the stock market, and maybe their particular stocks, and to the prices of their houses. Some highly respected economists have essentially agreed. As the late Nobel laureates Milton Friedman and Lawrence Klein have argued, the ultimate test of the worth of economics is the accuracy of its predictions.[1]

If that is the case, then the financial crisis of 2007 to 2008 and the subsequent Great Recession and slow recovery since have probably changed a lot of minds about economists, but not for the better. Few economists warned of these events in advance or in time for most people to sell their stocks or not to borrow so much against their houses, or buy them at all before housing prices in many areas began to fall in 2006. If instead many economists had issued their warnings in time, maybe policy makers in the United States and elsewhere would have clamped down on extending easy credit to many U.S. homeowners who couldn't afford them, especially for mortgages requiring little or no money down, thus minimizing the growth of the housing bubble. Maybe elected officials wouldn't have pressed the two housing giants, Fannie Mae and Freddie Mac, to buy or guarantee so many securities backed by subprime mortgages that later went sour. And maybe financial regulators would have pressed the nation's banks, especially the largest banks, to fund more of their assets with shareholders' money so they would have had a greater cushion against mortgage losses that later would bring some of them down and put others in the desperate position of having to take government investments to keep them afloat.

But none of that happened. Indeed, even the two economists thought to be in the best position to predict future hard times and to recommend measures to avoid or at least minimize them—Federal Reserve Chairmen Alan Greenspan and Ben Bernanke—publicly indicated that the economy was doing pretty well up until the crisis. They didn't even warn that when the housing market turned downward and borrowers began defaulting, the rot would slow the rest of the economy. Perhaps they each believed these things would happen but as public officials whose every word is sliced and diced by the media and the public, they couldn't voice their misgivings out loud without triggering mass panic and thus the very crisis they wanted to avoid.

Nonetheless, to be fair to both of these distinguished economists, they were in good company: Many other highly credentialed economists didn't issue such warnings either. Moreover, Alan Greenspan later apologized for not reining in the subprime mortgage lending boom earlier, while at least in my view (one that I know is not universally shared), Ben Bernanke's extraordinarily innovative easy-money policy helped save the U.S. economy from a far worse recession than actually happened, one that was the worst since the Great Depression of the 1930s.

The failure of the economics profession—with a few notable exceptions like New York University's Nouriel Roubini and Yale's Robert Shiller—to see the crash coming has pretty much tarnished the reputations of all economists since. It has also promoted deep soul-searching among economic forecasters about how to improve their models so that they will be better able to warn the rest of us of future trouble with enough time to head it off, or at the very least to keep its impacts to a minimum.

I wish them luck because they have an uphill battle. Economic forecasters as a whole have never had a very good track record of predicting the turning points in the economy, either the beginning of recessions or recoveries. In his latest book, Greenspan argues, in my opinion persuasively, that forecasters have an especially difficult time calling financial crises and sudden downturns when economies, and especially banks, are highly leveraged—that is, when they operate with thin cushions of reserves or capital to absorb losses when economies hit bumps in the road or asset bubbles deflate.[2] When that happens, financial panics can lead to sharp downturns that cannot easily be seen in advance.

Nonetheless, a major thesis of this book is that prediction is not what all economists do and the worth of economic ideas should not be measured by the success or failure of the few who attempt to make predictions. This proposition is important, I submit, not only for those who make policy—elected and appointed officials—and for the wider voting public, but also for those who run and create the businesses that produce the goods and services we want to buy and in the process generate the incomes with which to pay for them.

Indeed, through the years I have found many in business to be skeptical about economists who spend their time in the Ivory Tower and not in the trenches where business is actually done. How is it possible, people in business often ask, that economists can really understand what is going on in the real world if they are not actually working in business? Others in the business world are simply innocent about the economics profession. I can't resist repeating this story that Hal Varian, Google's chief economist whom you will meet in Chapter 3, told me about someone from the human relations department at Amazon, which now has a chief economist but was then looking for one, asking of Hal the same question my own mother asked me: "Now, could you tell me what it is that economists actually do?"[3] Presumably, Amazon has figured that out by now.

The truth is that relatively few economists actually engage in economic soothsaying or prediction. Yes, let me repeat that, or phrase it in a slightly different way: The popular perception of what most economists do is wrong, and I intend to show that in the chapters that follow.

A third and even more important reason I have written this book is to tell readers, even economists, that some economic ideas have proven to be extremely important in launching or improving the performance of many businesses. In doing so, I will focus on U.S. businesses, because the United States is the country where I was born and live, and thus has the economy I know best. But readers from or interested in other countries should find the following material useful as well. Many businesses elsewhere around the world are modeled on successful businesses launched in the United States, so if economics is useful here, it can be useful anywhere. In Part II of the book, I show how policy ideas urged by economists, once they were adopted, actually led to the creation and growth of many businesses, a fact of which their founders, current executives, and employees may not even be aware.

Although I have not quantified the business impact of economic ideas with precision, I plan to show you that collectively the notions discussed in this book have created trillions of dollars of income and wealth for the United States and the rest of the world, hence the title of the book. Along the way, I hope to teach some economics through examples, ideally reawakening your interest in the subject if you took it long ago, but without the graphs, charts, and maybe lots of equations you were required to solve but whose relevance you did not immediately (or ever) grasp. Likewise, if you are running or thinking about creating a business, perhaps one or more of the stories in the chapters that follow may quiet your skepticism about the importance of economics in business, or maybe even inspire you to change the way you or your company operates. Finally, and I know this is a long shot, there may be a chapter or two in here that inspires some economists to change the way they teach the subject, by relating at least some economic ideas to their practical uses or consequences in business settings.

I focus primarily on the positive contributions of economists to business because they have been largely overlooked, in my opinion. The financial crisis and the Great Recession have provided many examples where economic ideas have been misused and taken too far—some derivative financial instruments that went bust and took a good portion of the U.S. economy with them last decade are perhaps the best known to this generation of readers—and I will briefly discuss those where it is relevant to do so. But I am deliberately going light on these instances for two reasons: They already have been discussed extensively by others, and where economic ideas have been misused, it was those who engaged in the misuse rather than economists or their ideas that were at fault.

This book is written in the spirit of *Better Living Through Economics*, edited by Vanderbilt economist John Siegfried, who also was a long-time secretary of the profession's main professional organization, the American Economic Association.[4] This useful book contains essays by some leading economists on how various economic ideas have changed society through the adoption of public policies urged by economists. There is a bit of overlap between Siegfried's book and this one—especially in my later discussion of some policy-related topics—but most of what readers will find here is new, even my gloss on public policies in the second section of this book. It is the business perspective in this book that I believe is unique and one that I know that business readers will appreciate, and hopefully others will too.

Organization of the Book

This book takes key insights from various economists—some, but not all, rewarded for ideas with one of the two leading prizes for economists—the Nobel Prize or the Clark Medal, both described in detail in Appendix A—and show how these concepts, knowingly or unknowingly, have been applied in real businesses to make real money, and also in the process to benefit consumers in the United States and elsewhere around the world.

Let me clarify, by the way, whom I mean by economists—mostly, but not exclusively, individuals with PhDs in the subject. I take a broader view because the main purpose here is to focus on economic *ideas*, so along the way you will not only meet some famous economists but also some statisticians, specialists in finance, psychologists (one, Daniel Kahneman, has even won the Nobel Prize in Economics), or business executives or entrepreneurs who have commercialized an economic idea. For me, since it's the ideas that count, I will give the originators credit for being economists if the content of their ideas is related in some fashion to how the economy or some portion of it really works.

I have been privileged to know, and occasionally work with, many of the economists (so broadly defined) whose work is featured in this book. I feel a bit like Forrest Gump since I have had the good fortune to meet and know so many outstanding members of the profession during some very exciting times. My personal connections to the entrepreneurs and business executives are fewer. Where relevant, I will tell you a few personal stories about the individuals I know, in sidebars throughout. I do this not out of vanity—I have just been lucky enough to know these people—but instead because I believe this will help humanize both the individuals and the subject of economics, which I have learned over the years, can be intimidating (or boring) to many.

Each chapter of the book is devoted to one or several related economic ideas and to one or more economists who developed them. You will learn something about why some of the economists went into the field and, in particular, what led them to their ideas. The chapters contain similar information about a number of entrepreneurs and business leaders, and their companies that commercialized these ideas. Along the way, I'll mention or introduce you to some very interesting and (believe it or not) readable books by certain economists, so if nothing else, consider this book a reader's guide to some of the best popular economics writing by those who really know their stuff. At the same time, I apologize to the many worthy economists whose great ideas have not made it into this book because of space limits and my judgment that their research does not bear directly on the business-related themes of this particular book.

The chapters in the book are structured in three broad groups. The first part includes chapters that center on ideas that have directly found their way into certain businesses. In some cases, there is a straight line from the ideas to the businesses. In other cases, the line is not so clear, or the lines are parallel: that is, economists came up with a given idea that businesses thought of independently and found a way to make money off it. In a few cases, the economists learned from the businesses. Whichever way the causation runs, I simply want to demonstrate the importance of the ideas themselves as a way of illustrating the usefulness of economic insights, regardless of who thought of them first.

The second part focuses on economic ideas that have influenced public policies that created opportunities for a surprisingly wide range of companies to emerge and grow and, in the process, have changed much of the way business is done in this country. Many economists (including me) make it their career because they believe it will help them influence policy in some way for the better, not so much out of a desire to run for office (although many politicians have studied the subject in college and a few even have had graduate degrees), but through their writing and, for some, as advisers to elected officials or government agencies. Each of the chapters in the second part of the book discusses economic ideas that have powerfully changed governmental policy, specifically facilitating the deregulation of industries where conditions never or no longer warranted it, and in turn unleashed major, positive forces for existing and new businesses in the U.S. economy.

The concluding part of the book peers into the future by identifying a few economic ideas already in circulation that are waiting for potentially large business applications or policy changes that will create platforms for many businesses in the future, many that almost certainly cannot now be imagined. The last chapter in this part of the book concludes with some thoughts about the future of economics as a separate academic discipline, and the implications this might have for business in the future.

At the end of each chapter I summarize some of the main takeaways or "bottom lines." I haven't said enough in this introduction to warrant a bottom line for this chapter, but to whet your appetite for what's in the rest of the book and to justify the "trillion dollar" claim in the title of the book, here are a few things you will find as you read further:

- Economists have been instrumental in implementing and designing auctions in a variety of companies that collectively have market values in the hundreds of billions of dollars, or more.
- Economists have built the mathematical backbone for minimizing costs in much of the transportation industry.
- Statistical techniques developed and refined by economists are increasingly being used in the sports industry (and not just in baseball!).
- Economists have contributed to a growing "matchmaking" industry, of human organs and whole people (in the "marriage market").
- Economists and their insights helped spawn the growth of index investing and financial options contracts (collectively involving several trillion dollars).
- Without the deregulation of the transportation industry and the breakup of AT&T, events in which economists played prominent roles, Internet retailing would not exist on nearly the scale that it does today, if at all.
- Economists also played prominent roles in encouraging the deregulation of the prices of oil and natural gas without which energy firms would not have had the financial incentives to make the technological breakthroughs that have dramatically increased U.S. oil and gas production, reversing the "energy pessimism" that has overshadowed the country and world since the early 1970s.

Not bad for a relatively small profession, if you ask my opinion.

My Personal Interest (and Bias)

I find economics to be a fascinating and exciting subject. While I had some interest in it before attending college, I really got turned on to it by the best teacher I have ever had, a then young, dashing, and brilliant economist from India, Jamshed Ghandi, at the Wharton School of Finance at the University of Pennsylvania (the nation's first undergraduate school of business, which later added a famed master's program and a limited PhD program). As my choice of schools implies, I went to Wharton to learn about business, and specifically corporate finance, a subject I then only vaguely understood. Although my enthusiasm for choosing economics as a major waned a bit after taking the standard introductory level course in my freshman year—an experience I'll bet many readers and countless other former college students have had—that attitude changed completely the following year when I had the great fortune and privilege to take Ghandi's seminar in finance, which was really about macroeconomics. Ghandi had a reputation for being a very tough but fair grader, and an outstanding teacher, a reputation he maintained long after I took his course and graduated.

You will find as you read through the book that other economists were attracted to the subject in the same way that I was, through the gifts of one special teacher, admittedly a not unusual way in which many people choose their professions. In my case, what appealed to me most about economics is that it was a practical way to apply mathematics, which I was good at, but not good enough to be a mathematician, or even to be a physicist (a trait shared by other famous economists, too, although the field has become more mathematical over time, and the very best economists tend to be those who are both mathematically gifted and can express themselves well in writing). That is because, as MIT Professor Robert Solow reportedly once quipped, "Little boys don't grow up wanting to be economists, they have to learn about it later in life." (He made this remark at a time when it was rare to find women economists, a situation that has changed significantly, as it has for other professions).

For students who are thinking about taking an economics course, I hope this book will help you get through the graphs and equations and understand, at least at some level, that they actually have been or can be useful. For those who have suffered through an economics course and want an easy way to go back and remember some of what you learned, or perhaps learn a few new things with business relevance, then hopefully this book is for you.

I realize that those running a business or working in one are perhaps my toughest audience. Many of these readers are probably skeptical that economists have very little understanding of the real world, or their particular business. One of the noted economists featured in a later chapter, Franklin Fisher of MIT, told me a great story that encapsulates this attitude.

The building at MIT that houses both the business school and the economics department is called the Sloan building, named after one of America's leading industrialists, Alfred P. Sloan, who built General Motors (in the good old days, long ago). When the MIT president at the time told Sloan about the plans to name the building after him, he reportedly replied something to the effect, "That's all very nice and I'm grateful, but only if you move all the economists out of the building." They weren't moved, but Sloan's attitude is not at all unusual in business, in my experience, and I fully understand it.

Sloan's skepticism about the usefulness of economists uttered many decades ago persists elsewhere. Even a famous historian, Harvard's Niall Ferguson, has climbed on the anti-economist bandwagon. Worrying about how America has lost its way (in his book by that name),[5] Ferguson singles out the profession for failing to recognize how increasing bureaucracy and regulation are stifling American entrepreneurship, a position with which I am sympathetic. I personally applaud Ferguson for turning his attention to the importance of entrepreneurs in advancing innovation, a theme I have stressed in my own past writings and discuss later in this book, and even agree with his assertion that "[n]ot many economists talk about [institutional impediments to entrepreneurship]," a situation I spent nine years as research director at the Kauffman Foundation trying to rectify (even recommending the funding of historians like Ferguson himself to study the subject, which he clearly has). It's his diagnosis of the reason why economists ignore these impediments, echoed by many in business—"because not many economists run businesses"—that I want to counter.[6]

By the end of this book (maybe even before), I hope all readers will come away with a different impression of at least some economists, and more importantly, with a more positive view about the importance of economic ideas or the way economists tend to think. I may not be able to tell you everything about economics you might benefit from knowing, but ideally it will be enough for you to realize that Keynes was right when he famously uttered that practical men (he wasn't thinking of women) have little idea of the extent to which their beliefs and actions have been heavily influenced by the writings of some defunct economist. Most of the economists you will meet vicariously in this book are not yet defunct, but alive and well and still contributing to the ongoing process of understanding how economies work, and still coming up with ideas that real people in real businesses are using to improve their lives and those of their customers, suppliers, and employees.

Finally, to those with a business background you should know that this is not your standard business or economics book. It will not give you or your company five steps to success, or seven steps to happiness. It will not tell how certain companies were built to last, went from good to great, or fell from grace. I will attempt, however, to draw out some general lessons your business may be able to use from each chapter. As noted earlier, you'll find those lessons in "The Bottom Line" section at the conclusion of each chapter.

So, sit back and actually enjoy reading about economics. It will make me happy if you get even half the pleasure reading the book as I have in researching and writing it (feel free to skip things you already may know or anticipate you will disagree with).

Notes

1. The statement about Friedman is in Alex Rosenberg and Tyler Curtain, "What Is Economics Good For?," *New York Times Opinionator*, August 24, 2013, and Klein's statement is from Glenn Rifkin, "Lawrence R. Klein, Economic Theorist, Dies at 93," *New York Times*, October 21, 2013.

2. Alan Greenspan, *The Map and the Territory: Risk, Human Nature, and the Future of Forecasting* (New York: Penguin, 2013). For an excellent summary of the book and a reflection on Greenspan himself, see Gillian Tett, "Crash Course," *Financial Times*, October 26–27, 2013, 19.

3. Interview with Hal Varian, July 15, 2013.

4. John Siegfried, ed. *Better Living through Economics* (Cambridge, MA: Harvard University Press, 2012).

5. Niall Ferguson, *The Great Degeneration: How Institutions Decay and Economies Die* (New York: Penguin Group, 2012).

6. Niall Ferguson, "How America Lost Its Way," *Wall Street Journal*, June 8, 2013, C1, http://online.wsj.com/article/SB10001424127887324798904578527552 326836118.html. It is getting ever-harder to do business in the United States, argues Niall Ferguson, "and more stimulus won't help: Our institutions need fixing."

Chapter 2

An Easy Introduction to Economics

If you've made it through the first chapter, you're now probably asking an important threshold question: How much economics do I have to know to understand what follows? The answer is, not much, and what you do need to know before you plunge in, I will now tell you. For readers who have taken economics but forgotten a few things, this refresher may also be helpful. In whatever camp you fall, you will learn the rest of what might be useful to know before you read coming chapters. You will also discover how the economic ideas featured in these chapters use or build upon one or more of the following concepts.

Rationality

First, most economists assume that all actors in the economy behave rationally—that is, they act in their self-interest, even if that interest includes altruistic behavior, from which many people derive pleasure. Actually, the notion of pleasure, or utility, is a philosophical idea that predates modern economics and is associated with the British philosopher Jeremy Bentham, who argued that people act in such a way as to maximize their total utility. More sophisticated versions of this concept have appeared since in the writings of many economists, but the notion is that people are made happier more by the pleasure they derive out of doing various activities and, yes, buying things, than from accumulating money per se. Now, it is true that a large majority of people would rather have more money than less, but all of us know that money is not the only thing that drives people's behavior or makes them entirely happy (often it doesn't). The key notion for economists, whom one would assume care only about money, is that whatever people value—and money and the things it can buy are certainly important—they act in the workplace and as consumers to maximize what they value. In that sense, they are said to be rational.

As for businesses, the calculus is simpler, and is generally assumed to be all or almost entirely about money—profits, to be precise. Standard economics textbooks don't tell firms how to reduce costs or enhance revenues in order to maximize profits, but rather assume that whatever technologies are available for producing goods and services, firms will pick the cheapest ones available to them (some may be proprietary to other firms, giving them a leg up in the competitive race), while selling as much as consumers want at prices set by the market (see next subject). Business schools specialize in teaching future and current business leaders techniques for minimizing costs while maximizing sales. What many business leaders may not realize is that some of the material they learn from their business school professors originated from economists, some of whom you will meet, as well as their ideas, in later chapters.

The assumption of rationality is important to most economists for two reasons. If actors are rational, then it is easier to predict how they will behave. Consumers will thus buy less of something the more expensive it is, while firms will do the opposite, eagerly producing more of it the higher the price. I'll have more to say about this famous supply and demand analysis in a moment.

A related advantage of the rationality assumption is that it makes economic analysis more mathematically tractable—important to economists—since mathematics has become the lingua franca of academic economics. You can have a good idea, but unless it can be expressed mathematically, you are unlikely to be taken seriously among your academic peers—and you'll have a very small chance of ever winning a Nobel Prize (you'll meet one famous exception in a later chapter). A number of critics, including many economists themselves, believe the field has become too mathematically abstruse and less relevant to the real world than it used to be. Although I personally find some merit in this critique, I also recognize that economists have used or improved upon a number of mathematical methods to develop important insights and techniques that are used in many businesses today, as I demonstrate in later chapters without writing a single equation!

Other critics, including some economists, have attacked the rationality assumption, especially by individuals. People oftentimes are emotional and they do not have the time or inclination to search out all of the relevant alternatives before buying or selling, and thus do not always pick the perfect or the optimal outcome. One economist, Herbert Simon, a longtime professor at Carnegie Mellon University, even won a Nobel Prize for showing how and why many individuals and firms may be content to settle on an acceptable outcome or one that satisfies rather than optimizes. Simon, and other economists who have elaborated on his work, has also used the term *bounded rationality* to describe how people often behave: They are rational, but within limits, not wanting or having the time to explore and examine each and every possible option or choice they might pick.[1] Research in psychology and a branch of economics called behavioral economics (more about this subject in a moment) shows that offering consumers too many choices can be suboptimal for society—a phenomenon known as choice anxiety.[2]

Perhaps the most articulate and vociferous defender of the (unbounded) rationality assumption is another Nobel Prize winning economist, and probably one of the most recognized names in economics, the late Milton Friedman (see the following box). Among his many writings, Friedman penned an essay on just this subject in the 1950s, arguing that it didn't matter whether *everyone* in the economy behaved rationally. The key was that the marginal actor—that last purchaser of a particular item—behaved "as if" he or she were rational.[3]

Milton Friedman: Capitalism's Defender

To economists of my generation, there were three figures who towered above them all. You will meet two of them in this chapter. The first is Milton Friedman.[4]

Freidman found economics, like many others, at college through the influence of two professors, Arthur Burns and Homer Jones, who then were teaching at Rutgers University, which Friedman attended on scholarship. But even after finishing college, Freidman was torn between pursuing a career as an applied mathematician or economist, and received graduate scholarships in both subjects. Freidman claims a toss of the coin determined the outcome, though he acknowledges that the challenge of figuring out how countries can escape severe depressions—it was 1932—also played a role. The world would not have been the same had the coin toss turned out differently.

At the University of Chicago, where he attended graduate school, Friedman was heavily influenced by Jacob Viner, then a leading theorist of international trade, but also by other members of an outstanding faculty. At Chicago, he met and later married another student, Rose Director, the daughter of Aaron Director, a Chicago faculty member who had a profound impact on many economists.

After graduate school, Friedman joined the faculty at the University of Wisconsin briefly but then went to work at the Treasury Department during World War II, helping to devise the withholding tax system for income taxes (an assignment that Friedman has written his wife never forgave him for, perhaps not entirely tongue in cheek). After the war, Friedman eventually found his way back to Chicago, which was his academic home throughout his teaching career, before he moved in his later years to the Hoover Institution at Stanford.

Friedman's academic work was far ranging. He established the monetarist branch of macroeconomics, which emphasized the exclusive role of the money supply in determining inflation; developed a theory of economy-wide consumption; revised an understanding of the tradeoff between unemployment and inflation, which Friedman argued was true only in the short run; and became an ardent advocate for flexible exchange rates, a policy that has governed international markets since the demise of the Bretton Woods system of fixed rates established after World War II.

Friedman also wrote for a popular audience and was the author or promoter of a wide range of policy ideas, including an all-volunteer military force and vouchers for elementary and secondary schools. He wrote articles for newspapers and magazines throughout his career, most notably *Newsweek*, alternating with Paul Samuelson of MIT (whom you will meet later in this chapter).

Friedman also dispensed policy advice to leading Republican politicians in the United States and to leaders of many foreign countries. Although his writings and research did not directly influence business, his tireless advocacy of free market policies found a warm reception among many (but not all) in business.

His *Capitalism and Freedom* is one of the most influential economics books of all time (up there with John Maynard Keynes' classic *General Theory of Employment, Money and Interest*, and a lot more readable). His widely popular book, *Free to Choose*, coauthored with his wife, Rose, was made into a television documentary. He was awarded the Nobel Prize in 1976, and died in 2006 at the age of 94.

The emphasis on that marginal buyer or seller has a long history in economics, and is perhaps most associated with a famous nineteenth century economist, Alfred Marshall. The central insight of the marginalist revolution can be illustrated with a paradox that perplexed the great Adam Smith: Why are diamonds—frivolous and nonessential consumer goods—so much more expensive than water, an essential necessity of life? The answer, the marginalists taught us, is that although water has greater total utility, diamonds have greater marginal utility, and therefore command higher prices.[5] That is to say, the value of one extra diamond, because diamonds are so scarce, is much higher than an extra drop of water, which generally is much more plentiful (though in many parts of the country or the world, water is becoming increasingly scarce, and is generally not priced to reflect that scarcity).

"Thinking on the margin" means to consider the economic consequences of the *next step forward*.[6] That is, individuals and firms should consider only the additional costs and benefits of the next unit—not prior sunk costs—when making decisions. Since we can't do anything about the past, it's best to focus on the present and the future if we want to maximize utility or profits. Admittedly, this is often hard to do. If we've sunk a lot of money into a project or an item, it is often difficult to walk away from putting even more money into it, even though if we stop and think rationally about it, we may never recover what we've put in already.

The emphasis on marginal thinking nonetheless has huge implications for how economies behave. In particular, as long as the last (or marginal) buyer and seller meet at a price both can agree upon, that is all that matters for markets to clear. It doesn't matter that many uninformed or less-than-rational buyers (less so sellers) are in the market.

Economists have debated Friedman's as-if metaphor for years, and this is a debate I have no desire or need to resolve, because I will provide examples of ideas that are essentially on both sides of the debate that have found their way into the business world. The efficient markets hypothesis associated with the setting of stock prices, the subject of Chapter 8, is a clear example of Friedman's hypothesis at work, and real money has been made by enterprising entrepreneurs using that concept.

At the same time, there is a newer school of economists who have paired with psychologists, or drawn from their literature, who draw out the implications of behaviors that are not always rational in the way either Friedman or other economists would define. These behavioral economists, such as Herbert Simon, have noticed many situations in which people do not always act rationally, and the results in the marketplace do not look like they follow Friedman's as-if assumption.

Behavioral economists look at the way people actually behave and find out that context matters. For example, setting the default option can lead to very different outcomes. Take, for example, the seemingly simple choice of whether to set aside a percentage of people's salary each month in a tax-deferred savings account to build up money for retirement, commonly called 401k accounts (or variations of them). If you tell workers they have to affirmatively opt in to such automatic salary deductions, they are much less likely to save than if you switch the default setting to an opt out—that is, everyone is presumed to sign up unless they affirmatively decide not to. Or changing the food options in a school cafeteria toward healthier food can nudge kids to choose healthier and less fattening items.

One popular book featuring behavioral economics is *Nudge*, co-authored by a lawyer, Cass Sunstein of Harvard Law School, and economist Richard Thaler of the University of Chicago.[7] Sunstein and Thaler focus on policies that firms and governments can take to nudge people toward decisions that are better for them and for society as a whole. When met with the objection that these policies take away people's freedom, the two authors respond that almost every decision that people must make is framed in a certain way, and that accepting one particular framing over another always happens, either implicitly or explicitly. They would rather have those decisions made explicit and create contexts that enhance the broader social welfare.

Behavioral economics has had an important impact on the world of finance, as you will learn in Chapter 8. The development of the field has many intellectual fathers, but one of the most influential is not even an economist at all, but rather a psychologist, Daniel Kahneman. Readers who want a nontechnical guide to his work should read his popular book *Thinking, Fast and Slow*.[8]

Markets

A second economic proposition it would be useful to know is that in capitalist economies—those in which individuals and firms can own and trade property, including goods and services—the market is the central institution that sets prices, rather than any governmental body (there is a limited exception to this rule, discussed shortly).[9] Prices, in turn, are really important in any economy—even in the former communist countries—as key signals to guide the behavior of producers and consumers. Hold that thought, however, until I quickly define the term *market*.

Actually, there are multiple kinds of markets, and each tends to be suitable for different kinds of goods and services. One kind of market is an organized exchange, like the stock markets (there are many of them, but that is a detail), where millions of people and institutions submit and buy and sell orders for stocks and more complicated financial products known as derivatives (such as options or futures contracts whose values are derived from the value of some other underlying financial instrument or commodity). Exchanges are ideal for completing trades and thus determining the prices of fungible or standardized items, such as a stock certificate, or many commodities, such as oil, corn, or wheat.

In the old days, human specialists and traders who worked on the floors of stock exchanges would match buy and sell orders, or complete the transactions themselves, hoping to profit from a later trade. Today, computers do the matching and complete much of the trading (all this is discussed in greater detail in Chapter 12).

More commonly, when economists refer to the market they are thinking about the aggregation of millions or billions of uncoordinated actions of buyers and sellers of often very different goods and services. In most cases, the items are offered on a take-it-or-leave-it basis by a vendor (a retail outlet, restaurant, or a service provider such as a doctor or a lawyer). Most items now for sale on the Internet are offered the same way. If buyers like the price, they purchase; if they don't they go somewhere else, either on foot, by car, or by clicking their computers, or touching their phones, each hooked to the Internet. Providers who have difficulty selling their wares eventually may lower their prices, while those who can't keep up with demand may raise them. Although there may be no single market clearing price for every good and service, the market in the aggregate tends to iterate so that prices for identical items or services converge. There are exceptions to this tendency, when prices are not readily apparent, as is generally the case in health care, but even in that sector, there should be movement over time toward greater transparency, which should lead to more price convergence.

Despite its flaws, this common notion of the market is pretty amazing. Several years ago, the economics writer for the *New Yorker*,

James Surowiecki, wrote a wonderful book, *The Wisdom of Crowds*, which I found not only highly thought provoking, but a good way of illustrating the virtue of markets. The book's main thesis was that when people can act independently without knowledge of what others are doing, large groups of them, on average, often are able to make better predictions than experts.[10] In much the same way, the uncoordinated actions of billions of people and firms each day (if you count multiple transactions by the same people, just in the United States alone) do a far better job than any central planner could not only to ensure that just about everything that people want they can get, as long as they are willing to pay a market-clearing price.

The great Austrian economist Friedrich Hayek, writing in the middle of the last century, argued that prices are the most important piece of information in any economy. Knowing the price of an item and the prices of the items and labor required to produce it (or deliver it in the case of a service, like health care) tells producers whether they can earn a profit making (or delivering) it, and if so how much to make. Likewise, the first question most buyers ask or want to see about anything they are interested in purchasing is the price. To be sure, information about quality is important, and in the age of the Internet, it is more available than ever before, either for free (ratings are provided on products and sellers on many websites) or for modest costs from for- and nonprofit entities like *Angie's List* and *Consumer Reports*, respectively.

Prices also have two other key relationships. Generally, the higher the price of any item, the more of it producers will be willing to make, but the less of it consumers will be willing to purchase. As standard economics textbooks then show—and this may be the single thing from taking a course in the subject that former students remember—these propositions can be graphed, with an upward sloping supply curve and a downward sloping demand curve. The point at which the two curves cross is the market-clearing price.

There is a third kind of market institution, the auction, which was thought to be reserved for determining the price for unique items, such as art and other collectibles. In Chapters 3 and 11, I discuss how auctions, even though they have a long history, have become much more widely used in recent decades in the physical and virtual worlds for many, many more items or services. In each case, economists helped business discover ways to generalize the auction so it is capable of being used routinely, while they have also persuaded policy makers to use the device for allocating scarce publicly owned goods, such as the electromagnetic spectrum that has enabled the incredibly rapid growth of wireless telecommunications.

More broadly, in many cases what appears to be scarce can be made less so through the signaling function of prices. High prices attract investment that expands capacity and entrepreneurs who invent or discover cheaper ways to provide the scarce resource or commodity. One of the best examples is the combination of horizontal drilling and chemical fracturing techniques that have transformed the energy landscape over the past few years. It took a while, but the high prices of oil and natural gas stimulated the development and widespread use of these innovations. Had oil and natural gas prices still been regulated, as they were in the 1970s, the energy revolution probably never would have happened. Economists played an important role in facilitating this outcome, a story told in Chapter 10.

Market Failures

While markets are superior to central planners in sending the right signals for the production and consumption of most goods and services, this is not always the case. Markets can fail to maximize efficiency under certain conditions, although economists often disagree about the extent to which these failures occur and whether the governmental fixes represent improvements or are appropriate in the first place.

Perhaps the best-known cases in which markets fail involve externalities, both negative and positive, which are not taken into account by private actors. An example of a negative externality is when manufacturers generate pollution and harm third parties; they will tend to produce too much because, in the absence of taxes or regulatory mandates, the producers or consumers do not pay for the costs of pollution. In a famous article published in 1960, Nobel laureate Ronald Coase of the University of Chicago showed that, in theory, government intervention is not required to internalize such externalities since the producers of pollution and those harmed can negotiate a solution.[11] In practice, however, there are typically so many who are harmed that it is too costly for them to band together to conduct such a negotiation.

The standard answer to the externality problem therefore that is advocated by many (maybe most) economists is to impose taxes in the amount of the damage caused by the polluters. This idea goes back to Arthur C. Pigou, an economist who outlined such an approach in the early twentieth century.[12]

A carbon tax is a notable example of a Pigouvian tax. The basic logic is simple: Taxing the emissions from pollution sources forces the emitting parties to internalize the costs imposed on society. A carbon tax could reduce both greenhouse gas emissions and the federal budget deficit, which is why many economists from both sides of the political spectrum have advocated it.[14] I have a lot more to say about a carbon tax, or its rough equivalent—cap and trade—in Chapter 14.

Conversely, the benefits of some goods may not be easily captured by a single purchaser, such as the security provided by local police or a system of national defense. Similarly, the benefits of basic research and developments in the physical and health sciences spill over or accrue to the larger public, including many companies or potential companies that are capable of using the fruits of the research, together with their own proprietary knowledge, to develop new goods and cures. Likewise, some of what policy makers now call basic infrastructure—such as roads and sewers—benefits society at large. Even education has positive externalities, since although individuals benefit personally from attending and doing well at school, many of them later use the knowledge they pick up along the way to develop new scientific advances or to launch new companies that benefit the public. For example, one estimate is that inventors reap only about three to four cents of every dollar in benefits they generate for society as a whole.[15]

These various public goods must be financed by some governmental entity, or otherwise there will be insufficient volunteers to pay for them—that's why we have taxes. (Another reason is to support various social safety net programs, notably Social Security, Medicare, and Medicaid that transfer income from working members of society to those who no longer can work, such as the aged and disabled, and, most recently in the United States, those with insufficient income to purchase affordable health care.)

You will learn in later chapters of several ways in which public goods have found their way into business applications. In particular, the federal government has funded several important fields of study that have led to breakthroughs in economic science, which in turn have been used in business—the very premise of this book. The National Science Foundation supported Internet search technologies, which eventually sparked the interest of two Stanford computer science graduate students, Sergey Brin and Larry Page, who founded Google, now one of the world's leading Internet search companies which has benefitted from the application of economic ideas (about which you will read in Chapter 3). In addition, during and after World War II, the fields of linear programming and operations research were funded by the Office of Naval Research, which generated mathematical techniques for minimizing costs (the subject of Chapter 4).

A second way in which the market can fail is if sellers (more typically) have superior information than buyers. Economists call this *information asymmetry*. Normal people call it unfairness. In some cases, markets can solve the problem; for example, by consumers demanding and willing to pay for warranties against defects. But in some situations, warranties, backed up by arbitration or the availability of the judicial system to resolve disputes, are not enough. Requiring appropriate disclosures, which sometimes can be excessive with too much fine print, is the standard additional remedy for information asymmetry. Mandatory disclosures are especially important for services, such as insurance, where what consumers are buying are promises by the sellers to make payments, contingent on some event (such as disability, damage to your house or your car, or your death) far into the future. These regulations are supplemented, as in the case of banks as well, with financial soundness requirements and regular supervision of these financial institutions to give customers comfort that the firms that are holding their money will be able to give it back to them when they want it (banks) or deserve it because of losses covered under their policies (insurance).

The third source of market failure occurs in rare cases when the structure of the market itself limits the market to one competitor because the average costs of serving more customers continue to fall even as more goods or services are sold. For example, if the investment to build a network is so large relative to the size of the market, then the average costs of supplying the service may continue to decline even as more customers are added (this is in contrast to most goods after which at some point, both the average cost and the marginal cost, or the cost of serving additional customers, turn up well before all customers in the market are served). Traditional examples of such natural monopolies are the old wire-based telephone network (unlike newer mobile telephone services where competition is not only possible but has proven to be highly desirable) and the distribution of everyday utilities, such as electricity, natural gas, and water.

How does or should society deal with natural monopolies? The textbook answer is with price regulation: capping rates at some level that enables the monopoly provider to earn an appropriate return (given the modest risk) for its investors, but no more. Over time, different approaches to monopoly price regulation have been developed, as will be discussed in Chapter 11. Price regulation of monopolies is the exception to the proposition that markets are always better at setting prices than governments.

Believe it or not, there are cases in which, sometimes given the right governmental rules, private actors can help correct certain market failures and make money at the same time. I devote parts of several chapters in this book to explaining how this is either already being done in some cases, or in others, could be done in the future, either initially or more extensively than has been allowed so far.

For example, in the case of pollution, environmental regulators have shown increasing interest in adopting an idea thought up by economists: allowing polluters to trade allowances to emit a maximum amount of certain pollutants (sulfur dioxide being the first example). Such cap-and-trade systems encourage those that can most efficiently reduce pollution below some level to do so, while requiring those who do not have this capability to pay the social cost of exceeding the limit. This is more cost effective for society as a whole than simply requiring every polluter to meet the same standard, regardless of its costs (although many economists believe pollution taxes, such as a carbon tax, are a more efficient way to get to the same result, the politics of enacting such taxes has proved even more difficult than persuading Congress to extend cap-and-trade to carbon-based air pollution). So-called emissions trading also opens up business opportunities for exchanges to handle these trades, opportunities that could be expanded if cap-and-trade systems were more widely adopted for other pollutants, as I discuss in Chapter 14 in the concluding part of this book.

In the case of information asymmetries, newspapers and magazines have long been a source of information for consumers about specific products, although less so about service providers. Customer ratings of some professionals, such as doctors, are beginning to be available on the Internet. At the same time, as surely all readers of this book know, the Internet has been steadily, and in more recent years rapidly, undermining the economic feasibility of print publications, largely because information can be distributed to additional customers at essentially zero cost without the need for additional paper and trucks to deliver the product into buyers' hands. So far, those information providers that are making money in the Internet age are using some variation of a free service available to anyone who accesses the Internet coupled with a pay wall for premium content. Time will tell whether this, or another, business model will succeed.[16]

In the meantime, there is one business that has done much to solve the information asymmetry problem in financial markets, and that is Bloomberg LP. I discuss the success of the particular Bloomberg technology and business model in Chapter 3, which although it cannot be traced to the idea of any particular economist, highlights the importance of the economics of improving transparency.

As for the regulation of monopoly, several chapters in Part II of the book show how the government has inappropriately regulated certain sectors of the economy that never were or no longer display the declining cost characteristics of natural monopolies—transportation and telecommunications. These are instances of what some economists have called government failure and serve as a warning to those who quickly embrace government intervention as the immediate solution to market failures. Most economists will tell you that government should only intervene where the costs of market failures outweigh the costs of government failure, a calculation that admittedly is often difficult to make in the abstract or without sufficient experience to test the outcome; further, by that time, since government intervention has become the status quo it tends to be very difficult to change, let alone eliminate.

My main purpose in the second section of the book, however, is to tell the story of how economists have had a powerful impact in persuading federal officials to establish the right policy platform—deregulating prices and entry in industries where it never was or no longer is appropriate—that quickly facilitated the rise of a whole new range of businesses and business models that have literally remade much of the U.S. economy in the process. This is a story that has benefited many businesses, and yet they, as well as many readers, are probably unaware of it. It is also a story of how economists have had a powerful impact on business *indirectly* by doing what most economists believe they are best at—convincing policy makers of doing what economists believe is in the best interest of society.

Oh, one more thing: There have been through the years a number of critiques of markets, along the lines that it is immoral or unjust to let markets allocate many inherently nonmarket things or institutions: like organs, or votes, or even who gets tickets to concerts. One of the best works of this genre is a thoughtful book by Harvard political scientist Michael Sandel, *What Money Can't Buy*.[17] He's right, of course, to a certain extent, but as an economist, I believe he overstates his case. The alternative to allocation by price is allocation by queue. That may be fair in some eyes, but it's a method that doesn't provide an economic incentive for innovation or enhanced supply to eliminate or reduce a shortage of an item that may be in scarce supply. Economist Timothy Besley has provided a thoughtful critique of Sandel's views on these matters.[18] Readers who want more philosophical discussion of what is sure to be an ongoing debate over the role and limits of markets in any society are well advised to consult both these works.

The Macro–Micro Distinction

Another economic concept it would be useful for you to know before exploring the rest of the book is the distinction between what economists call macroeconomics, which covers how entire economies perform, and microeconomics, which concerns itself with how individual households and firms behave. In most college courses, the two subjects are typically taught in different semesters.

Macroeconomists try to understand what drives the performance of the overall economy, and ideally how to mitigate extreme cyclical fluctuations. They monitor various indicators, with which many readers may be familiar, such as the growth of GDP and inflation, the unemployment rate, and the trade balance, but they continue to argue about the fundamental causes of variations in these indicators.

When I was an undergraduate majoring in finance (really a subfield of economics) in the late 1960s and early 1970s, and later in the mid-1970s when I was completing my graduate training in economics, macro was much sexier and more interesting for members of the profession and at least for students like me than micro. In my undergraduate years, the big debate was whether monetary policy or fiscal policy (changes in taxes and government spending) was more effective in mitigating the ups and downs of the overall economy. The main protagonists were two early Nobel Prize winners, Milton Friedman of Chicago, who argued that the money supply affected only the rate of inflation and who was skeptical of the impact of fiscal policy, and Paul Samuelson of MIT (see accompanying box), who had more faith in the effectiveness of both monetary and fiscal policy.

Paul Samuelson: A Twentieth Century Legend

The two other great economists of the twentieth century, at least in my view, were John Maynard Keynes, the British economist whose writings really established what we now routinely call macroeconomics, and Paul Samuelson, who among his amazingly diverse contributions put Keynesian theories into mathematical language. He was awarded the second Nobel Prize in Economics for just a small portion of his research, notably, his *Foundations of Economic Analysis*, written when he was a graduate student and which sufficed for his PhD thesis. It also earned him the first John Bates Clark award ever awarded by the American Economic Association. Numerous other awards graced him during his long career.

Ironically, Samuelson earned his undergraduate degree in economics at the University of Chicago, the intellectual home of staunch defenders of free markets, whose views Samuelson later did not always share. This was especially true of Milton Friedman, who was Samuelson's academic foil through much of both their careers. Samuelson earned his doctorate at Harvard, but thereafter joined the faculty at MIT, where he remained until he died at the age of 94 in 2009.

Samuelson published research on virtually every major topic in economics, or as he stated in one essay about his life, he "had his finger in every pie."[19] Not surprisingly, therefore, he authored (and later coauthored, with William Nordhaus of Yale University, one of many of Samuelson's outstanding students you will meet in Chapter 14) an introductory economics textbook that for several decades was the leading one in the field (I used it in my freshmen year at Penn).

Like Friedman, Samuelson wrote for popular magazines, including *Newsweek*, and counseled politicians, most notably candidate and then President John F. Kennedy, and President Lyndon Johnson.

Samuelson influenced so many people and students that inevitably he had a major effect on business simply through his teaching. He was also an avid investor, and you will meet in Chapter 8 a legend in that field (John Bogle) who traces one of his important innovations to Samuelson's work in finance.

Later, as I was in graduate school, the United States suffered through stagflation in 1973 to 1974—a combination of high inflation and high unemployment—that some claimed could not be easily reconciled and so demanded a new macroeconomic paradigm. The result was a new skepticism about the ability of any governmental policies to have a long-run impact on unemployment, but there was still a strong worry that excessive monetary growth would lead to runaway inflation. The result was a new, quasi-Keynesian synthesis that asserted there was a natural rate of unemployment that the government could affect marginally in the short run through fiscal and monetary policies, and perhaps might nudge lower through better education and training in the long run. Still, there remained a number of skeptics, three of whom eventually won Nobel Prizes (Robert Lucas of Chicago, Thomas Sargent of the University of Minnesota, and Edward Prescott of Arizona State University), who questioned the effectiveness of *any* governmental policies to affect the economy even in the short run. Once the financial crisis and recession of 2008–2009 was under way, the intellectual and political fights about the impact of macroeconomic policies broke out again and continue to this day.

This is what the public, to the extent it follows economics, most sees about the field: vigorous and sometimes ad hominem arguments with seemingly no consensus. But as I asserted at the outset of this chapter, relatively few economists actually are involved in these disputes or spend much of their research time seeking to resolve them. Much more day-to-day work is spent by many more economists attempting to understand the behavior of the sub-units of the macro-economy— individual firms, industries, and consumers. These activities are lumped under the broad field of microeconomics, and it is the insights of some of this work that are the focus of this book.

In recent years, and especially in the wake of the global financial crisis, macroeconomics has become a more humble science. Prior to the crisis, many economists were convinced that our understanding of the macro economy, including the nature of economic fluctuations and the effects of fiscal and monetary actions, was overall pretty solid.[20] The financial crisis, however, severely challenged many of the assumptions and conclusions that had gained consensus among many macro economists over the years. It turns out that it is extremely difficult to estimate, assess, or forecast many dynamics in the macro economy with any reasonable degree of certainty. Indeed, one of the most contentious policy debates during the financial crisis concerned the unknown effects of the fiscal stimulus: Was it too small or too large? What would be its impact on consumer spending, unemployment, or GDP? It's simply impossible to run experiments with the economy. For these reasons, macroeconomics remains an imperfect science at best.[21]

Microeconomics, on the other hand, is a much better understood segment of the field for at least two reasons. First, understanding and predicting the behavior of individuals and firms is much easier than predicting what happens in the entire economy, which is really the summation of literally millions of micro units. Second, micro economists often have richer data and more tools at their disposal (such as running experiments) to better understand and predict consumer and firm behavior. To be sure, microeconomics is also an imperfect science, but as I demonstrate throughout this book, many of its key insights have spurred innovation and led to trillion-dollar benefits to the economy.

Economic Growth in the Short and Long Run

There is one branch of macroeconomics that plays a background role for much of what follows, and this involves attempts to understand what really drives, and ideally predicts, the rate of growth for entire economies over the *long run*. This is a distinctly different subject from what determines the quarterly or annual ups and downs of the economy, which is what most macroeconomists spend their professional lives trying to understand.

Economists often discuss long-run growth in terms of an economy's potential growth rate. This is the rate at which total output (putting aside how it is distributed) is capable of growing, assuming those who are willing and able to work have jobs. This doesn't mean the unemployment rate is zero, but rather because of the frictions in the labor market and the mismatch at any time between the qualities employers seek in employees and the skills of available workers, full employment is taken to mean the lowest unemployment rate that is consistent with stable inflation. Until the 2008–2009 recession the so-called natural rate of unemployment in the United States was thought to be in the neighborhood of 5 percent. Since the recession, with so many workers out of jobs for so long and skills requirements continuing to increase, there seems to be a rough consensus that the natural rate of unemployment has inched above 5 percent, perhaps closer to 6 percent.

Assuming this to be the case, then the long-run growth rate of the United States economy, or any economy, is at once simple because it is a mathematical identity, but also inherently complex because one large component of that identity is virtually impossible to project with any accuracy, even by the best of economists.

The simple mathematics are that total output growth equals the sum of the projected growth of the labor force and the growth of productivity, defined as output per worker. Of the two halves of this equation, productivity is far more important, and it is also the most difficult to project. That is because the easiest component of productivity growth to predict, that which depends on the projected growth in equipment and buildings that enable workers to be more productive, is also of lesser importance. By far the most important factor affecting productivity growth, at least in countries that have the most advanced technology, is the growth of innovation, or new and more highly valued products and services and methods of generating and delivering them.

Innovation and growth matter because they determine the rate at which general living standards advance. The average American has about 10 times the income of one living at the beginning of the nineteenth century because of the wave of innovations that now characterize modern life: indoor plumbing, air conditioning, modern means of communication and transportation, huge advances in medical care, and amazing advances in information technology. Similar benefits are enjoyed by the average citizens of other, now rich or almost rich, countries in Europe (despite that continent's post-2008 difficulties), in parts of Asia (Singapore), Latin America (Chile), Canada, and Australia. Meanwhile, much of the rest of the world wants to be like the rich world, and China and India are racing ahead as fast as they can to catch up (though on a per capita basis they still have a long way to go).

Averages, of course, conceal how income and wealth are actually distributed. A society can be relatively rich on average by both measures, but have extremes of poverty and prosperity. As the former Secretary of Labor Robert Reich has quipped, "Shaquille O'Neal [the former 7 foot-plus center for the Los Angeles Lakers] and I [Reich] have an average height of six feet."[22]

The Equity–Efficiency Tradeoff

Ideally, there is a balance between distribution and growth. Societies need some degree of inequality in order to give incentives to the high performers to want to continue to work hard and to innovate, and thereby lift the economic fortunes of everyone, even those at the bottom. But too much inequality can leave the rich feeling physically vulnerable, behind their gated communities and with their personal bodyguards, while stoking support for leaders, even in quasi-democratic regimes, such as Venezuela when it was led by Hugo Chavez, who favor populist policies that force money and wealth to be redistributed to the poor.

Many (but not all) economists believe in a limited amount of redistribution—it has been the basis for the income tax code in the United Sates and other advanced economies—as a way of giving families at the bottom of the income distribution at least some chance to help themselves and their children have access to goods and services, most importantly education, that will enable them to improve their lives and climb up over time into better stations in life. It remains a stubborn fact that your own incomes are heavily influenced by the socio-economic status of your parents.[23]

In addition, redistribution provides a safety net for the aged, those with limited skills and therefore limited incomes, and those temporarily out of work. In doing so, redistribution is a form of social glue that can help keep a society together, especially one as heterogeneous as the United States. But too much redistribution can drive those at the very top to invest in nontaxed assets (such as municipal bonds) or even to leave for other countries, which private jets and Internet access make it easier to do.

More broadly, there has always been an ongoing conversation about not only redistribution but also about the proper role of government in the economy: When is it appropriate for the government to intervene in the economy? The standard textbook answer is that government intervention can be justified on both efficiency and equity grounds.[24]

The efficiency rationale is that the government should intervene in instances where there is market failure. As we have seen, market failures deliver outcomes that do not maximize efficiency for society. That is, the pie is not as large as it could be, so the government can intervene and make it larger for society.

The second rationale for government intervention has to do with equity, and particularly redistribution—the size of each person's slice of the pie. The utilitarian view posits that since an extra dollar is worth more to a poor person than to a rich person, society would be better off if some amount of redistribution were allowed. However—and this is a huge point—too much redistribution, changing the size of each person's slice, can shrink the size of the entire pie. Why? Because of incentives, the most productive and rich members of society may be less willing to work hard and innovate if they see a larger share of their pie taken away and given to less productive or less well-off individuals.

The subject of distribution is a hot button issue that deserves its own very different book from this one. It is a topic that involves both positive and normative economics—another big distinction in economics. Positive economics is the branch of economics concerned with explaining phenomena without making value judgments as to the merits or fairness of a given outcome. Normative economics, on the other hand, is the branch of economics that specifically deals with expressing how things *should be*, not just the way they *are*.

The debate about redistribution and whether to greatly expand it through much higher taxes, specifically a global wealth tax, really heated up in 2014 with the publication of *Capital in the 21st Century*, by French economist Thomas Piketty.[25] Since this book is about how economics is used in business, I will not wade into either the technical or policy aspects of this already bestselling book, but simply note that it exists and has clearly become a lightning rod for both economists and noneconomists alike.

One much less controversial but I believe equally important book relating to the subject of distribution, and one that I highly recommend to readers, is *The Race between Education and Technology* by Claudia Goldin and Lawrence Katz. These two highly regarded Harvard economists advance the view that most economists would agree with—that eventually the best way to narrow income inequality is to widen opportunities for education, especially among those in disadvantaged neighborhoods and in single-parent families.[26]

This challenge grows harder when technology is racing ahead, rapidly increasing the minimum level of skills workers need to secure even moderately well-paid jobs, while public resources available for teaching those from disadvantaged homes are under stress. Tyler Cowen, one of the more ingenious economists of this generation, has written a provocative, disturbing, but also very persuasive book, *Average Is Over*,[27] which argues that the U.S. economy (and by logical extension other rich country economies) is really becoming two economies: one for those whose earnings put them in the top 20 percent of incomes, and another for the other 80 percent. The keys to being in the top 20 percent are facility with information technology and ability to market oneself, a characteristic of successful entrepreneurs.

There is no amount of redistribution that will rectify this 20/80 situation without severely undermining incentives for growth. Nor, in Cowen's view, is education the whole answer. People in the bottom 80 percent have to be motivated to learn the skills that can put them in the top 20 percent, which in the process would increase that figure. Figuring out how to encourage students and adults to constantly retrain themselves to be equipped to deal with fast-moving technology is one of the great challenges of our time.

Whether or not Cowen turns out to be right that at least for the next couple of decades the 20/80 division will continue and possibly widen, economic growth can still increase the incomes of even those at the bottom of the income distribution in each society. The poorest Americans today are better off than those in the middle and upper classes of the nineteenth century, and that is because of the invention and commercialization of many of those technologies listed earlier that characterize our modern society and have powered its growth.

As for the rest of the world, literally billions of people today are living above the level of extreme poverty—one or two dollars a day—because of economic growth, especially in the once really poor countries, China and India. If you care about all people living better and longer lives, you cannot be opposed to economic growth.

Innovation and Growth: The Role of Economists

In the meantime, the main focus in the following chapters is on one aspect of economic growth that even many economists have not well recognized: how ideas of economists have contributed and, if given the chance, will continue to contribute to innovation and growth and thereby enhance human welfare. The importance of this theme is best understood if I first give you some context about the much broader discussion about the prospects for future growth that is being vigorously debated among some academic economists, and, I predict, is not likely to die down anytime soon.

Shortly after the recovery from the Great Recession of 2008–2009 began, the same Tyler Cowen to whom I have just referred penned a short e-book (later published in print), *The Great Stagnation* (as an e-book, this was first of its kind in economics, a format that is beginning to be more widely used). In brief, the book's main thesis was that the United States, even as a technological leader, has already picked all the low-hanging fruit available for increasing growth: moving women into the labor force, topping out the percentage of the population that goes to college, and wringing about as much innovation as it can from its universities and private sector. The future outlook for productivity growth at least for the next several decades therefore looks dim, in Cowen's view, much more pessimistic than the long-term forecasts of somewhat less than 2 percent per year issued by the Congressional Budget Office (which is more than a percentage point below the 3 percent pace in the "golden" quarter century after the end of World War II and during the revival years of the 1990s).[28]

Cowen's dour view about the future was reinforced with another, even more pessimistic outlook painted by one of America's leading macro economists, Robert Gordon of Northwestern University, in two widely read academic studies.[29] Gordon's story, broadly speaking, is that the information technology revolution was never what it was cracked up to be, while the innovative streak that drove growth in the United States and other advanced countries dating from the Industrial Revolution, has run its course. Gordon went out on a limb, at least relative to other economists, and projected that productivity would essentially stop growing at all at some near point in the future.

Among academic economists, the leading rebuttal to Cowen's and Gordon's pessimism was advanced in another e-book (later also published in hard copy), *The Race Against the Machine*, authored by two technology economists, Erik Brynjolfsson and Andrew McAfee. These authors argue that Moore's law—the historical doubling of computing power every 12 to 18 months named after Intel cofounder Gordon Moore—will continue making the information technology industry even more productive, while improving productivity in a wide range of sectors using IT, such as education and health care. At the same time, as Cowen would write more expansively later, the two authors worried that continued IT-driven innovation would widen income inequalities.[30] Brynjolffson and McAfee have since published a second book, *The Second Machine Age*, which amplifies the themes of their first book.[31]

Brynjolfsson's and McAfee's optimism about future productivity growth is shared in a shorter study published in 2013 by Martin Baily, former chair of President Clinton's Council of Economic Advisers and some of his colleagues at the McKinsey Global Institute.[32] MGI subsequently put out a much lengthier report identifying twelve disruptive technologies that should continue to power growth in the future. Most of these technologies already exist and some are already commercialized, including: the wireless Internet, increased cloud computing, driver-less cars, and 3D printing, among others—but the MGI authors argue that they will improve in quality and in market penetration, and thus impact, over time.[33]

Former Federal Reserve Chairman Ben Bernanke weighed in on the debate over future productivity growth in a commencement address he gave at Bard College in May 2013, siding with the optimists. After discussing how radically different the life of an average American has changed over the past century, due to the development or diffusion of a wide range of innovations that make up modern life as we know it now, Bernanke did what most economists do when they talk about the future: They extrapolate, in some broad sense, and say there is no reason why the future should differ fundamentally from the past.[34] The story of civilization is one of continued innovation, at least since the Industrial Revolution, and why should that story change?

This debate about the pace of future growth in the U.S. economy and elsewhere surely will continue as long as there is human activity. The outcomes matter, for a number of reasons. First, as noted earlier, how fast the economy grows determines the rate of improvement in average living standards (admittedly putting aside that pesky issue of distribution). For example, if per capita income (one way of measuring productivity) grows at 2 percent, average incomes and thus living standards will double every 36 years. Raise the growth rate to 3 percent, and the doubling time shortens to 24 years.

Second, not only the pace but also the nature of innovation and in which industries it is concentrated determines the rate at which major social challenges and problems are solved or at least abated. For example, advances in battery lives could dramatically change the mix of autos on the road. Or different kinds of medical breakthroughs will extend the lives and ideally improve the quality of life of people with the affected diseases. Continued improvements in pollution control or carbon storage technologies, among others, will have important impacts on the nature and pace of climate change. And so on.

Third, the rate of productivity growth will have an important effect on the trajectory of the federal budget deficit in the future. Every official governmental body that has looked at this issue—the Congressional Budget Office, the General Accountability Office, and the trustees of the Medicare and Social Security trust funds—has projected that without some combination of major changes in benefits of the major entitlement programs (Social Security, Medicare, Medicaid, and potentially health care under the Affordable Care Act) and tax increases, the long-term outlook for federal deficits is not sustainable. At some point, investors (domestic or foreign) will demand much higher interest rates on the debt issued to finance these programs and the rest of the government, and those higher rates will lead to much slower growth or most likely a deep recession.

These budget forecasts all assume continued productivity growth of about 1.5 percent and total growth (counting continued growth of the labor force) at about 2 percent. If future growth falls short of that projection, then the day of reckoning will come sooner rather than later; conversely, if productivity turns out to grow more rapidly than currently projected, federal policy makers have more time to make these very difficult political choices (which, to date, very few elected officials have wanted to make). Other advanced countries that have even more rapidly aging populations than the United States and broad social safety programs face similar challenges.

In short, the pace of innovation could not be more important to the welfare of residents here and elsewhere around the world. Yet when virtually all those with an interest in the subject think about innovation, they think of physical or at least virtual things: new and better machines, software, or apps. The same is true of economists, who tend to focus on easily measureable indicators of innovation, such as research and development expenditures (which are an input into the innovative process rather than measures of innovative outputs), or patents (which are very rough measures of innovation but do not reflect its commercial value). The key point is that each measure, however flawed, has some connection to new products, services, or processes of production.

The Bottom Line

Economists are fond of saying "there is no free lunch." By that they mean that an inherent fact of the world is that there is scarcity *at any one time*. There isn't enough capital or oftentimes the right labor, or people with the right skills, to go around, and so the central problem in any society is how to allocate them.

The economic answer, at least in capitalist societies, is to let markets allocate, and they do this principally by setting prices—or actually, allowing all economic units, households, and firms, to set prices through the combined effects of their willingness to supply and pay for goods and services.

The challenge of established businesses or those founding new businesses is to use the prices that the markets are setting to guide their future activities. Those firms earning high profits at current prices stimulate others to enter their markets, thinking that they can do a better job at a lower price. Even harder, but crucial to economic advance, is for firms and entrepreneurs to figure out what markets are not delivering to people now that consumers *would want* if only someone gave it to them. In the age of the Internet, entrepreneurs have been making money developing new platforms like eBay or Amazon that make it possible for many other entrepreneurs to build their businesses, some of which satisfy those latent consumer desires.

Markets fail for any number of reasons, however. This is where government can play a useful role helping them work better. But as we will see in later chapters, government can make mistakes, too, just like businesses. Only it's often more difficult in the political world to get rid of an institution or a practice than it is in the ruthless world of the market, which drives out of business what isn't working.

The central premise of this book is that economists and their ideas can and have played an important role in helping many businesses and entrepreneurs in many different industries be successful. In the process, economists have the same or similar impacts on productivity and human welfare as the more conventional kinds of innovation that come to mind when economists and non-economists alike think about this subject. It is surprising, at least to me, that of all people, economists haven't figured this out, or done more to promote the value of what they do for a living.

I have one conjecture why this is so, and to find out what it is, turn the page to the introduction to the first section of the book.

Notes

1. Herbert A. Simon, "Rational Choice and the Structure of the Environment," *Psychological Review* 63, no. 2 (1956): 129–138.

2. See, for example, Barry Schwartz, *The Paradox of Choice: Why More Is Less* (New York: Ecco Harper Collins, 2003). For another critique of the rationality assumption, see Robert J. Shiller, "The Rationality Debate, Simmering in Stockholm," *New York Times*, January 18, 2014, BU6, http://nyti.ms/1j49qDf.

3. Milton Friedman, *Essays in Positive Economics* (Chicago: The University of Chicago Press, 1953).

4. This description is drawn from Milton Friedman, "Milton Friedman," in *Lives of the Laureates: Twenty-three Nobel Economists*, ed. William Breit and Barry T. Hirsch (Cambridge, MA: MIT Press, 2009), 65–77.

5. Steven E. Rhoads, "Marginalism," in David R. Henderson, *Concise Encyclopedia of Economics*, www.econlib.org/library/Enc/Marginalism.html.

6. Library of Economics and Liberty, "Margin and Thinking at the Margin," www.econlib.org/library/Topics/College/margins.html.

7. Cass Sunstein and Richard Thaler, *Nudge: Improving Decisions about Health, Wealth and Happiness* (New York: Penguin Books, 2009).

8. Daniel Kahneman, *Thinking, Fast and Slow* (New York: Farrar, Straus & Giroux, 2011). See also the landmark article he coauthored that helped launch behavioral economics: Daniel Kahneman and Amos Tversky, "Prospect Theory: An Analysis of Decision under Risk," *Econometrica* 47 (1979): 263–91.

9. Several years ago, I collaborated with two wonderful colleagues in exploring four basic types of capitalism practiced around the world and their varying effectiveness. See William J. Baumol, Robert E. Litan, and Carl J. Schramm, *Good Capitalism, Bad Capitalism, and the Economics of Growth and Prosperity*

(New Haven, CT: Yale University Press, 2007). Five years later, I joined one of these coauthors to elaborate the advantages of one particular form of capitalism, that in which entrepreneurs are the central actors, Robert E. Litan and Carl J. Schramm, *Better Capitalism: Renewing the Entrepreneurial Strength of the American Economy* (New Haven, CT: Yale University Press, 2012).

10. Surowiecki, James, *The Wisdom of Crowds* (New York: Anchor, 2005).

11. Ronald H. Coase, "The Problem of Social Cost," *Journal of Law and Economics* 3, no. 1 (1960), www.jstor.org/sici?sici=0022-2186(196010)3%3C1:TPOSC %3E2.0.CO;2-F.

12. Library of Economics and Liberty, "Arthur Cecil Pigou," www.econlib.org /library/Enc/bios/Pigou.html.

13. Ibid.

14. Laura D'Andrea Tyson, "The Myriad Benefits of a Carbon Tax," *New York Times*, June 28, 2013, http://economix.blogs.nytimes.com/2013/06/28 /the-myriad-benefits-of-a-carbon-tax/.

15. William D. Nordhaus, "Schumpeterian Profits and the Alchemists Fallacy," Yale Working Papers on Economic Applications and Policy, Discussion Paper No. 6, http://www.econ.yale.edu/ddp/ddp00/ddp0006.pdf.

16. For one highly persuasive optimistic projection about the future of the news business, which runs counter to the rampant pessimism among those currently in the business itself, see Marc Andreessen, "The Future of the News Business: A Monumental Twitter Stream All in One Place," http://a16z .com/2014/02/25/future-of-news-business/.

17. Michael J. Sandel, *What Money Can't Buy: The Moral Limits of Markets* (New York: Farrar, Straus & Giroux, 2012).

18. Timothy Besley, "What's the Good of the Market? An Essay on Michael Sandel's What Money Can't Buy," *Journal of Economic Literature*, LI, no. 2 (2013): 478–496, www.aeaweb.org/articles.php?doi=10.1257/jel.51.2.478.

19. Paul A. Samuelson, "Paul A. Samuelson," in Breit and Hirsch (2009), 49–64. My portrait of Samuelson draws heavily on this autobiographical essay.

20. Jeffrey A. Miron, "A Little Humility Would Help," *New York Times*, www .nytimes.com/roomfordebate/2012/04/01/how-to-teach-economics-after -the-financial-crisis/a-little-humility-among-economists-would-help.

21. Ibid.

22. Robert Reich, "The Biggest Risk to the Economy in 2012, and What's the Economy For Anyway?" *Robert Reich*, http://robertreich.org/post/16773820312.

23. Julia B. Isaacs, Isabel V. Sawhill, and Ron Haskins, *Getting Ahead or Losing Ground: Economic Mobility in America* (Washington, DC: The Pew Charitable Trust, 2008).

24. Jonathan Gruber, *Public Finance and Public Policy* (New York: Worth Publishers, 2005), 1–22.

25. Thomas Piketty, *Capital in the 21st Century* (Cambridge, MA: Belknap Press, 2014).

26. Claudia D. Goldin and Lawrence F. Katz, *The Race between Education and Technology* (Cambridge, MA: Belknap Press of Harvard University Press, 2008).

27. Tyler Cowen, *Average Is Over: Powering America Beyond the Age of the Great Stagnation* (New York: Dutton, 2013).

28. Tyler Cowen, *The Great Stagnation: How America Ate All the Low-Hanging Fruit of Modern History, Got Sick, and Will (Eventually) Feel Better* (New York: Dutton, 2011).

29. Gordon outlines his arguments in two papers: Robert J. Gordon, "Revisiting U.S. Productivity Growth over the Past Century with a View of the Future," National Bureau of Economic Research, www.nber.org/papers/w15834; and Robert J. Gordon, "Is U.S. Economic Growth Over? Faltering Innovation Confronts the Six Headwinds," National Bureau of Economic Research, www.nber.org/papers/w18315.

30. Erik Brynjolfsson and Andrew McAfee, *Race against the Machine: How the Digital Revolution Is Accelerating Innovation, Driving Productivity, and Irreversibly Transforming Employment and the Economy* (Lexington, MA: Digital Frontier, 2012).

31. Erik Brynjolfsson and Andrew McAfee, *The Second Machine Age: Work, Progress, and Prosperity in a Time of Brilliant Technologies* (New York: W.W. Norton, 2014).

32. Martin N. Baily, James M. Manyika, and Shelabh Gupta, "U.S. Productivity Growth: An Optimistic Perspective." *International Productivity Monitor*, March 2013, 3–12, www.csls.ca/ipm/25/IPM-25-Baily-Manyika-Gupta.pdf.

33. James Manyika et al., "Disruptive Technologies: Advances That Will Transform Life, Business, and the Global Economy," McKinsey Insights & Publications, www.mckinsey.com/insights/business_technology/disruptive_technologies.

34. Ben S. Bernanke, "Economic Prospects for the Long Run," Bard College Commencement speech, www.federalreserve.gov/newsevents/speech/bernanke20130518a.htm#fn2.

Part I

THE POWER OF ECONOMIC IDEAS: DIRECT USE IN BUSINESS

As promised in Chapter 1, this first part of the book contains chapters outlining how economic ideas have *directly* made money for firms, by enhancing revenues, cutting costs, facilitating innovation, or some combination of all three. In some cases, the entrepreneurs or businesses that implemented these ideas were acutely aware of them and their origins, and so the line between idea and outcome is easy to grasp. In other cases, businesses used an economic idea without knowing it, and economists later validated it, theorized about it, or quantified its impact. In a few cases, economists and businesses pursued their ideas in parallel, each seemingly unaware of the ideas or efforts of the other, though I suspect this may change over time (maybe some from each camp will read this book and make this prediction come true). All routes to business success are broadly consistent with the overall thesis of this book and with the quote from Keynes about the power of defunct (and not-so-defunct) economists and their ideas.

Chapter 3 begins with a discussion of how economic ideas have influenced how firms set prices. To be sure, in highly competitive markets, firms are price-takers: They take what the market dictates. But in a surprising number of situations, markets take a while to settle down and, especially in new markets or circumstances, economists have offered useful advice about how those markets should be created and prices set.

Chapter 4 turns to the other side of the coin: minimizing costs. Here, too, business can figure out how to cut costs to the bone without the help of an economist. But in many kinds of businesses where things must be moved around (like planes or trucks) or supplies, materials, and inventory must be managed, minimizing costs becomes a lot more difficult to do without the aid of some formal techniques. Indeed, an entire field of study, known as operations research, grew out of the work of mathematical economists. You'll meet the founders and the work they spawned in this chapter.

Chapter 5 addresses a seemingly technical subject, empirical economics, which leads in surprising directions. Economists test their propositions through the use of increasingly sophisticated statistical techniques, so in one sense economics is part applied statistics, part theory. After providing a brief history of how the uses of these techniques in the business world has changed over time, I introduce a surprise: the extension of similar techniques into sports. That's right, sports. With the publication of *Moneyball*, the same kinds of techniques economists have long used to test their hypotheses and to generate forecasts of economic variables have been applied by a new generation of quants to the performance of certain athletes and teams, and thus indirectly to the financial performance of their owners. In "Beyond Moneyball" I only scratch the surface in discussing how what started as a hobby in the garage of baseball guru Bill James has now spread to multiple sports, while creating a new academic specialty to boot (couldn't resist the pun).

Chapter 6 discusses the one exceptional pattern in this part, the parallel interests in experimentation in the worlds of economics and business. Of the two fields, experiments are newer and more unconventional among economists, who traditionally either theorized about the working of the economy or its constituent components (in increasingly sophisticated mathematical terms), or used the statistical techniques profiled in Chapter 5 to test their theories. It is hard to stop the real world, apply a treatment to one population, and compare what happens to a control group, as medical researchers commonly do. Nonetheless, you will learn in Chapter 6 that this is changing, and there is growing interest in and work among economists in using human subjects (students and businesspeople) to test theories. As for business, experiments have long had a place in this world: What else, after all, do most entrepreneurs and many established firms do except constantly experiment until they get things right so that people or other firms want to buy what they have to sell? With the rise of the Internet, running experiments has become far less costly, and the testing of the look and feel and the specific content of websites, among other things, has become routine.

Chapter 7 addresses a topic you won't find (at least yet) in many textbooks: the economics of matchmaking. This is a relatively new branch of the field, and it addresses markets where non-price attributes are even more important than prices for allocating resources. Think about the job market, or the dating market, and you get the idea. The chapter outlines how economists have made important contributions to our understanding of these markets, and growing matchmaking businesses, facilitated by the Internet, have listened to them. I loved (again pun intended) working on this chapter and hope you have as much fun reading it.

In Chapter 8 I finally get around to the topic with which I opened the book, the world of finance and how it has been affected by the ideas of the economists (or financial economists, as they may prefer to call themselves). I know in the wake of the financial crisis the temptation of some (maybe many) readers is to ask: What good have economists been for finance; aren't they partially to *blame* for the crisis? I will address that issue in the policy part of the book in Chapter 12. Chapter 8, however, outlines for you a number of important *positive* contributions of economists and their ideas to finance that have led to new financial products (think indexed mutual funds and exchange traded funds) or that have greatly facilitated the pricing of other products (think options, which have been a mixed blessing). For those inclined to think better of economists, the positive tone of Chapter 8 will not be a surprise: If economists can't help those in the financial world, which is all about money, then how can they possibly be of use to firms in other industries? It turns out, if you are persuaded by Chapter 8, that economists needn't worry about the answer to that question.

Before beginning the chapters in this part, some readers may be tempted to ask a different, but important question: If the economic ideas surveyed in this book are so good and valuable, why are economists even necessary to think them up? One answer, which economists trained in the University of Chicago's Department of Economics would give, is that ordinary people are smart enough to figure out by themselves the good ideas they need to make money and they don't need to consult economists to help them to do it. Firms and their customers know what's in their best interest or act as if they know. That's a good answer for a lot of ideas, but I also believe an incomplete one.

Not everyone who has no economic training, or who hasn't read or hired someone with this background, came to every idea laid out in this part on their own, nor could they be expected to. That would be like saying that ordinary people, without training in science, could be expected to come up with all of the discoveries that scientists in all kinds of disciplines have made over the centuries. To believe this to be true reminds me of the old joke about what an economist, presumably one trained in free market economics at Chicago, said when he or she was told there was a $20 bill on the sidewalk: "No, that can't be, because if it was there it already would have been picked up."

But we all know there are plenty of $20 bills, some even larger than that, that are left on sidewalks all the time, just as there are ideas remaining to be discovered, or at least widely implemented, in both the physical and social sciences (and many economists think they are leaders of the pack among social scientists). You will find some of those ideas in the remaining chapters of this book, beginning with the chapters in this part.

Chapter 3

The Price Is Right

O ne of the earliest television shows I watched as a young child was *The Price Is Right*, hosted for many years by Bob Barker. I loved the show so much that occasionally I would feign illness to stay home from school (exactly how will remain a secret) to watch.

At this writing the show is still on and I suspect it will remain a television staple for years to come. There may be a few readers of this book who haven't seen *The Price Is Right*, but for those who haven't, the format is quite simple. Three contestants are chosen from the audience to participate in a two-round contest in which they are shown various items and asked to guess the price of each. A key rule is that a contestant automatically loses if the price is too high, but the contestant closest to the right answer on the low side wins a prize. The prizes are larger in the second round than in the first, and typically the winner from the first two rounds plays a guessing game one final time, by themselves, for one large prize.

Ask people in business and they'll tell you that after coming up with a product or service to sell—a task whose difficulty I do not want to understate—the first decision they must make is to figure out what price to charge. They are like the *Price Is Right* contestants, with one big difference: When businesses set prices it is not a game; it can be a (business) life or death decision. As one of the most respected and thoughtful entrepreneurs I've met, Norm Brodsky (with his coauthor

Bo Burlingham) has underscored in the best popular book I've ever read about entrepreneurship, *Street Smarts*, it's much easier to lower prices on things that aren't selling than to raise them even if they are.[1]

That is because when businesses set a price, they are setting customers' expectations about the nature of the product or service. Is this a luxury item, in which case a higher price can act like a status symbol? Or is this a product or service very similar to many others in the marketplace where customers carefully compare prices on comparable items, something that is far easier to do in this age of the Internet than ever before? If all consumers need to do is check their phone or their personal computer, or go to a search engine and find the best price at the most convenient location or by ordering online, then you'd better set price at or below the market if you want sales. In either event, unless prices for all goods and services are rapidly rising, prices tend to be sticky, so getting to the right price quickly, in most markets, is important.[2]

Of course, if you're selling something that already is well known, the market—the combined interactions of lots of buyers and sellers—will reveal the price, and that's what you'll charge. Actually, you may set the price at a slightly lower level if you think you can capture more sales that way. Or perhaps you'll charge a bit more, if you can differentiate your product or service with a little something extra that no one else, or perhaps only a few of your competitors, is offering.

What happens if you are an entrepreneur or an executive at an established firm introducing a *new* product or service? How do you know what to charge for something that hasn't been tried yet?

Here's what the economics textbooks will tell you, which often is not enough, or is at least less than satisfying. At a minimum, you will want to charge enough to cover at least the costs of manufacturing, or what economists (and accountants) call short-run variable or marginal costs. These are the costs associated with selling just the extra one or perhaps several items. Examples include the materials that go into making a product, but maybe not much else, not even the cost of workers. In the very short run, employers won't change their workforce to make one more or less widget or to see one more or one less customer. Over a bit longer run, labor costs are variable, and so it may be appropriate to allocate the average amount of additional labor required to produce an extra item to the variable cost side of the ledger.

Of course, if all you're doing is trying to cover your marginal costs, you won't stay in business very long, because to get it started, you or any business typically had to lay out money for fixed costs—rent, equipment, and so forth. Plus, if you're really being rational, you'll want to count as a fixed cost the "cost of capital" or what you and other funders (friends, family, angel investors, or in the rare case, venture capitalists) expect to earn on their investments, given the amount of risk involved (I'm not counting bank debt as a source of funds, unless your business is well established and it has access to a bank loan; many entrepreneurs use mortgage or credit card financing, but are not in a position to get an ordinary commercial loan unless they pledge personal assets to secure it).

So, ideally, you'll want to charge a high enough price to generate a return on capital, after covering variable and fixed costs. You won't know what the price is, however, unless you also make some projections about the amount you hope to sell—the number of widgets, or the number of customers or clients (in case you're in the service business)—over some reasonable period of time. Add up all the costs, divide the volume expected, and you'll have the cost per unit, and hence the price. Sounds easy, until you begin the guesswork of how well your product or service will sell, something you may not know for a long time. That's why the best you can do is price by trial and error, or you can fix a price and add more value to the product or service over time and hopefully convince customers to buy it.

The latter strategy is one that Michael Bloomberg and his company has used to price its service, financial information. Bloomberg didn't consult an economist about the strategy, but over time he found it really worked. I start with his example, even though it runs counter to the central objective of this book: to convince you how important economists are or can be. The story introduces a degree of humbleness that economists should have but often don't.

The Bloomberg Way of Pricing

Even if I hadn't gone to work at a Bloomberg company, I would not have hesitated to call Michael Bloomberg and the company he and his colleagues built a true American success story. Born to a middle class family in Massachusetts, Bloomberg went to college at Johns Hopkins (a school he had barely heard of in high school), studied engineering, and had a very successful career at Salomon Brothers trading bonds until, at the age of 39, he was unexpectedly and summarily let go in the wake of a company reorganization.

Though he left the company with $10 million, surely enough for most anyone to retire on, Bloomberg had other ideas and ambitions. From his experience as a bond trader, he knew how opaque that market was—there was (and still is) no equivalent of a New York Stock Exchange or NASDAQ for bonds—so anyone who wanted to buy and sell bonds had to get their quotes and complete their trades through intermediaries like Salomon. In the language of economics, this was a market imperfection that Bloomberg realized could be fixed in a profitable way.

He did so by building what has become known as the Bloomberg terminal, which, in the days before the Internet, was a personal computer-like device with limited capabilities that was connected through a private line into a data center that provided up-to-date feeds of bond quotes. Over time, thousands of additional features—in the forms of commands—were added to the offering, including quotes and offers on an expanding array of financial instruments (equities, derivatives, and foreign exchange) and increasingly sophisticated analytic tools (such as the Black-Scholes-Merton options pricing formula, which is discussed in Chapter 8).[3]

The strongest markets for the Bloomberg terminal are financial traders, in commercial and investment banks, and institutional buyers of securities and financial information. Along the way, Bloomberg realized that quotes and prices of financial instruments were not enough: It would be critical to add a financial news operation to the offering, since traders wanted not only the prices but the information that induced markets to change the prices of these instruments. Over time, under the direction of its founder, Matt Winkler, Bloomberg News became one of the leading sources for news of any kind in the world.

One other important feature of the Bloomberg terminal makes it a very valuable feature for customers: the chat function. Invented before instant messaging became a big hit outside the financial world, Bloomberg discovered, largely by accident, that traders valued the short bursts of characters Twitter users (who came much later) would recognize as abbreviated tweets that the terminal would transmit in real time between traders and other terminal subscribers.

I mention this brief history without noting price. It was and remains a fundamental philosophy of the company that the price of the terminals does not vary from customer to customer—there are no discounts, except for nonprofit universities and for purchasers of more than one terminal. The one-price policy was meant to provide simplicity for the company's sales force, and also to let all customers know they were getting the same deal and no one else was getting a special one.

Bloomberg has also charted a different technological path. In an age when virtually all information services providers, in any field, offer their customers data and information through the Internet, housed increasingly in the cloud, from its start the main Bloomberg terminal (unlike some of Bloomberg's other recently acquired or launched vertical businesses) has continued to provide data, analysis, tools, and chat services through dedicated private communications lines accessed through proprietary terminals on a subscription basis. This has turned out to be an advantage in the age of cyber threats, relative to individual websites and even to companies relying on the cloud. In addition, even with rapid broadband connections, there is some latency (or lags) in Internet responses. Fast responses to commands over private dedicated networks give Bloomberg terminals an important advantage in the world of financial transactions, where milliseconds count.

The importance of these various non-price means of competition appears, at least on the surface, to violate one of the first rules about market economies elaborated in the second chapter—the centrality of price signals in a market economy. On closer inspection, however, this is not the case.

That is because while the nominal price of the Bloomberg terminal essentially has remained flat in real (or inflation-adjusted) terms, its services (and those of its subsidiaries, or verticals) are continuously augmented with new information and functions. This means that the quality adjusted prices of the Bloomberg offerings decline over time, an approach that is central to the company's efforts to differentiate itself from its competitors. My personal experience with a Bloomberg business reinforces this lesson, and also demonstrates how ideas with economic content can be thought up and implemented without a lot of formal economic training.

It's now time to evaluate cases where this isn't always true, where economists and their ideas have had a much more direct causal impact on how businesses have developed and prospered. In particular, I want to focus on the surprisingly large number of transactions in the modern U.S. economy that are based on a very different type of mechanism for setting prices: some variation of an auction.

Auctions

Auctions as a means of setting prices and allocating ownership have a long history. Auctions were used as early as 500 b.c. in a way that would be considered abhorrent today: selling women as wives. Auctions also were used in Roman times for selling off war plunder. In America, Pilgrims auctioned off crops, livestock, slaves, and even entire farms. Even today, individuals and lenders routinely use auctions to sell property, while upscale auction houses sell collectibles.[4]

A common theme runs through these uses: Most of them tend to be for items in limited supply and thus are unique. But auctions were also used for fungible financial instruments, such as shares of stock, which until relatively recently were sold on the floors of exchanges through what was called the open-outcry system. A single auctioneer, namely the specialist, would match multiple buyers and sellers on a running basis throughout the trading day, with prices moving up or down depending on the balance of purchase and sale orders. Today, as noted in Chapter 1 and discussed in more detail in Chapter 12, all but the very largest buy and sell orders for stocks are matched electronically by computers, while futures and options contracts (to be discussed in more detail in Chapter 8) are still sold and bought by human beings.

Outside of these seemingly unusual contexts, one wouldn't think of auctions as being the standard mechanism for setting prices in any economy. Nonetheless, one pioneering economist (more accurately, a mathematician) in the nineteenth century, Leon Walras, imagined the prices of all the goods (he wasn't thinking about services) traded in the economy being set through a series of hypothetical auctions. Walras calculated that economies would be in equilibrium when prices of all goods had iterated, through an auction-like procedure, to their market-clearing prices, or the highest price at which all goods offered would be sold. To this day, many economics textbooks and journal articles reference the Walrasian auctioneer in some fashion.

It turns out, however, that the best-known auction system—where items for sale are sold at the highest prices—is only one of many different types of auctions discussed in the economic literature that have found their way into actual use. Moreover, with the introduction and increasing popularity of the Internet, the costs of conducting auctions have gone down dramatically, so auctions are now used in many more contexts.

In much of the rest of this chapter, I describe different types of auctions, how they came to be, and how a number of them are now the pricing method of choice in a number of markets. Chapter 11 expands on auctions, in a very different setting—where a government entity requires the use of an auction because it is the most efficient way to allocate a limited resource (for example, the electromagnetic spectrum) while earning revenues for the government.

Airline Seats

In this age of constant, though often irritating (but cheaper) air travel, I'll bet this has happened to you at least once. You arrive at the gate for your flight and are about to begin the boarding process, and then one of the attendants announces that all of the seats for the flight have been sold and he or she begins offering travel vouchers for future flights so the airline can get excess travelers off the plane. The vouchers go quickly and often for not much money if there are more takers than slots available, but I've been on flights, and I'll bet you have too, where the gate attendants have raised the voucher price until all the seats are reassigned.

The auction itself seems like such a natural way to clear the market in airline reservations, but it actually is a relatively recent practice, dating from the late 1970s when American Airlines first introduced the idea, after receiving a green light from the agency that used to regulate airline fares, the Civil Aeronautics Board (CAB). Before then, airlines randomly bumped passengers on overbooked flights, and in the process generated a lot of ill will. To avoid that outcome, airlines deliberately did not fill their planes and thus flew with less capacity than they do now, a circumstance that made customers more comfortable, but reduced profits for the airlines. To compensate, airlines had to raise prices higher than they otherwise would be to cover the cost of partially empty planes.

If you've read this far, you've already guessed where the airlines got the idea for auctioning overbooked flights—yes, from an economist. Actually, any economist could have told them to do this, but it took a bold one, Julian Simon, to raise and actually push the idea, and another economist to allow the airlines to implement it.[5]

Bold is certainly a word one associates with the late Julian Simon, who spent most of his academic career at the University of Maryland. If Simon were still alive, I'll bet (and he was fond of bets) he wanted to be remembered for some of his other, controversial but far-sighted ideas, so I'll give you a taste of those before returning to the story about his epiphany with applying auctions to the airline seat market.

Simon is likely best known for two mutually reinforcing propositions, and one related bet. The first proposition is that higher population growth is almost always good. More people means more brains devoted to solving the world's problems, provided people are educated. The largest population growth in world history—the roughly six-fold increase between 1800 and today—coincided with the largest growth in per capita incomes and living standards, disproving any claims that population growth suppresses economic growth.

The second proposition is that the world has an inexhaustible supply of natural resources. One cannot simply extrapolate into the future the growth of current consumption of any commodity or seemingly scarce resource, such as oil, and then divide by the current estimate of the total worldwide reserves of that commodity or resource. As demand outruns current supplies, prices rise, which triggers additional investment to expand supplies, locate new reserves perhaps using new technologies (think of the recent shale oil and gas revolution enabled by the combination of hydraulic fracturing and horizontal drilling, discussed in Chapter 9), or to find alternatives. In addition, higher prices encourage consumers to reduce their demand, to become more efficient, and to use alternatives.

This basic economic principle, which economics students typically learn in any introductory course, was the basis for Simon's classic rebuttal, *The Ultimate Resource*, to the now infamous Club of Rome study published by MIT scientists in the early 1970s that predicted the world would eventually run out of resources. The prediction was based on a simple extrapolation of past consumption trends indefinitely into the future.[6]

Simon didn't merely write academic papers asserting these views; he put his money where his mouth (or pen) was. In 1980, he made a famous wager with Stanford environmental scientist Paul Ehrlich, who worried that the combination of rising population and resource scarcity would lead to soaring prices of basic commodities. Simon disagreed and made this bet: 10 years later, the prices of five metals would cost less than they were selling for in 1980; Ehrlich took the opposite position. Simon won.[7]

Simon's urging of auctions as a way to clear a market with a fixed supply—in this case seats on a particular airplane—was related in a way to his skepticism about scarcity. Let prices do the work of allocating the seats even if the plane were oversold. Simon argued that by letting auctions clear the prices of full planes, airlines would work hard at booking more seats in advance, without fear of offending some ticketed passengers by not letting them on the plane, as was the custom before the auction practice became widespread.

Simon thought up his auction idea in the 1960s, when airline fares were strictly regulated, so at the same there was no way it could be implemented. Toward the end of the following decade, however, Simon took the notion to Alfred Kahn, who was then chairman of the CAB, which not only had long regulated airline fares but also approved which airlines could fly particular routes. You will learn a lot more about the remarkable Kahn in Chapter 9, which discusses the major business impact of his campaign to eliminate airline price and entry regulation and the CAB that oversaw it. Simon struck at just the right time, since Kahn and his colleagues on the board shared the predisposition of other economists who, except in rare cases of natural monopoly, argued that market forces should be allowed to determine prices rather than government regulators. Kahn and the rest of the CAB therefore were easily persuaded—though Kahn cleverly called the idea the volunteer bumping plan—and overbooked flights have never been the same.[8] (The bumping plan did not differentiate seat prices by where they were located, which would have introduced an additional attribute and thus a source of service differentiation, into the auction. This may have been more theoretically pure, but in practice, the gate agents needed to fill planes quickly when they were overbooked so they could take off reasonably close to on time).

Unfortunately, some airlines did not let auctions really clear the airline seat market, but rather offered a take-it-or-leave-it deal, and thus some continued random bumping. Writing in 2010, the editors of the *Wall Street Journal* criticized the Department of Transportation, which had residual authority over the airline market after the CAB was abolished in 1978, for seeking to regulate what clearly should be an unregulated market. The *Journal* editors had the right answer for this problem: Get rid of the artificial rules, and go auction all the way.[9]

Airline seat auctions not only cleared seat markets where the airlines permitted them to do so, but they benefited the airlines and passengers in other not-so-obvious ways. Airlines gained from fuller flights, knowing that it was better to overbook and give a voucher to a few customers if they had to, in a way that made the customers happy. At the same time, fuller flights enabled the airlines to spread the fixed costs of flying their planes across more paying passengers, which allowed them to charge lower fares. One of Simon's former colleagues writing in 2009 cited estimates that auctions of overbooked seats led to combined airline-passenger benefits of $100 billion over a 30-year period (a figure fully one-tenth of the trillion-dollar figure cited in the title of this book).[10]

Google and Online Ads

By far the most famous use of auctions in recent years is by Google for its online ads, which are a major source of that company's revenues and profits. Two economists played an important role, one directly, the other as inspiration.

Google's extraordinary rise in so short a time to become one of the most valued, admired, and feared (by some) companies in the world is now well known—or easily found out from the multiple books written about the firm.[11] One of those authors, Steven Levy, also has written an excellent account of how the company stumbled onto auctions as a way of selling advertising.[12]

According to Levy, Google's cofounders, Sergei Brin and Larry Page, wanted advertising to be one way of monetizing the value of the keywords that users type into their Internet search engine algorithm, but no more important than the revenues they anticipated from licensing the search technology and selling servers. As it turned out, of course, advertising has become the overwhelmingly dominant source of Google's revenues and profits.[13]

Early in the company's history, the firm sold two kinds of ads. The ads at the top of the right hand side of a web page were displayed once a search term was entered and were sold in the traditional way, through human sales representatives who sold keywords, such as *perfume* or *shoes*, to specific companies or their advertising agencies. Advertisers would pay based on the number of views of their ads regardless of how many times users clicked through them. The second kind of ad, listed lower down the right side of the page, was sold directly online at a fixed price.

Levy reports that the two individuals Brin and Page had put in charge of the company's advertising efforts, Salar Kamangar and Eric Veach, were barely out of college, and had majored in biology and computer science, respectively. Although neither had a background in economics or business, they thought it made more sense to auction the online ads at the bottom of the page rather than have Google guess their value by setting a price, while retaining a human sales force to sell the higher valued ads at the top of the page. Under their new AdWords Select system, small- and medium-sized businesses—the main online advertisers at the bottom of the search results page—would be asked to submit sealed bids for specific keywords in advance. Each time users typed in those keywords, Google's algorithms would determine almost instantaneously the winning bids, and rank them in order on the page.

The order of placement, by the way, introduced an element of uniqueness into each ad, which fit the general nature of auctions, which tend to be used for differentiated goods or services. In Google's case, the exploding volume of searches—now into the billions a day—has created a vast market for slightly differentiated ads.

Kamanger and Veach came up with a significant innovation, however, in designing their auction, inspired by an auction-based ad system then being used by GoTO, an early search engine competitor of Google's. As Levy reports, and various economists have pointed out, even sealed bid auctions can be gamed in order to avoid the winner's curse—a bid that is substantially higher than the second-highest bid so that the winner feels like he or she has overpaid (which is often the case). This can lead each bidder to bid low; if all bidders behave this way, the seller will end up receiving too low a price. To avoid this outcome, Veach thought up on his own—reportedly without reading the economic literature—an alternative to the highest bid auction. The winning bidder would pay one penny more than the *second-highest* bid, with the rest of the ad order determined by the ranking of the other bids. This way bidders wouldn't have to worry about overbidding, since the second place bid in effect would act as a safety net.

Without knowing it, Veach's second-price auction essentially replicated an innovation for which a Canadian economist, William Vickery, won the Nobel Prize in Economics in 1996. Vickery's Nobel win was bittersweet because, at the age of 83, he died three days after being named. In doing so, he became the only Nobel winner to have never actually received the prize, but it may have been some consolation to Vickery (while he was alive) and to his family, that the second-price auction widely was called the Vickery auction before his death and since.

Until Vickery came along, most of those who thought about auctions, including Walras, simply assumed that they worked best when whatever was being put up for sale went to the highest bidder. But Vickery had a very different and counter-intuitive notion: that the highest bidder still wins the auction, but pays that *second highest* price bid, a result that Veach at Google had reached largely for programming reasons. Vickery mathematically proved that this result holds more generally, both for bids conducted by sealed bids (where the bids are secret) and an open outcry or public auction, where by definition, the winner pays a bit more than the second-place bidder (but most likely less than the winner would have been willing to bid).[14]

It is not clear what motivated Vickery to study the auction process or to become interested in the subject, but we can take an educated guess by looking at other subjects that occupied his attention. Among the many topics he covered in his research, both macroeconomic and microeconomic in nature, he was concerned throughout his career about institutions that established proper incentives, especially under conditions of scarcity. For example, he is widely regarded as one of the fathers of charging for congestion, an idea that has been tried in a few places and, as I predict in Chapter 14, will be more heavily used in the future. Charging cars or planes during more congested times of the day is just another price-based way of allocating a fixed resource, much like using an auction to set a price for a unique item.

Shortly after agreeing to take the chief executive's job at Google, Eric Schmidt persuaded Hal Varian, one of the profession's leading experts on the Internet economy, to begin part-time consulting work for the company (the deal was proposed and consummated at a party in New York City in January 2002). Varian studied auctions and in his own work built on Vickery's; see the following box for Varian's background.

Hal Varian

Hal Varian's migration to Google is an all-American success story. Having grown up on an orchard in Ohio (though one of his ancestors was the mayor of New York), he clearly had broader horizons for his future.

They developed through his schooling, and in particular, like another famous economist, Paul Krugman, the noted *New York Times* columnist and Nobel Prize winning economist, Varian was entranced with Isaac Asimov's *Foundation Trilogy* (I was, too, but Varian and Krugman took their enchantment to much greater heights). Varian was especially struck by Asimov's theme that society could be structured through mathematical relationships. When Varian went to MIT as an undergraduate, he took courses in psychology and political science before ending up with economics, which he realized was the subject most closely aligned with Asimov's vision: It purported to model people's behavior mathematically in a way that none of the other disciplines did.

Varian went from MIT to Berkeley, where he earned his MA in mathematics and then his PhD in economics. He has had an unconventional, and highly productive, life ever since,

(*continued*)

working his way through the academic ranks at MIT, Stanford, Oxford, the University of Michigan, and then back to Berkeley, where he became the first dean of Berkeley's School of Information Sciences. In the process, he turned what had been a modestly boring field of library science into the study of managing large bodies of data, what the world now knows as Big Data.

Since the mid-2000s, he is most widely known as a highly successful corporate economist who made the transition from academic life to being an entrepreneur with ease, first as a consultant to and later as chief economist for Google. Had Varian gone to college today, he might have been a neuroscientist or perhaps a computational geneticist, fields that today also employ highly mathematical techniques to model human behavior. Google and his fellow economists are glad Varian grew up in an earlier era and became an economist instead.

When Varian asked Schmidt what he wanted advice about, Schmidt suggested that Varian begin by taking a look at the auction process that Kamanger and Veach had designed. Levy reports, and Varian confirmed to me, that after studying Veach's auction process, he told Schmidt that Google had designed its auction perfectly. Later, Varian also wrote that Google's adoption of what is also known as a second-price auction had "nothing to do with Vickery auctions: It was primarily an engineering choice design."[15] Varian's response nonetheless made it easier for Google's managers to take the next logical step: converting all of Google's ads to an auction-based system and, in the process, dispensing with any human salespeople. This seemed very risky at the time because no other business sold its ads this way, nor were advertisers accustomed to such a system. Google had to persuade—actually *teach*—them how to use an auction. Many resisted at first, but eventually, the ad auctions became highly successful and the main source of the company's revenue.

Google adopted several important adjustments to its auction process to ensure that ads are targeted to the right audiences. One amendment is to add a quality adjustment score, so when a user types in the words "Oklahoma City restaurants" the quality adjustment process, which is part of Google's secret sauce, assigns the highest scores to all restaurant ads that include the words "Oklahoma City." This modification weeds out restaurants from all locations outside Oklahoma City. Knowing that Google will do this encourages all restaurants to bid more than they might otherwise, which maximizes ad revenue for Google not only through the higher prices advertisers are willing to pay, but through the greater number of clicks on the ads, which trigger payments by advertisers to Google.[16]

Google's auction also differs from the standard Vickery auction, which is designed only for one winner. Instead, Google auctions off positions, with a first place winner, second place right below, third place below that, and so on. Accordingly, while the company goes with the second-highest price for the winning auction, the other lesser prices are charged, in order, to those bidders who win those lesser positions. Google constantly is fine-tuning its auction procedures, just as they fine-tune its search algorithm, using simulators to quickly get to the core of a problem rather than a series of A/B tests (discussed in Chapter 6) that can be quite expensive.

An entire industry has grown around Google's auction process, with advisers charging advertisers on how best to respond to Google's auctions. Varian has done his best to help advertisers participate in Google's auctions by explaining the company's auction procedures and how to participate in the auctions in a highly viewed YouTube video (Google bought YouTube in 2006), which I highly recommend for readers interested in the subject. One important takeaway from the video lecture cannot be overemphasized: the importance of concentrating on the *incremental cost of the ads and the value an advertiser expects to receive from them* rather than the absolute value.

Remember from Chapter 2 that prices are set by the last incremental purchaser, not by all those who have gone before. This simple insight is critical to advertisers bidding for positions on Google and for the company's own marketing efforts. For advertisers, the amount they should bid for any position should reflect the incremental revenue they expect to gain from any additional clicks for which they have to pay Google, not the *total* revenue for that position. To bid any more puts advertisers in a position where what they have paid is exceeded by any additional revenue they may gain from being a slot or two higher in the advertising pecking order.

By the same reasoning, Varian explains, Google's marketing efforts to interest more advertisers concentrate not on the already thick markets for most popular words, where there are many advertisers and the spread between their bids is narrow, but rather in thin markets for less-popular words, where the additional bids, if calculated according to the incremental value principle, are likely to yield the company more revenue. Admittedly, this type of thinking may run counter to some business instincts, which are to double down on customer segments that are already producing much revenue. The more sensible course, as a general rule, is to focus marketing in segments that are less popular but where the upside gain, compared to the incremental costs of marketing, is greater. Because it is not always easy to make these calculations, which require data and the analytical power to interpret them, Varian has dubbed "marketing as the new finance."

Google uses auctions for other parts of its business, such as allocating servers between its business units. Most famously, the company used an auction process when it decided to offer some shares to the public in 2004 rather than going the traditional route of hiring an investment bank to sell shares and set the price. The particular process Google used for its initial public offering (IPO) is called a Dutch auction. The auctioneers (the investment banks that carried out the auction and that were eager for the business) accepted bids for both quantity and price, and then determined the highest price at which all of the shares being offered would be sold. Take, for example, this hypothetical. The company wants to sell 2,500 shares: One bid comes in at 1,000 shares at $104, another for 800 shares at $103, still another at 700 shares at $102, and so on. The clearing price is the price at which the sum of the quantities bid equals the shares put up for sale at the price at which this occurs, which in this hypothetical would be $102 or lower.

Companies using this method do not have to use the exact clearing price, however, in order to help ensure a "pop"—a jump in the stock price above the IPO price, shortly after the IPO—for investors who initially buy the stock. Having a pop reduces the chances that some initial purchasers will welch on their commitments to follow through with the stock purchases (they may be disinclined to do that if the stock price trades below the IPO price shortly thereafter, meaning that if the purchases were honored, the buyers would immediately suffer loss). Google adopted a variation of a pure Dutch auction in large part for this reason, according to Varian (who advised on the structure of the auction, along with other leading economists he brought in as consultants on the matter).

A natural question arises: Why don't all companies going public use an auction like Google did to manage their IPO, rather than continue to use investment banks to set the IPO price, as is still routinely done? One answer to this question is that few private firms have the kind of public recognition before their IPOs that Google has. As a result, companies going public may feel the need for investment banks to drum up demand for their stock before the offering actually takes place. In other cases, well-known private companies may want an investment bank to set a high price to effectively cash in on the bank's fame or that of the firm's founder. A good example is Facebook, which was one of the world's best-known privately held companies when it went public in 2012 but which did not use an auction to set its IPO price. That may have turned out just fine for Facebook since its stock price fell for some substantial period of time after the IPO, leaving investors upset, but it allowed Facebook's owners to sell fewer shares to raise the money they were seeking than would have been the case had the initial price been lower.[17] (Within a year of the IPO, Facebook's stock price had more than recovered from its initial post-IPO decline.) Of course, we will never know if Facebook could have fetched an even higher price had it used an auction to set its IPO price.

Another reason why some private companies may prefer an investment bank to set the stock price is that the bank also buys all the shares before they are resold to the public. This gives companies going public certainty about how much money their offering will raise, rather than risk taking in a lower amount if the stock were sold through an auction. Whether investment banks will continue to dominate the IPO process, or whether more firms going public will turn to auctions to set their opening prices, may not be decided for some time.

Getting back to Google, Hal Varian's life certainly changed after his meeting with Eric Schmidt. Several years after assuring Schmidt about the wisdom of using the Vickery auction, Varian left his tenured job as professor of economics and dean of Berkeley's School of Information Sciences to become Google's full-time chief economist. Varian has hired a team of statisticians and econometricians (a unique type of economist I discuss further in Chapter 5) who have applied economic and statistical ideas in a wide range of areas in the company. One well-known success is Google Trends, which allows users to graph over time the number of times particular search terms have been requested. This tool has been adapted by Google to show trends in the flu in different geographic areas, before official government warnings, or can be used by anyone to predict other variables, such as the unemployment rate by looking at trends in search words or phrases like "unemployment claims."

Varian is modest in claiming parentage for other ideas for which he and his team have been instrumental at Google. Upon some coaxing, he volunteered to me a few examples (I am sure there are more, but Hal is not the kind of person to toot his own horn). Among the various innovations at Google to which he contributed were the occasional use of A/B testing (a subject I discuss in greater detail in Chapter 6), and the introduction of quality assurance techniques to assure that Google's new products do not have bugs. He also has brought other well-known economists to consult with the company, mostly those with research experience relating to auctions. And he has been a pioneer in developing or overseeing the development of various techniques for discerning patterns in very large bodies of data, or "Big Data," a subject we explore in several later chapters of this book.[18]

Other Uses of Auction-Based Pricing

Google has not been the only pioneer of auctions on the Internet. Another leading success story is eBay, which has become famous for its auctions, too. eBay's history is amazing in a different way from Google's because the former's success does not rest on having unique (and secret) software, or in using an alternative to the conventional high-price auction, but rather in using the power of the Internet to make virtual auctions economic in a way that physical auctions never could. I will not discuss eBay further, despite its huge success and importance, because there is no unique economic idea to credit for the company's success, nor do I have any evidence that any of the sellers on eBay (some of whom have become commercially successful largely by taking advantage of eBay's auction platform) or buyers use economists to assist with their bidding strategies. Many of the buyers on eBay, for example, have learned through experience that it can pay to wait until the last minute to submit a winning bid, a strategy some economists might recommend but one that anyone can figure out.

However, there are instances where economists have played important roles in advising participants in auctions or those operating an auction platform. For example, in 2008, economists helped design and manage a then-controversial auction platform for setting benchmark prices for wholesale milk. The market has since taken off, and celebrated its fifth-year anniversary in July 2013.[19] Likewise, economists also helped Ocean Spray establish a quarterly auction to sell its intermediate product, cranberry concentrate.[20]

And then there is the remarkable case of Stanford economist Susan Athey, the first woman to win the coveted Clark Medal awarded (now each year) to the economist under 40 doing the most promising work in the field.[21] Athey has conducted research on a wide range of microeconomic topics, beginning with timber auctions as an undergraduate at Duke, which led to later work establishing the virtues of sealed bids to help avoid collusion among bidders for government contracts. But what got her attention from the business community—Microsoft's former and longtime President Steve Ballmer in particular—was her research on the digital advertising market. Ballmer reportedly was especially interested in her view that the market required more than just one competitor (Google), and so he summoned her to his Redmond office, where eventually Athey spent a full year, and has continued ever since as Microsoft's chief economist while also teaching at Stanford.

Like many economists, Athey has strong mathematical training, supplemented by computer science, both of which she studied in college. She also is a prodigy, having entered college at the age of 16 and earning her PhD at Stanford at the young age of 24. Her doctoral dissertation, which suggested a new way to model uncertainty, helped her become one of the most highly sought after young faculty members in the country at the time. She chose to begin her research and teaching career at MIT, moving to Harvard, and then later returning to Stanford.

In Chapters 6 and 11, you will meet other economists who have wrestled with the intricacies of auctions in different contexts, where the government has either mandated the use of auctions (for electricity in some states) or is an active seller itself of something the private sector very much desires (like the scarce electromagnetic spectrum used for telecommunications or U.S. Treasury bonds). These auctions can be quite complicated, as can be the strategies bidders use for achieving successful outcomes. It will not surprise you to learn that economists have played important roles in these situations.

Conditional Offer of Purchase (Name Your Price): Priceline

One of the fascinating things about the Internet is that it has created opportunities for not only hundreds of thousands, if not millions, of new businesses, but also new business models. Priceline, the first website allowing customers to name their price to potential suppliers of travel services, is an example of such a new model.

Priceline was born out of a series of brainstorming sessions convened by an already highly successful pre-Internet entrepreneur, Jay Walker. Walker made his initial smaller fortune by founding the Synapse Group, a company that processed magazine subscriptions using the credit card network. He sold a controlling interest in the company in 2001 to Time Warner for over $600 million.[22]

Walker was not content to sit on his success, however, especially once the Internet became more than an academic curiosity in the early 1990s. Walker could see in broad terms that the Internet would fundamentally transform business, but he wasn't sure exactly how, so he assembled a small group of his associates, including software engineer Scott Case. The team eventually came up with the business that became Priceline, where Case became its chief technology officer.[23]

Like many entrepreneurs, Walker was looking not only for something different and scalable, but an idea that could be patented so the company would have intellectual property to protect. His opening was the Supreme Court's decision in 1988 in *State Street Bank v. Signature Financial Group*, making clear the patents were available for business methods (although that principle had been established by the Supreme

Court as early as 1790, the U.S. Patent Office rejected the theory during the computer age until the Supreme Court resurrected it). Amazon would later get a patent for its one-click button that enables customers to purchase online. Although many academic scholars have since argued that patents should not be issued for business methods because they can inhibit innovation if not easily worked around (as Barnes & Noble and other companies did by adding a second click to get around Amazon's one click), business method patents are still available, although the courts have made them more difficult to get after the Supreme Court ruled in *Kappos v. Bilski* that a business method patent was not appropriate for a tax-efficient method of hedging commodity price risks (even where a mathematical formula is involved).

The business method that Walker and his team came up with, and soon patented, was the *conditional purchase offer*, and they built Priceline around it. Here's how they came up with the idea.

Any unsold seats on a given flight or unbooked hotel rooms for any given day disappear after the flight takes off or the day is over. As Walker explains it, he and his team brainstormed how to solve three interrelated problems confronting all sellers of perishable merchandise, of which airline travel and the hotel business are prime examples:[24]

- How can sellers discount the seats or the rooms (or any perishable item, for that matter) and attract new buyers without encouraging or allowing other buyers who are willing to pay full price from also taking advantage of the discount?
- How can regular, full-price customers be discouraged from delaying their purchases in order to receive last-minute discounted fares or prices?
- Because sellers cannot see the demand curve for their products (how many buyers there are at each price), they cannot discover it without lowering their prices in a way that cuts into their profits.

The conditional price offer solves all of these problems by initially offering a more restricted version of airline tickets and later other travel services, and asking customers to submit conditional *offers*—not bids. The offers had to be binding and Priceline assured they were by requiring those making the offers to give their credit card information at the time of making the offer. The conditional price offers had no effect on full price or regular customers, nor did these customers have any incentive to submit last-minute low-price offers for what, in essence, were somewhat impaired versions of the normal service: flights whose times or departure airports (within a given radius of the customer's departure location) only Priceline could control.

Walker recounts that he had difficulty at the beginning persuading airlines to participate. Each feared that selling seats at cheaper prices, even at the cost of not selling any at all, would somehow dilute its brand. TWA, which is no longer flying, thought differently and was the single exception. Eventually, others followed suit.

Walker and his cofounders realized that this business model would appeal only to leisure travelers (and perhaps a few business travelers really trying to save money) who cared only about price and were flexible on other terms. In more technical terms, Priceline was targeting the most price-sensitive customers on the demand curve for travel, and ignoring the rest (thus engaging in a variation of Ramsey pricing, which I describe below, but with the twist that customers rather than vendors set the price).

The rest, as they say, is history. Using a series of clever television ads, starring William Shatner from *Star Trek*, Priceline quickly became a phenomenon in the late 1990s, had some growing pains after the Internet bust, but has gone on to become one of the leading travel booking sites on the web. Walker left the company long before all of this success was achieved, moving on to patent inventions relating to vending machines and inventing and manufacturing casino games.

So where, you may ask, is the economist or the economic idea in the Priceline story? The answer is Walker himself, who was trained in college, at Cornell University, in its well-known industrial and labor relations program, which essentially is all about microeconomics. In other words, Walker studied in school the fundamentals of demand curve analysis that eventually he would one day apply to help build a major Internet-based company resting on a unique business model. Walker's story proves that one of the best ways of transferring economic ideas from the Ivory Tower to business is through the entrepreneurial efforts of single individuals trained in economics.

Different Prices for Different Folks

It doesn't take an economist to tell you that different people are willing to pay different prices for the same item or service. That is because people have different preferences. The demand curve you see in standard economics textbooks is downward sloping, meaning that as prices fall, consumers want more units. This reflects the fact that consumers (or businesses needing supplies) at the very top of the curve are willing to pay much more, and are generally less sensitive to variations in prices, than those at the bottom at the curve.

Many different economic ideas have flowed from this very simple insight, and a number of them have found their way into commercial practice. Let's begin with perhaps the simplest case, a situation where there is only one seller, or a monopolist. In the 1920s, a young math prodigy in the United Kingdom named Frank Ramsey (see following box) formally proved that such a firm would maximize its profits if it could charge higher prices to those least sensitive to price changes (in formal terms, those whose demands are price-inelastic) than to customers who were more price sensitive (in economic jargon, those with price-elastic demand). Ramsey formalized his finding by proving that the optimal strategy for a monopoly firm is to set a markup over variable cost that is inversely proportional to the consumer's elasticity of demand (sorry, I couldn't resist, but in plain English it's the formal equivalent of everything in the paragraph that precedes it).

Now, in the real world, the prices that monopolies like public utilities charge are limited by regulation precisely because consumers have no other choices. So for practical purposes, Ramsey's proof is of most direct use to regulators rather than the firms themselves, though firms that earn their monopolies fair and square, through hard work, luck, or foresight, or by owning a lawfully granted patent can maximize their profits following his strategy. The major objection to Ramsey pricing is on grounds of equity, because some consumers who highly value the product of the monopoly, say electricity, may also have modest means, and so many believe it is unfair to charge them more than well-heeled consumers.

Frank Ramsey: The Life of a Genius Cut Short

Frank Ramsey's life is interesting, but tragic.[25] Ramsey was born in 1903 to an accomplished father, Arthur Ramsey, who was a mathematician and president of Magdalene College at Cambridge University in England. His mother, Mary Agnes Stanley, raised four children.

Ramsey demonstrated intellectual prowess at a very young age, showing wide-ranging interest in literature and mathematics. He was said to have suffered from mild depression and developed an intellectual interest in psychoanalysis, even to the point of being psychoanalyzed by a disciple of Sigmund Freud.

Following in his father's footsteps, Ramsey began his studies at Cambridge at the age 16. While there, he attracted the attention of Keynes and Arthur Pigou, another of Cambridge's leading economists at the time, both of whom urged Ramsey to turn his mathematical mind to economics.

He did so with relish, producing a number of papers, the most famous of which led to the theorem about monopoly price discrimination developed as a by-product of a seminal paper on taxation.[26] The pricing theorem is now widely known as *Ramsey pricing* in his honor. Keynes called another of Ramsey's papers about economic growth "one of the most remarkable contributions to mathematical economics ever made."[27]

In January 1930, about three months after the infamous stock market crash, Frank Ramsey, having suffered from chronic liver problems, entered Guy's Hospital in London to have an abdominal operation. He never went home. Developing jaundice after the operation, he died shortly thereafter. He was 26. Economists to this day speculate about the professional greatness Ramsey would have achieved had he lived a normal life span.

The central notion at the core of Ramsey's contribution—that firms should be permitted to price discriminate according to consumers' sensitivity to price—is actively now used and accepted in many markets, even those served by more than a single producer. Before I show you this to be the case, I want to be clear what I am *not* referring to: the tendency of firms to charge different prices for *essentially different, although related products* because some of them come with different, more highly valued features. Think of fancier hotel rooms within the same hotel carrying a higher price than standard rooms, or first-class airplane tickets with wider seats and better service that cost more than those in coach.

The price discrimination on which I focus instead is the difference in price for the *same* room or the *same* coach seat or the *same* cruise ship cabin that firms charge depending on when you book the reservation. As one of the architects of airline deregulation, former dean of the Yale Management School and distinguished law professor Michael Levine has demonstrated in considerable detail, these situations have two major things in common: (1) they each involve the delivery of a service that has "common costs" that must somehow be recovered, ideally at the maximum profit possible, and (2) the booking or departure times are fixed according to a preset schedule.[28]

For example, an airplane or cruise ship has many seats, all made possible by investment in the vessel itself, plus all of the fixed costs of the crews who steer and maintain it. These costs do not vary if one extra passenger boards (except perhaps minor cleaning costs, and perhaps some snacks if the passengers are lucky). In addition to figuring out how to charge passengers to cover these costs, the firms also confront another challenge: The reservations for available seats are made at different dates and times. Should passengers who book early (typically leisure travelers) be given a relative discount, in the hope that those who book at the last minute (often business users) will want to pay more? The main challenge confronting each of the firms providing these services is to figure out what to charge each customer in order to maximize the firms' profits.

You will learn more about Levine in Chapter 9 but, for now, all you need to know is that he was one of the first academics, government officials, and then business executives to wrestle with these problems in a very real business setting. Shortly after airline fares were fully deregulated in 1979, he was recruited to run Continental Airlines. At the time, it was a risky move, because historically people who ran airlines were former airline pilots, not trained lawyers who also had a

deep understanding of economics. Levine brought his technical experience gained in government, combined with economic training after
law school under the tutelage of future Nobel Prize winner Ronald
Coase of the University of Chicago (who we will meet in later chapters), to Continental and to the airline industry more broadly. His key
innovation: He began the process of charging different prices for the
same seats (or seat equivalents) to different customers depending on
their likely sensitivities to prices. This explains why today prices of
airplane seats and hotel rooms can and do change continuously, often
within each day and certainly within a week in the case of airlines.
Increasingly sophisticated yield management, or what are sometimes
called dynamic pricing programs, are now in place throughout both
industries, a clear example where an economist had a powerful impact
not only on their own business but also in other industries.

Much later in his career, after teaching at a number of leading law schools and serving for a time as dean of the Yale School of
Management, Levine developed his more general theory about pricing
in industries with common costs and fixed allotments. Levine's analogy
to the pricing of different parts of a cow for meat is highly instructive:
Why is it that hamburger is cheaper than prime rib or other parts of
the animal? It is not simply because there may be more of the former than the latter; the different prices reflect differences in consumers'
tastes that are reflected in differences in willingness to pay for certain
cuts of meat. Likewise, travelers manifest similar differences when they
book a cruise ship or plane reservation at different times. Levine credits
Frank Ramsey with inspiring dynamic pricing in competitive settings,
not just in elasticity-based pricing by a monopolist.[29]

Another variation of Ramsey pricing, also widely in use, is peak
load pricing by utilities, which charge more for electricity when overall
demand is high—say during the summer afternoons when air condi-
tioners are running full blast seemingly everywhere in hot climates—
than when it is lower. In part, peak load prices may reflect the higher
costs of fuel to power electric generators than during base load periods, but they also reflect differences in willingness to pay. The more
price-sensitive consumers respond to these price differences by adjust-
ing when they use their appliances, and that is precisely why peak-load
pricing promotes energy efficiency.

Until Levine and other economists showed the generality of charging on the basis of consumers' price sensitivities, it was widely assumed that only monopolies could engage in price discrimination. Instead, Levine and others showed that the presence of price discrimination should not always be taken as evidence of monopoly power, and that, in fact, it was more likely evidence of the common cost problem that many firms in a variety of contexts confront, since virtually all firms have fixed costs they need to recover in order to remain profitable. Levine, in particular, however, demonstrated this to be a widespread problem, not one limited to special circumstances. Other economists, such as William Baumol, whom you will meet in the next chapter, have also demonstrated this.[30]

It is well recognized that price differentiation can only work if users being charged higher prices cannot arbitrage their way to lower prices—that is, being able to buy a low-priced item and immediately turn it around and sell it as a high-priced one. Arbitrage is a lot easier to do when selling physical commodities, which is why we don't see much price differentiation for goods. Furthermore, if price-insensitive users can pose as price-sensitive users to whom low prices might be charged, then even providers of travel services might find it difficult to engage in price discrimination.

The Bottom Line

Prices are among the most important—some will say *the* most important—signals in any economy. In purely competitive markets, with well-established products and services, firms have little or no choice about what prices to charge. The market tells them, although perhaps first through trial and error.

For new products and services, however, firms have a lot more choice, and this is where economists have proved their worth. Not in all cases, to be sure, such as the Bloomberg terminal, where an entrepreneur decided on a pricing strategy and his successors (when Bloomberg was serving as mayor of New York) stuck with it, with remarkable success.

But in other contexts, such as Internet search, and in more conventional physical markets for services in limited supply, such as the travel industry, economists have had important and, I would argue, powerful effects on how business is conducted. Indeed, without the innovations of economists (and engineers acting like them, in Google's case), certain businesses would not have grown as rapidly as they did, and may not even have survived to this day. If you're searching for the trillion dollars of value I promised you in the title of the book, you've found much of it here in this chapter about pricing like an economist.

Here are some key practical takeaways from the successful use of economic ideas in pricing:

- Where you don't know what price users will pay for your service or commodity, consider an auction, such as a Vickery or second price auction.
- If you have excess demand for a service with limited shelf life, such as a plane ticket, also consider an auction to clear the market.
- Even if you're not a monopolist, there may be a way to engage in price differentiation, if customer arbitrage is difficult or expensive.

Notes

1. Norm Brodsky and Bo Burlingham, *Street Smarts: An All-Purpose Tool Kit for Entrepreneurs* (New York: Portfolio, 2010).

2. Alan S. Blinder, *Asking about Prices: A New Approach to Understanding Price Stickiness* (New York: Russell Sage Foundation, 1998). Price and wage stickiness, at least downward, is a fundamental tenet of Keynesian economics, and is a topic of seemingly never-ending controversy among many macroeconomists.

3. Michael Bloomberg and Matthew Winkler, *Bloomberg by Bloomberg* (New York: John Wiley & Sons, 1997). The material about pricing is drawn from this book and my own experience at Bloomberg Government, an information services subsidiary of Bloomberg LLP.

4. Mike Brandly, "Mike Brandly, Auctioneer Blog," *Mike Brandly Auctioneer Blog*, http://mikebrandlyauctioneer.wordpress.com/auction-publications/history-of-auctions.

5. Julian L. Simon, "An Almost Practical Solution to Airline Overbooking," *Journal of Transport Economics and Policy* II, no. 2 (May 1969): 201–202.

6. Julian L. Simon, "The Ultimate Resource," *American Journal of Physics*, 53, no. 3 (1985): 282.

7. The metals were copper, chromium, nickel, tin, and tungsten.

8. Julian L. Simon, "The Airline Oversales Auction Plan," *Journal of Transport Economics and Policy* 28, no. 3 (September 1994): 31–23.

9. "Auctions for Overbooking," *Wall Street Journal*, June 8, 2010, http://online.wsj.com/article/SB10001424052748703303904575293011757655060.html.

10. Jan Dennis, "Airline Overbooking Policy Well Known and So, Too, Should Be Its Creator," News Bureau, University of Illinois, August 3, 2009, www.news.illinois.edu/news/09/0803overbooking.html.

11. Steven Levy, *In the Plex: How Google Thinks, Works, and Shapes Our Lives* (New York: Simon & Schuster, 2011).

12. Steven Levy, "Secret of Googlenomics: Data-Fueled Recipe Brews Profitability," Wired.com, May 22, 2009, www.wired.com/culture/culturereviews/magazine/17-06/nep_googlenomics?currentPage=all. The rest of the personal material about Varian I obtained in a personal interview with him on July 15, 2013 (and through earlier conversations I had with him during the course of our careers). In the interest of full disclosure, I wrote a white paper on behalf of Google with Hal Singer in 2012, defending one of Google's search practices.

13. In 2012, Google's advertising revenue accounted for almost $44 billion versus $31 billion in revenue from Google websites. See: "2012 Financial Tables," *Google Investor Relations*, July 10, 2012, http://investor.google.com/financial/tables.html.

14. William Vickery, "Counter-speculation, Auctions, and Competitive Sealed Tenders." *Journal of Finance* 16, no. 1 (1961): 8–37, http://onlinelibrary.wiley.com/doi/10.1111/j.1540-6261.1961.tb02789.x/pdf.

15. Hal R. Varian, "The Economics of Internet Search," *Rivista di Politica Economica* (November–December 2006): 177–191. www.rivistapoliticaeconomica.it/2006/nov_dic/pdf/Varian_eng.pdf.

16. For this reason, the Google ad auctions are not pure Vickery auctions. For a technical explanation, see Hal R. Varian, "Online Ad Auctions," *American Economic Review* 99, no. 2 (2009): 430–434. http://pubs.aeaweb.org/doi/pdfplus/10.1257/aer.99.2.430.

17. Some investors who bought the stock on the first day were also caught up in a computer glitch that prevented trades in the stock from being completed for several hours on the NASDAQ exchange on which the company's shares were listed. At this writing, several class action investor lawsuits are still pending against NASDAQ over this incident.

18. For a thorough overview of these techniques, see Hal. R. Varian, "Big Data: New Tricks for Econometrics," *The Journal of Economic Perspectives* 28, no. 2 (Spring 2014): 3–28.

19. For more information about this platform, see www.globaldairytrade.com.

20. See www.cranberryauction.info. The economists who assisted in establishing both this auction platform and the earlier one for milk, which they also manage, are from CRA International, a firm I discuss briefly in Chapter 5, and with which I previously have been affiliated as a senior consultant (but not on auction-related matters). I am grateful to Brad Miller at the firm for providing me with this information.

21. Aki Ito, "Stanford Economist Musters Big Data to Shape Web Future," Bloomberg.com, www.bloomberg.com/news/2013-06-26/stanford-economist-musters-big-data-to-shape-web-future.html.

22. "Jay Walker," Speakers Platform, www.speaking.com/speakers/jay-walker .php.

23. Scott Case, "Interview on Jay Walker and the Origins of Priceline," interview by Robert E. Litan, June 2013.

24. Unpublished memorandum provided by Walker to the author.

25. D. H. Mellor, "Cambridge Philosophers I: F.P. Ramsey," *Philosophy* 70 (1995): 243–262.

26. Frank P. Ramsey, "A Contribution to the Theory of Taxation," *Economic Journal* 37, no. 14 (1927): 47–61 www.uib.es/depart/deaweb/webpersonal/ amedeospadaro/workingpapers/bibliosecpub/ramsey.pdf.

27. John Maynard Keynes, "Frank Plumpton Ramsey," *Essays in Biography* (New York: Harcourt, Brace and Jovanovich, 1933).

28. Michael E. Levine, "Price Discrimination Without Market Power," *Yale Journal on Regulation* 19, no. 1 (2002): 1–34.

29. Ibid.

30. William J. Baumol, "Predation and the Logic of the Average Variable Cost Test," *Journal of Law and Economics* 39, no. 1 (1996): 49. See also Levine, 6–8. I was privileged to work with Baumol and my colleague Carl Schramm in writing *Good Capitalism, Bad Capitalism, and the Economics of Growth and Prosperity* (New Haven: Yale University Press, 2007).

Chapter 4

Minimizing Costs

I f you're running a business or just running your life, you don't have
to be an economist or take a course in economics to understand
how to cut costs. It's a matter of choice and arithmetic. What things
and services do you believe are essential to carry out the business, or to
live the life the way you want? What are you willing to pay for them?
If you're on a budget—most people are and so are all businesses in one
fashion or another—then controlling costs is one of the most important
things you regularly do or should do.

Of course, not everyone is successful in this endeavor, which is
why some people and businesses go bankrupt—they live beyond their
means. As a nation, the United States has lived beyond its means for
years, borrowing from foreign governments and individuals to maintain
a level of spending that cannot be financed solely by domestic incomes.

There is nothing inherently wrong with this imbalance if the borrowed funds are used productively, that is, put to work earning more
income in the future, whether by expanding the ability to produce more
goods and services or, in the case of individuals, through the acquisition
of skills that will command a premium in the labor market. Borrowing
for professional school, putting aside whether the school has done a
good job of minimizing its costs, generally (though not always, just ask
a lot of recently minted lawyers) is a good investment for those who
earn their degrees. Borrowing to finance more and bigger houses, as

many did during the years running up to the financial crisis, did not turn out to be such a good investment.

I digress on purpose, since the simple lesson of the last paragraph bears repeating precisely because through the years it so often has been ignored. The main subject of this chapter, minimizing costs, is a close cousin of the maxim to live within your means, with a twist: here I am going to tell you how certain techniques for minimizing costs have been developed by economists or experts in related disciplines and are now widely used in business. Because these techniques are not obvious to the untrained eye, nor are they typically taught in introductory courses in economics, they are fitting subjects for this book.[1]

Optimization

Economists have a lot of favorite words and optimization is one of them. The word is uttered in the context of *constraints*—the fancy word for saying that there is no free lunch. Firms seeking to maximize profits are really engaged in optimizing their performance given the constraints of the demand for their products and their costs.

Actually, costs are not a given, but something to be optimized, or actually minimized, on their own. Mathematicians and mathematically oriented economists have developed techniques to help firms do this with precision rather than relying on hunches. Here's a short history, in plain English, of the field.

The Diet Problem

One of the earliest uses of the specific optimization tool on which I focus in this chapter—linear programming—was to solve the diet problem, which is an easy way to begin to understand the power of the technique. The diet problem is to find the way to minimize the cost of food subject to the constraint that the diet meets an individual's minimum daily nutritional requirements. Later versions of the problem added another condition, one of diversity, so that one doesn't end up eating only one or two foods.

To solve this problem first requires some information about key inputs: the cost of individual items of food per serving (such as corn, milk, bread, and so forth) and the nutritional content of the servings of these items (amounts of particular vitamins and calories). If the diversity constraint is added, then one must add the maximum number of servings per item in a day. Since the costs and outputs rise in a linear fashion as the food variables increase—one pound of butter costs twice as much as half a pound, and so on—this is a linear programming problem: The total cost of the menu is the objective function that one wants to minimize, while the constraints are the minimum acceptable daily nutritional values and the ceilings on the quantities of the different food items needed to ensure diversity.

Today, this problem is readily solved by typing in the required amounts in an application program available on the Internet.[2] But before the age of the computer and, later, the Internet, someone had to come up with the mathematical technique for solving it, by hand (as is the case for virtually every other formula now easily solved by computers and often available on the Internet). The great Russian mathematician Leonid Kantorovich and American professor George Dantzig (see the following boxes) independently came up with the simplex method for doing this. Nobel Prize–winning economist George Stigler of the University of Chicago also outlined his own linear programming-based solution to the diet problem.[3]

The simplex solution method, which can be found in any textbook on operations research, or on the Internet,[4] entails a process of trial and error: successive calculations are made, with improving results, until an optimum is reached. This is much like everyday life, the way humans learn from their mistakes, constantly becoming better—though unlikely perfect—in any endeavor they undertake. We will encounter the trial and error process in Chapter 6, when we discuss the use of experiments in both economics and the business world.

Linear programming was used for far more than solving diet problems. During World War II, the U.S. military secretly used the technique that Dantzig had largely developed as a way of reducing costs. After the war, the technique was described in the academic literature, and thereafter used widely in industry, for scheduling airline and shipping routes, planning the outputs of oil refineries, and minimizing costs for firms in the electricity and telecommunications industries.[7]

George Dantzig

George Bernard Dantzig—yes, his parents gave him his first two names in honor of George Bernard Shaw—was a long-time professor of operations research at the University of California at Berkeley and later Stanford University.[5]

Dantzig inherited his aptitude for mathematics from his father, who also was a mathematician. Born in Germany, his family emigrated to the United States early in the twentieth century, initially moving to Portland, Oregon, and later to Baltimore and then to Washington, D.C. During the family's time in the nation's capital, Dantzig's mother worked as a linguist at the Library of Congress while his father tutored math at the University of Maryland, from which Dantzig earned his undergraduate degree in mathematics and physics. He obtained his doctorate in statistics at the University of California at Berkeley, after serving in the U.S. Air Force Office of Statistical Control during World War II. During his time in the Air Force, he developed techniques for allocating airplane production in an efficient manner.

One event during Dantzig's graduate studies has become legend. During one of his statistics courses, the teacher and Dantzig's eventual thesis adviser wrote two famous unresolved problems in statistics on the blackboard. As he was late to class, Dantzig thought they were homework problems, and a few days later handed in the solutions. Several weeks later, the adviser told Dantzig that he had just solved two of the most difficult, unresolved problems in statistics, and on that basis alone the statistics department awarded Dantzig his PhD.[6]

After the War, Dantzig first worked at the Rand Corporation, then moved to the University of California at Berkeley and later to Stanford. During the course of his career he won many professional prizes for his work, which found its way into practical uses in a wide range of industries described in the text.

In academia, linear programming became the foundation of the field of operations research, a cross between economics and math, to which a number of other prominent economists, such as Kenneth Arrow, Tjalling Koopmans, and Robert Dorfman, made important contributions (some won Nobel Prizes for their other work).[8] William Baumol, who is profiled later, wrote a classic textbook explaining various operations research techniques.[9]

The Transportation Problem

As indicated earlier, linear programming has been applied in many industries, primarily with the objective of minimizing costs. The founders, executives, employees, and consumers in these industries have many unseen and mostly unknown (outside of the economics profession itself) economists and mathematicians to thank.

One of the more widely known applications of linear programming is known as the transportation problem, outlined by a French mathematician, Gaspard Monge. Simply stated, this problem involves figuring out the least costly way of sending outputs of some items—say raw materials—from where they are sourced (for example, in mines or in forests) to destinations for further processing into finished goods. The sources may not be equally productive, the costs for sending the materials or supplies may differ from one route to another, and the distances between the various sources and destinations also vary. Figuring out how much to send from each source to each destination via a route that minimizes overall costs is the essence of the transportation problem.

Instead of sending materials to different locations, imagine you are running an airline that is sending people from and to different places. Suppose further there are multiple routes the planes can fly (in the old days, as we will see in Chapter 9, one had to get government approval before flying any route, which was essentially impossible for new entrants); your airline has a limited number of planes, each with a fixed number of seats; the market conditions dictating the prices you can charge for seats are constantly changing; some costs rise in a linear fashion as the numbers of flights increase (salaries for pilots, flight attendants, and maintenance personnel, whether they are employees or contractors); and other costs are linearly related to the route distance (principally fuel). Assuming you can get landing rights and gate slots at the takeoff and landing airports, the transportation problem for airlines becomes: What combination of routes will maximize your profits? Or, if you don't know the prices the market will let you charge, at the very least, what combination of routes will minimize your costs given the size of your workforce, salary structure, the number of your planes, and total miles they can fly?

It doesn't take much thought to realize that this is a really complicated problem, one that grows exponentially more difficult the larger the airline, and thus the more planes and routes the airline can fly. As William Baumol noted in his textbook on the subject of operations research, there are literally billions of different combinations of inputs and outputs that are theoretically possible even for a firm with fewer numbers of products and constraints than are involved in setting the traffic patterns for today's airlines.[10] Picking out the one or the few items that minimize costs or maximize profits is thus akin to finding the proverbial needle in the haystack. But with a powerful detection device such as linear programming, aided by modern computers, one can yield the result in seconds or less. Now you can understand why transportation companies, like airlines, trucks, and railroads, can and do use programming techniques to solve these problems and to update the solutions on a regular basis.

It took more than century before a method for solving the transportation problem, as Monge identified it, was invented. Leonid Kantorovich first devised a solution to the problem during World War II. Refinements since then have enabled transportation problems to be solved through techniques simpler than the simplex method developed initially to cope with standard linear programming problems. In addition, the structure of the transportation problem has been used to develop ways of optimally assigning jobs where employees can make the most valuable contributions, in what economists have called the assignment or matching problem, a subject I take up in Chapter 7.

Critical Path Method

A variation of linear programming, widely used in large organizations to manage large projects with multiple interdependent tasks, is critical

Leonid Kantorovich

The original giant in operations research, the one who first discovered the simplex method for solving linear programming programs (Dantzig later replicated and refined it), was the great Russian mathematician and economist Leonid Kantorovich. He was born in 1912 in Russia.

Kantorovich was a mathematical prodigy, beginning his college education at Leningrad University at the age of 14, where he eventually earned his PhD and became a full professor in the faculty of mathematics at the age of 22.

Kantorovich eventually worked for the Soviet government, developing linear programming after being assigned the problem of optimizing production in the plywood industry. During World War II, he was put in charge of safety. In the depth of the famous winter of 1941 to 1942, during the siege of Leningrad, he walked between cars on the ice of Lake Ladoga so he could better calculate the optimal distance between cars on the ice to ensure the cars did not sink. After the war, given its command-and-control economy, the Soviet government adopted linear programming to plan its economy.

In 1949, Kantorovich was awarded the Stalin Prize, and for his courage during the war he was given the Order of the Patriotic War, both remarkable given his Jewish background and the infamous anti-Semitism in Russia and later in the Soviet Union. He won the coveted Lenin Prize in 1965 for his work.

In 1975, Kantorovich shared the Nobel Prize with Tjalling Koopmans (one of my mentors in graduate school who kindly took me under his wing). Kantorovich was not aware until the 1950s that linear programming techniques had been independently developed in America after he developed them. He died in 1986.

path analysis. CPM involves listing all of the activities or tasks that are required to complete a project, such as constructing a building or an airplane, or undertaking a research and development project; the estimated time to complete each task; and the extent to which the various activities are dependent on one another (you can't build the first, second, and third floors, and so on, until the foundation and each of the preceding floors is completed).

Using just these values, mathematical techniques—similar to those involved in linear programming—have been developed for determining the quickest path to completing the entire project.[11] Since time is money, the quickest path is generally the one with the least cost, though sometimes, there are risks associated with the fastest path. In these situations, there are tradeoffs between getting it right and getting it done at least expense.

Today, many companies follow the logic of CPM but use diagrams to analyze it. One of the most commonly used diagrams is the Program Evaluation and Review Technique, or PERT chart. CPM, PERT, or some variation is commonly used by major weapons contractors, by the military itself, and by software companies—or firms that require multiple tasks, pursued in parallel and interdependently. CPM software is also widely available to assist companies in organizing complex projects at minimum cost.

The Role of Government and Other Thoughts on Programming Problems

Up to this point, I have mentioned government only in passing, largely in connection with satisfaction of the needs of the military in both the United States and Russia during World War II. But the U.S. government, the Office of Naval Research in particular, played an important role in funding basic research in linear programming in the United States after the end of the war. Along with the role the government played in launching the Internet (also initially for military purposes), and later in supporting research on Internet search algorithms, the government did what most economists routinely have called on the government to do: to support basic research with broad public benefits that would not otherwise be funded by individual companies at the socially optimal level because the gains from the research would be too widely diffused.

There are two other aspects of linear programming that deserve mention before moving to our next topic. First, for each application of linear programming to minimizing costs there is a dual that calculates the way to maximize profits. Essentially, all the signs in the original problem are reversed (instead of the constraints being expressed as amounts greater than a given sum, they are stated as being less than a particular amount). In addition, the objective is changed from minimization to maximization. The reference above to maximizing profits in the airline example, or extending it to maximizing profits in any plant with multiple outputs and inputs, are examples of duals of a cost minimization problem.

Because the values of the inputs into a production process represent the amount by which an additional input, say of labor or a certain material, contributes to the profits of the firm, economists call these values "shadow prices." For example, suppose your firm had a linear programming dual in which the objective was to maximize profits and one of the constraints is that each employee works no more than 40 hours per week. The dual calculates, among other things, the additional gain in profits from having employees work a marginal unit, say an average of one more hour per week. The result, or the shadow price of labor, would be marginal value of an additional hour of work—a number you might like to have in comparing that figure to the overtime hourly pay the law may require you to pay those employees.

Second, linear programming derives its name from the fact that all the key relationships, say between costs and output, are linear—that is, they are multiplied by the same constant factor. Not all relationships in the world work that way, however. Typically, output per unit of output falls as more is produced—this is the notion of diminishing returns. The opposite of diminishing returns is economies of scale, which arise when the average cost of something falls the more of it is produced.

In either situation of diminishing or increasing returns, some or possibly all of the relationships between costs and output can be *nonlinear*—that is, the graph of such a relationship is not a straight line. Not surprisingly, techniques for solving nonlinear programming problems have surfaced, and represent an advance over the initial linear programming solutions. As a general rule, where one has diminishing returns, the linear programming solution will recommend too few activities, products, or routes (in the case of transportation networks discussed next). Conversely, in the presence of increasing returns or economies of scale, the linear solution will recommend too many activities, products, or routes. Since the real world is often not linear (though it may be close enough), nonlinear programming solutions are often more realistic.

William Baumol

I could have profiled William Baumol in almost any of the chapters in this book, that's how versatile and prolific he has been throughout his distinguished career, which marks him as one of the greatest American economists of the last half century. I chose to do it here, however, because he published extensively on linear programming and operations research techniques in the early stages of his career, and as the endnotes indicate, I draw extensively in this chapter from the latest edition of one of his textbooks on these subjects.[12]

Baumol spent most of his academic career as a professor of economics at Princeton University and then after his "retirement" (which never happened), as professor of economics and director of the entrepreneurship center at New York University's Stern School of Business. He is one of the rare breed of economists who is both mathematically gifted and who writes clearly and engagingly.

During his long career—he was still working on a number of book-length projects past the age of 90—he developed novel insights, tested important hypotheses, and wrote about an astonishingly wide range of microeconomic and macroeconomic subjects: the theory of contestable markets, growth theory, monetary economics, macroeconomic fluctuations and dynamics (the subject that introduced me to Baumol as a junior in college when I used his textbook on this subject), and the economics of the performing arts (live theater, orchestras, dance performances, and so on, which is not an accident, since he is an accomplished artist as well). He is the coauthor, with Alan Blinder (another of America's great economists, and one of its best writers, profiled in Chapter 12), of multiple editions of an introductory economics textbook.

Baumol may be best known for the disease named after him. Baumol's disease asserts that the costs of some economic activities are condemned to rise at a rate significantly greater than the economy's rate of inflation because the quantity of labor required to produce these services is difficult to reduce. Since the Industrial Revolution, labor-saving productivity improvements have been occurring at an unprecedented pace in most manufacturing activities, reducing the cost of making these products even as workers' wages have risen. However, in some service industries (such as health care, education, and the live performing arts, among others) automation is not always possible. As a result, labor-saving productivity improvements in these activities occur at a rate well below average for the economy. Therefore, the costs in these service industries increase at a much faster rate than that of inflation. Yet even Baumol recognizes that technology— sound recordings in the case of music and the various Internet-based methods of education that continue to proliferate— may help to alleviate his productivity disease.

During 2005 to 2007, I was privileged to coauthor (with Carl Schramm) a book and a number of articles on entrepreneurship and capitalism with Will Baumol. I consider the book, *Good Capitalism: Bad Capitalism*, my best to date (outside of *this* book), and collaborating with Baumol was the reason why.

Learning by Doing

Toward the beginning of the last chapter, I recounted the standard textbook approach to pricing—set your price at marginal cost, or a truly competitive market will force you to do it. In addition, economists typically assume diminishing returns set in at some point in business. It is progressively harder and more costly, for example, to squeeze out cost savings as one produces more of an item. Or if you've heard the phrase "Let's first pick the low-hanging fruit," you're hearing an application of diminishing returns. The phrase implies that once the easily picked fruit—likely the fruit on a tree that is most visible—is picked, it is more time-consuming, and thus more costly, to fumble through the tree looking for the hidden pieces.

There are important real-world exceptions to both these notions—that is, price should be set at marginal cost, and that diminishing returns rule the world. I lump the exceptions under a single label: Learning by doing.

The phrase suggests its own definition, but first I want you to know what it is *not*. First, learning by doing is different from economies of scale. The latter arise when the average costs of producing extra units just keeps falling the more a firm produces. As output expands, there is more stuff to divide those fixed costs into, so average costs fall. Note this can happen even if the marginal cost of additional units remains the same (we will see in a moment what happens when this assumption is relaxed). Economies of scale are typically found in industries or sectors requiring large capital investments at the front end, as in utilities, oil refineries, railroads, and, in the Internet age, with heavy advertising to build brand awareness.

Learning by doing also is not the same as another widely used term often associated with the Internet: *network externalities*, which are roughly the demand side equivalent of economies of scale on the supply or cost side. Network externalities exist when a service, such as telephone service or a social media network, becomes more valuable as the number of users increases (Metcalfe's law, named after the computer scientist Robert Metcalfe, refers to the observation that the value of a network increases with the square of the number of users).

Network externalities are prevalent in the software world and in mobile communications, which each have operating systems on which applications software, or apps, are overlaid. Here, too, a virtuous circle operates: The more apps that exist for a particular operating system, the greater will be the demand for the system. Likewise, the more popular the operating system, the greater are the incentives for applications programmers to develop apps that run on that system. In the presence of network externalities, it is hard to dislodge the dominant player—not always the first one, by the way—since new entrants must somehow persuade users or applications developers to abandon a platform in which they have invested time and money and one in which they already have a high degree of comfort (and for these reasons, they are sometimes said to be locked in).

So, if we're not talking about economies of scale or network externalities, then what do economists mean when they refer to learning by doing, and why is the concept so important? As you might guess, the answer is actually pretty simple. When workers engage in some task more frequently and routinely, they are likely to get better at it, just as most athletes, musicians, or almost any professionals, improve with practice.[13] In the workplace, the worker who learns by doing may be getting paid the same rate per hour (and very likely will continue to be until an annual or more regular pay review is conducted), but because he or she is becoming more productive, then the cost per unit is falling. That's learning by doing: when marginal costs fall as output increases.

In fact, this is generally what happens in most manufacturing plants. It would be surprising if it didn't. At the same time, however, at some point the learning levels off, the productivity advances diminish, and the effect slowly comes to a halt. If you were graphing the impact of learning by doing, you might see a steep upward slope in productivity (or conversely a steep downward slope in per unit cost) as production increases, followed by a leveling off, so that the overall productivity graph looks like an S (or an upside down S for unit costs).

But there is at least one notable product that has long been an exception to this pattern—integrated circuits or computer chips. Gordon Moore, one of the cofounders of Intel, uttered a famous statement some time ago that has been enshrined as Moore's law: Computing power doubles roughly every 18 months, which means that the cost of computing comes down by 50 percent over the same period. This has been happening for decades, despite some skeptics who thought the trend would stop. So far, there has been no S curve in semiconductors.

This fact has important macroeconomic implications because so much hardware and software is linked to the processing capability of integrated circuits. But for my purpose here, I want to stress one key and often overlooked aspect of Moore's law: what it suggests as an optimal pricing strategy, which in turn has important implications for cost control.

The standard economics textbook tells readers that prices in competitive markets equal marginal costs. It turns out, however, that this equality does not describe the optimal pricing strategy for an innovative firm in perhaps a new market, where learning by doing is expected to last for a long time—as in semiconductors. If a firm is reasonably certain that its marginal costs will continue to fall as more output is produced and purchased, then the firm will want to set a price for its product *below* its current marginal cost. Doing so will generate additional cost-reducing demand, which in turn will help establish the firm as a market leader. Admittedly, Moore's law may not have been evident when semiconductors were first used, but once the silicon revolution was underway, then it became safer for the two major firms in the industry (Intel and AMD) to set their prices with each new generation of chips on the assumption that firms and their workers would learn by doing.

But how many firms are in industries that will end up having Moore's law equivalents of their own—decades of falling marginal costs that will give firms sufficient confidence to price below marginal cost at the outset? It is doubtful that there are that many, but who really knows?

The only way to find out is for truly entrepreneurial firms to try learning by doing pricing and then find out. I'm not optimistic that this will be a successful strategy for many firms, based on Norm Brodsky's observation cited at the beginning of Chapter 3: It's a lot easier to lower prices from having set them too high than to raise them once you've realized that you've set them too low. Where you set prices at first establishes important expectations among purchasers about your price points, and once those expectations are established, it is dangerous to upset them.

There is another rationale for setting prices below marginal cost, however, which is a loose intellectual cousin of learning by doing. This is the notion of the first mover's advantage—the idea being that if a company with a truly new idea or way of doing things gets a sufficient head start on future competitors, it can establish a brand presence that is impossible, or at least very difficult, for others to overcome. Amazon in Internet retailing (first starting with books) fits this model.

Yet even this example has its limits. Other companies that have not been first movers have refined earlier companies' efforts to become dominant players in their industries. Microsoft is perhaps the most notable example. While it did not charge for its Internet browser, the company made its fortune on operating systems and applications software for personal computers, and later did well in video game consoles. In each of these segments, Microsoft was not the first mover, but financially among the best movers. And as far as I know, in none of these profit-making markets did Microsoft set a price based on learning by doing.

The Bottom Line

There comes a time in many businesses when the common-sense maxim—just keep your costs down—just isn't good enough. As this chapter has sketched out only on the surface, powerful mathematical techniques, developed initially by mathematicians and later refined by economists, were developed just prior to and during World War II, that have enabled firms in many industries with multiple outputs and inputs, or with business models built around transportation networks of some kind (of goods, people, or electrons), to figure out on a continuous basis how best to deploy limited resources to minimize costs or maximize profits.

Importantly, these techniques do not require a lot of data. Problems or challenges growing out of the need to make sense of masses of data are another area where economists have made great contributions, and they are the subject of the next chapter.

That is not all. In some cases, what it costs to produce an item depends on how much of it is made. In the semiconductor industry and perhaps in a few others, it can make sense—and it is the profit-maximizing strategy—to price what a firm is producing so low that the market literally forces the firm to produce more than it may initially had planned for or thought it possible to produce in order to *compel* the use of the learning curve to reduce costs.

The propositions in this chapter are not self-evident. They take some economic knowledge. Hopefully, you are beginning to see that economists are even more important to success in business than you may have thought before picking up this book. That conclusion is reinforced in subsequent chapters.

Notes

1. I am indebted to Roger Noll, who made valuable suggestions regarding the organization of this chapter, and to William Baumol, who reviewed the chapter for accuracy and made a number of valuable substantive and editorial suggestions.

2. See, for example, Joseph Czyzyk and Timothy J. Wisniewski, "The Diet Problem: A WWW-Based Interactive Case Study in Linear Programming," Mathematics and Computer Science Division, Argonne National Laboratory, http://citeseerx.ist.psu.edu/viewdoc/summary?doi=10.1.1.47.5308. For an earlier version of this challenge, see George Dantzig, "The Diet Problem," http://dl.dropbox.com/u/5317066/1990-dantzig-dietproblem.pdf.

3. George Stigler, "The Cost of Subsistence," www.jstor.org/stable/1231810.

4. See, for example, this video, which tells one how to solve a linear programming problem in Excel: www.youtube.com/watch?v=I3pckP_8T-k.

5. This profile draws on his obituary in *The New York Times* by Jeremy Pearce, May 23, 2005.

6. Sira M. Allende and Carlos N. Bouza, "Professor George Bernard Dantzig, Life and Legend," *Revista Investigación Operacional*, 26, no. 3, http://rev-inv-ope.univ-paris1.fr/files/26305/IO-26305-1.pdf.

7. Joe Holley, "Obituaries of George Dantzig," *Washington Post*, May 19, 2005, p. B6, http://supernet.som.umass.edu/photos/gdobit.html.

8. William J. Baumol, *Economic Theory and Operations Analysis* (Englewood Cliffs, NJ: Prentice Hall, 1972), 70.

9. Ibid.

10. Ibid., 83.

11. One of the pioneering works in the field is James Kelly, "Critical Path Planning and Scheduling: Mathematical Basis," *Operations Research* 9, no. 3 (May–June, 1961).

12. This profile is based on the author's personal knowledge about Professor Baumol and correspondence with him.

13. The writer Malcolm Gladwell made this observation a central theme of his book *Outliers: The Stories of Success* (New York: Little, Brown & Co., 2008). Gladwell argued that to do anything really well requires at least 10,000 hours of practice.

Chapter 5

Beyond Moneyball

A ll sciences—social and scientific—have their techniques for validating hypotheses. Economics is no exception. Its practitioners make heavy use of increasingly sophisticated statistical techniques to try to sort out cause and effect and make predictions.

Except in the situations I discuss in the next chapter, empirically oriented economists do not have the luxury of conducting experiments to test their hypotheses, as do their counterparts in the hard physical sciences. Instead, economists must try to tease out relationships and infer behaviors from what is already going on in the real world, which cannot be stopped and restarted to suit the needs of economists who want to know what is really happening.

In this chapter, I will take you through a tour of the statistical method economists most commonly use—regression analysis—first by briefly explaining the concept and its origins, then discussing its use during the heydays of large forecasting models (the era when I learned economics) and later during the waning popularity of those models. I will also discuss how the tools of economics have been used to analyze complex challenges and solve real-world business disputes, in what is called the economic consulting industry. I will then introduce you to the exciting world of sports analytics, in which statistical and economic methods have played a central role. I conclude with an application of the Moneyball concept, popularized by Michael Lewis, to policy and business.[1]

Consider this introduction to a basic statistical technique (which I promise will be painless) as a worthwhile investment in understanding the really fun stuff in the latter half of the chapter.

A Brief Guide to Regression Analysis

Suppose you are a farmer with a reasonably large amount of acreage and you grow corn. You have historical data on the amount you plant, the volume of your crop in bushels (we will ignore prices since they are outside your control because you compete in a highly competitive market), and the amounts of fertilizer and insecticide you apply. Now suppose an agribusiness conglomerate comes to you and talks you into buying its special supplement which it says will enhance your crop volume, based on data supplied from the company's experience with other farms, and apply it after planting.

Months pass and you reap your crop. Amazingly, it's up 10 percent compared to the year before. Can you say with confidence that the application of the supplement did it?

Of course you can't. A whole lot of things influence your crop output, some within your control like the fertilizer, the insecticide, and the supplement, and other factors, such as amount of rain, days of sun, daily temperatures during the growing season, and so on. Ideally, you'd like to control for all factors other than the application of the supplement, so you can know with some degree of confidence whether and to what extent that supplement worked or didn't.

How would you go about addressing this challenge? Well, it turns out that some very smart statisticians in the early part of the nineteenth century developed techniques to enable you to do precisely this. Furthermore, these same techniques, known as *multivariate regression analysis*, have been taught to undergraduate and graduate students for decades in statistics and social science classes, in some cases even to advanced high school students.

Regression analysis enables economists (or other social and physical scientists) to understand the relationships of different variables. In the farming example above, an economist or statistician would estimate an equation to understand how different independent factors (such as the special supplement, the fertilizer, the amount of rain, the days of sun, the temperature, and so on) cause an effect on crop output—the dependent factor.

It turns out that when the data are collected and organized, an economist or statistician, or, frankly, many analysts with even less formal training, can estimate an equation to find out if the 10 percent increase in your crop output was in fact caused primarily by the application of the special supplement, or if instead the other factors had a larger effect. The beauty of regression analysis is that it enables the analyst to estimate the effect of every causal variable on the key dependent variable, controlling for the effect of all other causal variables that you want or need to explain and influence, such as crop output.

It could be the case, for example, that the special supplement contributed very little to your increased crop yield and that instead the amounts of fertilizer, rain, and sun were the most important factors. If that is true, you have valuable information: There's no need to buy the special supplement. Simply keep using the fertilizer and make sure your corn gets enough water (the sun you can't control). You could even cut back on the insecticide, since the regression results may have shown a negligible effect.

Besides helping you to understand how different factors relate to each other, regression analysis can be used to predict the value of one variable if you know the values of the factors that you think affect that variable. For example, with regression analysis, you can get a fairly good idea of roughly how much output your crop will yield next month under different scenarios (a lot of rain, few days of sun, and so on) based on historical data that you've collected. That is the magic of statistical analysis.

In the real world, knowing not only the *direction* of the effect of a given factor on another (positively or negatively), but also the approximate *size* of that effect, can be extremely valuable. In a sense, many decisions in business, sports, public policy, and life involve questions about the unknown effect of changing one factor. Will adding the special supplement cause your crop output to increase? Will revenues increase if we raise ticket prices, and if so, by how much? What are the main determinants of economic growth? Regression analysis can be used to answer these and many other questions.

Although I spend the rest of this chapter highlighting some of the ways regression analysis and other statistical techniques have been used in the business world, I want to add a word of caution. There is an old saying: "There are lies, damn lies, and statistics;" implying that, given enough time and ingenuity, one can prove just about anything with statistics. That overstates things, but there is some truth to the saying. Careful choice of the time periods and the specifications of equations to be estimated can generate the results a particular researcher wants. Or, better yet, in this age of essentially costless computing, it is easier than ever to engage data mining to run regressions mindlessly to see which equations best fit the data and then proclaim that one has found the truth.

The best way to guard against data mining, used in its pejorative sense (there is a more positive use of the term I will discuss later), is to test estimated equations out of sample, or in future periods after the period used to estimate the equation. Clearly, an equation that does a poor job predicting future values of the variable of interest, or the dependent variable, calls into question the value of the explanations it purports to advance from the historical data. Conversely, equations that do relatively well predicting future values inspire confidence in the validity of the regression results, which brings us to the first business use of regression analysis—predicting the future.

The Business of Forecasting

The business of economic forecasting as we know it today has its roots in the Keynesian revolution during the Great Depression and World War II. One of the pioneers of econometrics and macroeconomic forecasting was a Dutch economist, Jan Tinbergen, who is credited with developing the first national comprehensive model of how an entire economy works. Having done it first for his home country, the Netherlands, in 1936, Tinbergen produced a model of the American economy in 1938 for the League of Nations in Geneva, Switzerland.[2] Tinbergen's initial model is considered a precursor to the large forecasting models solved by computers today. In 1969, Tinbergen and Norwegian economist Ragnar Frisch shared the very first Nobel Prize awarded in economics, "for having developed and applied dynamic models for the analysis of economic processes."[3]

American economist Lawrence Klein created the first large comprehensive forecasting model of the U.S. economy (see box that follows). Having studied for his PhD under Paul Samuelson at MIT during World War II, Klein built a more robust version of Tinbergen's earlier model in order to estimate the impact of the government's policies on the U.S. economy.[4]

Lawrence Klein

Lawrence Klein is widely acknowledged to be the father of macroeconomic econometric models. Born in Omaha, Nebraska, in 1920, Klein grew up during the Great Depression and went to the University of California, Berkeley for college, where he studied economics and mathematics. He earned his PhD at MIT and thereafter joined the econometrics team at the Cowles Commission of the University of Chicago (now the Cowles Foundation), where he began the challenging task of, in his words, "reviving Jan Tinbergen's early attempts at econometric model building for the United States."[6]

During the late 1940s and 1950s, Klein traveled around the world and performed pioneering research in econometrics and macroeconomic modeling. Shortly after World War II, Klein used his model of the U.S. economy to correctly predict—against conventional wisdom—an economic expansion rather than another depression.[7] At the University of Michigan, Klein worked with a graduate student, Arthur Goldberger, to develop what later became known as the Klein-Goldberger Model, an early U.S. macroeconomic forecasting model. Klein left Michigan because the university denied him tenure due to his earlier temporary post-war affiliation with the Communist Party, which he joined simply to speak at a particular event (a decision he had long renounced, to no avail).

Klein then moved to Oxford for a short period before being invited in 1958 to join the faculty of the University of Pennsylvania. He promptly began work on a series of models that became known as the Wharton Models, which ultimately

(continued)

contained thousands of equations solved by computers to forecast a wide range of macroeconomic variables. The following year, he was awarded the John Bates Clark Medal for his pioneering work in macroeconomic modeling. The University of Pennsylvania was his academic home for the rest of his life.

Beginning in the early 1960s, Klein began consulting on forecasting for both private and public sector clients around the world. In the late 1960s, Klein played a critical part in initiating and leading Project LINK, a large and ambitious research project aimed at coordinating econometric models in different countries.[8]

Klein founded Wharton Econometric Forecasting Associates as a nonprofit organization within the University of Pennsylvania in the late 1960s, which was later sold to a private publishing company. Over the years, WEFA became one of the world's leading forecasting organizations, and Klein remained engaged in special projects even after the firm merged with Data Resources Inc. (DRI), WEFA's main competitor, and formed Global Insight in 2001.[9]

Klein was awarded the Nobel Prize in Economics in 1980 "for the creation of economic models and their application to the analysis of economic fluctuations and economic policies."[10] Klein lived to the age of 93 and died at his home in 2013.

Finally, one personal note: I will be forever grateful to Professor Klein for recommending me for my first job at the Brookings Institution after completing my undergraduate studies at the University of Pennsylvania. At Brookings, I had the great privilege of serving as the research assistant for Arthur Okun, another of the great economists of the latter half of the twentieth century, who at 39 became the youngest chair of President Johnson's Council of Economic Advisers (and who tragically died at the young age of 51 of a heart attack). My career would have never been the same without Klein's kind and extremely generous gesture to a (then) young college student.

By the 1960s, Klein was the undisputed star in the field of fore-casting. Through a nonprofit organization set up within the University of Pennsylvania known as Wharton Econometric Forecasting Associates (WEFA), he would regularly perform and sell forecasts to both the private sector and governments around the world.[5]

During roughly this same period, Klein and other economists at the University of Pennsylvania collaborated with Franco Modigliani (another future Nobel Prize winner) and his colleagues at MIT, and with economists at the Federal Reserve Board to build the Penn–MIT–Fed macroeconomic model of the economy. That model has been successively refined through the years, but it is still the work-horse of the Fed staff in preparing their forecasts for the meetings of the Federal Open Market Committee, which sets monetary policy and conducts other business of the Fed.

Klein and WEFA's foray into econometric forecasting attracted other entrants. Among the more notable, and for a time the most suc-cessful, was Data Resources Inc., founded by the late Harvard econ-omist Otto Eckstein and Donald Marron, a former CEO of Paine Webber (a brokerage firm bought by UBS bank in 2000). During the 1970s and 1980s, DRI and WEFA were the dominant macroeconomic forecasting firms, projecting not only the outlook for the entire econ-omy but for specific industries. Both firms also provided one-off stud-ies of particular subjects using their econometric engines—their large bodies of equations, based on the use of regression analysis and histori-cal data on multiple variables.

Through much of this period it seemed as if the macro models had unlimited futures but then, as in other industries, disruptive technolo-gies combined to make the macro forecasting business, as a commercial operation, much less profitable. One of these technologies was older and in use for some time before it helped seal the fate of the large macro models, namely software for regression analysis and other sta-tistical techniques that individual users could use on their own main-frame and later minicomputers. Robert Hall is one of the nation's leading economists; he has long taught at Stanford and at this writ-ing is the head of the committee of the National Bureau of Economic Research that pinpoints the dates at which expansions end (recessions) and later begin. He also developed one of the most popular programs of this genre, TSP (Time Series Program). Hall did this while he was a graduate student in economics at MIT.

Hall's and subsequent versions of TSP refined by Berkeley's Bronwyn Hall were important, but it was a hardware innovation—the personal computer—combined with the statistical software packages then available that really disrupted the macro modelers. Armed with a PC, a statistics software app, and some data, virtually anyone with enough training could build his or her own, much smaller models without paying substantial annual sums to the macro modelers for either macro or industry-specific (micro) forecasts. And that is precisely what many customers of the macro modelers eventually did.

Macro-model customers moved away from the models for other reasons as well. For one thing, they were so large, with so many equations, that they were not transparent. Users couldn't easily understand how a change in one or more of the input variables translated into changes in projected outputs. They simply had to trust the model, or the modeler, since it was also unclear how often and to what extent those running the models adjusted their forecasts with judgmental factors that reflected the modelers' own beliefs about whether to trust the unadjusted projections of their models.

Another contributing reason for the decline in macro modeling was the so-called Lucas critique, outlined by eventual Nobel Prize winner Robert Lucas of the University of Chicago. Lucas demonstrated that fiscal and monetary policies were influenced by some of the factors driving the forecasts of macro models, so one could not draw reliable conclusions about the impacts of certain policy changes by using the models. In technical terms, Lucas showed that fiscal and monetary policies were not truly independent variables.

Another problem that has plagued not only the macro models but also users of regression analysis is how to distinguish between causation and correlation. Two or more variables may be highly correlated with the variable to be projected, say GDP, but it may not be clear they cause or determine GDP. Although Clive Granger developed a statistical method for addressing this problem—an achievement that earned him a Nobel—the macro models did not correct all of their equations for it.

Yet another challenge to the macro models was posed by the rise of VAR models (technically vector autoregression models) that were statistically fancy ways of just extrapolating past data into the future. VAR models often outperformed the structural macro models. One of the leading exponents of VAR models is another Nobel Prize winner, Christopher Sims of Princeton University. Both VAR and the macro models had difficulty predicting turning points in the economy, or the beginnings of recessions or expansions.

The decline of the large-scale macro-model business has not ended forecasting, however. Numerous forecasters, on their own or working mostly for financial companies, offer forecasts built with PCs and off-the-shelf software and are routinely surveyed by popular news outlets such as the *Wall Street Journal*. At the same time, several large-scale commercial models remain (Moody's, Macroeconomic Advisers, and IHS, which also bought Global Insight). The Fed and the International Monetary Fund, among other official entities, continue to use their own large-scale macro models.

Many businesses and other governmental organizations—notably the Congressional Budget Office and the Council of Economic Advisers—use an average of the major forecasts of key macroeconomic variables, such as GDP growth, inflation, and unemployment, compiled by Blue Chip Economic Indicators. This approach adapts the wisdom-of-crowds approach (really the wisdom of *experts*) to forecasting, which has been widely popularized by the journalist James Surowiecki of the *New Yorker*.[11]

The Business of Economic Consulting

In the 1970s the tools of economics, and particularly econometrics, began to be widely applied to solve real-world business and legal challenges by new firms in what is now known as the economic consulting industry.

Whereas the business of forecasting involves primarily macroeconomic models dealing with the national economy, the business of economic consulting involves the application of microeconomic tools to the challenges that individuals and firms face, rather than whole economies. In particular, the economic consulting firms formalized the business of providing economic expertise in an expanding array of legal disputes, addressing such questions as causation, valuation, and damages. Today, economists from various consulting firms are routinely used as experts, on both sides, in legal disputes involving antitrust, patent, discrimination, and torts (personal injuries) issues, among others. In addition, economists are frequently found in various regulatory proceedings at all levels of government.

The rise of economic consulting also coincided with the development and growth of the field of law and economics, taught in both law schools and economics departments. One of the fathers of law and economics, Richard Posner, has had a tremendous influence on the way many judges analyze and decide cases. Posner, a law professor with economic training who later was appointed to be a federal circuit judge, is widely regarded as the most prolific legal scholar and judge of his generation. In 1977, he cofounded, with his University of Chicago Law School colleague William Landes, Lexecon, which became one of the more successful economic consulting firms. Lexecon is now part of the global firm FTI Consulting.[12] Other successful competitors in the economic consulting business include Analysis Group; The Brattle Group; Cornerstone; CRA International; Economists, Inc.; Navigant; and National Economic Research Associates, or NERA. (Full disclosure: during the course of my career I have had a part-time relationship, as many economists do, with several of these firms.)

The growth of the economic consulting industry as we know it today would not have been possible without the technological revolution of the past thirty years. In particular, many of the innovative tools and methods used in economic consulting, such as regression analysis, depend on the use of advanced computers, network services, and software to store and analyze large quantities of data.

The contribution of the economic consulting industry to the economy should be put into some perspective, however. Since the litigation-consulting component of the business consulting industry is linked to specific disputes, the economists who participate in these matters assist in transferring wealth from one pocket to another, which may outweigh any enhancements to the productive efficiency of the economy to the extent that the quantification of damages assists the legal system to deter undesirable behavior. The latter impacts encourage resources to move to more productive activities. Whatever the net impacts of litigation consulting may be, it is uncontestible that economic consultants could not do their jobs and the audiences they address—judges, regulators, and sometimes legislators—could not interpret the consultants' work without relying on the methods of analyses developed by academic economists and statisticians.

Franklin Fisher

While Lawrence Klein and Otto Eckstein were showing the real-world application of large-scale regression analyses, another econometrician, Franklin Fisher, now emeritus professor of economics at MIT, was publishing papers on econometric theory. Fisher's research and econometric methods have been widely used by empirical economists for decades, both in academia and in the economic consulting business.[13]

Fisher did his undergraduate work at Harvard, where initially he did not know where and how to apply his prodigious mathematical skills. He roamed around the Harvard course offerings until his section leader in an introductory history course suggested that Fisher try economics. He followed the advice and was smitten.

One of his early undergraduate essays in economics was brought to the attention of Merton (Joe) Peck, a leading expert in industrial organization at Harvard (who coincidentally a number of years later taught me at Yale and was one of my PhD thesis advisers). Peck forwarded Fisher's work to Carl Kaysen, another leading industrial organization expert also at Harvard. Kaysen also had an unusual experience for an economist: In the 1950s he spent a year as an economic clerk for Judge Wyzanski in the famous antitrust case brought by the Justice Department against the United Shoe Company.

In any event, Kaysen was so taken with Fisher's paper that he took the unusual step of becoming Fisher's tutor, while also helping him be immediately admitted into graduate level courses. Somewhat like my mother who questioned the value of

(continued)

an advanced economics degree—because that was where Fisher was clearly headed—Fisher's mother came to see Kaysen around this time to express her skepticism, but apparently was assuaged.

Fisher became fascinated with econometrics in particular by working on an empirical research project with one of his professors, and then went to graduate school at MIT, where he taught his entire career after earning his PhD at the school. Fisher published some of the leading theoretical papers in econometrics in the 1960s, but later turned to more practical empirical uses of econometric tools to understand particular problems once he realized that theoretical econometrics was moving in the direction of pure mathematics. Fisher's interest in econometrics, like that of other economists, was more practical.

One demonstration of this bent was that Fisher became one of the early outside directors of the economic consulting firm Cambridge Research Associates (CRA), a firm formed by John Meyer and several colleagues. Fisher has remained affiliated with CRA (and MIT) ever since.

Data Analytics and Big Data

Earlier I referred to the practice of data mining in the pejorative sense in which it was used during much of my career. My, things have changed. With the rise of the Internet, mobile telephones, and the proliferation of various kinds of databases, both public and private, the term now has both negative and positive connotations, but very different from those associated with those just running regressions. The negative associations overwhelmingly reflect concerns about intrusions of personal privacy by the government or private companies. The positive aspects of data mining, now associated with Big Data, relate to the ability of analysts to uncover patterns in very large data sets in a short period of time that can lead to new drugs and other products, new services, and new ways of producing or delivering them.

It is not my purpose here to debate the pros and cons of mining Big Data and how to limit its downsides, but rather simply to point out that the analytical techniques used for extracting useful information from large data sets include (but are not limited to) regression analysis in its various forms. These techniques are used in businesses to analyze customer behavior in the real world and on the Internet; pharmaceutical companies looking for new cures; meteorologists looking to improve their forecasts; financial institutions seeking to improve their detection of fraud; and, as will be discussed in the next chapter, by firms conducting continuous experiments (often on the Internet) seeking to refine their product and service offerings to consumers. Expect more uses and benefits from Big Data as more firms, and even the government, devote more resources to data analytics.

I am aware that the main practitioners of data mining are statisticians rather than economists. Indeed, Google, with a huge amount of data due to the vast number of searches conducted on its website each day, has many more statisticians than economists on its staff for analyzing data.[14] Nonetheless, economists can be useful in structuring these analyses, highlighting what to look for, as well as in designing and interpreting the results of the experiments aimed at improving customer experiences. Businesses are increasingly recognizing this to be the case, and they are hiring economists in increasing numbers (after pretty much ignoring them in the preceding two decades).[15]

Love it or hate it, Big Data is here to stay. There is a growing literature on the topic that is difficult to keep up with. At this writing, I highly recommend two books cited in the endnote for those interested in the subject.[16] An earlier book, *Super Crunchers*, by economist and lawyer Ian Ayres of Yale Law School, anticipated the growth of Big Data analytics and is also worth reading if for no other reason than he was way out front on this topic before it became as popular as it has become.[17]

One final observation about all this is worth noting. The Big Data movement came largely out of the business world rather than academia, and thus is the exception to the rule of this chapter (although it is roughly consistent with the course of events described in the topic areas covered by the next two chapters). At this writing, in mid-2014, universities are just beginning to catch up to industry's need for a whole new generation of data scientists—individuals who have training in multiple fields, primarily statistics and computer science, but also economics and perhaps one or more of the physical or biological sciences. As just one example, Georgetown received a $100 million donation in September 2013 to launch a new public policy school, one of whose primary missions will be data analytics. Carnegie Mellon and the University of California at Berkeley already have made their marks in the field. I expect a growing number of other schools to join them in the years ahead.

Econometrics and Sports: Moneyball

It may not exactly be Big Data, but the data generated by athletic performances is certainly interesting to millions of Americans and the owners of the teams who put them on the field. Perhaps no sport is more measured or attracts more data geeks than professional baseball. The best-known sports geek of them all is Bill James, who helped launch the baseball data revolution from a makeshift office in the back of his house in Lawrence, Kansas. James and his craft were catapulted into fame by Michael Lewis in his book *Moneyball* (the basis for the movie of the same name).[18]

Moneyball entails the use of statistics to discover and exploit the inefficiencies in the valuation of individual players (baseball in the first instance) to determine how and to what extent these players contribute to their teams' performance. The book *Moneyball* credits the Oakland Athletics and its manager, Billy Beane, with being the first practitioner of this mode of analysis but in fact other teams were making use of some of the same techniques, now also widely referred to as sabermetrics, at or near the same time.

The fundamental idea behind sabermetrics is to identify the key variables that most contribute to the performance of both players and teams. Since you are now familiar with the basic premise of regression analysis, you won't be surprised to learn that the Oakland A's used various forms of it to evaluate baseball players' batting statistics (and also their fielding statistics) in college and the minor leagues to discover overlooked or undervalued players to build a relatively inexpensive winning team. Put another way, teams practicing moneyball use baseball data to find undervalued players in much the same way that Warren Buffett and other value investors use financial data to discover undervalued stocks (one of the topics covered in Chapter 8).

Today, virtually all baseball teams engage in some form of moneyball, although none to my knowledge use it exclusively. More typical is the way the St. Louis Cardinals employ it—two different teams of experts, traditional scouts who rely on their gut and feel from observing young prospects, and the quants or analysts who go by the numbers, are mixed together to decide who to draft and trade. The stakes are huge, and no one has yet perfected the art of picking all the right people. The Cardinals' scouting staff, for example, analyzed all of the baseball draft results from all teams between 1990 and 2013 and found that if a club signed nine players from a single year's draft (in which more than 20 players are taken by each team, counting all rounds) who eventually made it to the major leagues, that would put the team in the 95th percentile of all teams (namely in the top two).[19] Comparable data for just the more recent years, when presumably many, if not all, teams are using analytic techniques to help them identify talent, are not available, and one hopes are better. Still, picking young baseball players who are likely to have successful professional careers remains part art and part science, though moneyball techniques are pushing things in the scientific direction.

This is evident from the large and growing interest in sports analytics among fans of all types of sports teams, as well as among academic scholars. For example, if you're into sports and want to know how a clever economist can come up with really interesting insights into what works and doesn't, at least statistically, I highly recommend *Scorecasting* by Tobias Moskowitz (the economist) and L. Jon Wertheim, executive editor of *Sports Illustrated*.[20] For a thorough discussion of the uses and limits of sabermetrics in baseball, where it all started, you can't do better than *The Sabermetrics Revolution: Assessing the Growth of Analytics in Baseball* by Benjamin Baumer (a mathematician) and Andrew Zimbalist (one of the leading "sports economists" in the country, baseball in particular).[21]

The growing academic and real-world research in sports analytics turns out, not surprisingly, to be of more than academic interest. The annual MIT Sloan Sports Analytics Conference, for example, has become the premier forum for discussing the growing importance of the application of analytics to a range of sports. The conference has attracted growing numbers of attendees since its founding in 2006, and representatives from all major sports and all corners of the country come to it every year to discuss the latest trends and developments.

Can all sports be moneyballed? In other words, is it possible to apply analytics to the other major sports—football, basketball, hockey, and soccer—to discover and exploit different inefficiencies? Are individual sports like golf or tennis easier to moneyball? Are there certain sports that simply can't be moneyballed? And perhaps most important to the vast majority of us who are not professional athletes, can or will a type of moneyball be used to assess our performance in the workplace?

The answers to all these questions seem to be yes, although it will take more time for analytical techniques to penetrate some sports than others. The speed of adoption in various sports will depend on the types of variables and metrics that are unique to each sport, and whether that data can be collected, analyzed, and exploited effectively. Some sports, like football, are more team-oriented and therefore have less individuality than baseball. The insights of moneyball and economics suggest, however, that there could be a lot of low-hanging analytical fruit in sports other than baseball, since they haven't been explored as extensively yet.

Basketball is one sport outside of baseball where moneyball is starting to make inroads. At the 2011 MIT Sloan Sports Analytics Conference, for example, the backdrop in the main panel room featured a picture of Kobe Bryant taking a fadeaway shot just as Shane Battier was sticking his hand in Bryant's face. The image illustrated a well-known analytical finding by the front office of the Houston Rockets (Battier's team at the time): Bryant is a much less efficient scorer (as is likely the case with most other players) when a hand from an opposing player obstructs his view.[22]

Still, one sign that basketball has a way to go to catch up to baseball in analytical techniques is that professional basketball teams have been reluctant to discuss what measures they look at, citing the information as proprietary. Only when these measures become standardized and are widely adopted by all teams and made public, analogous to on-base percentage and similar publicly available baseball statistics, is moneyball likely to become part of the mainstream in basketball or any other sport.

As for the workplace, most companies already have a variety of ways in which they measure the performance of their employees, both by the quantity and quality of their output. There is an entire human relations sub-industry that has grown up around this subject. As sports analytics become increasingly sophisticated and well accepted across a number of sports, do not be surprised if some of the lessons from the athletic world spill over into the corporate world (and perhaps vice versa).

Bloomberg Sports and William Squadron

You can't engage in moneyball or any sort of statistical exercise without data. In the pre-digital world, Bill James was the king of baseball statistics. In the digital age, the data king in baseball, and potentially in soccer and other sports, is Bloomberg.

At one level, this should not be surprising because Bloomberg is a financial data company. Sports data are no different, though behind every hit or pitch is also a video, which makes it unlike financial data. Bloomberg Sports, overseen by William Squadron, has brought baseball data to a whole new level: The type, speed, and location of every pitch and its aftermath (taken, swung at, hit, and where) are fully integrated in a single system. The Bloomberg Sports database enables managers and players to know instantaneously the tendencies, or probabilities, of how specific pitchers will fare against specific batters, ideally in specific situations (with runners on base or none at all) and vice versa, all based on their prior histories.

Although he is not an economist, Squadron brings a unique set of skills, as an attorney, and more importantly, as a business innovator in the sports industry over the course of his career. He and Fox Sports colleagues Stan Honey and Jerry Gepner spun a sports technology company out of News Corp

(continued)

(owner of the Fox television network) that is perhaps best known for developing the yellow line that magically appears on TV screens during football games to indicate where the first down marker is, as well as showing the K Zone—the strike zone—for each pitcher-batter combination in televised baseball games.[23] Later, Squadron moved to Bloomberg where he is showing how the back office of data is crucial to the further development and refinement of statistical techniques applied to the sports business (just as large databases, or big data, are the foundations for a growing data mining industry).

Regulatory Moneyball

I concede that after all this talk about sports, economics, and statistics, it may be somewhat of a letdown to conclude this chapter by talking about regulation. But Cass Sunstein, one of the nation's leading legal scholars and a former regulatory official, has cleverly explained that the main task of regulators is or should be the practice of *regulatory* moneyball.[24] Given the huge impact that federal and other regulations have on business and society, discussion of this topic alone would justify the trillion dollar label in the title of this book and hopefully that fact alone will pique your interest.

Yes, I did say trillion, and that and more may be the aggregate costs and benefits of just the body of federal regulation, even more counting state and local regulation. Admittedly, there remains a debate over the precise price tag, which I do not intend to resolve. My main purpose here is simply to focus on technique—the act of comparing the benefits and costs of rules before implementing them.

You would think such a simple idea—which many economists over many decades have championed—would not be controversial, but it has been one of the most contested notions in the policy arena over the past several decades. In fact, I began my career, after finishing law and graduate schools, as a staff economist at the Council of Economic Advisers

(CEA) in 1977, when the political discussion about using cost-benefit analysis (CBA) in regulatory decision making, something which most people informally and routinely do in their everyday lives, was quite intense. The discussion and debate over CBA continues to this day.

Here's how it all started. The precursor of CBA in the federal government was the inflation impact statement (IIS), which the administration of Gerald Ford required executive branch regulatory agencies to prepare before issuing final rules. The Carter administration, led by the Council of Economic Advisers, reformulated the IIS as something closer to a full cost-benefit analysis. CEA also headed a multi-agency Regulatory Analysis Review Group, which was formed to review the analyses of agencies' proposed rules.

After President Reagan was elected, he further formalized the regulatory review process by issuing an executive order creating the Office of Information and Regulatory Affairs within the Office of Management and Budget. OIRA exists to this day, and is viewed as an important institutional check on the quality of cost-benefit analyses performed by executive branch regulatory agencies, whether or not their underlying statutes permit the balancing of costs against benefits in issuing rules themselves. Some agencies therefore don't use CBA to make decisions under some statutes, although the analytical technique tends to find its way into decision making indirectly in many cases.

Although CBA has been controversial through the years—consumer and many environmental groups generally have opposed its use while business has been more friendly—every president since Reagan, both Democratic and Republican, has reaffirmed and refined its implementation. Several contentious issues remain, however. One is the appropriate discount rate to apply to likely benefits and costs in future years (the future values are discounted because a dollar today is more valuable than one received in later years). A second issue relates to the values assigned to avoiding deaths and injuries, in particular whether these values should be adjusted by age (if so, then a strictly economic calculus would assign greater values to avoiding deaths and injuries to younger than to older people).

Does regulatory moneyball have limits? Of course it does. Many benefits of regulatory rules, for example, cannot be monetized or quantified in any objective or scientific way. In addition, there are ethical issues involved in assigning values to lives, discounting them to take account of time value of money, or varying them by age.

In the end, however, regulatory moneyball (or CBA) is an input—a very important one, but not the only one—into regulatory decisions, just as real moneyball (sabermetrics) has become one, albeit not the only, important factor in the sports business.

The Bottom Line

It is hard to know where economics ends and statistics begins because the two fields are so intertwined. This is clearly the case in academia, where empirical economics is essentially applied statistics. In business, statistical analysis is becoming more important, especially in the age of big data. Companies using statisticians to refine their marketing or their production processes may not be aware of the close connection between economics and statistics. Nor may some sports enthusiasts be aware of the growing role of statistical analysis by the teams and players they root for. But one of the defining features of twenty-first century economies will be their reliance on and use of techniques for data analysis. Economists played a major role in this movement at its inception and will continue to help shape it in the future.

At the same time, economics as a separate academic discipline will also be affected and shaped by big data and the growing importance of analytical techniques in academia and the business word. I close the book in Chapter 16 with some thoughts about this topic.

Notes

1. Michael Lewis, *Moneyball: The Art of Winning an Unfair Game* (New York: W.W. Norton & Company, 2004).

2. *New York Times*, "Jan Tinbergen, Dutch Economist and Nobel Laureate, Dies at 91," June 14, 1994.

3. David Henderson, "Jan Tinbergen" in *The Concise Encyclopedia of Economics* (Indianapolis: Liberty Fund, Inc., 2008).

4. Ibid., "Lawrence Klein."

5. Lawrence R. Klein—Biographical, www.nobelprize.org.

6. Ibid.

7. Henderson, *Concise Encyclopedia*, "Lawrence Klein."

8. "The Prize in Economics 1980," press release, www.nobelprize.org/nobel_prizes/economic-sciences/laureates/1980/press.html.

9. "Lawrence R. Klein–Biographical," www.nobelprize.org. See also Glenn Rifkin, "Lawrence R. Klein, Economic Theorist, Dies at 93," *New York Times*, October 21, 2013.

10. "The Prize in Economics 1980."

11. James Surowiecki, *The Wisdom of Crowds* (Norwell, MA: Anchor Press, 2005).

12. Larissa MacFarquhar, "The Bench Burner," *New Yorker*, December 10, 2001, 87.

13. This profile is based largely on a personal interview with Professor Fisher, June 10, 2013.

14. Based on personal communications with Hal Varian, Google's chief economist.

15. Bob Tita, "In-House Economists Are Hot Again," *Wall Street Journal*, February 27, 2014.

16. Viktor Mayer-Schonberger and Kenneth Cukier, *Big Data: A Revolution That Will Transform How We Live, Work and Think* (Chicago: Eamon Dolan/Houghton Mifflin Harcourt, 2013); and Bill Franks, *Taming the Big Data Tidal Wave: Finding Opportunities in Huge Data Streams with Advanced Analytics* (Hoboken, NJ: John Wiley & Sons, 2012).

17. Ian Ayres, *Super Crunchers: Why Thinking by the Numbers Is the Best Way to Be Smart* (New York: Bantam Books, 2007).

18. Lewis, *Moneyball*.

19. Ben Reiter, "Three Days in June," *Sports Illustrated*, October 28, 2013, 34–39.

20. Tobias Moskowitz and L. Jon Wertheim, *Scorecasting: The Hidden Influences Behind How Sports Are Played and Games Are Won* (New York: Three Rivers Press, 2011).

21. Benjamin Baumer and Andrew Zimbalist, *The Sabermetrics Revolution: Assessing the Growth of Analytics in Baseball*: (Philadelphia: University of Pennsylvania Press, 2014).

22. Marc Tracy, "Which Sport Is Most Immune to Moneyball?" *New Republic*, March 7, 2013. See also Michael Lewis, "The No-Stats All-Star," *New York Times*, February 13, 2009.

23. For a great description of this enterprise, see Hank Adams, "Why It's Never Been More Fun to Watch Sports," *The Atlantic*, October 2013, 18–20.

24. For more details on the subjects discussed in this section, see Cass Sunstein, *Simpler: The Future of Government* (New York: Simon & Schuster, 2103).

Chapter 6

Experiments in Economics and Business

Economics, at least as it was taught to me, was a non-experimental social science. Like others in this category—sociology, anthropology, or political science—economists could not, it was thought, conduct experiments and test hypotheses like their counterparts in the hard sciences. The chemist, the physicist, or medical researchers can control for all factors other than the one hypothesis he or she wants tested. The economist could do no such thing, but instead had to figure out how an economy already working actually worked. Or, as one common joke has put it, the economist's job is to explain how something that works in practice works in theory.

Business pretty much worked this way, too, and for many firms it still does. Individuals or entrepreneurs invent stuff and then try to sell it. The farsighted and strong-willed ones are successful. Henry Ford knew what kind of car the masses of Americans would buy, and what his Ford Motor company would make: a simple black Model T. If consumers didn't like it, they could go elsewhere. Likewise, Steve Jobs was famous for knowing what electronic devices consumers wanted and what they wanted the designs to look like. And he was mostly right. There are countless other examples of other companies and entrepreneurs who behave with such self-confidence and have been rewarded with success.

This chapter is about a very different way of thinking—the use of experiments in both economics and business, that has affected both domains but in parallel fashion. So far, there has been essentially no cross-pollination of lessons learned in the two arenas.

Nonetheless, I devote an entire chapter in this book to experimentation, for multiple reasons. First, experimentalism is the way much, if not most, of the world operates. It is not just scientists who first formulate hypotheses and test them, but also empirically oriented economists, which is most economists these days, who go about their business in the same fashion, although not in precisely the way that scientists do. Increasingly, many businesses are also borrowing scientific testing principles before and during the introduction of new products and services, as well as refining those they already are selling.

Second, experimental techniques are on the cutting edge of both economics and the business world and for that reason alone they deserve attention.

Third, my idealistic hope is that practitioners from each domain will begin to learn more from each other and, in particular, that some of those reading this book will not only draw that conclusion but actually apply it in their daily endeavors.

In what follows, I distinguish between two types of experiments. In economics, I first speak of laboratory experiments, which have their analogue in focus groups in the business world, since each type of experiment is conducted outside of the real world in an effort to improve the accuracy of predicting how those who live and work in that world will behave or react. I then turn my attention to field experiments, or those conducted with real-world subjects: randomized controlled treatments (RCTs) in economics (borrowed from pharmaceutical testing), and A/B testing and variations thereof in the business world. I close the chapter by discussing the importance of experimentation in innovation and entrepreneurship, which drives economic growth and thus, in a sense, blends the two separate worlds of academe and business I discuss in the chapter.

Economics in the Lab: Vernon Smith and Experimental Economics

The notion that economists could learn something from a lab-like setting was so heretical that it took an iconoclastic economist from my hometown, Wichita, Kansas, to begin changing the way economists think and the way at least some economics research is now done.

That individual, Vernon Smith, did what came naturally not only to hard physical scientists, but to many businesspeople every day: He began to experiment, initially with students in his classrooms at the various universities where he has taught, and later in more controlled settings with students or other young people outside the classroom.

Unlike most other economists, who we know about only through their own writings or in some cases through essays or biographies written about them by others, we know about Smith both through his professional work and his remarkably candid autobiography.[1] I draw heavily on that work in summarizing Smith and his ideas here. One other note: Unbeknownst to me as I was drafting this part of the book, Bloomberg View columnist Megan McCardle was finishing up her own terrific book, *The Upside of Down*, which also discusses Smith's work in detail. I recommend her book to you for a lot of reasons, but if you want to know more about Smith and his experiments, you'll find it there.[2]

Smith devoted much of his professional life to experimental economics by accident, mostly through his teaching, where he quickly became unsatisfied with the conventional material that was then and still is found in most economics courses. He credits in his autobiography the university that first hired him after graduate school, Purdue, and the chairman of its economics department in the 1950s and 1960s, Em Weiler, with nurturing his interest in experiments as a way of demonstrating to students how Smith believed economies, and more importantly the actors within them, really behaved. He refined his notions about experimental economics at numerous other universities, but mostly at the University of Arizona.

Drawing on the pioneering work of Harvard economist Edward Chamberlin, who used mock auctions to demonstrate how supply and

Vernon Smith: Iconoclast

Smith's background is unlike most other economists I have known or those you have read about in this book, and almost surely contributed to his skeptical, questioning approach to economic research.

Smith's early life, though it predated the Depression, sounds a lot more like *The Grapes of Wrath* than the relatively sheltered academic lives of the typical economist, whose fathers, and in some cases mothers, taught at a university, or at least a high school, and thus had homes where one was expected to grow up and pursue an intellectual career. Smith's father worked for a railroad and did not earn much. As a result, Smith grew up relatively poor, in a household where intellectual discussions were rare.

Reading his autobiography, it was amazing to me how from his essentially hardscrabble background Smith found his way from North High School and Friends University in Wichita, Kansas, to the California Institute of Technology for his undergraduate degree, and later to Harvard University for his PhD (he switched to economics along the way at the University of Kansas, which he attended as a graduate student after college).

Smith began his varied academic career at the Krannert School of Management at Purdue, but moved through many other universities, staying the longest (26 years) at the University of Arizona, where he conducted much of the experimental work that eventually earned him a Nobel Prize. Smith has also taught at Stanford, Brown, George Mason, and, most recently, Chapman University in southern California, which gave him the resources to open an experimental economics lab using local area high school students, among others, as subjects.

During the course of his career Smith has published on a broad array of topics outside experimental economics, including finance and natural resources. Almost unique among academic economists, Smith shared his byline on a number of his important papers with his undergraduate students at the University of Arizona who helped him design and computerize a number of his experiments.[3]

demand curves work, Smith greatly expanded the use of experiments to confirm basic economic propositions. Like Chamberlin, Smith used students in classroom settings to make bids and offers, illustrating in the process how prices and quantities of a hypothetical commodity converge to their theoretical competitive equilibrium. He found in the course of running these experiments that it doesn't take a large number of competitors to generate the competitive result found in the supply and demand graphs that populate introductory economics textbooks.

Smith worked with various colleagues over the years to refine his experiments, and to show they could be applied outside the classroom and in the real world. In his words, Smith confirmed to me that by far the most practical application of his ideas was in the design of bidding procedures for wholesale electric power, which he developed in conjunction with Stephen Rassenti at Arizona. Initially, Smith and Rassenti proposed such a system for the power commission in the state, which rejected the ideas as too impractical. Ironically, they were picked up and implemented in the 1990s in New Zealand and Australia, and also by the electric utility company Ohio Edison.[4]

It is difficult to overstate the extent to which Smith's work was long viewed to be out of the mainstream by the rest of the profession, where members spent their time either theorizing or using regression analysis and other statistical techniques (in both cases, using increasingly sophisticated mathematics) to test those theories. The standard view is that economic behavior could only be discerned when people or firms were using their own money in real-world settings. The notion that lessons could be drawn from laboratory settings where individuals were given play (or even small amounts of real) money and then tasked with spending it or using it in some fashion for purposes designed by the experimenters was not only the exception rather than the rule, but looked down on by many mainstream economists—until Smith was awarded the Nobel Prize, of course.

As evidence, consider the fact that fully 8 percent of all the papers published in several leading economics journals in 2011 used experimental methods or fell into the experimental economics category.[5] That figure was up from essentially zero in 1973, the first year covered by the study. That same study also showed a sharp upward trend in empirical papers published with the author's own data set, and downward trends in empirical papers using other data sets and purely theoretical papers.[6] The sharp shift toward experimental economic research is no doubt heavily due to the fact that Smith's influential work legitimized the field.

There is still the nagging question, though, about the extent to which economic experiments, conducted in laboratory settings, can be extrapolated into the real world with people's own money on the line. Smith and his colleagues have shown that despite the skepticism, many various theoretical economic propositions can be confirmed through such experiments, while the experimental methods they have devised can be used more frequently in business settings.

As I discuss shortly, businesses increasingly have been taking up that challenge, but in a different way than Smith and other experimentalists have gone about their work; that is, by using methods approximating the randomized controlled experiments in the field that are the gold standard for assessing the efficacy and dangers of pharmaceuticals or evaluating various social policy interventions. And businesses appear to have done so without being prodded by economists.

Lab Experiments in Business: Focus Groups

Before I get to that story, however, it is interesting to summarize how some businesses have used a similar laboratory approach to that used by the economic experimentalists. The experimental method to which I refer is the focus group. Movie studios use them to test potential audience reactions to different plots, especially endings. Advertising firms use this technique, along with politicians, to refine their messages, increasingly tailored to very different audiences. Some firms use focus groups to identify products or product areas that consumers might be attracted to. Go to the web and type in "focus groups in business" and among the entries that immediately pop up are articles suggesting that entrepreneurs use focus groups, formal or informal, to test the viability of their ideas before committing much time and a lot of money to new enterprises.

There is a limit, of course, to the effectiveness of focus groups. By construction, they tend to be small, and thus may not be representative of larger populations. Also, what may seem to appeal in a small-group setting may not be readily accepted or welcomed when introduced into the wider marketplace, which is one reason companies may roll out new products or services in certain test geographic areas, getting feedback and introducing refinements before marketing to a much wider audience or market.

At the same time, if they are properly run, focus groups can yield insights in ways that mass experiments, which often call for binary (yes or no) responses, cannot. Focus group participants may volunteer in an unstructured setting ideas or reactions unanticipated by the focus group organizers. This can lead to "aha" moments that change messaging or product designs, or even foster new ideas that firms were not originally planning to pursue.

Economic Experiments in the Field: Randomized Controlled Trials

Economists for years have borrowed techniques from the social sciences, engineering, and mathematics to model or infer individual or collective behaviors. In recent years, a small but growing band of economists, led initially by Michael Kremer of Harvard, and in a much more expansive fashion by Esther Duflo of MIT and Abhibit Banerjee of Harvard, has looked to a favorite technique used in medicine and program evaluation: randomized controlled experiments. Duflo, who earned her PhD and has since taught at MIT, won the Clark Medal in 2010 and a MacArthur genius award in 2009.

RCTs compare treatment and control groups to test whether the tested medicine or policy intervention has had a statistically significant impact.[7] Among the interventions the above-mentioned economists have tested are whether putting cameras in school rooms reduces teacher absences (it does), and whether microcredit programs encourage entrepreneurship in poor countries (also a yes).

Kremer, Duflo, and Banerjee are not the only economists who conduct RCTs. Roland Fryer of Harvard uses the method to test the impact of various school interventions, such as paying kids in some manner for their achievements. The late Elinor Ostrom, a political scientist who won the Nobel Prize in Economics for her work (joining several other non-economists), conducted pioneering experiments validating that groups can self-organize to share resources.[8] Tyler Cowen even argues in his new, important book *Average Is Over* that the future of economics, and indeed possibly all social sciences, lies in a merger into a single social science, in which researchers will specialize in the crunching of large bodies of data, some from experiments. The empirical results will drive the theory, not the other way around.[9] I have more to say about this projection in Chapter 16.[10]

One critique of RCT in economics and the social sciences relates to the transferability of the results from the specific experiments being conducted to other contexts. For example, it might be true that installing cameras in schoolrooms in India reduces teacher absences, but that result may be unique to a particular site or to wider region within India if not the entire country. It is not clear whether the same result would be obtained in different countries with different cultural norms and expectations. The same critique can be applied to other RCTs.

Nonetheless, RCTs remain the gold standard not only in medicine but also in the evaluations of programs funded by foundations, schools, hospitals, and other organizations. Even if the results from one experiment in one setting are not generalizable to other organizations in other settings, the findings are likely to be used, and properly so, in the specific contexts where the tests are conducted.

Business Experimentation in the Field

Well before academic economists had discovered the use and power of RCTs, business began using real-world experiments, modeled loosely or closely on RCTs, to fine-tune their products, their marketing strategies, designs of their web pages, and so on. The pioneers on the front lines typically have not been economists, but they have acted like economists in using experimental methods to hone their business strategies and, in some cases, build great companies.

James Manzi, one of the leaders in this field whose efforts I will describe shortly and who is profiled in the accompanying box, has outlined the history of business experimentation.[11] In his telling, the true pioneers of the practice were the founders of Capital One, today one of the nation's largest credit card companies, whose success Manzi attributes to continuous and extensive experimentation.

Capital One was launched by two former Strategic Planning Associates (SPA) consultants, Rich Fairbank and Nigel Morris, who attacked the credit card customer base as if it were one giant laboratory. Do customers respond better to solicitations in blue or white envelopes? Send out solicitations to two groups and see if there is a statistically significant difference. Apply the same approach to virtually everything else the company does, including employee selection, collection policies, cross selling of different financial products, and do as many as 60,000 experiments a year, and that is how Capital One was built. No single experiment was a "home run" but the "singles" from thousands of successful experiments incrementally improved the company so that in 25 years, Capital One grew from nothing into a major Fortune 500 company and one of the largest credit card lenders in the United States.

That is Manzi's personal experience with how business experiments work: They provide incremental rather than disruptive improvements that over time add up to either major breakthroughs or significant additions to companies' bottom lines.

The Internet unleashed a huge jump in business experimentation because it became so easy to do. Rather than sending out large batches of different colored envelopes and waiting for sales results, one can change the color or design of websites on a daily or even more frequent basis, and offer the different impressions to different sets of randomly chosen website visitors. If the comparisons are limited to just two sets of customers they now have a name—an A/B test—and we have Google to thank for introducing them.

Google has been conducting just these kinds of experiments for more than a decade, making small tweaks here and there to its website results and other aspects of its business. The company does all this with a growing army of statisticians picking, in each case, whether the A or the B design prompts the best reaction from website visitors, or clicks of ads, or so on. Indeed, Google runs so many A/B tests simultaneously that almost everyone who visits the site is probably being tested whether they know it or not. Put another way, there is no single Google website, but many different ones being tested at the same time.

Other companies actively using A/B tests include Amazon, Netflix, and eBay.[12]

A semi-science has since grown up around the proper construction and administration of A/B tests, given that many other firms, whether Internet-based or still grounded in the physical world but with an Internet presence, use them. One well-known company providing a free tool for anyone or any firm that wants to conduct its own A/B test is Optimizely, founded by two ex-Google employees, Dan Siroker and Pete Koomen, who honed the testing technique for the Obama presidential campaign in 2012. An entrepreneur and writer, Eric Ries, has written the bible for A/B testing by tech startups, *The Lean Startup*. Ries and his book have even encouraged a whole lean-startup movement.[13]

Not all A/B-type tests are run on the Internet, because most commerce, after all, is still conducted in bricks-and-mortar facilities. One of the leading companies facilitating experiments in that context is Applied Prediction Technologies, founded by James Manzi (see the following box). Since its founding in 1999, APT has grown to the point where, according to Manzi, 30 to 40 percent of the largest U.S. retailers, hotels, restaurant chains, and retail banks in the United States had used or were using APT's experimentation platform as of 2012.[14]

James Manzi: Analytical Pioneer

Although he is not a formally trained economist, he has the analytical tools and certainly acts like one, though in a business setting. Manzi backed his way into the analytics and experimentation business by accident, like many entrepreneurs with other businesses.[15]

Manzi studied math and science in his undergraduate years at MIT, with the intention of going on to get his PhD in either mathematics or physics. But after a year in graduate school at the University of Pennsylvania, Manzi realized he was better suited for a business career, one where he could use his considerable analytical skills.

He gained his first job at AT&T's research labs, and shortly thereafter, at the age of 23 joined a newly formed consulting firm, Strategic Planning Associates (SPA). SPA specialized in applying analytical techniques to help companies determine which of their many lines of business offered the most opportunities and how to maximize profits pursuing them. Manzi used a variety of mathematical techniques, drawing on his earlier training, in multiple consulting assignments with the company.

With this experience under his belt, Manzi took the entrepreneurial plunge in 1999, launching with two other partners Applied Predictive Technologies. As noted in the text, APT has become a major force in enabling bricks-and-mortar businesses to conduct real-world experiments.

Innovation and Entrepreneurship: Experimentation as the Foundation of Growth

There is one other connection between experimentation and economics I cannot resist closing this chapter with, and it relates to entrepreneurs, many of whom are experimenters by nature, and whose importance to the economy I believe cannot be overstated. With the exception of a few economists like the great Joseph Schumpeter, Israel Kirzner, and a famous economist I am about to reveal, this was not generally well recognized among mainstream economists (and still isn't in some quarters) until relatively recently. So this is a case where business has been out in front of economics, but economists are catching up and have begun to provide practical research that even the most skeptical entrepreneurs will find useful.

The reason I can make these claims is that I spent nearly a decade of my life on the periphery of entrepreneurship, but at the center of entrepreneurship *research* when I directed research for the Kauffman Foundation, the world's largest foundation devoted primarily to advancing entrepreneurship. During the near decade I was there (2003 to 2012), Kauffman greatly expanded its support of mainstream economists to study various aspects of entrepreneurship, and in particular, its connection to innovation and economic growth. The list is long, but a sample of the notable economists who were funded included William Baumol of NYU (profiled in Chapter 4), Edmund Phelps of Columbia University (profiled below), Amar Bhidé of Tufts University (who had already made his mark in the field with a landmark study of innovative entrepreneurs),[16] Josh Lerner of Harvard Business School, Steven Kaplan of the University of Chicago, and Alicia Robb, formerly of the Fed staff and at this writing a senior fellow at Kauffman itself.

I benefited greatly from frequent interactions with these remarkable individuals and many others, as well as from reading their research when writing two books on entrepreneurship and economic growth, one with an economist profiled earlier in this book (William Baumol) and the president of the Kauffman Foundation, Carl Schramm,[17] and the sequel which Schramm and I coauthored.[18] I learned more from writing these books, all the while enjoying the process, than from any other books I had previously written (until this one!). Although the books are very different (and of course I encourage readers of this book to read them), they have a common theme: Entrepreneurs, defined as those who commercialize new products, services, or ways of producing or delivering them, are among the most important, and arguably *the* most important, drivers of innovation and growth in average living standards.

Edmund Phelps

One sign that mainstream economists are taking entrepreneurship and its crucial connection with innovation more seriously is the shifting research agenda by one of the profession's leading macroeconomists, Edmund "Ned" Phelps, who won the Nobel Prize in 2006. Through much of his career, Phelps' research focused on inflation and unemployment, and the theory of economic growth.

Phelps' latest book, *Mass Flourishing*, makes the case for entrepreneur-driven innovation as one of the major drivers of economic growth, but worries about various impediments to such innovation today.[19] His book extends his earlier work emphasizing the importance of cultural factors that influence entrepreneurial propensities.

Phelps is from Illinois, went to Amherst for undergraduate studies, and earned his PhD at Yale University. During the course of his prolific academic career, Phelps has held positions at the RAND Corporation, Yale, the University of Pennsylvania, and Columbia, where he cofounded the Center on Capitalism and Society.

On a personal note and with full disclosure: Although I saw him from afar when I was a lowly research assistant at the Brookings Institution in the 1970s and witnessed his presentation or discussion of papers at the semiannual meetings of the *Brookings Papers on Economic Activity*, I got to know Phelps much later in life (for both of us), while I was at the Kauffman Foundation. The Foundation supported Phelps' work and the launch of his Center, and thus played a part in encouraging Phelps' research and writing about entrepreneurship and innovation during the post-Nobel phase of his career.

There are many ways to classify such innovative entrepreneurs. The distinction I believe to be most relevant to this chapter, and thus this book, is between those who are convinced they know better what consumers eventually will want than consumers themselves and are highly unlikely to change their minds—think Steve Jobs, Larry Page, and Sergey Brin—and those entrepreneurs who start with one idea (typically written in detail in a business plan), but often quickly shift to another after some initial encounters with consumers and the marketplace. The latter category includes the entrepreneurial equivalents of scientists, those who have a hypothesis (the business plan) about how a business can be profitable, and then test it through refinements in the products or services they sell to consumers. These experimental entrepreneurs keep experimenting until they get it right.[20]

I know of no studies that attempt to determine what portion of successful entrepreneurs are inspirational and those that are experimental, but my own impression is that most fall into the second camp or, at the very least, have both elements as part of their nature. As a matter of logic this stands to reason, since I cannot count how many times I have heard the adage, from economists and businessmen (and women), that what makes an entrepreneur different is that he or she sees opportunity where others see only problems. This is a variation of the advice I have heard many successful entrepreneurs give to aspiring entrepreneurs: Channel your entrepreneurial passions into fixing, for commercial gain, the problems that you personally have found to be highly irritating or frustrating. Successful entrepreneurs who are motivated in this fashion even if they succeed on the first try are combining both inspirational and experimental traits.

My guess is that few entrepreneurs succeed on their first try, and thus need to experiment or, to be blunt, to fail, often repeatedly, before achieving success. The secret economist I mentioned earlier who came to this conclusion much earlier than I did was Albert O. Hirschman, certainly one of the more unusual economists of the twentieth century, as should be evident from his profile in the following box.

Albert O. Hirschman: Unconventional Pioneer

The life of Albert O. Hirschman is one more suited to a spy novel than an economist, and fortunately it has been captured in a remarkable biography of the man and his ideas.[21]

Hirschman's amazingly varied life began in Berlin where he was born. As the rise of Nazism became evident, he left Germany (with his family's blessing) during his teenage years to study economics in France, England, and Italy, receiving his doctorate from the University of Trieste in 1938, just before the outbreak of World War II. An activist as well as intellectual, Hirschman punctuated his studies for a brief time by fighting against General Franco in the Spanish Civil War. After France surrendered to Germany, Hirschman risked his life again to help artists and intellectuals escape from Europe (and the Nazis) to the United States through the Pyrenees mountains in Spain and then to Portugal.

Hirschman immigrated to the United States during the early years of World War II, landing a fellowship at the University of California at Berkeley. He later joined the U.S. Army, which fortunately used his intellectual skills in the Office of Strategic Services (the predecessor to today's Central Intelligence Agency). After the war, his academic career took him to a number of universities, in and outside the United States, which gave him a unique perspective on economics and societies.

Hirschman practiced an eclectic, word-based economics that is out of fashion today. He was a true public intellectual, drawing insights from multiple disciplines to look at the world the way it is—dynamic, messy, and complex—and not the way many economic theoreticians imagine it to be, simple, mechanical, and easily subject to mathematical description and analysis.

Though he was perhaps best known for his classic *Exit, Voice, and Loyalty*—which finds a role for each noun in any economy—Hirschman also makes some highly useful insights about entrepreneurs and their economic importance.[22] In my paraphrasing of his description, the typical entrepreneur is not the swashbuckling risk-taker, but someone who embarks on a path that is so obvious to him or her that it would crazy to *not* do it, and thus is more accurately characterized as a "prudent" risk-taker. We know, by the way, from much modern research that for many, if not most, entrepreneurs, this is true—an insight that was drilled into me during many encounters I had with entrepreneurship researchers while I was at Kauffman.

But in Hirschman's telling, here is where experimentation enters the picture. After launching his or her venture, the typical entrepreneur encounters any number of unexpected obstacles: Manufacturing the product is more difficult than expected, or consumers are not as enthusiastic about the initial version of the product or service as the entrepreneur anticipated. The successful entrepreneur is one who finds ways to overcome these obstacles, many times completely changing course again and again before hitting on what it is that consumers really want. The resulting success is often due more to accident than design, although the perseverance, and even madness (to outsiders), of the entrepreneur also play a critical role.

Hirschman describes this sequence of events in one of his essays, which Malcolm Gladwell recounts in his excellent review of Adelman's biography of Hirschman.[23] This essay describes Hirschman's studies of large paper mills that were constructed in Pakistan with the intention of being supplied by bamboo forests from China. After those forests unexpectedly died, the mill's operators improvised by building alternative supply chains, which ultimately made the mills more profitable than they would have been otherwise. Hirschman generalized from this experience by claiming what in my own experience rings true: Entrepreneurs typically start on a path they do not see as risky at all, then something happens that upsets their expectations and, being too far into their projects to turn back, they are forced to improvise. Those who get over this hump, or mountain, of unexpected trouble are the surviving entrepreneurial successes.

Hirschman's account of entrepreneurship is similar in spirit to the much more recent description offered by Scott Adams, the creator of the *Dilbert* cartoon series. Adams has penned a thoughtful and highly readable account of both his life and how repeated failures ultimately help lead to success in almost any endeavor, including the founding and growth of a new firm.[24]

So much for economic descriptions and analysis about entrepreneurship and its role in economic advances, which are of interest to economists and to policy makers. But what have economists to say that can benefit entrepreneurs?

Here progress has been slower, in large part because producing this impact has not been high on many researchers' agendas, and because reaching would-be and actual entrepreneurs is difficult. For one thing, whether entrepreneurs are inspirational or experimental, they are the type of people who do things for themselves, not the kind who consult books and articles, even though it is easier to do than ever before in the age of the Internet. For another, if they do read materials related to their chosen paths in life, entrepreneurs understandably are likely to be partial to things written by other entrepreneurs based on their own real-world experiences rather than by academics or journalists. Who can blame them?

There are limitations, however, with many of the entrepreneurial advice books one sees in bookstores or online. Too many are too general to be of much practical use, while others draw on personal anecdotes that do not often translate to the problems faced by particular entrepreneurs in their specific businesses. From an academic perspective, the advice books tend to be far from scientific because entrepreneurs (or consultants) turned authors are not trained to assemble large data sets and analyze them to draw general conclusions.

Even with these caveats, I can still safely recommend one popular book, coauthored by a successful entrepreneur, that I believe is the best practical guide for entrepreneurs ever written: Previously titled *The Knack*, its most current edition is entitled *Street Smarts*.[25] The authors are Norm Brodsky, who has moonlighted for years as a columnist for *Inc.* (in my view, the best of the popular magazines for entrepreneurs) and his *Inc.* editor and coauthor Bo Burlingame, who has written widely about entrepreneurship for years.

As for the economists, they are slowly catching up, using the analytical and empirical tools of their trade to elicit insights from different data sets collected about entrepreneurs. One the best of this genre is the classic *The Origin and Evolution of New Business* by Amar Bhidé, now an economics professor at Tufts.[26] Bhidé interviewed the founders or top executives of 100 companies no more than eight years old that had made the *Inc.* 500 in 1989, a list published each year by *Inc.* magazine of the fastest growing privately held companies over the previous four years. He supplemented this sample with another 200 case studies of successful entrepreneurs compiled by his students (when he taught at Harvard Business School), which he found to broadly corroborate the findings from his more formal sample.

Bhidé's purpose in writing his book was to uncover the keys to entrepreneurial success by identifying factors common among successful entrepreneurs. One of his main findings was that most founders had capital constraints, or limited money to start their ventures, which were generally financed by the founders' own savings and borrowings

(from credit cards and mortgages). Only 5 percent of the sample companies—and these were among the most successful private firms—were
funded initially by more formal sources, such as venture capital firms.
Subsequent research supported by the Kauffman Foundation over the
years has confirmed this result.

Bhidé also confirmed that successful entrepreneurs mostly improvised or experimented as they went along. Few wrote or adhered to business plans, the focus of so much coursework and many entrepreneurial
competitions since. The companies did not have seasoned professionals at
the top (except for those financed by VCs, who often replace founders
with more experienced executives when putting money into new companies), but generally were run by founders who were struggling and
adapting as they went along. These findings emerged from both Bhidé's
formal sample and from his students' case studies. For readers who want to
learn more, I strongly urge reading Bhidé's study, which has stood the test
of time, and has been largely reinforced by more recent comprehensive
studies of entrepreneurship, such as Noam Wasserman's sure-to-be-classic
The Founder's Dilemmas, which I discuss shortly.

One drawback of the Bhidé study, however, is that it suffers from
survivorship bias, because he looked only at many of the most successful companies. That was his objective, of course, but in doing so he
implicitly made no attempt to establish a control group that inevitably
would have had many unsuccessful or relatively less successful companies in his sample. Those less successful might also share some of the
traits or keys to success Bhidé found among the most successful entrepreneurs, but we will never know.

While I was at Kauffman, the foundation's largest monetary commitment to entrepreneurship research was the funding of the most
comprehensive longitudinal data set of new firms ever assembled about
U.S. firms. This Kauffman Firm Survey (KFS) followed 5,000 firms
established in 2004 (the year the study was launched) for eight straight
years, asking over 100 questions of their founders or top leaders. By
doing this, the KFS enables researchers to test numerous hypotheses
about the factors driving entrepreneurial success, although it too suffers from a form of survivorship bias, though one not as severe as in the
Bhidé study. The reason is that many firms fail or merge, dropping out
of the KFS database over time, which means that only the survivors

report the most complete data histories. However, unlike the Bhidé study that deliberately chose 100 of the most successful enterprises as the basis for its analysis, the KFS sample includes surviving firms that exhibit various degrees of success. Numerous researchers have made use of the KFS to author papers, including those of one of Kauffman's own senior fellows, Alicia Robb.

As of this writing, however, by far the best and most recent empirically based study of and guide for potential and actual entrepreneurs in my opinion is *The Founder's Dilemmas*, by Noam Wasserman of the Harvard Business School.[27] Wasserman's exhaustive treatment of virtually all aspects of the early stages of launching a new business is based on the experiences of nearly 10,000 founders, almost 20,000 executives, in about 3,600 startups over a 10-year period from 2000 to 2009. The book is chock full of advice, backed by an extensive analysis of the data on a wide variety of topics, including: whether to found companies alone or in teams; the issues that come up in teams that tend to lead to success or failure of the enterprise; the often tension-filled discussions about how to split up equity and compensate founders and their employees; hiring issues; and when to stay with the company (and if so, how to transition toward founder and management succession), or to sell out to a strategic buyer. This brief summary just scratches the surface of an enormously impressive book, which I believe is must-reading for anyone thinking about or in the process of founding a business. The book and its research provides clear evidence that academics can provide practical advice, provided they go out, like Wasserman, and talk to real people doing the things that entrepreneurs care about and that academics want to analyze.

The Bottom Line

Experiments are a part of everyday life and of many disciplines and pursuits, including both economics and business. Yet the movements toward experimentation in both lines of endeavor have developed, at least up to now, quite independently of one another.

This eventually will change. Both economists and those actively engaged in business now use experiments in laboratory settings and in the field. As this continues, I expect that businesses will call upon economists more frequently for their advice and their research lessons. Likewise, if economists are asked more frequently for their advice, expect to see them produce more business-relevant research.

Of the firms engaged in experimentation, perhaps the most important to the overall economy are new ones (speaking only of the United States), since they drive innovation, especially disruptive innovation, which determines the pace of economic growth. We may not need economists to start new businesses, but the better their research about what accounts for successful entrepreneurship, the larger should be the number of successful entrepreneurs and their companies. Or so we should all hope.

Notes

1. Vernon L. Smith, *Memoirs* (Bloomington, IN: Author House, 2008).

2. Megan McCardle, *The Upside of Down: Why Failing Well Is the Key to Success* (New York: Viking Adult, 2014).

3. This profile draws heavily on Smith's memoirs cited in endnote 1.

4. Author's e-mail correspondence with Vernon Smith, June 6, 2013, and Stephen Rassenti, Vernon L. Smith, and Bart J. Wilson, "Using Experiments to Inform the Privatization/Deregulation Movement in Electricity," *Cato Journal* 21, no. 3 (Winter 2002): 515–544.

5. Daniel S. Hammermesh, "Six Decades of Top Economics Publishing: Who and How?" *Journal of Economic Perspectives* 51, no.1 (2013): 152–162.

6. The findings in this study were subsequently corroborated and refined in Daniel S. Hammermesh, "Six Decades of Top Economics Publishing: Who and How?" *Journal of Economic Literature* LI, no. 1 (March 2013): 162–172.

7. Much of their research is summarized in Abhijit Banerjee and Esther Duflo, *Poor Economics: A Radical Rethinking of the Way to Fight Global Poverty* (Cambridge, MA: Public Affairs, 2013). See also *What Works in Development? Thinking Big and Thinking Small*, ed. Jessica Cohen and William Easterly (Washington, DC: Brookings Institution Press, 2010).

8. James Manzi, *Uncontrolled: The Surprising Payoff of Trial-and-Error for Business, Politics, and Society* (New York: Basic Books, 2012), 195.

9. Tyler Cowen, *Average Is Over: Powering America beyond the Age of Stagnation* (New York: Dutton Books, 2013), 225–228.

10. For another discussion of randomized controlled experiments in economics see "Random Harvest," *The Economist*, December 14, 2103, www.economist .com/news/finance-and-economics/21591573-once-treated-scorn-randomised -control-trials-are-coming-age-random-harvest.

11. Manzi, *Uncontrolled*.

12. Information for this paragraph in part from Brian Christian, "The A/B Test: Inside the Technology That's Changing the Rules of Business," *Wired*, April 25, 2012, www.wired.com/business/2012/04/ff_abtesting.

13. Eric Ries, *The Lean Startup* (New York: Crown Business, 2011).

14. Manzi, *Uncontrolled*, 147.

15. This profile is based on Manzi, *Uncontrolled*, and an interview with him, October 9, 2013.

16. See Amar Bhidé, *The Origin and Evolution of New Business* (New York: Oxford University Press, 2000).

17. William Baumol, Robert E. Litan, and Carl Schramm, *Good Capitalism, Bad Capitalism, and the Economics of Growth and Prosperity* (New Haven, CT: Yale University Press, 2007).

18. Robert E. Litan and Carl Schramm, *Better Capitalism: Renewing the Entrepreneurial Strength of the American Economy* (New Haven, CT: Yale University Press, 2012).

19. Edmund S. Phelps, *Mass Flourishing: How Grassroots Innovation Created Jobs, Challenge and Change* (Princeton, NJ: Princeton University Press, 2013).

20. *The Economist* magazine devoted an entire special report in its January 18, 2014, edition called "A Cambrian Moment," about experimentation as the key to tech startups in particular.

21. Jeffrey Adelman, *Worldly Philosopher* (Princeton, NJ: Princeton University Press, 2013).

22. Albert O. Hirschman, *Exit, Voice, and Loyalty: Responses to Decline in Firms, Organizations, and States* (Cambridge, MA: Harvard University Press, 1970).

23. Malcolm Gladwell, "The Gift of Doubt," *The New Yorker* (June 24, 2013): 74–79. The book about Hirschman is Adelman, *Worldly Philosopher*.

24. Scott Adams, *How to Fail at Almost Everything and Still Win Big* (New York: Penguin, 2013). This is also one of the main themes of McCardle's excellent book, *The Upside of Down*.

25. Norm Brodsky and Bo Burlingame, *Street Smarts: An All Purpose Guide for Entrepreneurs* (New York: Penguin, 2010).

26. Bhidé, *Origin and Evolution of New Business*.

27. Noam Wasserman, *The Founder's Dilemmas: Anticipating and Avoiding the Pitfalls That Can Sink a Startup* (Princeton, NJ: Princeton University Press, 2012).

Chapter 7

Matchmaker, Matchmaker

A t a fundamental level, economics is about resource allocation, or who gets what? Mainstream introductory textbooks suggest that prices play a critical role in the answer. Those willing and able to pay the going price for goods and services sold in the market get what suppliers make available. In competitive markets, this outcome is said to be efficient.[1]

However, there are many examples of markets where price is not the governing factor in decisions, if prices exist at all. Consider some of the most important decisions people make: where to go to college, which job to choose, or which person to marry. Price is important in two of these cases, but not in the third, and even in the first two, price is often or generally not the most important factor in the decision.[2]

So how do these nontraditional markets work, where matches may be made based on a certain set of rules and characteristics that are unique to each setting?[3] Answering that question is the subject of this chapter, in which I introduce you to a new branch of economics called market design, a field devoted to making markets work more efficiently by better matching supply with demand.

I will begin with a brief and gentle introduction to the economics of matchmaking. I then discuss two major applications of market design and matching theory in the real world, including one where business is clearly at stake (the job market) and the other where the Internet has enabled much larger businesses to develop, such as the dating market. I conclude with some bottom line observations.

Unlike the subject of the last chapter, where economists and businesses using experiments developed more or less in parallel, there has been considerable cross-fertilization among economists and businesses in the world of matchmaking. Given the stories you are about to read, I wouldn't be surprised to see a lot more such cooperation in the years ahead.

A Gentle Introduction to Market Design and Matching Theory

Matching is one of the most fundamental functions of markets. As we have seen in previous chapters, prices are the matchmakers in traditional markets. Indeed, Adam Smith, the father of modern economics, marveled at the way consumers and firms operated in a market economy and responded to prices, acting as if guided by an invisible hand that leads markets to allocate resources efficiently. All of this you will find in any standard economics textbook.

A new field of economics, not yet found in most introductory or even intermediate-level economics textbooks, is developing. That field is market design, which recognizes that well-functioning markets depend on detailed rules. For example, supply and demand drive both the housing market and the job market, but someone who wants to buy or sell a house goes through similar but also some very different steps than those taken by job seekers or employers.[4] Market designers try to understand the specific rules, characteristics, and culture of each market in order to fix them when they're broken, or to build markets from scratch when they're missing.[5]

Think of market designers as the engineers of economics. Just as civil engineers apply principles of physics and mechanics to design bridges, market designers apply the principles of economic analysis— competition, incentives, information, economies of scale—to design exchange mechanisms or improve existing markets.[6]

Matching theory essentially comes from two subfields of economics: game theory—the study of strategic behavior, in which particular rules and market characteristics play an important role in an outcome—and experimental economics, which is about conducting empirical work and testing theories in the real world.

To understand the field of market design and the economics of matchmaking, remember the discussion in Chapter 2 about how traditional markets can fail, or why markets for certain goods or services are sometimes missing in the first place: where there are externalities, information asymmetries (one party knows more than the other about a particular product or service), or public goods. A classic example is pollution, which imposes costs on third parties and therefore leads to overproduction when the producer does not internalize these environmental costs. Sometimes, the private market can solve these problems (if the polluters and those affected by it are small in number and thus can negotiate a solution), and in other cases, the government is better suited to provide remedies, which include taxes, subsidies, and regulation.

In the context of market design, market failure refers primarily to the specific rules (or lack thereof) and characteristics of markets that sometimes impede efficient matching. In particular, there are three kinds of market failure that the market designers study:

1. Markets can fail to provide *thickness*, or to bring together enough buyers and sellers to transact with each other to make a real market.[7]
2. Markets can fail to overcome *congestion*, or to provide participants with enough time, or with the means to conduct transactions fast enough to make satisfactory choices when faced with many alternatives.[8]
3. Markets can fail to make it *safe* for participants to reveal or act on confidential information they may hold.[9]

The primary motive for economists interested in improving market design is to correct these market failures, and more broadly, to make markets work more efficiently by better matching individual suppliers with purchasers or those on the demand side of transactions. As such, market designers are interested in improving both traditional markets governed by a price mechanism and nontraditional markets, where the scarce goods to be allocated are heterogeneous and indivisible and prices may not be key to reconciling supply and demand. Examples of the latter include which students go to certain schools, which workers get specific jobs, and who receives which transplantable organ.[10]

Many of the examples we will explore in this chapter involve nontraditional markets, but it is also useful to briefly consider the ways in which market designers can improve traditional markets that are governed by a price mechanism. Take auctions and online marketplaces, discussed in Chapter 3, for example. While in theory it seems straightforward that buyers and sellers in these settings would arrive at an efficient outcome, in practice it is actually very difficult to present buyers and sellers with only the markets and products or services they are interested in. That is, while it is easy to provide a platform to draw participants to a marketplace, there are numerous inefficiencies that arise when buyers and sellers cannot find the relevant products or services, either due to information asymmetries, congestion, or a lack of thickness. In these situations, market makers can improve price-driven markets by better matching supply and demand in accordance with the rules and institutional culture of each market.

Two of the pioneers of market design and matching theory are Lloyd Shapley and Alvin Roth, who were awarded the Nobel Prize in Economics in 2012. The Nobel committee recognized Shapley's and Roth's extensive work across a multitude of disciplines and settings, from abstract theory developed in the 1950s and 1960s by Shapley on stable matching to the empirical and practical work conducted by Roth since the early 1980s (see the following boxes for brief overviews of the work of each economist).

Lloyd Shapley

Lloyd Shapley, like a number of Nobel Prize winners in economics, did not get his formal training in the subject. Nonetheless, during the course of his career, he made significant contributions to game theory, market design, and matching theory, and was recognized by the Nobel committee in 2012 (along with Alvin Roth) for the importance of this work.

Shapley was born in Cambridge, Massachusetts, in 1923 and enrolled at Harvard University in the early 1940s, but couldn't complete his degree, because like many other young men at the time, he was drafted and served in the U.S. Army from 1943 to 1945. Shapley returned to Harvard after the war and graduated with a degree in mathematics in 1948. He then worked as a research mathematician at the RAND Corporation before going to Princeton University to obtain his PhD in mathematics. While there, he mentored and befriended John Nash, a fellow future Nobel laureate, and the protagonist in the book and movie *A Beautiful Mind*. Shapley can even be credited with that title when he described Nash as having a "keen, beautiful, and logical mind."[11]

At Princeton, Shapley's major contribution to game theory was his introduction of what has come to be known as a Shapley value—a payoff derived from a set of axioms applicable to every cooperative game. The value and related measures of it have been widely applied in numerous settings over time, including in the quantification of the impact of voting rules on the influence of individual voters, in legal decisions concerning electoral districting and representation, and in accounting problems of cost allocation.[12]

Shapley also made some of the earliest and most important theoretical contributions in matching theory. In a seminar paper he coauthored in 1962 with David Gale, Shapley explored the idea of stable matching—allocations where no individuals perceive any gains from further trade.[13] In the paper, titled "College Admissions and the Stability of Marriage," Shapley and Gale presented a model of a two-sided matching in which men and women—or students and colleges—expressed preferences for their matches. In particular, Shapley and Gale proposed a deferred-acceptance algorithm (since known as the Gale-Shapley algorithm) for finding stable matching, for instance, where no couples would break up and form new matches that would make them better off.

Since 1981, Shapley has been affiliated with the University of California, Los Angeles (UCLA), where he is currently a professor emeritus.

One of the primary distinctions market designers make when analyzing markets is that of centralization versus decentralization. Some markets have centralized clearinghouses that match supply and demand (even if prices are absent). Other markets are decentralized and do not have a central authority to allocate resources.

For example, consider the market for medical residents, with hospitals on the demand side and new doctors (residents) on the supply side. In the early twentieth century, medical students would apply for positions in hospitals during their final year of medical school. However, as competition for new doctors increased, by the 1940s hospitals began hiring students much earlier than before—often almost two years before graduation.[14] Due to the uncertainty and insufficient information about medical students' plans of where they wanted to work two years later, as well as the lack of viable alternatives that were available to each student, the market began to lose thickness over time.

By the 1950s, hospitals and medical organizations addressed this problem by establishing rules concerning when offers could be made. That soon led to congestion because hospitals were not giving medical students enough time to make decisions. To solve this problem, medical groups organized a centralized clearinghouse to better match supply with demand called the National Resident Matching Program (NRMP), which is still in use today and is a version that Alvin Roth redesigned in the 1990s to improve its efficiency (see box on Alvin Roth later).

As the NRMP example demonstrates, introducing a centralized clearinghouse can improve a market that previously, in the words of market designers, could unravel, and fail to produce an efficient outcome. This solution raises a question, however: Can all decentralized markets be made more efficient by introducing a centralized clearinghouse to match supply with demand?

According to Clayton Featherstone, a former post-doctoral fellow who was mentored by Roth at Harvard Business School and who now conducts research in market design and matching theory at the Wharton School of the University of Pennsylvania, the potential gains of having a centralized clearinghouse must be weighed carefully against the potential gains of having numerous smaller exchanges compete with each other for market participants.[15] As always with market design, details matter; so it depends on the market in question.

For example, as we will see below in the dating market, there are currently several dozen viable dating websites available to individuals, each offering a different interface and user experience, with some catering to very specialized audiences. This is a case where the net benefits of a single clearinghouse are not sufficient to justify the costs.

There is a good counterexample, however, and it is the market for kidneys. This is a market that Roth has thought a lot about and has helped to greatly improve in the past few years. In the United States, as in many other countries, commercial trade in human organs is illegal, mostly for ethical reasons, which is why the market for kidneys is sometimes described as a repugnant market. Kidneys therefore are allocated in the United States through a donation system that matches patients with donors. There are currently about 70,000 patients in need of a kidney transplant, yet only about 11,000 a year receive them.[16]

Since people are born with two kidneys and can live healthy lives with just one, a person can donate a kidney to someone in need. However, since the patient and donor may be incompatible (because of differences in their blood types, for example), they would have to locate another such pair in which the donor in one pair could donate a kidney to the patient in the other pair, and vice versa.[17] Up until the early 2000s, these so-called paired exchanges were rare because it was difficult for people to locate compatible patient-donor pairs.[18]

In this situation, then, it is clear that the market lacks thickness and would benefit from having a centralized kidney exchange to bring together more compatible donor pairs and thereby permit the transplantation of many more kidneys. Roth and his colleagues M. Utku Unver and Tayfun Sonmez argued exactly this point in a 2004 article.[19] Kidney surgeons in New England were receptive to the idea and, with the help of Roth and his colleagues, the 14 kidney transplant centers in that area were brought together to create the New England Program for Kidney Exchange. Roth believes there is a substantial business opportunity for someone to organize a single, national kidney (and other organ) clearinghouse. In fact, Congress has established a national pilot program for kidney exchanges that is being operated as a nonprofit organization (like the New England organization). Kidney transplants not only offer vastly greater quality of life for patients than dialysis, but also save money; by one good estimate, $60,000 per Medicare beneficiary.[20]

Where there are cost advantages to a single clearinghouse, such as in the market for kidneys, economists cite this as evidence of economies of scale. With kidneys, what matters is that the number of patient-donor matches is maximized. However, as we will see in the example of dating websites, there is more room in that setting for product differentiation and, indeed, that is partly what has contributed to that market's decentralization, which ends up benefiting consumers because greater competition leads to the differentiation that consumers want.

Alvin Roth

Alvin Roth is one of the pioneers of market design and has made significant contributions to matching theory, game theory, and experimental economics. Born in New York City in 1951, Roth went to high school in Queens, where he dropped out in his junior year and began taking weekend engineering classes at Columbia University.[21] After a professor there suggested that he apply to college, Roth was admitted formally to Columbia and graduated with a degree in engineering in 1971. He went to Stanford University to complete his graduate work, receiving both his masters and PhD in a branch of engineering called operations research, which uses mathematics to improve decision making, often in the face of uncertainty (see Chapter 4, which discusses this field in greater detail).

Roth has taught at multiple universities —the University of Illinois, the University of Pittsburgh, Harvard, and Stanford— applying his training in operations research to explore topics in game theory, including market design and matching theory.

In the early 1980s, Roth recognized the real-world relevance of the Gale-Shapley algorithm (explained in the box on Lloyd Shapley earlier). In particular, in 1984 Roth studied the algorithm used by the NRMP clearinghouse to match new doctors with hospitals and discovered that it was closely related to the Gale-Shapley algorithm proposed decades earlier.[22] By the 1990s, there were signs that the NRMP clearinghouse was encountering problems. As the number of female medical students grew over the preceding decades, dual-doctor couples were often looking for work in the same region, and this presented a challenge to the system: Many new doctors were no longer using it, a sign that it was not producing stable matches. In 1995, Roth was asked to redesign the system and modernize it to produce stable matches and improve its efficiency. The new algorithm, which he designed with Elliott Peranson, was adopted by NRMP in 1997 and is still in use today.

In recent years, Roth has applied the Gale-Shapley algorithm in a variety of other settings. In 2003, for example, Roth helped to design New York City's public high school matching system. Before 2003, the city's allocated spots through a complicated process that involved repeated rounds of applications and rejections, resulting in tens of thousands of unstable matches every year. The new algorithm that Roth implemented, based on the theoretical work of Gale and Shapley, resulted in a 90 percent reduction in the number of unstable matches. Today a growing number of school systems, including Boston's, have begun to apply Roth's techniques to improve their matching mechanisms.[23]

Another significant contribution by Roth to market design and matching theory is the market for kidney donors and patients, as discussed in the text. Roth's most recent projects include helping redesign the job markets for gastroenterologists and economists, and setting up a nationwide kidney exchange, which would provide far more thickness and stable matches than any of the existing regional clearinghouses.

As is evident from the multitude of diverse applications of his work, Roth is a pioneer of applying sophisticated economic theories to solve practical problems. For his contributions to market design and matching theory, Roth was awarded the Nobel Prize in Economics in 2012 (along with Lloyd Shapley) and remains active in field experiments to this day as a professor of economics at Stanford University and emeritus professor of business administration at Harvard Business School.

Matchmaking in the Labor Market

In recent years, another market that has benefited directly from the research of Shapley, Roth, and other market designers is the labor market—perhaps the most important matching market of all. As discussed, Roth's work in the medical labor market greatly improved a system that was in danger of falling apart, or unraveling. That is, there were signs that the centralized clearinghouse was not producing stable matches, and so medical students were often avoiding the mechanism altogether and finding matches on their own.

In this section, I describe situations where the insights of market designers have produced positive business impacts in the labor market in general, helping to better match supply (job seekers) with demand (employers). In particular, algorithms are increasingly playing matchmaker to improve the efficiency of the labor market and the likelihood that the matches that take place are stable in the first place—often a significant problem in many companies.

Let's start with the fundamentals. At a basic level, job hunting and hiring are a lot like dating. Both involve information asymmetries, costly and drawn-out search processes, and complex sets of criteria.[24] And though money can play a role, it's not necessarily the central factor in hiring, and less so in dating (and where it is, one or both sides are interested not only in wages paid today but in the future earning power of the other). Instead, the primary consideration is about the particular qualities of people that are thought to lead to enduring matches. In the labor market, much is made of concepts like fitting the company culture and compatibility of skills.

Yet we all know from personal experience that many employer–employee relationships do not work out, or in the language of the literature on matching theory, a substantial share of the matches between employees and employers are not stable. Put differently, there are probably millions of employee–employer matches that, if broken up, could lead to new matches that make all parties involved better off. Of course, it is not realistic to expect a perfect equilibrium in which every employee and employer is completely satisfied with their matches. But the insights of the market designers suggest there is room for improvement.

Some businesses have begun to make this possible. AfterCollege, Inc., for example, has developed software that thinks and acts like a human recruiter, examining the characteristics of stable matches so a computer can recommend vacancies to job seekers and candidates to hiring managers.[25] Another popular online job matching service is provided by LinkedIn, the company that perhaps more than any other has upended corporate recruiting in the past decade. The company has taken advantage of its vast database of about 200 million career profiles to create an algorithm that notifies recruiters about "People You May Want to Hire."[26] LinkedIn's growth is a testament of its growing popularity among employers and potential employees alike.

LinkedIn's algorithm is a microcosm of what market design is all about: understanding the institutional details of a given market in order to improve the way it matches supply and demand. For example, LinkedIn discovered from mining its own data that computer engineers migrate back and forth between New York and San Francisco frequently; accordingly, its algorithm is designed to show specific companies in California a few candidates from New York, but it wouldn't show them candidates from, say, Reno, because there is very little mobility between that market and Silicon Valley.[27] The same logic can be applied to match job seekers and companies in finance in New York and London, for example.

The algorithmic approach to the matching of job seekers with employers differs from traditional hiring in at least two important respects. First, firms using algorithms focus on a broader set of employee traits than just education and experience to help employers find talent by adding cognitive ability, personality traits, and cultural fit to produce better candidates.[28]

Second, the new job matchmaking companies have harnessed the power of technology, and in particular the benefits of data analytics, to create algorithms that better match supply with demand and produce more stable matches.

Companies like AfterCollege, CareerBuilder, Burning Glass, and oDesk are taking advantage of their rich databases to mine information and identify traits that are better predictors of successful matches in the workplace. oDesk, for example, is the nation's largest online market connecting businesses to remote contractors. In 2011, it introduced an algorithm that generates recommendations of best-match candidates to businesses, resulting in more filled vacancies and more stable matches.[29]

The new job matchmakers still face an important challenge, however. The best predictors of stable matches—characteristics like creativity, personality, and cultural fit—are the ones that are the most difficult to quantify and therefore the hardest to incorporate into an algorithm. That is partly the reason why traditional measures like education and experience continue to be widely used despite their tenuous connection to efficient matches.

So what, if anything, can matchmaking firms do to fix this problem? The answers may come from academia. Amy Kristof-Brown, an expert on person–environment fit who earned her PhD in organizational behavior and now teaches at the Tippie College of Business at the University of Iowa, has found that optimal fits based on company culture reduce turnover and create stable matches.[30] She has advised RoundPegg, a firm that seeks to quantify the elusive concept of company culture by measuring a variety of indicators with surveys to get at the attitudes and beliefs of individual employees.[31] In this way, companies' cultures can be quantified and then matched to the specific attributes of each job seeker in order to create more stable matches.

Another example is a startup called Good.co, which specializes in improving labor market matches involving millenials—those born in the 1980s and 1990s—many of whom are now entering the labor force in large numbers.[32] Good.co uses surveys to assess job seekers' personalities and make recommendations about workplace fits based on qualities that have proven to yield successful matches. Like Good.co, dozens of other startups have launched in recent years with the goal of improving labor markets by using surveys and other data-driven tools to explore the characteristics that lead to enduring matches.

Matchmaking in the labor market is turning out to be a win-win-win-win business. Job seekers and employers both are better off from more stable matches. Matchmakers profit from improving existing markets or creating new ones from scratch when they're missing. And society benefits from better matches in the workplace, which should lead to higher productivity, greater innovation and, over time, a higher standard of living. In this way, market designers and the matchmakers in the labor market who use their insights help achieve a fundamental goal of economics: to improve the general welfare and increase the wealth of nations.

Matchmaking and Online Dating

As we just discovered with matching in labor markets, hiring and dating have a lot in common. In fact, many market designers have for decades considered them to be so similar as to be synonymous.[33] Like hiring workers, dating has problems associated with information asymmetries, long search processes, and complex criteria, so it is not surprising that the Internet has facilitated matchmaking in both markets. In addition, as you will see shortly, economists have developed a number of insights that have been applied to improve the online dating world and thus create more stable matches, sometimes in ways that differ from the solutions being implemented by matchmakers in the labor market.

Online dating sites offer two things that neither traditional matchmakers nor chance encounters at, say, bars, shopping malls, or workplaces entail. One is the vastly greater choice available to market participants online.[34] Using the framework of market design outlined earlier, online dating sites provide much more thickness than traditional settings. The other potentially large benefit of online dating is that, as with matchmaking in the labor market, the companies in this space tend to claim they have scientifically proven ways of finding the perfect matches for their users.

It will take much time and study to determine which, if any, of these claims for scientific validity have merit. In the meantime, it's instructive to see how economists have helped some of the online sites overcome one of their initial obstacles.

Unlike the markets for medical doctors, kidneys, and schools in which there were plenty of potential customers on both the demand and supply sides, the online dating markets struggle with attracting as many women as they do men. In particular, with little refereeing by the online sites, men would flood the inboxes of attractive women, who in turn would ignore most of the messages because it is difficult and very time-consuming to separate spammers from good prospects.[35] Women thus faced a needle-in-the-haystack problem. Or, to borrow a term from market design, many of these dating sites had encountered congestion problems, preventing markets from creating efficient and stable matches. So how was this problem solved?

One website, Cupid.com, hired Muriel Niederle, an expert market design economist from Stanford, as an adviser to the firm. In 2005, at the suggestion of Niederle and economist Dan Ariely (then at MIT, now at Duke), Cupid.com began to allocate electronic roses to its male members.[36] The logic of this change was based on the fact that the marginal cost of sending another message to a new member was essentially zero, which encouraged too many men to send messages to women's inboxes. What if, the economists asked, communications were made more costly? If the number of messages people could send were limited—in this case to two electronic roses per month—then men would have an incentive to reveal their true preferences and signal their interest to the women that they wanted to impress. In short, the economists argued that the scarcity of roses would motivate suitors to be selective, and so members who weren't serious would essentially be weeded out of the process.

According to Eric Straus, CEO of Cupid.com, the results were "a wonderful thing." The electronic roses increased a suitor's chances of getting a reply by about 35 percent.[37] The majority of online dating sites have followed suit and implemented various mechanisms to increase the cost of communication between members. In fact, one site, whatsyourprice.com, has literally put a price tag on not just the cost of sending a message to another member, but on the dates themselves. Men bid for dates with women, and if a proposed price is accepted for a date request, the suitor is supposed to pay the woman the amount they agreed upon when they meet on their first date.

Whatsyourprice.com is an extreme example of where prices can be used in a setting that most people would never consider to be a traditional market. Instead, the trend with the majority of dating sites has been to introduce algorithms designed to create efficient and stable matches. For example, the psychologists at eHarmony claim that the algorithm at this well-known dating site has the ability to identify the key traits that contribute most to stable matches and enduring relationships. Much like the labor market sites devoted to identifying the real characteristics that yield successful relationships in the workplace, eHarmony asserts that the traditional traits that lead to many relationships, like physical attraction, are in fact poor predictors of stable matches. The site instead arranges matches by using the results of long questionnaires that its customers fill out. The company doesn't let customers search for partners on their own, a method the company thinks is inferior compared with its advanced algorithm.[38]

Over the years, other dating sites, which include match.com, chemistry.com, and okcupid.com to name a few, also have claimed that their algorithms produce better matches and longer-lasting marriages compared with alternative methods. However, many of these online sites preserve their intellectual property—their algorithms—as trade secrets, thereby making it virtually impossible to confirm with any degree of certainty whether their claims are valid.

It is nonetheless conceivable that the operators of one or more of these sites one day will develop sufficient confidence in the reliability of their algorithms to open up these databases for independent researchers to study. Indeed, it may only take one to get the ball rolling. If one site's methodology is verified by highly respected researchers, other sites may be compelled by market pressures to open up their databases as well to other researchers. But even if none of this happens, eventually the good sites will drive out the bad or not-so-good ones or, hold your breath, a government agency like the Federal Trade Commission may compel the sites to publish their marriage rates and other indicators of dating success (such as length of marriages) as the sites mature.

As for the business opportunities associated with online matchmaking, the title of a recent book on the subject—*Love in the Time of Algorithms*—makes it clear that dating sites are here to stay. Indeed, with an estimated $2 billion in annual revenues in North America alone, third-party, for-profit matchmaking is a booming industry.[39] Techniques used to make matches will surely improve over time, as will the design of the markets themselves, with likely better and more stable marriages the result. Let's hope.

The Bottom Line

As important as prices are in clearing most markets, they are not the deciding factor in some markets where buyers and sellers, or those on each side of the market, are looking to match specific non-price characteristics. Just as the house in gambling establishments always collects the "vig," matchmaking businesses in an expanding array of both traditional and nontraditional markets are likely to grow by earning fees from the matches they arrange. Hopefully this chapter has explained how and why economists may help them and their customers along the way.

Notes

1. Jonathan Gruber, *Public Finance and Public Policy* (New York: Worth Publishers, 2005), 3.

2. The Royal Swedish Academy of Sciences, "The Prize in Economic Sciences 2012: Stable Matching: Theory, Evidence, and Practical Design," www .nobelprize.org/nobel_prizes/economic-sciences/laureates/2012/popular-economicsciences2012.pdf.

3. Leon Neyfakh, "The Matchmaker," *Boston Globe*, www.boston.com/ bostonglobe/ideas/articles/2011/04/03/the_matchmaker/.

4. Alvin Roth, "The Art of Designing Markets," *Harvard Business Review*, http:// hbr.org/2007/10/the-art-of-designing-markets/ar/1.

5. Ibid., 1.

6. Hal Varian, "Avoiding the Pitfalls When Economics Shifts," *New York Times*, www.nytimes.com/2002/08/29/business/economic-scene-avoiding-pitfalls-when-economics-shifts-science-engineering.html.

7. Muriel Niederle, Alvin E. Roth, and Tayfun Sonmez, "Matching and Market Design," In *The New Palgrave Dictionary of Economics*, 2nd ed., ed. Steven Derlauf and Larry Blume (Hampshire, UK: Palgrave Macmillan, 2008).

8. Ibid.

9. Ibid.

10. Ibid.

11. Quote from his biography at the time of his winning the Nobel, which is a major source for this profile. Cynthia Lee and Judy Lin, "Colleagues Applaud Lloyd Shapley's Nobel," *UCLA Today*, http://today.ucla.edu/portal/ut/ colleagues-at-ucla-applaud-lloyd-239730.aspx.

12. The American Economic Association, "Lloyd Shapley," www.aeaweb.org/ PDF_files/Bios/Shapley_bio.pdf.

13. The Royal Swedish Academy of Sciences, "The Prize in Economic Sciences 2012: Stable Matching: Theory, Evidence, and Practical Design," October 2012,

www.nobelprize.org/nobel_prizes/economic-sciences/laureates/2012/popular-economicsciences2012.pdf.

14. Alvin Roth, "The Art of Designing Markets," *Harvard Business Review*, 3, http://hbr.org/2007/10/the-art-of-designing-markets/ar/1.

15. Interview with Clayton Featherstone, October 18, 2013. I am grateful to Featherstone for discussing many of the insights of market design and matching theory described in this chapter.

16. Roth, "The Art of Designing Markets," 2.

17. Ibid.

18. I appreciate the help that Clayton Featherstone provided in making the point in this paragraph.

19. Alvin E. Roth, Tayfun Sonmez, and M. Utku Unver, "Kidney Exchange," *Quarterly Journal of Economics* 119, no. 2 (2004): 457–488.

20. Economic Report of the President (2013): 171.

21. Susan Adams, "Unfreakonomics," *Forbes*, www.forbes.com/forbes/2010/0809/opinions-harvard-alvin-roth-freakonomics-ideas-opinions.html.

22. The Royal Swedish Academy of Sciences, "The Prize in Economic Sciences 2012."

23. Ibid.

24. David Zax, "Falling for the Job," *Time*, http://content.time.com/time/magazine/article/0,9171,2151168,00.html.

25. Aki Ito, "Algorithms Play Matchmaker to Fight 7.7% U.S. Unemployment: Jobs," Bloomberg News, www.bloomberg.com/news/2013-04-03/algorithms-play-matchmaker-to-fight-7-7-u-s-unemployment-jobs.html.

26. George Anders, "Who Should You Hire? LinkedIn Says: Try Our Algorithm," *Forbes*, www.forbes.com/sites/georgeanders/2013/04/10/who-should-you-hire-linkedin-says-try-our-algorithm/.

27. Ibid.

28. Zax, "Falling for the Job."

29. Ito, "Algorithms Play Matchmaker."

30. Zax, "Falling for the Job," 4.

31. Ibid.

32. Ibid.

33. Ibid., 2.

34. *The Economist*, "The Modern Matchmakers," www.economist.com/node/21547217.

35. Ito, "Algorithms Play Matchmaker."

36. Mark Whitehouse, "Job-hunting Takes a Line from Dating," *Wall Street Journal*, www.stanford.edu/~niederle/WSJ.Matching.htm.

37. Ibid.

38. Zax, "Falling for the Job," 4.

39. Seth Stevenson, "Love Bytes," *Slate*, www.slate.com/articles/technology/books/2013/02/dan_slater_s_love_in_the_time_of_algorithms_reviewed.html.

Chapter 8

Economists and Mostly Good Financial Engineering

We now come to the chapter about economists and finance. Given the bad reputation that the subject has earned in the wake of the financial crisis, I purposely delayed discussing it until I've put you in a better mood.

Seriously, economists, or actually financial economists, have made major contributions to our understanding of the way not only how the financial sector works, but also how the overall economy operates. Modern economies would not exist without modern financial sectors and systems, for finance is the lifeblood of all economies. When it works as it is supposed to, financial institutions and markets are not just abstract middlemen, but essential institutions that enable people and firms to save and diversify their wealth. Just as clogged arteries and malfunctioning hearts can debilitate or kill people, finance gone wrong can do the same to economies. That is why financial engineering, in some quarters, no longer has the desirable connotations it once did. As an aside, most of those innovations that turned out wrong were not invented by economists, although many economists, including some famous and important ones, were late in realizing precisely how wrong they turned out to be.

In Chapter 12, I discuss a few ways in which economists have contributed to policy measures that have provided the platforms that have enabled or encouraged certain financial innovations or practices which I believe have had positive economic effects.

This chapter is not about policy, however, but about financially related economic *ideas* that collectively have had major business implications. I will concentrate on three of the most important ones, as well as on the economists who thought them up, and a few of the business visionaries who put them to profitable, socially productive uses.

Not Putting Your Eggs in One Basket: The Rise of Index Investing

If there is one adage that many investors have been told by their financial advisers, or by many books on investing, it is "Don't put all your eggs into one basket." In other words, do your best to diversify. True, this won't make you a killing, unless you make a lot of money from some other endeavor, save a lot of it, and then put *that money* into a diversified portfolio of stocks, bonds, and some alternative assets (like real estate, or even gold). Then the laws of compound interest will take over, and if you live long enough, your wealth will be substantial.

There is a competing investment philosophy that is diametrically opposed to this bit of conventional wisdom. Attributed to a wide number of people, one of whom was Andrew Carnegie, the founder of U.S. Steel (once a mighty industrial powerhouse), this notion is to concentrate on only one investment, and then watch that particular "basket" very carefully. I have heard this quote from some businessmen before, and frankly, it strikes me as much better advice for people engaged in business than those deciding how to invest someone's money.

Business calls for single-minded focus on what a firm and its employees do best. The national analogue to this notion is the principle of comparative advantage, probably one of the least understood and yet most important insights from economics. This principle says that nations (or firms or people) are best off if they concentrate on what they do best compared to others, even if they are absolutely better at doing a lot of things better than others. The principle implies that businesses are thus better off if they are focused on just one or a few things.

Investing is different. One can earn more and take less risk overall by diversifying. But what is the optimal amount of diversification? That was a question that Harry Markowitz asked in the early 1950s. His answer, roughly 20 to 30 stocks, and the methodology he used to derive it, earned him a Nobel Prize in 1990. Several years earlier, in 1981, Yale economist James Tobin (one of my graduate school mentors and favorite teachers and people) also won the Nobel Prize for related work.

Some ideas win Nobel Prizes while others become popularized, either by journalists or other economists. The notion that portfolio diversification is the best way to invest in the market provides such an example. When investors think of the concept, the individual who most often comes to mind is neither Markowitz nor Tobin, but longtime Princeton economics professor and frequent op-ed columnist Burton Malkiel, who penned one of the most famous popular books about investing, *A Random Walk Down Wall Street*. Originally published in 1973, the book has since had 10 editions.[1]

Ideas can have real-world commercial impacts in many different ways. Sometimes, entrepreneurs and executives at established firms read a book or an article with a clever idea and they proceed to make it operational. Others get commercial ideas from economists they hire as consultants. And frequently, as you will see in this book, entrepreneurs are motivated by an economic idea they learn while attending school.

John "Jack" Bogle, the founder of the Vanguard family of mutual funds, is a prime example of the last way economists have had an impact. Bogle reports that he was heavily influenced by both Malkiel and Paul Samuelson (profiled in Chapter 2), two of the champions of indexing and critics of active money management, especially by individual investors, both in writing his senior thesis at Princeton on the idea of index funds and then actually implementing that idea at Vanguard.[2] In 1976, the firm launched its S&P index fund, shortly after Malkiel published his first edition of *A Random Walk Down Wall Street*.

The rest, as they say, is history. Not only did Vanguard go on to sponsor funds based on other indices, but other funds copied Vanguard's model and did the same and then some. Eventually, numerous mutual funds offered all kinds of sector-specific funds, each with its own index.

It is difficult to overstate the importance of the indexing revolution in the mutual fund business, which up to Bogle's time operated entirely through funds that were actively managed by stock pickers, and accordingly charged comparatively larger management fees (typically 1 percent or more of the assets of the fund each year) than index funds (where the fees tend to fall in the range of 10 to 20 basis points, or 0.1 to 0.2 percent of assets). Bogle has shown in his extensive writings how this difference in fees mounts up over time, especially for long-term investors, taking away half or more of their total returns.[3] Furthermore, economic research has consistently documented that indexed funds have generally generated better returns for investors than actively managed funds. Investors have noticed, moving more of their money over time to indexed products: The share of all equity mutual funds that are indexed more than doubled from 1998 to 2012 (8.7 percent to 17.4 percent).[4] If one adds in the newer exchange-traded funds discussed next, indexed products accounted for fully one-third of both stock mutual funds and ETFs in 2013.[5]

There is one downside to indexing, however: Index funds or their shareholders have no incentive to monitor the managers of the companies that make up the index, or to exercise voice rather than exit, to use Hirschman's terminology. But there are still many investors who can and do perform this monitoring function, so it is not clear how much of a loss of oversight the trend toward indexing has actually caused.

In the past two decades or so, the exchange-traded fund (ETF) was developed by other financial entrepreneurs; it was modeled on the index approach that Bogle had pioneered. An index-based ETF essentially holds a fixed basket of stocks and trades like a stock throughout the day, unlike a mutual fund, which reprices only at the end of each trading day. In addition, an ETF has tax advantages over a mutual fund, which passes through its gains and losses on a pro rata basis to shareholders, with the decision to sell or buy being made by the fund manager. In an ETF, that decision is made by the ETF holder, who controls his or her own tax consequences.[6]

The ETF has made inroads into the institutional investment world for the above reasons, so much so that many mutual fund companies now offer ETF products themselves. Moreover, some innovators have designed ETFs whose stock holdings are actively managed. Still, as of 2012, assets held in ETFs accounted for only 9 percent of all assets managed by investment companies.[7]

What started then as a simple, but important economic insight from Harry Markowitz, elaborated by Samuelson, and popularized by Malkiel—that one gains superior returns given any level risk by diversifying an equity portfolio—eventually transformed the investment world.

Efficient Markets and Their Implications

It took an economist following an unlikely route to this subject to take the logic of index investing to the next theoretical level: If it makes sense to diversify, that must be because it is rare (see Warren Buffett), if impossible, to consistently outperform the market as a whole.

Eugene Fama was that individual, and for his research work he was awarded the Nobel Prize in Economics in 2013 (see following box). Fama won the prize for his development of the efficient markets hypothesis (EMH), which is one of the most cited, contentious, and often misunderstood propositions in economics. Nate Silver, the statistician and political forecaster (among other things), has done one of the best jobs I have seen translating the hypothesis into plain English and I will summarize his description here.[8]

EMH has a number of versions, each stronger then the next. In its weakest form, EMH postulates the findings just stated: Future stock price movements cannot be predicted from past statistical patterns.

The second, semi-strong version of EMH, is that trying to pick stocks that are undervalued—the kind of thing that Warren Buffett does remarkably well—is a sucker's game. All relevant information about the fundamental value of a company is instantaneously reflected in its stock price, so there is no room for investors or traders to consistently make money trying to guess which stocks will outperform the average, or won't.

How then can one explain Buffett's success (and that of a few others, like Peter Lynch, the famed investor who managed Fidelity's Magellan Fund in its early years for roughly two decades)? Fama's answer, like that of other EMH defenders, is luck. In any large number of coin-flippers there inevitably will be a few who consistently pick which side of the coin comes out on top. But the winners clearly have no special insight into coin flipping.

Buffett had a rejoinder to that answer, which he supplied in a famous debate he had at Columbia University in 1984 with another EMH defender, Harvard Business School professor (emeritus) Michael Jensen. The event celebrated the fiftieth anniversary of the publication of the bible of value investing, Graham and Dodd's *The Intelligent Investor*, which advocates an investment style that is the very antithesis of EMH. After Jensen presented the coin-flipper analogy, Buffett replied by identifying nine other money managers who managed very different portfolios and yet had outstanding investment records. This result, he argued, could not be the result of random flips of the coin.

The accounting of this exchange comes from Buffett's unofficial and widely celebrated biography, *Snowball*, whose author, Alice Schroeder, reports that the audience applauded Buffett's answer.[9] And for what it's worth, most money managers side with Buffett; how could they not, for to embrace EMH would deny the value of their profession, picking stocks?

Schroeder goes on to say, however, that EMH may still have provided a valuable function by discouraging the average investor from managing his or her own money. In addition, she notes that there are now multiple versions of EMH that essentially say that EMH works for the most part, but not always.[10]

The third, strong form of EMH is that even traders with private information cannot consistently outperform the market. Silver states that not even most EMH supporters believe this extension of the theory.

Silver also adds an important caveat to the three forms of EMH that Fama himself would insist on. Each applies only to *risk-adjusted returns*. Some investors willing to take above-average risks may be able to outperform the market, but only because of their risk taking, not because they have superior stock-picking ability. Their annual returns also will fluctuate more widely than a market-wide portfolio.

EMH critics, and there are many, cite the stock market's sharp occasional falls as disproving the hypothesis. EMH defenders respond that market fluctuations do not refute the core proposition of the theory: namely, that no one can consistently outperform the market, except by taking more risk, or by chance.

Eugene Fama

Eugene Fama didn't start out wanting to be an economist when he enrolled in college at Tufts University. His first interest was in Romance languages, but like many who get turned on to something else, Fama's life was changed after working as an assistant to a professor who ran a stock market forecasting service.

Fama's work interested him in poring through past stock market data to discover patterns that might support a profitable investment strategy. The professor told him to test each strategy on a forward-looking basis, taking into account the costs of buying and selling the stocks—what economists call transactions costs—and as Nate Silver describes it, "almost always" the strategies failed.[11]

But the work and the hunting changed Fama's intellectual interests entirely. He abandoned any thought of pursuing Romance languages and instead went to the University of Chicago's business school to earn his PhD in finance (or what I have been calling financial economics). His dissertation focused on whether one could extrapolate the investment performance of mutual funds from their past performance (analogous to stock-picking exercises of his undergraduate years), based on data from the decade of the 1950s.

Lo and behold, the striking answer was that one couldn't! Just because a fund had a good run in the past, an investor could not count on a continuation of that performance in the future. Fama also established the same result for the wide number and variety of technical analysts—those who attempt to divine the future movement of stock prices from their past patterns charted on a graph.

In short, Fama found that no one actively managing money, not even the best mutual fund managers, could consistently beat the market, or the performance turned in by an average of all stocks.

In 2013, Fama was awarded the Nobel Prize for his pioneering financial research. As discussed shortly in the text, he shared the prize with two other researchers.

If picking stocks is a losing proposition, and indexing is the way to go, can anyone make money using the insights of EMH? The answer is yes, and one of the clearest examples is Dimensional Advisers, founded by one of Fama's former Chicago graduate students, David Booth.

Booth got the idea for his company after being an adviser to pension plans for large companies in the late 1970s, which then were heavily invested in large-capitalization stocks. He eventually wondered why these companies' treasurers were not also investing in small-cap stocks, or those of small or young public companies, as well.

Booth didn't wait for the answer, or for anyone else to implement the idea. In 1981, he and a graduate school colleague, Rex Sinquefeld, launched Dimensional Advisers with the explicit objective of building what was, in effect, an index fund of small-caps, even before such indices existed—in other words, the reverse of Vanguard's innovation of building the funds to replicate existing indices. Dimensional added value stocks, or those with low ratios of price to book value, to the mix of its portfolios for its investors.

The EMH theory was not the only basis, however, for Dimensional's success. Booth and his colleagues introduced several important trading innovations, which the fund also credits for its success. One innovation was to buy stocks throughout the day, rather than only at the closing, when index funds are priced. This saved trading costs and enhanced the funds' performance. A second innovation was to parcel out orders to different brokers and tell them to be patient, and not to buy unless there was plenty of volume, or when many sellers were around. The founders did not want orders being executed when only a few sellers were able to command higher prices than in thicker markets. These instructions created competition among brokers for getting stock at the cheapest prices, which increased returns for Dimensional's fund investors.[12]

This second practice has changed with the advent of high frequency trading, conducted by computers using trading algorithms for buying and selling stocks. Dimensional has adapted by developing its own ordering systems that bypass brokers. Later in the company's history, Dimensional used the research findings of the company's academic advisers (see box on David Booth that follows) to develop funds that invested in large-cap stocks, including companies in international markets, and fixed-income funds as well. As the firm's investment vehicles diversified, Dimensional broadened its marketing strategies, opening foreign offices and seeking funds from individuals with defined contribution pension plans. Dimensional's official history makes clear that its economic advisers were critical to each stage of the company's success and expansion.[13]

David Booth: Putting EMH to Work in the Investment World

David Booth is one of the humblest billionaires you'll ever meet, and also a very generous one. I met him while we happened to be sitting next to each other on a shuttle bus ride at an event at Dallas several years ago. After introducing ourselves, and he said his name was David Booth, I thought a moment and then blurted out, "Are you the David Booth who just bought the Naismith papers (the original rules of basketball) and donated them to the University of Kansas?" He said yes.

That question came to me because just before this bus ride, the *Kansas City Star*, the largest newspaper in the city where I was then living, had just reported the multimillion-dollar purchase of these papers by Booth and his donation. I also realized that he was the same Booth for whom the University of Chicago's Business School had been renamed after his very generous donation to the school where he received the training in finance that ultimately led to his great success.

Booth then briefly told me his life's story, how he had grown up in a modest house on Naismith Drive near the University of Kansas and why he had purchased and then donated the Naismith papers because of his love of basketball and the University of Kansas, which he attended as an undergraduate (both parts of his background resonated with me since I am a Kansas native, and a huge fan of the basketball teams of all Kansas universities).

(continued)

> From Kansas, Booth went to Chicago's business school with the intention of earning his PhD in finance studying under Fama. Booth greatly enjoyed learning from Fama and served as his teaching assistant, but ultimately came to the conclusion that he was better suited for the investment world than academia. So he left Chicago before getting his PhD and entered the world of money management, first at Wells Fargo working on index funds, and later at A.G. Becker.
>
> Booth credits his teacher Fama with the inspiration for his hugely successful entrepreneurial career in money management. Fama, Kenneth French (another well-known financial economist at Dartmouth), and Robert Merton (another Nobel Prize winner), along with a handful of other academic stars in financial economics, are consultants to Dimensional, illustrating another important principle Booth explained to me: Start with a good idea but surround yourself with a lot of other people who are smarter than you to help implement it.[14]

Behavioral Finance

The Nobel Prize for Economics has often gone to multiple economists in the same year. The year 2013 was one of those years, for not only did Gene Fama win for his work on EMH, but Robert Shiller of Yale University (see the following box) was a co-winner (along with Lars Hansen, Fama's colleague at the University of Chicago) for his work on financial economics, too. But what was relatively rare in this award is that Fama's and Shiller's research reached opposite conclusions.

Whereas Fama argues that financial asset prices are efficiently determined, Shiller was recognized by the Nobel committee for his research going back to the early 1980s showing that stock prices vary far more frequently than dividends,[15] suggesting stock prices can and do move for reasons that may have nothing to do with the fundamental earning power of their companies. This means that stock prices can overshoot in both directions, forming bubbles in good times (when, in Warren Buffett's terms, investors are greedy) and being excessively deflated in bad times (when Buffett says that investors are fearful). To Fama and other proponents of at least one of the stronger forms of EMH, it makes no sense to talk of stock price bubbles because prices are always efficient.

Shiller was also in the vanguard of a school of financial economics called behavioral finance—a branch of a broader school of behavioral economics, discussed in the second chapter. Finance behaviorists, including not only many academics but also many professional and amateur stock pickers, believe there are too many ways in which stock price movements depart from one or more versions of EMH. Thus, some investors and hedge funds buy and sell on momentum, believing they can predict stock prices over some future period (which may be much shorter than a day) based on past prices. Other investors have observed and acted on past oddities in stock pricing—such as the tendency that persisted for some time for stock prices to rise during the first week in January (after professional investors have sold off some stocks at year-end for tax or other reasons), or the apparent tendency of the worst performing stocks in the Dow Jones Industrial Average or the worst performing mutual funds to outperform the market as a whole for some period ahead.[16] Academic financial economists continue to debate the validity and importance of behavioral finance.

There is one proposition on which both Shiller and Fama very likely would agree, however: In the short run, stock prices are unpredictable and therefore it is prudent for most investors to buy and hold broad index-based instruments (mutual funds or ETFs). Shiller would be the first to tell the average investor that he or she cannot rely on some of the statistical oddities that some investigators may have found in the past that generated risk-adjusted returns, outperforming the market as a whole (what finance professionals call *alpha*). To this extent, then, Shiller's work provides just as much intellectual support for the indexing movement as does Fama's (Shiller would also argue, however, that in the long run it is fundamentals, namely the underlying earning power of companies, that determine stock prices and that such prices revert to a long-run average of price-to-earnings ratios).

EMH proponents, meanwhile, deny that the oddities various behaviorists claim to have discovered are stable, largely because once they have been identified for all investors to see, enough may jump on the opportunities until at least some of the oddities disappear, or, in finance language, are arbitraged away. Shiller and other behaviorists may agree with this to some degree, but would add that market misalignments or bubbles can persist for some time before they are corrected or punctured, a proposition that EMH proponents would not accept.

Behavioral finance has important implications for policy makers, which is why the debate over its merits has an importance that extends beyond the world of investing. If it is true that financial markets are prone to manias and bubbles, as not only the behaviorists believe but as one of their intellectual godfathers, the late Hyman Minsky, argued in his many writings, then there is a case for preemptive government policies aimed at thwarting these tendencies.

In the aftermath of the financial crisis, such policies have been called macro-prudential regulation, to distinguish them from the traditional micro regulation and supervision of individual financial institutions. Macro-prudential regulation was legitimized by the Dodd–Frank Wall Street Reform and Consumer Protection Act of 2010, which created an interagency committee (the Financial Stability Oversight Committee or FSOC) to monitor the economy for signs of bubbles in different asset markets and to take steps to keep them from growing too large. It will be quite a trick if regulators can pull this off, but the intellectual underpinnings of the effort clearly lie in behavioral finance.

Robert Shiller

Robert Shiller is a native of Michigan, and earned his undergraduate degree from one of the state's flagship universities, the University of Michigan. His master's and PhD degrees in economics are from MIT, where he wrote his thesis on interest rate determination under the supervision of another Nobel laureate, Franco Modigliani. Shiller's Nobel came in 2013, as noted in the text.

Ironically, Shiller is one of the few economists of recent years who was widely known even before he won the prize. That is because Shiller predicted the deflation of not one, but two asset bubbles. His widely popular book, *Irrational Exuberance*, which focused on the excesses in the stock market, was published in March 2000, or just one month before stock prices, especially those of newly public Internet companies, crashed. Later in the decade, but well before housing prices began to turn down in 2006 and 2007, Shiller presciently warned in both writing and in media appearances of an emerging bubble in residential real estate prices, fueled by the excessively liberal extension of subprime mortgages.

Shiller is not your typical ivory tower economist. He has long displayed a strong interest in applying his ideas to the real world. One of his best-known endeavors is his partnership with Wellesley economist Carl Case in forming and publishing the Case–Shiller index of residential real estate prices, which was purchased and is being maintained by Standard & Poor's. Unlike other such indices, which report average prices of all homes sold within a given time period and geographic area, Case–Shiller follows the prices of the *same* homes in 20 cities around the country and thus doesn't change when the mix of lower and higher priced homes changes.

Valuing Options: Upsides and Downsides

This book began with the observation that economists suffered a hit to their prestige on account of the financial crisis of 2007 to 2008 and the subsequent Great Recession. In many popular accounts, financial derivatives played an important role in these events and, by implication, derivatives have taken on the characteristics of an unprintable (at least in this kind of book) four-letter word.

I address derivatives in more detail in Chapter 12, which discusses the impact of economists on policies affecting the financial sector.

Here, I want to discuss both the positive and not-so-positive impacts that one economic advance relating to a particular derivative, the tradable financial option contract, has had on the financial industry, and business more broadly.

An option is just one form of a derivative, or a financial instrument whose value is derived from the value of some other more fundamental financial contract. For example, a futures contract is one that requires the holder to buy or sell a particular commodity, or more recently an index of stocks, at a particular price before the end of some time period (typically six months). In contrast, an option contract simply gives the holder the *right* to buy or sell that instrument—let's use a stock—at a given price before some maturity date. An option to buy is a call and an option to sell is a put. The price at which the option is exercised is called the strike price.

For example, consider IBM selling at $200 per share. An investor could buy a range of calls at different strike prices, from below $200 (in which case the option is said to be *in the money* because the market price is above the strike price) to well above $200 (in which case the option is *out of the money*). You would buy a call if you thought IBM's price was going up. If you did this because you had shorted IBM (bet against it), you would be hedging that position (since the gains on the option if IBM's price increase would be offset by your loss on the short). If you bought the call simply because you wanted to bet on IBM's stock price increasing but didn't want to shell out the full $200 per share, then you'd be speculating.

Options also allow purchasers to take advantage of *leverage*, since the price of an IBM option with a strike price of $210 may be $5 a share, which may double if IBM's market price rises by $5. In contrast, a $5 increase in a stock with a base price of $200 would represent only a 2.5 percent gain (5/200). Better yet, the option limits your downside loss, which is only the cost of the option itself. In effect, an option is like paying an insurance premium for a limited time on the value of a stock.

I ran through this example for a call, but the same analysis applies, in reverse, to put options, which purchasers would buy if they thought the price of stock was going to fall. As with calls, purchasers could buy a put as a hedge or for speculative reasons.

Speculation: A Practice Much Misunderstood

Some readers may see the word speculation and immediately have a negative gut reaction. After all, weren't speculators somehow responsible for the financial crisis? And don't speculators add to market volatility, which somehow is bad for the market?

There is an abundant literature in economics journals on the virtues and drawbacks of speculators, but on the whole, financial economists support the presence of speculators (some call them noise traders as opposed to fundamental traders) for at least two reasons:

1. Hedgers need someone to take the other sides of their trades, and there may not be equivalent volumes of offsetting hedgers to do this; speculators are essential to fill the gap.
2. Speculators add volume to the market for any financial instrument, which makes them more liquid—that is, easier to buy or sell without moving the price.

Although options have traded for hundreds of years in other locales, the Chicago Board Options Exchange (CBOE) was the first exchange authorized to trade financial options in the United States, opening for business in April 1973. Not coincidentally, two financial economists, Fischer Black and Myron Scholes, some months before had developed an options pricing formula that traders would be able to use easily to make informed purchase and sale decisions. The Black–Scholes paper was published shortly after the CBOE opened.[17] At around the same time, Texas Instruments introduced a pocket calculator that had the Black–Scholes pricing formula embedded in it.[18] Later, Robert Merton published a paper generalizing the Black–Scholes result.[19]

The Black–Scholes–Merton (BSM) options pricing formula has since become one of the most widely used formulas in economics, used by traders at banks, hedge funds, nonbank firms, and other financial institutions around the world. Two of the developers of the formula, Scholes and Merton, received the Nobel Prize in 1997 for their work.

The prize is not without controversy, however, on two counts. One reason is that two hedge fund traders, Ed Thorp and Sheen Kassouf, had earlier developed and used a proprietary formula for pricing warrants, which are options to buy stock that were then (and still are) issued with other securities, such as convertible bonds (bonds that can be converted to stock). The Thorp-Kassouf formula was similar to the one developed by Black and Scholes, but was not made public in the form of an academic journal article (although a trading strategy relating to their formula had been published elsewhere).[20]

Second—and coincidentally less than a year after Scholes and Merton received their Nobel—Long-Term Capital Management (LTCM), a large hedge fund in which Scholes and Merton had been partners, collapsed and had to be rescued (at the instigation of the Federal Reserve) by its bank creditors.[21] The fund collapsed largely because its founders assumed that extremely unlikely events—precipitated by the 1997 financial crisis in Russia—or so-called *tail risk* could not occur, but in fact did.

Still, neither the prior work by Thorp nor the LTCM debacle can detract from the importance of the BSM breakthrough. It is widely understood that the options market—where today options on a range of financial instruments are traded on multiple platforms around the world—would not have developed as rapidly and deeply as it did had the BSM equation not been invented and widely publicized (and not held closely as the proprietary tool of one hedge fund).

Although the BSM formula itself is complicated (and can be found not only in the original articles but in financial economics textbooks),[22] with the advent of pocket calculators and later apps for personal and tablet computers, any trader can easily use it to figure out what price to bid or ask for an option simply by punching in a few key known or easily estimated parameters: the disparity between the current market price of the underlying financial instrument on which the option is written (say, a stock or a stock index) and the strike price; how volatile the stock historically has been; the time left before the option expires (its current maturity); and the interest rate for borrowing funds.

Here's the intuition behind each of these parameters, each holding the other factors constant. For example, an option is worth more the closer the market price is to the strike price, the more volatile the movements are in the underlying stock price (making it more worthwhile to invest in the option), the more time is left to exercise the option, and the lower the interest rate (which, among other things, measures the money foregone by not investing in an alternative asset).

The original Black-Scholes equation used a number of unrealistic assumptions. Merton later revised the equation and removed some of the assumptions. But the BSM model is still not perfect: Most notably, it underestimates extreme moves in the markets, of the kind that upended LTCM (tail risk, again), and incorrectly assumes that transactions are costless (though the costs have come down hugely since the equation was first published, largely due to the deregulation of brokerage commissions, discussed in Chapter 12). Even with these limitations, traders continue to use it as they widely view the BSM model as a sufficient approximation of the true value of an option.

The easy pricing of options made possible by the BSM model has had major effects, both welcome and unwelcome, on the real economy outside of Wall Street and Chicago where options and their underlying financial instruments are traded.

Let's take the good part first: the positive impact of stock options on the formation and growth of new companies. All new companies have the common challenge of conserving cash. This is true even for the fortunate few that receive seed financing from one or more angel investors, or even more rarely, from a venture capital firm. Outside financiers want founders to do everything to conserve cash, especially cash they provide in return for shares in the company.

Worried about drawing down their cash reserves, founders of new companies turn to stock options as a way of partially compensating new employees, whom they will need, at some point, to make their companies grow. From the vantage of the founders, options are better than giving stock outright (even if its sale is restricted), since the options will only be exercised if the company does well (depending on the strike price), and meanwhile the founders will not have given up equity ownership slices of their companies (diluting their shares or those of their investors). From the employees' vantage, the options are like long-shot tickets in horse racing: If they pay off, they can bring riches.

Although publicly held companies have granted their senior executives, and in some cases other employees, stock options for some time, they became a dramatically more important component of compensation after Congress, at the request of the Clinton Administration, denied companies the ability to deduct as expenses for tax purposes executive salaries in excess of $1 million. As often happens with legislation with good intentions—this one aimed at narrowing the widening disparity between compensation paid to top managers and other employees of publicly held companies—this particular proposal had some undesirable unintended consequences, which illustrate the downside of the increased use of options.

In particular, with companies no longer allowed to deduct high salaries as expenses, they were incentivized to accept demands by top executives for stock options in lieu of cash above the $1 million cap. From a tax point of view, this was ideal for the executives, since the tax rate on any capital gains from an increase in their company's stock price was considerably lower than the highest marginal tax rate on salary income. Even better, the executives didn't have to pay even the lower capital gains taxes until they exercised their options, which could be years away. Options also benefited the companies issuing them, because, for financial reporting purposes at the time, options were not recognized as an expense until they were exercised.

The problem with large option grants, however, was that they unintentionally gave some unscrupulous executives incentives to have their companies take big risks, or even to engage in accounting tricks, in order to goose the prices of the companies' stocks so that the executives could cash in their options with big gains. Because the options were just that—a right to buy stock at a potentially discounted price at a later point—they carried very limited downside risk. The worst the executives could suffer if their bets turned sour was to lose the value of the option.

Unfortunately, the potential downside to options was realized in the late 1990s and early 2000s when it was revealed that top executives of Enron, Worldcom, and Tyco, among other companies, cooked their companies' books and eventually led them into actual or near bankruptcy. Along the way, the executives cashed in bundles of stock options.

While it is impossible to prove cause and effect, it is difficult to escape the conclusion that at least for some executives who may have been predisposed to engaging in or encouraging deceptive accounting, the incentives provided by stock options could have been the decisive factor tipping them to actually do it.[23]

The corporate accounting misdeeds landed a number of the executives in jail for fraud, while spurring the enactment of sweeping legislation, the Sarbanes–Oxley Act of 2002, that subjected publicly held companies, their executives, directors, and accountants to a new set of corporate governance standards and other requirements that remain controversial to this day. Several years later, after a bruising quasi-political campaign, the official American and international bodies that set accounting standards changed the rules governing the reporting of options and required companies to record the value of options as an expense at the time they are granted, using the best methods available for that purpose. The BSM formula is one such method.

The Bottom Line

The ideas of economists, or a subset of them known as finance specialists, have had a powerful impact on the world of finance, and the firms engaged in the business. The indexed financial products business owes its origins to, or at least was accelerated by, the ideas of financial economists. The efficient markets hypothesis has found practical application in the world of investing, even though many money managers reject it, believing their stock picking can outperform the market. Also, some money managers and hedge funds engage in some form of momentum trading, a fact that behaviorists would cite to support their view of financial markets. It is not clear, however, what specific impacts academic behavioral finance specialists have had on the world of investing.

Finally, financial economists played a huge role in facilitating the rise of options trading and had an important influence on the use of options as employee compensation. This was more clearly a positive development for startups than it has been for established public companies.

Notes

1. Burton G. Malkiel, *A Random Walk Down Wall Street: The Time-Tested Strategy for Successful Investing*, 10th ed. (New York: W.W. Norton & Company, 2012).

2. Bogle's reference to Samuelson in particular can be found in his letter to the editor in the *Wall Street Journal*, October 19–20, 2013. As for Malkiel's influence on Bogle, I heard it directly from Bogle in a short speech he gave at a dinner held at Princeton in the early 2000s.

3. John C. Bogle, *The Battle for the Soul of Capitalism* (New Haven, CT: Yale University Press, 2005).

4. Investment Company Institute, *2013 Investment Company Fact Book*, Figure 2.13, available at www.ici.org.

5. Liam Pleven, "Family Wins Out for Bogles," *Wall Street Journal*, November 29, 2013.

6. For a guide to ETFs, see Gary L. Gastineaux, *The Exchange-Traded Funds Manual* (Hoboken, NJ: Wiley Finance, 2010).

7. Investment Company Institute, *Fact Book*, Figure 3.3.

8. Nathan Silver, *The Signal and the Noise: Why So Many Predictions Fail—But Some Don't* (New York: Penguin Press, 2012).

9. Alice Schroeder, *The Snowball: Warren Buffett and the Business of Life* (New York: Bantam Dell, 2008), 529–530.

10. Ibid.

11. Silver, *Signal and the Noise*. This profile draws heavily on Eugene F. Fama, "My Life in Finance," *Fama/French Forum*, Dimensional, 2013. See http://www.dimensional.com/famafrench/essays/my-life-in-finance.aspx.

12. Dimensional, *Dimensional Fund Advisors at Thirty, With Insights from David Booth and Eduardo Repetto* (Austin, TX: Dimensional, 2011).

13. Ibid.

14. Profile based on a personal interview with Booth, May 10, 2013; Pauline Skypala, "Still a Firm Believer of Market Efficiency," *Financial Times*, November 22, 2010.

15. The article in which this finding was published is one of the most cited articles in the history of the *American Economic Review*. Robert J. Shiller, "Do Stock Prices Move Too Much to be Justified by Subsequent Changes in Dividends?" *American Economic Review* 71, no. 3 (June 1981): 421–436.

16. For a fascinating compilation of a number of these oddities, see Richard Thaler, *The Winner's Curse: Paradoxes and Anomalies of Economic Life*, (Princeton, NJ: Princeton University Press, 1994).

17. Fischer Black and Myron Scholes, "The Pricing of Options and Corporate Liabilities," *Journal of Political Economy* 81, no. 3 (1973): 637–654.

18. Scott Patterson, *The Quants: How a New Breed of Math Whizzes Conquered Wall Street and Nearly Destroyed It* (New York: Crown Business, 2010), 40.

19. Robert Merton, "Theory of Rational Option Pricing," *Bell Journal of Economics and Management Science* 4, no. 1 (1973): 141–183.

20. Patterson, *The Quants*, 39–40.

21. Fischer Black died in 1995, and thus was ineligible for the 1997 award. He surely would have shared it had he lived.

22. One of the simplest expositions I have found is in Robert W. Ward, *Options and Options Trading* (New York: McGraw-Hill, 2004).

23. See George Benston, Michael Bromwich, Robert E. Litan, and Alfred Wagenhofer, *Following the Money: The Enron Failure and the State of Corporate Disclosures* (AEI-Brookings Joint Center on Regulatory Studies, Washington, DC: The Brookings Institution Press, 2003).

Part II

ECONOMIST-INSPIRED POLICY PLATFORMS FOR PRIVATE BUSINESS

All capitalist economies require a certain amount of legal as well as physical infrastructure to operate. Citizens and companies must know that the property they currently own or hope to own in the future is legally and physically secure. Likewise, consumers and businesses must have faith that their agreements will be adhered to by parties on the other side of transactions (counterparties) and, if not, that the agreements will be enforced by a well-functioning judicial system.

There are other aspects of the legal infrastructure that are helpful to business formation and growth. Ideally, licenses and fees to launch a business are kept to a minimum, but those that remain should be obtained as quickly as possible. The World Bank's *Doing Business* report annually ranks all countries around the world on the ease of launching a legal business.

Not as well recognized, but also equally important, are bankruptcy laws that enable failing firms to reorganize and not necessarily go completely out of business and strand customers and suppliers. Liability laws that assign responsibility for compensating injured parties to those whose negligence causes harm not only seem just, but also provide incentives to others to be careful. At the same time, corporate laws that limit the liability of shareholders for the losses of companies to the amounts shareholders invest are essential to encourage investment in new and existing enterprises in the first place.

This book assumes that these basic elements of an effective legal infrastructure are in place, although not necessarily in an ideal fashion in every location in the country. Indeed, there has long been and will continue to be tension between those who want more government regulation to protect against harms that business activity may cause and many in the business community who believe that regulatory burdens are already too high and need to be curtailed.

Although I will not attempt to resolve this particular debate, which likely has no end, the chapters in this second part of the book focus on industries where government has eliminated or significantly cut back what economists call economic regulation, which limits the prices of what firms in particular industries may charge and determines which firms may even enter an industry. Economic regulation is to be distinguished from what economists call social regulation, aimed at correcting market failures, such as pollution, or unequal information between buyers and sellers.

Although many businesses have been formed as a direct result of social regulation—think of those who make scrubbers that reduce emissions from electric power plants or airbag manufacturers that enable automakers to meet auto safety rules—I focus on economic deregulation and the economic arguments for it for two reasons.

First, as you will learn in the chapters that follow, economists have been arguing for years that the case for economic regulation for most industries has been weak or nonexistent, and thus most of it should be eliminated. This is not the case with social regulation in general, which is widely accepted in principle, but is argued over in its details (specifically whether certain rules have benefits that exceed their costs, and even if they do, whether the rules are the least restrictive alternatives available).

Second, when policy makers finally responded to the economists' critiques and cut back or eliminated economic deregulation, it opened vast new horizons for many new businesses or business models to launch and flourish. In effect, economic deregulation has become a policy platform on which many new businesses have been formed and innovations developed. In the process, the U.S. economy has been changed forever, for the good, or so I argue.

Much of this change was brought about by the urgings, research, and writing of economists, demonstrating how economists in these instances indirectly contributed to the success of many businesses, an outcome of which the founders, executives, and employees of these firms may only be dimly aware. The stories you will read in this part are important for people in all walks of life to understand and strengthen the central theme of this book: that economists and their ideas are really important, much more so than many people may realize.

The chapters share another common thread: Each deals with an industry that either helps define what it is to be a modern economy, or is an essential part of what makes that economy—the U.S. economy in particular—tick. Thus Chapter 9 deals with mass transportation; Chapter 10 is devoted to energy; Chapter 11 discusses telecommunications; and, finally, Chapter 12 deals with finance. It is difficult to imagine how a modern economy would work without advanced technologies and practices in each of these industries. That they exist now, although imperfect and constantly evolving, is due in significant part to the rules and institutions that govern prices and entry into these industries. Broadly speaking, economists have argued for decades that these industries are fundamentally competitive (if not when economic regulation was adopted then certainly now) and should not be subject to regulatory regimes more suitable for natural monopolies. It has taken policy makers time to catch up and act on this insight, and I believe this would not have happened, or would have occurred much later, had economists not first laid the intellectual groundwork for it all.

To be sure, financial deregulation has been somewhat an exception, essentially a mixed bag. As I argue in Chapter 12, certain ideas urged by economists were taken too far by the unscrupulous and the reckless that later contributed to disastrous results, including the misuse of stock options (discussed earlier in Chapter 8) and the failure to police the development of certain mortgage securities. But the origins of the 2007 to 2008 financial crisis, which among other things helped give the economics profession the bad reputation that I discussed at the outset of this book, are complicated and many. There were many policy mistakes along the way that economists did not support or of which they were largely unaware. At the same time, a number of financial deregulatory measures had desirable social impacts and led to the creation of businesses that have helped investors. They deserve to be highlighted and credited for their contributions.

Finally, if so much deregulation outside of finance was such an unqualified success, what took policy makers so long to make the necessary changes? This, too, is a complicated story that is outside the scope of this book, although it deserves a brief discussion before I get into the details of each deregulatory measure.

Briefly, there are two broad schools of thought about regulation and deregulation. One posits that regulation or deregulation is adopted to advance the public interest. It is as if legislators and regulators read and follow the basic economic textbooks and only regulate to correct market failures in the most cost-effective manner possible.

For example, the public interest view is broadly consistent with the introduction and elaboration over time of various forms of social regulation, which are aimed at protecting the safety of our air, water, food, and, in a financial sense, our financial institutions. In addition, the initial economic regulation of a number of industries that were characterized by natural monopolies—railroads, electric utilities, and telecommunications—also seems consistent with the public interest. But the extension and maintenance of economic regulation in these and other industries as technology weakened or eliminated natural monopolies does not sit well with the public interest view. Instead, the public interest was rescued only when policy makers finally listened to those economists who had pointed this out and began, in the late 1970s, to deregulate prices and entry in many sectors where it was no longer economically justified.

The alternative view of regulation is called *public choice theory* and is premised on the notion that, as a general rule, the industries subject to regulation, both social and economic, generally want it, even if some industry members protest that regulation is unnecessary or has gone too far. The reasons why firms would want regulation vary, but at bottom they boil down to making it too costly or impossible for competitors to enter their industry (economic regulation), or to give them some advantages over competitors that might not have the resources to comply with certain regulatory requirements (social regulation).

For decades, developers and supporters of the public choice model were in the distinct minority of economists, but the view gained respectability when one of its founders, James Buchanan, won the Nobel Prize for his work in the field. Other prominent economists who have developed this theory or aspects related to it include Buchanan's sometime collaborator, Gordon Tullock, Chicago's Sam Peltzman and George Stigler, and my colleague at Brookings for many years, Anthony Downs (whose book *Economic Theory of Democracy*, written as his PhD thesis under the supervision of another Nobel winner, Kenneth Arrow, helped lay the foundations for public choice economics).

Like its counterpart—public interest theory—public choice has its limits, too. Industry generally did not back the major legislation that authorized most social regulation—such as the Food and Drug Act, the National Highway Traffic Safety Act, the Clean Air Act, the Clean Water Act, and the Occupational Safety and Health Act—which were pushed by consumer and environmental groups and labor unions. Nor was industry universally behind much economic deregulation, though in some cases they were, as various chapters in this part will show.

In sum, there is no grand universal theory of regulation and deregulation that can explain each and every regulatory statute or major regulation. Rather, elements of both major theories, public interest and public choice, have played important but different roles at different times.

What I want to emphasize in this part of the book, however, is the important roles that economists played in the economic deregulation of many key industries in the U.S. economy, which in turn has had profound impacts on many firms. Many economists over the years have joined in this effort and deserve credit for building the intellectual case for deregulation where it has proved especially beneficial. I have pro-filed a number of these individuals in this part.

I want to conclude this introduction to Part II, however, by sin-gling out two particular economists who have had a major impact on the field and on my own thinking about regulation and the role of government during my own career, and yet who do not fall neatly within any one of the topic-specific chapters that follow. Readers who are interested can easily find their substantial body of work through any standard Internet search engine.

Roger Noll, now a professor emeritus at Stanford University where he taught economics for over two decades (and at this writ-ing is still teaching a seminar for advanced undergraduate economics majors), is one of those rare polymaths, who is always fun to talk with, and who constantly comes up with stimulating ideas that make the lis-tener want to explore further (no wonder he is such a great teacher). Blessed with a loud and infectious laugh, Noll has written on a wide variety of microeconomic subjects, including the regulation or deregu-lation of just about everything that matters, as well as topics relating to antitrust law and economics. Noll also taught at the California Institute of Technology and for a time was a senior fellow at the Brookings Institution. You might not see Roger's name attached to any specific sentence in the chapters in this part, or in earlier chapters, but he's there between many lines. I owe special thanks for his useful sugges-tions for topics in Chapter 11, in particular.

Lawrence "Larry" White, another longtime friend, has been a professor of economics at the Stern School of Business at New York University for most of his career. White is one of the leading specialists on what economists call industrial organization, the economics of anti-trust law, and on the economics and regulation of the financial industry. White has held a number of government positions that have informed his views: as a senior staff economist for President Carter's Council of Economic Advisers (where I first met him), as chief economist for the Antitrust Division at the Department of Justice, and as a member of the Federal Home Loan Bank Board (which used to oversee the sav-ings and loan industry). White's chapter on the influence of econo-mists in antitrust enforcement in John Siegfried's edited volume *Better Living through Economics*, cited in Chapter 9, is not only must reading for specialists in this field, but also makes clear how economists have taken over the thinking about how the nation's antitrust laws should be enforced. This has had and will continue to have important effects on how businesses with significant presence in particular markets are allowed to behave, and when it is most likely that mergers between firms will be challenged.

Noll and White are just two of the many economists who have influenced my own thinking through the years, and from whom I have learned, in conversation and through their written works. I also thank them for their friendship.

Chapter 9

Planes, Trains, and . . . Trucks

T his chapter may not be as entertaining as the movie with a similar title (with automobiles at the end instead of trucks), but I will promise you this: It will demonstrate how extraordinary things can happen when regulators and legislators pay attention to some very simple economic insights that had long been promoted by many economists before policy makers actually acted on them.

The insights center on the role that competition, rather than regulation of prices and entry, can and should play in markets that do not display characteristics of natural monopoly. The extraordinary consequences are the new businesses and business models in the world of transportation, as well as substantially lower prices than would be the case if prices and entry into the transportation business were still regulated. Indeed, I will bet that many consumers of these businesses, and even many of their founders, may not appreciate the extent to which they owe their good fortune to the power of some simple economic ideas that led to transportation deregulation in the late 1970s and early 1980s.

How did all this happen? The answer differs by industry. The public choice theory of regulation only explains the deregulation of air cargo transportation and rail traffic (where affected industries wanted it), but it doesn't explain passenger airline and trucking deregulation (industries in which firms liked the regulated life). In all these cases, however, economists from across the political spectrum were well ahead of the politicians and regulators in advocating deregulation.

Economists did not predict every outcome of deregulation, however. That is not surprising since markets have a way of developing and revealing behavior that few can anticipate.

The fact that each of the transportation industries reviewed in this chapter was deregulated, especially during a Democratic administration, was something of a miracle. I have already previewed the reasons why in the introduction to this section, but the circumstances that led to deregulation of each of the transportation modes are sufficiently different, as are the natures of the platforms that each created for business, that each deserves its own short discussion. Along the way, I highlight the role of economists in prodding the processes along. In the last part of the chapter I document the huge impact that transportation deregulation has had on the economy, and more relevant for readers of this book, on many businesses that would not exist in their present form, if at all, without deregulation.

Origins of Transportation Regulation

Since the invention of railroads, and later the car and the airplane, America has been a nation on the move. By one estimate, in 2007, total spending on transportation services amounted to $2.4 trillion, or about 17 percent of GDP,[1] roughly on a par with health-care spending as a percentage of the economy.

It's easy to take transportation for granted, except when something bad happens, like airplane crashes (which are much less frequent and generally less deadly than in earlier eras) or train derailments. But the fact is that our lives, as consumers, workers, and entrepreneurs, and as businesses, depend on fast and reliable transportation.[2] People use their cars to travel to and from work, to go on vacations, to visit friends, and to shop. We use mass transit—railroads, planes, buses, and subways—for business and pleasure. Businesses require transportation services to deliver their supplies and final goods to wholesalers and, increasingly (in the case of Internet sales), directly to consumers.

This is all true now, but it took roughly two centuries to reach this point, beginning with the invention of railroads in the early 1900s. Railroads began as steam engines, the technology that defined the Industrial Revolution, put on top of wheels on tracks. The tracks cost a lot of money and time to build. The process of laying them, beginning in the populated east coast, and later extending throughout the country, culminating with the cross-continental railroad track project after the Civil War, was an immense undertaking. It was made possible with the combination of foreign financing and lots of cheap unskilled labor. Those who want to know more about this amazing story can read any one of several classic books on the subject.[3]

Unlike the other modes of transportation to follow—airlines, and even more so, cars, trucks, and buses—railroads require substantial fixed investments to operate, which means there are significant economies of scale in operating them, and economies of scale limit the number of firms that can operate at a profit.

In other words, it makes little economic sense to build multiple tracks between the same locations. Unless the tracks can be shared, then only one railroad can operate on them, much like telephone, electricity, or cable lines in landline telecommunications. Each of these industries is liberated from the economies of scale problem when there are multiple methods or modes of transporting people, goods, or electrons from place to place. That is eventually what happened to railroads, which always had competition from barge traffic in rivers and lakes in some places (but not all), yet clearly found more competitors once airplanes and trucks were invented. As is discussed in Chapter 11, the same thing happened in communications once information was digitized and capable of being sent through the air as well as over wires.

But I am getting ahead of the story, if only to let you see where it eventually ends. At the beginning, when railroads made their debut, they quickly became the principal mode by which goods, the supplies that made them possible (like coal), and people were transported over long distances. After the Civil War, complaints arose from shippers who objected to the alleged monopoly prices that railroads were able to charge. More complaints followed after the discovery and later refinement of oil in the latter part of the nineteenth century, as large refiners (notably Standard Oil) were able to extract volume discounts at the expense of smaller shippers that had to payer higher rates.

In response, a number of states attempted to control railroad rates, but the Supreme Court overruled their efforts in 1886 as an unlawful encroachment on the Commerce Clause of the Constitution. Congress responded the following year by subjecting rail rates to price regulation overseen by one of the nation's earliest regulatory agencies, the Interstate Commerce Commission (the Comptroller of the Currency preceded it in the early 1860s, as the overseer of national banks authorized by Congress).

Although academics have disputed the need for the ICC in the twentieth century, one thing is clear: The agency and its mission were not demanded by the rail industry to which it was subject. Instead, the ICC and the rail rate and entry regulation it administered were definitely seen to be in the public interest.

The ICC's mandate was extended in the twentieth century with the invention of the car and truck—motorized competition for rail. This extension of regulation better fits the public choice model, but only halfway: While railroads later wanted trucks under a regulatory tent to contain competition with them, the same was not true of trucking firms until they and later their unionized workers, too, became accustomed to the comforts of regulation. As for rail, the ICC not only limited the prices trucks could charge, but also required approval of new routes. The agency subsequently added other rules, especially on what trucks could or could not carry on their return, to further limit competition between trucking firms and rail transport.

The airplane was the next major transport invention, proving its value initially in a military context during World War I. When the war ended, the postal service used airplanes to deliver mail, which prompted private operators to use them for carrying cargo. Rather than give the ICC regulatory control over the airlines, however, Congress in 1938 created an entirely new agency, the Civil Aeronautics Board (CAB), to oversee prices and entry into both the cargo and passenger airline traffic business. Since planes flew routes that took them over rail tracks, and yet could only operate with large fixed investments in airports, they looked to policy makers to bring them under regulatory protection, too. After all, were not airplanes simply railroads or trucks with wings (to paraphrase the economist Alfred Kahn's quip that planes were "marginal costs with wings")? Since flying over specific routes exhibited economies of scale in much the same way railroads did, wasn't there also a good public interest rationale to regulate prices and entry into the air traffic business as well?

Whatever theory best explains the creation of the CAB and the regulatory system it was supposed to implement, the CAB quickly moved after its creation to authorize a limited number of airlines fit to fly major point-to-point routes. No others were later allowed to fly these routes, at least as long as the CAB was in business.[4]

Airline Deregulation

Once established, the regulation of prices and entry into the major modes of mass transportation became something like the woodwork or plumbing in a house: just taken for granted. Incumbents that had their routes were happy with them, even though price controls limited their profits. In return, the authorized carriers were protected from competition with new firms in all of the different transportation modes.

There was one major loophole in this cozy system: Under the Constitution, which authorizes Congress to regulate *interstate* commerce, the CAB could only oversee travel *between states*. What the states did within their own borders was their own business.

For most states, this didn't really matter, because they were either too small or too sparsely populated to support multiple carriers within any transportation segment. This was not true in airline or truck traffic, however, especially in the two largest states (by land area): California and Texas. Both served their roles as laboratories well, especially regarding airlines.

Michael Levine, one of the pioneers of what would eventually turn into full-scale airline deregulation, and later William Jordan, published studies of *intrastate* air traffic in California in 1965 and 1970, respectively, and compared its cost to *interstate* travel over comparable distances. Their startling conclusion: Intrastate fares were roughly *half* the comparable interstate fares.[5] This finding reinforced the conclusion reached in an earlier, more academic study by one of America's then-leading industrial organization and trade economists, Richard Caves, of

Harvard University, that the airline industry displayed no evidence of economies of scale and therefore was not suited for price and entry regulation.[6] A subsequent study in the 1970s by economists George Douglas and James Miller (who later went on to head the Federal Trade Commission and the Office of Management and Budget) found that regulation led airlines to schedule too many flights, explaining their low load factors, while denying consumers the ability to choose cheaper, unregulated flights.[7]

It is difficult to understate how remarkable these economic studies were. Airlines were regulated, so it was thought, in order to *reduce* airline prices, ostensibly on the theory that air flight exhibited economies of scale and would enable airlines to exercise market power, or charge prices well above marginal cost. In fact, regulation shielded the major airlines from competition, and by encouraging them to compete on the basis of flight frequency rather than cost, the airlines responded by flying their planes roughly half-full. This had the effect of keeping average costs high, and likewise for passenger fares, which were regulated to ensure the airlines could recover their average costs with a profit on top.

The Kennedy Hearings

This crazy situation probably would have persisted for a long time—the airlines were happy with it, after all, and passengers didn't know what the world would look like with lower fares—but for a totally unexpected turn of political events.[8]

The origins lie in the decision by Senator Edward Kennedy, who upon learning in 1974 that he would be assuming the chairmanship of the ostensibly minor Subcommittee on Administrative Practice and Procedure of the Senate Judiciary Committee, cold-called one of the leading administrative law professors in the country at the time, Professor Stephen Breyer of the Harvard Law School (20 years later, Breyer would be sitting on the Supreme Court). Kennedy asked Breyer for a list of hearing topics leading to possible legislative reforms, and to come to Washington to direct the subcommittee's staff. Among the list of administrative law topics he provided, Breyer included the suggestion that Kennedy's subcommittee hold hearings to examine the impact of CAB's regulation of the airline industry. Breyer was steeped in the economics of the subject, which he taught his law students, but told Kennedy he could not take the staff director position fulltime given his tenured position at Harvard. Breyer suggested instead that he work on the subcommittee's staff during the 1974–1975 academic year, which coincided with his sabbatical. Kennedy accepted the deal.

Once on the job, Breyer quickly went to work organizing hearings that were held in 1975 that showcased the economists and their research, especially the contrast in fares between intrastate and interstate routes. The hearings stretched out over seven days, and brought in consumer advocates, officials from the CAB, and airline executives. It turned out that the only witnesses who favored the status quo were those who benefited from it, the industry and its regulatory agency. That coincidence, coupled with consensus among the economists that regulation was misguided, convinced Senator Kennedy that something needed to be changed.

Initially, the aim of the hearings was quite modest: simply to have the Antitrust Division of the Justice Department, as the arm within the Executive branch charged with protecting consumers from excessive prices, weigh in on regulatory matters before the CAB. As the hearings went on and as Kennedy became more engaged, he realized that the entire system of airline regulation eventually had to be dismantled. This was evident from the massive evidence compiled by the Senate committee report of the perverse effect of CAB regulation on airline entry and fares.[9]

Kennedy and Breyer both were politically savvy and aware that any move toward deregulation could bring the risk of higher fares on routes to smaller communities, an especially sensitive issue with rural state senators. The legislation that eventually deregulated airline traffic met this concern by authorizing subsidies for these routes.

Air Cargo Deregulation

The Kennedy hearings clearly got the airline deregulation ball rolling, and helped provide political cover for the Ford Administration to begin taking administrative steps to undo airline regulation, acting through the chairmanship of the CAB by John Robson. Robson took his first crack at the lowest hanging fruit, the aspect of regulation that none of the certificated carriers liked, air cargo regulation. Dating from the 1940s through the mid-1970s, only four carriers had certificates to fly cargo independently of passenger airlines (cargo could be flown in the belly of passenger planes but this was an exception), and had rejected other applicants seeking to carry both domestic and international air cargo.[10]

In the 1970s, the CAB relented and allowed a new company, Federal Express, to enter air cargo transportation, but at first only by flying small aircraft. Moreover, under the rules of the Interstate Commerce Commission (ICC) at the time, airlines could not transport air cargo by truck beyond 20 miles of an airport. Federal Express was severely constrained by this rule, which of course, appears totally anachronistic today. Both Federal Express and UPS now operate full fleets of planes and trucks that deliver all kinds of packages and cargo throughout the United States and all over the world. But in the highly regulated world before the 1980s, none of this was yet possible.

In 1976, Robson proposed an air cargo deregulation bill to Congress, but Kennedy was not able to convene hearings on both air cargo and passenger deregulation combined until 1977, by which time a new president, Jimmy Carter, had assumed office. The timing could not have been better. Carter and his domestic policy advisers had a strong commitment to transportation deregulation that went far beyond airlines. Given the strong backing of the air cargo airlines themselves, including the then upstart new entrant, Federal Express, Congress was able to pass an all-cargo deregulation bill by the fall of 1977, which President Carter signed into law in November.

Air Passenger Deregulation

Deregulating air *passenger* regulation was a heavier lift, because all of the established trunk carriers, with the exception of United, didn't want more rate freedom if it also was coupled with more entry. If deregulation of passenger traffic was going to be accomplished, it was going to take a combination of both administrative and legislative action.

President Carter saw this from the beginning, realizing he needed not just a CAB chairman who was committed to airline passenger deregulation, where it could be accomplished administratively, but other commissioners and staff who had the same objective. The administration's domestic policy advisers on these issues, Mary Schuman (then a young former staffer for Senator Magnuson), and Simon

Lazarus (former staffer at the Federal Communications Commission, and someone with whom I later practiced law and who has been a longtime friend), found that leader in Alfred Kahn. At the time, Kahn was the leading academic expert on regulation in the country (he is profiled in the following box). He was paired with another notable academic, Elizabeth "Betsy" Bailey (also profiled shortly), together with some high-powered economic staffers, Michael Levine and Darius Gaskins. Both Levine and Gaskins went on to have remarkable post-CAB careers (discussed in later profiles).

Alfred Kahn

There probably is no more venerated expert on regulation in the history of the economics profession than Alfred Kahn.[11] This is because Kahn was not only the author of numerous scholarly articles and several editions of the definitive textbook on the subject until the 1980s, but also because of his practical knowledge of the subject, and his engaging personality.

Kahn served in the 1970s as the chairman of the New York State Public Utility Commission, testified as an expert on regulatory matters in numerous legal proceedings, and was integral to the success of National Economic Research Associates (NERA, now NERA Economic Consulting), one of the leading economic consulting firms (discussed also in Chapter 5).

Kahn's rise to fame was not surprising given his early brilliance. Born to Jewish immigrants and raised in New Jersey, he graduated from high school at the age of 15 and from New York University at the age of 18. He earned his doctorate in economics from Yale during World War II. He thereafter served in the Army, and spent time at the Brookings Institution and the Antitrust Division at the Department of Justice. He began his teaching career after the war at Ripon College, where he quickly became chairman of the economics department. He moved to Cornell in 1947 where he remained (except for his

(continued)

detours in public service) through the rest of his distinguished academic career. As just one example of his versatility, Kahn was a noted singer on the Cornell campus, performing in numerous Gilbert and Sullivan productions.

Interestingly, Kahn's first choice of an agency to chair when contacted by the Carter transition team was the Federal Communications Commission. However, given Kahn's prior consulting work with Bell Labs, the Carter team thought Kahn would have an easier confirmation (and face fewer recusals) if he were nominated for the CAB. It was clearly the right choice. In two short years he became a father of airline deregulation.

From the CAB, Kahn moved on to become President Carter's anti-inflation czar in 1979, overseeing the newly formed Council on Wage and Price Stability (which was dismantled by President Reagan, and essentially made unnecessary by the anti-inflationary monetary policy of the Federal Reserve under the chairmanship of Paul Volcker). Kahn quickly became a popular figure in that position, despite the difficulty of his job—all he could really do was jawbone, because neither he nor anyone else had the statutory power to control prices and wages.

One mark of a person is whom they mentor and launch toward future success. Kahn taught many thousands of students during his career and I cannot pretend to know his impact from the classroom. But from personal experience, here are just a few examples of successful individuals who worked for him at the CAB and later when he was the inflation czar: Darius Gaskins and Michael Levine, both profiled elsewhere in this chapter, and Joshua Gotbaum, who worked for Gaskins at the Department of Energy before coming to work with Kahn. Gotbaum went on to have a highly successful career on Wall Street, administering the 9/11 recovery fund after that tragedy, running an airline, serving in a number of prominent posts in the Clinton Administration, and then as director of the Pension Benefit Guaranty Corporation during the Obama Administration.

On a personal note, I first met Kahn when I was a staffer at the Council of Economic Advisers (CEA) during the Carter Administration. Thereafter I had several opportunities to meet and talk with him on various professional matters, all memorable occasions. He was a remarkable individual and it was a privilege for me to know him.

Whether deliberately or not, Kahn and Senator Kennedy proceeded to act like a tag team whose actions reinforced the case for air passenger deregulation, leading to ultimate success. Kahn and his fellow CAB commissioners would take administrative deregulatory steps, setting the stage for Senator Kennedy, Senator Cannon (who had initially opposed deregulation but later joined forces with Kennedy), and eventually the full Congress, to see the virtues of going all the way.

For example, because neither Kahn nor Kennedy would have wanted airlines to increase their fares on certain routes out of the box, the CAB moved quickly in 1977 to grant permission to the airlines to *lower* their fares without filing new rates (which otherwise could have been contested and thus delayed for months, if not years). Although the airlines might have objected to lower fares, certainly consumers would not, so this was a clever political strategy that also validated the earlier-cited academic studies documenting lower rates on intrastate routes than interstate routes of comparable distance. The Kahn-led CAB also liberalized entry for carriers serving certain underserved airports such as Newark, Baltimore, or Chicago's Midway (all thriving airports today).

The CAB's air passenger initiatives, coupled with the success of air cargo deregulation, and the activism of Senator Kennedy, combined to push the landmark airline passenger deregulation bill into law by the end of October 1978. The law phased in deregulation over a five-year period and eliminated the CAB as of January 1985. Airline safety regulation remained at the Federal Aviation Administration, while authority for international airline negotiations and antitrust oversight was shared between the Department of Transportation (a mistake in my view) and the Justice Department.

Airline deregulation had some predictable, beneficial consequences—lower fares in particular—but also led to an unexpected restructuring of routes in the United States. The effects of airline deregulation on business, in particular, are explored in greater detail later in this chapter.

Elizabeth "Betsy" Bailey: Pioneer

When I was studying economics as an undergraduate there were very few women in the profession. Perhaps the best known was Joan Robinson, the acerbic and brilliant colleague of Keynes and other stars at Cambridge in the 1930s and later.

By the time I made it to Brookings as a research assistant, my first full-time job out of college, I became acquainted with Alice Rivlin, then a senior fellow at Brookings, who has become an icon in the profession; you will meet her in Chapter 14.

But no female economist I know has overcome the kind of discrimination against women in our society and in the economics profession more than Elizabeth "Betsy" Bailey.[12] After graduating with a degree in economics from Radcliffe, she took her first job in 1960 at Bell Labs as a technical assistant, a lower job ranking *because she was a woman* than her equivalently credentialed male counterparts. Bell Labs then had an incredible stockpile of economic and other scientific talent. The economists were devoted, as one might expect, largely to studying regulatory issues in the telecommunications industry. At Bell, Bailey toiled as a researcher for other more senior scholars for four years until the Civil Rights Act of 1964 changed her life.

That Act prohibited discrimination on the basis of race and sex in the workplace and other public places. Shortly after its passage, AT&T and other large companies began to change their employment practices. For Bailey, the changes meant that she was then able to obtain a master's degree in economics at nearby Stevens Institute of Technology, at company expense, like her male colleagues. She also was promoted and given wider recognition within Bell Labs. After gaining her master's,

Bailey was accepted for PhD work at Princeton. She already was working on her dissertation before enrolling there, and also had an article published in the prestigious *Bell Journal of Economics*, which quickly became the top journal for regulatory economics in the country.

As she was working on her PhD degree and after she completed it, Bailey continued working at Bell Labs, as one of the senior scholars herself. Shortly after President Carter assumed office, Bailey was called by the White House Domestic Policy Staff asking if she would be interested in filling one of the two Republican slots at the Civil Aeronautics Board. She was told that Fred Kahn, the dean of regulatory economists in America and an adviser to Bell Labs, was to become the chairman, but first she was asked if indeed she was a Republican. Not active in political life, Bailey thought a moment and then reported she had voted for some Republican candidates for office because they, more than Democrats in New Jersey, were more vocal in their advocacy for issues relating to child disabilities, an issue of great personal interest to Bailey. That answer was sufficient for the administration (an answer that seems quaint in light of the vastly increased partisanship in elected politics today), and in 1977 Bailey was sworn in as a CAB member, joining the board that launched the program of industry deregulation that no one thought was possible until then.

After the CAB, Bailey spent over two decades as a professor of economics at the Wharton School of Finance at the University of Pennsylvania where she continued her scholarly work in regulatory economics and industrial organization.

Trucking Deregulation

Once the deregulation ball began rolling with airlines in the late 1970s, it turned out to be hard to stop. Thank goodness, because that ball led to one of the most important, but largely unrecognized, policy reforms of that era: the deregulation of prices and entry into interstate trucking, and to a lesser extent, of railroads.

If price and entry regulation were not suitable for airlines, they clearly couldn't be for trucking, which had both major national firms and thousands of independents all competing against each other, but under the thumb of a command-and-control regulator, the ICC. Yet neither the trucking firms nor their unionized workers from the Teamsters wanted this system to change. Forget delivering services to shippers in the way they wanted. To those doing the driving, it was good to have the government approving routes, and thus effectively limiting competition, and allowing the truckers themselves to use effectively legalized cartels or rating bureaus to set shipping rates that the ICC routinely approved. The regulated system ensured that the firms would have profits from which they could meet union demands for high wages. Public choice theory cannot explain how this cozy system ever would have been eliminated.

But public choice does help explain how it all got started. It didn't take long after the automobile was invented and successfully commercialized for some companies to realize that these vehicles could do a lot more than carry people. With some modification, autos could be (and were) turned into trucks that would carry freight and directly compete with railroads but in a far more flexible fashion. Railroads were limited to carrying their loads down tracks, and once having arrived at their destinations, had to have their goods unloaded and put into the distribution chain—to manufacturing plants (if raw materials, like coal or metals), or to warehouses (if finished goods). The horse and buggy did much of this work, until the truck came along. And when that happened, the railroads faced a new kind of competition they hadn't seen, for trucks were not only useful for ferrying goods to and from railroad platforms, but they could also carry goods long haul instead of railroads themselves!

Dorothy Robyn's classic history of trucking deregulation (and later deregulation overall) pithily describes the chain of events that led to the industry's regulation, and although she doesn't explicitly embrace public choice theory as the explanation, her recitation of the facts demonstrates, at least to this author, the usefulness of the public choice framework.[13]

As Robyn tells it, the growing competitive threat posed by trucks to rail was not clearly evident until after World War I, during which the railroads were temporarily nationalized to support the delivery of men and equipment to their points of ocean departure for Europe. By the time railroads were returned to private hands in the 1920s, trucks had rushed into the vacuum for transporting goods and they clearly were a competitive force to be reckoned with. Using a time-honored tactic of harnessing the power of government to thwart competition, railroads first lobbied the states (reflecting the relatively weak power of the federal government at that point in history) to restrict entry into trucking and to set both maximum and minimum rates they could charge. By 1925, 30 states had enacted such regulatory restrictions.

The Supreme Court intervened by restricting the power of states to control *interstate* trucking traffic—the most important competitive threat to railroads that routinely crossed state lines—as a direct intrusion on the power of the federal government to regulate interstate commerce. So the railroad industry switched tactics, supporting a federal bill drafted by the national body representing the state utility commissions that gave states primary power to regulate trucks, while allowing appeals to be made to the ICC that then regulated rail. Truckers and labor opposed the bill. Advocates of public choice theory can claim victory with both stances: The railroads were acting in their economic interest to limit competition from a new technology and so wanted regulation, and they were opposed by the firms and employees using the new technology (trucks). It all made sense, but it also made for a standoff. The railroad-backed utility commissioners' bill went nowhere in Congress, until the Depression.

Then things changed, backed by President Roosevelt, who despite his reputation for being an antibusiness president, sided with the railroads, fearing that cutthroat competition between the railroads and the trucking industry would cause only more unemployment in the midst of the Depression. Even many truckers (but not the entire industry or the manufacturers that made trucks) switched sides and supported Roosevelt's National Industry Recovery Act (NIRA), which put most of the economy under the thumb of the government, but not the previous bill giving regulatory authority over trucks to the ICC that was perceived to be too much in the pocket of the railroads. Only after the Supreme Court struck down the NIRA as unconstitutional did the trucking industry give its support to what became the Motor

Carrier Act of 1935, which put trucks and rail under the regulatory control of the ICC. In 1948, Congress followed up by effectively delegating rate making authority for trucks to collective rating bureaus (analogous to similar arrangements in the insurance industry, which were sanctioned in the McCarran–Ferguson Act of 1944).

It is difficult for readers under the age of 40 or so, or those who never would have experienced the impacts of trucking regulation, to appreciate the complexity, indeed craziness, of what regulation of the trucking industry became. Imagine a world in which the nature of the cargo and prices for moving it were approved for every departure and destination. In such a world, trucks could carry goods one way, but had to return empty, or maybe half-full, because authority to carry full loads on that same return route would have been given to other firms. Imagine how such a world would or, more accurately, would *not* have accommodated the rise of Internet retailing and the transformative impact it has had on the U.S. economy. Hold that thought in your head until I resume discussing the impact of trucking deregulation on the American business landscape later in this chapter.

Even more so than with airlines, the obvious question is: How was it ever going to be possible to eliminate regulation of trucking? Unlike airlines, whose fares voters actually paid, the costs of truck shipments were (and still are) hidden in the price of goods that consumers pay. Only buyers of supplies and retailers pay trucking costs, and these can generally be passed on to the next purchasers. Moreover, to the extent deregulation of trucking would reduce shipping costs, the benefits to each buyer of trucking services would be small, as compared to the potentially large cut in wages, and possibly profits, earned by many truckers. Normally, such an imbalance in benefits and costs explains why status quos remain.

But the late 1970s were different and unique in several respects. First, once airline deregulation had been enacted, a precedent had been set for deregulating an even more diffuse industry, namely trucking, which clearly had no natural monopoly characteristics. Second, with Senator Kennedy again on board, the Carter White House took advantage of the momentum established by airline deregulation by helping to organize shippers and consumer groups to put pressure on Congress to take the next logical step and deregulate the trucking industry. Third, the ICC under the leadership of A. Daniel O'Neal in the early years of the Carter presidency took some initial administrative actions to loosen trucking rules, a process that his successor in 1980, Darius Gaskins, greatly accelerated. This was no surprise because Gaskins worked for Kahn at the CAB and, like Kahn, saw the virtues of a competitive, unregulated trucking market and persuaded his fellow commissioners of this view. Fourth, the general economic atmosphere at the time, another horrible episode of stagflation following the large increase in oil prices in 1979, had a silver lining for advocates of deregulation: It allowed them to claim that deregulation, which promised lower shipping rates, was needed to fight inflation. Alfred Kahn, by that time the administration's inflation czar, and Charles Schultze, the chairman of Carter's Council of Economic Advisers, were among those leading the charge for legislative deregulation using anti-inflation arguments.

It took all four of these factors to overcome decades of inertia, culminating in the passage of the Motor Carrier Act of 1980, signed into law by President Carter in July 1980. The Act eliminated government-sanctioned rating bureaus from setting interstate trucking rates (some states still maintained vestiges of intrastate controls after the 1980 Act), removed most restrictions on the commodities that specific truckers could carry, and got the government out of the business of approving routes and geographic territories for trucking firms. The Gaskins-led ICC moved aggressively after the Act to implement its key provisions.

Darius Gaskins: Multitalented Deregulator and Executive

Darius Gaskins is a unique economist, having achieved success in academia, government, and business. But like others featured here, his ascent to the top did not follow a straight line.[14]

His ultimate path certainly was not evident at the outset. A West Point graduate, he served as an engineer in the Air Force in the 1960s, working on the nation's space program. After the base on which he was serving shut down, Gaskins pursued his other

(continued)

passion, public policy, and thought he would make the most contribution (like many other economists, including your author) if he earned his PhD in economics. He went to a school known as much for its engineering as for its economics, the University of Michigan, and that is exactly what he did next (after obtaining a master's in engineering from the same school first).

Like other PhD economists, Gaskins went first from graduate school into the academy, the University of California at Berkeley, but didn't stay long. Following his passion for policy, he held a series of federal government jobs in the 1970s, at the Interior Department and the Federal Trade Commission where he became chief economist, before being enticed by Fred Kahn to be chief economist at the CAB. Once deregulation had been accomplished, Gaskins moved on to become chief of policy at the Department of Energy.

Kahn was instrumental in persuading the White House to nominate Gaskins for chairman of the ICC, a job in which he served from 1980 to 1981. During his short but highly influential tenure, Gaskins oversaw trucking deregulation, both administratively and with Congress, to help enact the Motor Carrier Act of 1980.

After his government service, Gaskins was attracted to the private sector, where he first took a job as a senior vice president at the Burlington Northern Railroad. He assumed the presidency of that company in 1985. Since 1991, Gaskins has been active in management consulting, and is a founding partner of Norbridge, Inc.

Railroad Deregulation

The deregulation of the railroad industry, for both passengers and freight, was different and easier than for airlines and trucks, because in this case, the industry wanted to be out from under the government's thumb. As we will see later, the industry, and the policy makers who listened to them, turned out to be right.

The introduction of regulation for rail differs from other industries, because it was motivated by a legitimate desire to curtail monopoly pricing by railroads in the late nineteenth century. As that monopoly eroded—due to stiff competition from autos for passengers and from trucks for freight—the case for having the ICC continue restricting entry while allowing the railroads themselves to set rates (a delegation of price regulation to the industry) also eventually fell apart. But it took an existential threat to rail for change to occur.

Given the rigidity of the collective rate making for railroad fares, railroads steadily lost traffic from the 1930s through the 1970s to other transportation modes, and for a number of railroads profits turned to losses. Deregulation was the only obvious answer to the industry's problems and it happened in two stages.

In 1976, Congress gave railroads some pricing freedom in the Railroad Revitalization and Regulatory Reform Act (known as the 4R Act). But shippers wanted more flexibility to negotiate their own deals with railroads. This is what they got when the Staggers Rail Act of 1980 was shepherded through Congress by the chairman of the House Commerce Committee, Representative Harley Staggers. This Act effectively deregulated virtually all aspects of the rail industry, except for safety and a requirement that railroads with bottleneck tracks or facilities give access to connecting rail lines (similar interconnection requirements were later imposed on regional telecom carriers after the breakup of AT&T and by the Telecommunications Act of 1996, subjects discussed in Chapter 11).

The route to passage of the Staggers Act was facilitated not only by industry support, but also by the momentum generated by the deregulation of the airline and trucking industries. If these two industries, which competed with railroads, could operate freely, it was hard to argue that railroads shouldn't be given the same treatment. Finally they were.

Deregulation's Impact:
The Transportation Industry

The deregulation of prices and entry in all sectors of the transportation industry has accomplished what the economists who supported it said would happen: It has lowered prices. One of the nation's leading transportation economists, Clifford Winston of the Brookings Institution, by himself and with colleagues, has documented this result in multiple academic publications, using a methodology that is now recognized as the gold standard in the way to conduct such studies.[15] Rather than simply look at prices or price trends before and after deregulation, Winston and his colleagues have constructed models to project what prices would have been in absence of deregulation and compare them to actual prices. Only by looking at these counterfactual examples can one know with any certainty whether deregulation has actually lowered prices. Nonetheless, it is still useful information to know that the pre- and post-deregulation data for airline prices, in particular, make clear the dramatic benefits deregulation delivered to consumers. Between 1978 and 2011, the real or inflation-adjusted passenger revenue yield (an average price measure commonly used in the industry) fell by almost one-half.[16]

Deregulation of transportation did have some unexpected results for the industries themselves, however, especially the airline industry, where at times the deregulation policy has been questioned (though it never has been reversed). The development of the hub and spoke system for airline routes was one unanticipated result, which on the whole has been a good thing by enabling travelers from non-hub locations to gain more frequent access to multiple destinations by flying to the nearest hub. Frequent flyer miles, a method airlines have used to ensure greater customer loyalty, was also an unanticipated result and a mixed blessing. Other things being equal, such customer loyalty arrangements can frustrate the ability of new entrants to entice customers away from established airlines, which diminishes competition. Nonetheless, even with these loyalty programs, the research shows that, on balance, average airfares are lower than they would have been under the old regulated system.[17]

A third development, which was entirely anticipated given the decline in fares, is much higher load factors, and thus less comfortable flights. Many readers may be too young to have experienced air travel when it was fashionable: People actually dressed up to fly. But because of its expense, air travel was limited to those with higher incomes and wealth. With deregulation, and the much lower fares it has brought, the panache has gone out of air travel—to put it mildly.

What is worse, at least from the passengers' point of view, is that in their quest to become profitable, airlines have substituted smaller, more fuel efficient, but less comfortable regional jets for the older, larger jets that the airlines used to fly. This source of reduced comfort is not deregulation's fault, however, since even in a regulated environment, airlines probably would have reacted pretty much the same way in response to higher fuel costs (unless the CAB would have approved passing on the higher costs to consumers).

Another result of deregulation that I do not believe was widely anticipated is the large variation in fares for essentially the same seats on the plane. This outcome was produced by yield management techniques that vary prices by when reservations are made. Airlines have also unbundled their services, generating another reason for fare variation. Passengers wanting a no-frills experience sitting at the back of the plane pay the least, while those wanting food, checking or carrying on baggage, entertainment, Internet service, and better seats, pay more for each of these items. Each of these developments—more fuel-efficient planes, unbundled pricing and service, and yield management—have led to much fuller planes, which has finally enabled many airlines to make money.[18]

It has taken a long time to get to this point, which many would say was unexpected. It is less surprising, however, if one considers the long time it has taken for the airlines to adjust their highly unionized workforces to a deregulated and more competitive environment. In this effort, the airlines ironically have been aided by multiple bankruptcies, which have afforded them leverage to gain concessions from unions, often repeatedly and by damaging employee morale. Another cost to the bankruptcies is that bankrupt airlines can keep flying while under judicial protection from their creditors. This has intensified competition, complicating efforts by all airlines to turn a profit. One response has been a rash of mergers, which airlines have sought in order to spread their fixed costs over larger route structures and passenger bases. The Department of Justice mostly accepted this consolidation until 2013, when the Department challenged the merger between US Airways and American Airlines. Like most challenged mergers in the past, this lawsuit was never tried because the parties worked out a plan of route divestitures (at this writing, the settlement had not yet been approved by the courts since some critics of the deal argue that DOJ gave too much to the merging parties).

Since airline deregulation was launched the industry has been in a constant state of upheaval. At first, a number of low-cost airlines entered the industry but, with the exception of Southwest, few have succeeded. Readers old enough may remember once popular upstarts like People Express and New York Air that have since disappeared, indicating that creditors are more apt to force liquidation of a new airline than a previously well-established carrier. A few newer airlines that offer better service, like Jet Blue, Alaska Air, and Virgin Air, nonetheless have survived, at least as of 2014 (Virgin's rights to fly domestically are severely restricted because it is a foreign carrier and the United States still has not liberalized much foreign carrier entry into the domestic market).

Developments in the air cargo side of the industry following deregulation have been more predictable but also revolutionary. FedEx has grown into one of the largest transportation companies in the world, followed closely by UPS. Both established integrated air and truck transportation systems, so they could deliver packages directly to their destinations rather than having to hand them off to another mode. This kind of integration, and the efficiencies and customer conveniences it has brought, never would have happened without deregulation of both airline and interstate truck travel.

As for trucks, all of the predictions about deregulation in this industry—which was never a natural monopoly—came true for both segments of the industry, TL (trucks loaded full) and LTL (trucks that are less than full). With entry controls gone, the number of TL companies exploded, from about 20,000 in 1980 to 55,000 in 1995. LTL truckers, meanwhile, gained much more flexibility without the regulation-era commodity traffic approval process. All in all, the industry became much more competitive and rates dropped, by at least 25 percent and perhaps more.[19]

Likewise, railroad deregulation also led to a major drop in freight rail rates, according to the Government Accountability Office, which also reported an increase in rail profitability.[20] How could that be? Because the drop in rates induced a substantial increase in traffic, as rail became a more viable competitor to trucks for freight shipments.[21]

Deregulation as a Business Platform

If the only outcomes of deregulating the transportation industry were lower prices, I would not have discussed the subject so extensively in this chapter. Rather I have done so because the deregulation of transportation has led to the formation of entirely new firms, while also fundamentally changing the way existing firms do business, or even stay alive. Indeed, it is hard to think how our modern economy would have developed over the past three decades, given the digital and Internet revolutions in particular, had the main transportation industries *not* been deregulated. In short, just as personal computing and mobile telephone operating systems have been platforms upon which entirely new apps firms were born, transportation deregulation has become one of the most important policy platforms for business in the late twentieth and early twenty-first centuries.

The key was not lower prices, although that helped. Instead, deregulation took the government out of the details of approving both prices and routes, and in the process turned firms that once offered services to customers on a highly rigid basis into flexible providers. And it was the flexibility created by deregulation—the ability of firms to get their goods from point A to point B using airplanes, trucks, or rail—that revolutionized the economy and the businesses operating within it.

Renaissance Deregulator, Airline CEO, and Scholar: Michael Levine

Michael Levine isn't a card-carrying economist—he never completed a PhD in the subject, but his insights, expressed in his articles and in his work, have had important effects on policy.[22] Levine's contributions to economic scholarship reflect his broad experience in both government and the private sector, as well as academia.

(continued)

Levine's unusual career was not surprising given his choice of undergraduate schools, Reed College, which has produced an eclectic array of interesting people (including Steve Jobs, who spent only a year passing through on his way to history). Levine went on to get his law degree from Yale, after which he spent what he claims was the most important educational year of his life, studying graduate-level economics with Professor Ronald Coase at the University of Chicago (a Nobel Prize-winning economist profiled in Chapter 11). Levine was especially taken with Coase's approach to economics, which was (and still is) rare in the field: to use logic or reason alone, without mathematics or empirical evidence.

Levine did not follow precisely the same course, however. In 1965, he penned what would turn out to be a highly influential article in the *Yale Law Journal* documenting how much lower intrastate airfares were than fares on interstate routes of comparable distances. This finding, which later became a major part of the intellectual case against continued airline regulation, also helped bring Levine to Fred Kahn's attention. When Kahn was selected for the CAB chairmanship, he asked Levine to direct the agency's domestic and international air divisions, one of the agency's top staff jobs.

After the CAB, in the 1980s, Levine turned to the private sector, taking senior executive positions at a number of airlines, including a stint as president at New York Air. It was during these assignments that Levine pioneered the development of the yield management pricing strategies discussed in Chapter 3.

After his private-sector experiences, Levine returned to academia, establishing an interdisciplinary law and economics program at the University of Southern California's Law School and the California Institute of Technology. He later held posts at other leading universities and from 1988 to 1992 was dean of Yale's School of Organization and Management. At this writing Levine is a research professor at New York University's Law School.

With all modes of transportation deregulated, shippers could pit the various modes against each other for long-haul traffic. For short-distance traffic, where trucks were dominant, the multiplicity of firms offered much competition. The result is what we have today, which was not the norm during the age of regulation: Any individual or company can call or make arrangements for transportation anywhere in the United States, obtain multiple quotes and shipping times, and then make a decision about who to engage and at what price.

This total freedom of movement has been the lifeblood of both existing and new businesses in the age of the Internet, and even before. In the 1980s when Japanese manufacturing techniques seemed to threaten the viability of many American firms, one of the Japanese practices most singled out for praise (and worry) was just in time (JIT) delivery. Used heavily by Japanese auto companies, JIT cut down on the need for large inventories of parts, and relied on systems of tracking sales and production so that parts could be ordered just as they were needed, with time allowed for transporting them from their sources to the production line. With few or no spare parts hanging around, the companies didn't need to spend cash to build stockpiles of parts to insert into the production line, but rather could rely on the parts being there as needed. To be sure, JIT systems were vulnerable to disruption (as the nuclear disaster at Fukushima in Japan proved in 2011) but, on the whole, they proved so successful that they were eventually adopted by U.S. manufacturing firms of all kinds. One of the early proponents was Michael Dell, who formed Dell Computer by using JIT to assemble the component parts of personal computers once they were ordered (that Dell later ran into trouble because PCs were being displaced by tablet devices in no way contradicts the importance of JIT, since tablet manufacturers also use JIT, as do many other manufacturers).

Now ask yourselves: Could JIT exist in a world where air, rail, and truck routes were tightly regulated? The question almost answers itself: of course not. If there is one word one associates with JIT it is *flexibility*, and no company relying on JIT to deliver parts and goods exactly when they are needed could compete successfully if it had to rely on transportation modes that were tightly controlled by an elaborate system of government approvals.

The other major force that has dramatically affected the U.S. economy over the past two decades, of course, is the Internet, and the rapid growth of web retailing. One company, Amazon, symbolizes the power of this phenomenon, but it is hardly the only one. Today, no retailing enterprise of any size can survive without an Internet presence, although the amount of "e-tailing" by conventional bricks-and-mortar companies has not picked up as rapidly as many may have thought.[23]

But just as there is a massive physical infrastructure that makes virtual reality possible on the jumble of wires, cables, and switches that constitute the Internet—there is a massive transportation network that enables Internet retailers of all kinds to deliver the goods that customers buy through third-party shippers, such as UPS or Federal Express. That is possible because these transportation networks can pick up ordered items virtually at any place, at any time, without the need to gain advance approval from a regulatory agency, as would have been the case before deregulation. Indeed, the only way companies like Amazon could have launched in a regulated era and promised multiple delivery options (other than the U.S. mail service) would have been to own their own transportation systems—trucks and planes—*at the outset*, something that few or any startups could have funded.

The Bottom Line

One huge irony is that the age of Internet commerce, seemingly untethered from the physical world, would never have developed as rapidly as it did without the fundamental policy reforms that transformed the physical transportation world in the late 1970s and early 1980s. Think about it: a world with far fewer retailers selling goods on the Internet than is the case now. Modern readers probably can't imagine it—and a major reason is that a lot of transportation economists established that it was the right thing to do decades before the deregulation reforms were adopted.

Likewise, modern manufacturing would not be what it is today without JIT. But JIT would also not have been possible had the transportation industry been as tightly regulated as it was before 1980.

The importance of deregulation of transportation, in short, is easy to overlook. Hopefully, this chapter brings to life the extraordinary contributions of economists who helped make this policy change a reality.

Notes

1. Clifford Winston, "On the Performance of the U.S. Transportation System: Caution Ahead," *Journal of Economic Literature* LI, no. 3 (September 2013).

2. Ibid.

3. See W. F. Bailey, *The Story of the First Trans-Continental Railroad—Its Projection, Construction, and History* (Minneapolis, Minnesota: Fili-Quarian Classics); Stephen Ambrose, *Nothing Like It in the World* (New York: Simon & Schuster, 2001).

4. Elizabeth E. Bailey, "Air Transportation Deregulation," in *Better Living through Economics*, ed. John J. Siegfried (Cambridge, MA: Harvard University Press, 2012).

5. Michael E. Levine, "Is Regulation Necessary? California Air Transportation and National Regulatory Policy," *Yale Law Journal* 74, no. 8 (July 1965): 1416–1447, and William A. Jordan, *Airline Regulation in America: Effects and Imperfections* (Baltimore: Johns Hopkins Press, 1970).

6. Richard E. Caves, *Air Transport and Its Regulators. An Industry Study* (Cambridge, MA: Harvard University Press, 1962).

7. George W. Douglas and James Clifford Miller, *Economic Regulation of Domestic Air Transport; Theory and Policy* (Washington, DC: Brookings Institution, 1974).

8. Much of the material in this section is based on an interview I had with Justice Breyer, October 17, 2013. See also Stephen Breyer, *Regulation and Its Reform* (Cambridge, MA: Harvard University Press, 1982).

9. U.S. Senate Committee on the Judiciary, Subcommittee on Administrative Practice and Procedure (1975), *Civil Aeronautics Board: Practices and Procedures*, 94th Congress, 1st Session.

10. Bailey, "Air Transportation Deregulation," 193.

11. This history is based largely on the author's personal knowledge of Kahn's background, but also on Thomas K. McCraw, *Prophets of Regulation: Charles Francis Adams, Louis D. Brandeis, James M. Landis, Alfred E. Kahn* (Cambridge, MA: Belknap of Harvard University Press, 1984).

12. Interview with Elizabeth Bailey, July 19, 2013.

13. This history of trucking regulation and subsequent deregulation draws heavily on perhaps the definitive book on the subject, Dorothy L. Robyn, *Braking the Special Interests: Trucking Deregulation and the Politics of Policy Reform* (Chicago: University of Chicago Press, 1987).

14. Interview with Darius Gaskins, July 7, 2013.

15. Winston, "On the Performance of the U.S. Transportation System," summarizes the various studies. See also sources in endnote 4 for economic benefits from airline deregulation alone.

16. Capital Group LLC, "Industry Note: Public Policy Success but Financial Failure," December 12, 2012 (brokerage research report provided to the author by Justice Stephen Breyer).

17. See Winston, "On the Performance of the U.S. Transportation System"; Bailey, "Air Transportation Deregulation."

18. For an excellent description of the new flying experience, with all its warts, see Bill Saporito, "Cabin Pressure," *Time*, September 9, 2013, 38–41.

19. See, e.g., Diane S. Owen, *Deregulation in the Trucking Industry* (Washington, DC: Bureau of Economics, Federal Trade Commission, 1998); Thomas Moore, "Rail and Trucking Deregulation," in *Regulatory Reform: What Actually Happened*, ed. Leonard W. Weiss and Michael W. Klass (Boston: Little, Brown, 1986); Clifford Winston, "U.S. Industry Adjustment to Economic Deregulation," *Journal of Economic Perspectives* 12, no. 3 (1998); Clifford Winston and Stephen Morrison, "Regulatory Reform of U.S. Intercity Transportation," in *Essays in Transportation Economics and Policy: A Handbook in Honor of John R. Meyer* (Washington, DC: Brookings Institution, 1999).

20. Jayetta Z. Hecker, "*Freight Railroads: Updated Information on Rates and Competition Issues*," Government Accountability Office, www.gao.gov/cgi-bin/getrpt?GAO-07-1245T.

21. Association of American Railroads, "The Impact of the Staggers Rail Act of 1980," www.aar.org/keyissues/Documents/Background-Papers/Impact%20of%20the%20Staggers%20Act%20April%202013.pdf.

22. Telephone interview with Michael Levine, June 26, 2013.

23. Shelly Banjo and Paul Ziobro, "After Decades of Toil, Web Sales Remain Small for Many Retailers," *Wall Street Journal*, August 27, 2013. http://online.wsj.com/article/SB10001424127887324906304579039101568397122.html.

Chapter 10

Economists and the Oil and Gas Revolution

M odern economies wouldn't be modern without the availability of various forms of energy—electricity, gasoline, diesel fuel, and natural gas. Except for the blending of gasoline with supplements like ethanol, the entire automotive and trucking transportation sector depends on crude oil. Natural gas, meanwhile, once thought to be a low-value fuel and confined to some manufacturing uses and fuel for running electric generators in peak periods, has become the hottest source of energy because it is turning out to be plentiful and is much cleaner to burn than oil or coal.

Even as late as the beginning of the Great Recession and in the early years of the recovery, however, there was deep pessimism among policy makers and the public about the prospect of continued dependence on foreign oil, especially from countries with less than friendly relations with the United States. This pessimism now seems like ancient history. In a few short years, the combination of hydraulic fracturing (fracking) and horizontal drilling has unleashed a massive increase in oil and gas production, by unlocking these fuels from shale formations throughout the continental United States. As a result, the dependence of the United States on foreign oil has dropped sharply and is widely projected to continue declining. Likewise, the price of natural gas, which is set more in domestic than global markets because it is less transportable, has also declined (though like the prices for other commodities, it also continues to fluctuate).

This chapter tells the story of how both oil and natural gas—essential to running a modern economy—came to be regulated and then deregulated, the latter consistent with a long line of advice from many economists. I'm not making the claim that the turnaround in U.S. energy markets is due solely to the economists—clearly, the development and use of new technologies, coupled with a revival of the entrepreneurial spirit in this sector, is mostly responsible. But I am making a modest claim that this turnaround would not have occurred had the prices of oil and gas been regulated during the past two decades, and some, if not much, of the credit for that goes to economists.

I also trace here how the oil and natural gas supply revolutions have affected virtually the entire economy. In this way, the energy revolution, enabled in significant part by sound economic advice, represents another policy-platform technology. Like the deregulation initiatives discussed in the previous chapter, an unregulated energy market has facilitated more rapid growth for existing businesses and contributed to the formation of some new firms.

The Origins and Decline of Price Regulation of Fossil Fuels

The stories of how the prices of oil and gas came to be regulated and then deregulated are very different, but they ended up at the same, right place.

The Oil Story

The regulation of crude oil prices came relatively late compared to natural gas. Apart from the four years of World War II when oil and virtually everything else was subject to price controls, crude oil prices were largely unregulated (except in Texas, where state authorities limited production in an effort to stabilize prices). This was true until the quadrupling of world oil prices caused by the Arab oil embargo of 1973–1974 prompted the Nixon and then Ford Administrations to limit the prices of "old" domestic oil (oil discovered before the embargo), while allowing newly discovered oil to be bought at world prices. As will become evident in the history of natural gas price regulation below, this split between old and new oil struck a compromise to keep a lid on most oil production in order to contain inflation while preserving incentives for producers to look for new oil.[1]

The problem is that once the government interferes with the pricing mechanism of the market, there is no telling how things will turn out—much like what happens when taking a loose thread out of a sweater only to discover that the sweater itself starts to become unraveled. A similar process happened with crude oil price controls.

Consider the following series of events. First, the cap on old oil, at about $3 per barrel, encouraged owners of existing wells to cut back production, which meant a cutback in fuels derived from crude oil. Shortages, manifested in long lines of angry motorists at gas stations, were the inevitable result. Second, government officials responded to this problem by introducing a system of odd–even rationing, so that drivers could only fill up on days on which the last digit on their license plates were odd or even (matching the day).

What is surprising, at least to this author, is that this complicated system of price controls and rationing was introduced and maintained by two successive Republican administrations, or those that ordinarily one would assume never to have the government interfere with the market, at least when it comes to setting or limiting prices. Reportedly, Nixon's chief economist, Herbert Stein, opposed both the general wage and price controls of 1971 and the oil price controls adopted after 1973, to no avail. Even a Republican administration turned out to be more fearful of both inflation and consumer anger at higher gas prices at the pump than they were of consumers upset by rationing. Roughly three decades later, it was another Republican administration, this one led by President George W. Bush, which abandoned free market principles again to rescue the banking system in order to avert a worse calamity. These episodes illustrate that crises cross partisan lines; they make it hard to stick with rules meant for more quiescent times.

The 1970s were a marked decade apparently, because at their end the nation and the world faced another large jump in oil prices, this one precipitated in early 1979 by a cutback in Iran's oil production and later a ban by the United States government on oil imports from Iran. These steps induced panic buying by oil traders and oil companies, which pushed crude oil prices from around $15 per barrel to $40 per barrel. With controls on domestic oil still in place, and consumers' experiences with the post–1973 oil price jump and long lines at gas stations that followed fresh in mind, lines began to reappear as many consumers sought to top off their tanks to ensure they always had enough gas to get where they wanted to go. Some states re-imposed the odd–even rationing system that had existed only a few years before to reduce the lines.

But then something surprising happened. Despite another bout of general economy-wide inflationary pressures, largely at the behest of his economic advisers, a Democratic presidential administration began dismantling the remaining system of crude oil price controls in April 1979, which ultimately was completed when President Reagan took office in 1981.

While Carter gave up controls with one hand, he took something from the oil industry with another, by tying oil price decontrol to a windfall profits tax on oil producers (computed as the difference between a base 1979 price and the average market price for crude oil over the year). The purpose of the tax was to recapture the profits owners of old oil would earn from decontrol. Congress agreed and imposed the tax as a quid pro quo for price decontrol in 1980.

The key point in this story is that despite some of the failures in Carter's energy policy, such as the synthetic fuels program that produced essentially no new fuel, and the controversies over the details of his energy plan, Carter's economists won the day. They persuaded the president to do something that his Republican predecessors could not bring themselves to do—end crude oil price controls—because controls were discouraging owners of these older wells from producing more oil. To be sure, the positive impact of oil price deregulation on production was limited largely because of the windfall profits tax. Nonetheless, deregulation reestablished the important principle that all crude oil prices, whenever oil is discovered, should be set by the market and not by regulators.

This principle proved to be hugely important in the 2000s when global oil prices again increased sharply. This time policy makers did not impose a date-based regime of oil price controls or a windfall profits tax, which allowed the market to clear without long lines and shortages. In addition, regulatory forbearance gave oil producers market incentives to marry new and existing drilling technologies that eventually led to the unlocking of vast amounts of oil from existing and newly discovered fields and in the process fundamentally changed the way policy makers have viewed the oil and gas markets.

The Natural Gas Story

Natural gas, oil's cleaner cousin, has a much more complicated regulatory history. Since the mid-1800s most segments of the natural gas industry—production, transmission, and local distribution—have been regulated in some manner. That is less true over the last few decades, however, with production prices no longer regulated and left to the free market. How that story unfolded is what I briefly discuss here.[2]

Natural gas was first used as a heating fuel after methods for extracting it from coal were developed. Since the economics of distribution favored natural monopolies, municipalities began regulating natural gas prices, at the point of delivery to consumers, as a way of protecting them against the power of the gas companies.

By the early 1900s, gas was being shipped between cities over intrastate pipelines. Since the economics favored the construction of only a single pipeline, which by that time typically transported gas from multiple sources (wells in addition to gas produced from coal), states began regulating intrastate rates on the same antimonopoly rationale. Eventually, pipelines were built across state lines, and state regulators attempted to follow them, but were slapped down by the Supreme Court in a series of cases in the 1920s. The Court held, quite understandably, that the Commerce Clause of the Constitution preempted the states from extending price controls on commodities such as gas shipped beyond their borders.

Interstate pipelines remained unregulated until Congress stepped in by enacting the Natural Gas Act (NGA) of 1938, which gave the power to set interstate pipeline rates (based on the cost of transmission) to the Federal Power Commission (the FPC later became the Federal Energy Regulatory Commission or FERC). In addition, Congress directed the FPC not to authorize the construction of new interstate pipelines where one already existed, effectively giving the agency both price and entry control over the pipeline business.

One thing the NGA did not seem to authorize, however, was the regulation of the prices gas producers could charge pipelines. That situation was short-lived because in the early 1940s the Supreme Court decided that gas producers affiliated with pipelines also were covered by the NGA. In 1954, the Court extended its ruling to cover unaffiliated gas producers, defining them as natural gas companies, thus bringing them within the ambit of the NGA's price control regime.

But how was the FPC going to regulate the prices of thousands of gas production wells? The answer is with great difficulty, if not impossibility. At first, the agency tried, unrealistically, to set prices for *each well*, based on its cost. This clearly proved to be impractical, so by 1960 the commission tried to set prices in five broad gas-producing regions, based on average costs of wells drilled in each region. That approach, too, took longer than anticipated and so in 1974 the commission adopted a national price ceiling of $0.42 per million cubic feet (mcf), a price that was lower than unregulated intrastate prices but still much higher than was allowed in many parts of the country before.

The below-market level for gas prices encouraged consumption, but discouraged the search for new gas, a recipe for eventual disruption, which a number of economists pointed out. They noted that the fragmented nature of the gas production market made it ill-suited for price regulation, paralleling arguments for deregulating transportation markets that also were a far cry from being natural monopolies, as discussed in the last chapter. The disruption eventually came when oil prices surged in 1973 to 1974 and many industrial and residential heating consumers who tried to switch to cheaper, regulated gas found out they couldn't.

Gas shortages were aggravated by the side-by-side existence of unregulated intrastate gas and regulated gas sold to interstate pipelines. If you were a producer, to which pipelines would you sell? Over time, more producers understandably picked intrastate pipelines, which made the natural gas market much less national in scope than crude oil, where no such distinctions existed, even when old and new oil were defined as part of the crude oil price controls introduced after the embargo-induced price jump. That price spike, by the way, widened the price differential between oil and gas (calculated at a common energy equivalent, British Thermal Units or BTU equivalents). With prices for natural gas suddenly relatively low, consumer demand for gas also spiked while additional supplies were not forthcoming. A severe gas supply shortage developed in the winter of 1976 to 1977, forcing the FERC to ration gas across the nation just as gasoline was being rationed.

Throughout this period and well before, economists well versed in the economics of energy had been calling for the deregulation of natural gas at the wellhead. With thousands of wells in business, it was impossible to call this industry a natural monopoly. Perhaps the most well-known economist making this argument was Paul MacAvoy, now emeritus professor at Yale's School of Management (where he was a former dean) and a former faculty member and dean of Rochester's Business School. MacAvoy also spent two years as a member of President Ford's Council of Economic Advisers at a critically important and convenient time in the history of natural gas policy, when natural gas supply curtailments or shortages reached a peak during Ford's tenure.[3] In the legal academy, Stephen Breyer of Harvard Law School and later a Supreme Court justice, also was a vigorous critic of natural gas price controls, citing MacAvoy's research.[4]

Backed by the intellectual firepower of the economics profession and coupled with the harsh realities of gas shortages, Congress finally began the lengthy process of dismantling production price controls in the National Gas Policy Act of 1978, which was part of the larger National Energy Act that the Carter Administration was pushing in an effort to make the nation less dependent on foreign sources of energy. The NGPA/NEA is yet another example where a Democratic president and a Democratic-controlled Congress did what free market Republicans had long been associated with—letting the market, rather than the government, set prices.

To be sure, the process was a gradual one. Wellhead prices on newly discovered gas were to be phased out over a seven-year period ending in 1985, while old gas would be forever subject to the pre-NGPA price limits. The rationale for the delay was that in an era of higher oil prices, a totally decontrolled gas market would lead to much higher gas prices and aggravate inflation, which was already a major national concern. In addition, the higher prices would hit colder, more Democratic areas of the country harder than the southern states, where less energy was needed to heat homes in the winter. The price limits on old gas, meanwhile, reflected the belief at the time that no additional gas could be recovered from wells that had already been drilled (erroneous as it later turned out with the development of enhanced recovery techniques), so why give producers of this gas a windfall?

The process of unwinding price controls even for new gas at the wellhead proved to have more complications than may have been originally thought. Even though pipelines blended the cost of newly discovered gas with old, regulated gas, average prices increased, inducing users to reduce their demand, relative to what pipelines expected. This mattered greatly, because after the NGPA became law, many pipeline companies believed that unregulated gas prices were going to continue to increase and so they signed long-term "take or pay" contracts with producers in an effort to lock in prices for substantial periods of time. When demand and average prices fell below expectations, a number of pipelines were stuck paying more, on average, for gas than they could sell it for.

Ultimately, all of the major distortions in the gas market were removed when Congress enacted the Natural Gas Wellhead Decontrol Act of 1989, which put all natural gas prices, including the price of old gas, on a path to decontrol by 1993. Since then, all natural gas prices have been determined by market forces, although because of differences in transportation arrangements, and differing local supply and demand conditions, the costs of gas delivered to customers still exhibits some regional variability. Other orders by FERC during the 1980s and 1990s also freed pipelines to deliver gas on a dedicated basis to certain, mainly industrial, users.

So, the lesson in all this history is that economists, such as MacAvoy, who argued that the price of natural gas at the wellhead should have been deregulated long ago were right all along. Had their advice been heeded, then many of the distortions associated with the natural gas market after the 1973 to 1974 oil embargo could have been avoided. Still, it is important that the policy eventually turned out right (except for the continued regulation of old gas), and helped set the stage for the technological revolution in oil and gas discovery that eventually came.

The Oil and Gas Supply Revolution

Now, it's time for full disclosure: My father, a highly intelligent man whose education was cut short by the Depression, was a reluctant independent oil producer, and I sort of grew up in the business. I assure you that this background does not explain my opposition to price controls on oil; readers by now will have understood that, like virtually all economists, I am opposed to such controls in any industry that is not characterized by natural monopoly. Indeed, I spent much of my dinner-table time getting into vociferous arguments with my dad about the wisdom of all the tax breaks from which oil producers (and thus I indirectly) have benefited.

But Dad was wise, and among the many things about his business he told me (much of which went in one ear and out the other at the time because after seeing him struggle anxiously for so many years, I knew early on I never wanted to be in the business) was that eventually enhanced recovery techniques would unlock substantial additional amounts of oil and gas from existing wells, and most importantly *our* wells. So, he urged that when he passed away (which he did in April 2011, at the age of 99) I should hold on to his oil producing properties for this reason alone, since not only would the requisite technology arrive, but the price of oil would rise sufficiently high, if left unregulated, to make it economically attractive to deploy the technology (Dad ventured nothing about gas prices because he wasn't a gas producer).

If only both of us had listened to his advice, but we didn't. As Dad approached the age of 92 his main wells needed substantial additional investment to keep them pumping and I was too busy working elsewhere, so a combination of risk aversion on the part of Dad (understandable at his age) and my inability to manage not only the reinvestment but any subsequent operation of the wells if the investment worked led Dad to sell out. Shortly thereafter, oil prices began to jump sharply, and several years later the fracking revolution was in full bloom, so the buyer of Dad's wells made out handsomely. Perhaps the only upside to this story for readers I hope—apart from confirming that an oil and gas technology revolution was inevitable and totally foreseeable—is that had we kept the property, I might be doing something very different and not have written this book!

The only thing that neither Dad nor I could have known at the time (this was in 2004) is how quickly the technological revolution in enhanced recovery would come. The revolution, in fact, was like other innovations—a combination of two separate, but related, technologies that combined to allow a quantum leap in results (the proverbial 1 + 1 = 3 synergistic result, rare but occasionally real).

One of the technologies, hydraulic fracturing, or fracking, has been the most controversial, but it is hardly new. My dad was doing it on his wells in the 1960s, and according to my research, it has been in use in some form in the oil industry since the late 1940s. The idea behind it is very simple and is suggested by the name: Highly pressurized liquid (typically water, sand, and some chemicals) is injected in an oil or gas producing well to break up the rock at the bottom so that it releases more oil and gas, which is pumped to the surface.

Fracking has become a much bigger deal in the last decade or so because it has been combined with newer directional drilling technology.[5] When my dad was in the oil business in the 1950s through much of the 1970s, oil producers drilled downward in a straight line for oil since that was the only way known for doing it (some producers would drill at a slant, if they had rights to the underground oil or gas on adjacent lands, which some of them did not, but the drilling still would proceed in a straight line). With directional drilling, oil companies (or their contractors) can essentially snake their way down the holes they drill in the ground, using motors and drills attached to pieces of pipe that can be attached in such a way that oil and gas can be found in multiple pockets underground using one wellhead. This eliminates the need to punch multiple holes in the ground, each drilled straight down, which collectively is far more expensive than using directional drilling techniques from a single wellhead. Directional drilling is especially cost effective in offshore locations where oil can be found, often only at very deep levels underground, using very expensive drilling platforms.

If one combines directional drilling with the fracking of so-called tight formations of shale or similar rock, then vast new horizons open up for recovering oil and gas from locations that otherwise never could be reached. When you see the fracking revolution referred to in the popular media, what the writers really mean (knowingly or unknowingly) is the *combination* of fracking with directional drilling.

The fracking or unconventional drilling revolution has been a major surprise, catching a lot of people, many of them quite knowledgeable, off guard. Until quite recently, there was much talk that U.S. oil production had peaked and was forever headed downward, which meant that the United States was destined to become ever more reliant on foreign-produced oil.

For example, it took only one quick look at a graph of U.S. oil production over time to become convinced that this peak oil thesis, named after geophysicist M. King Hubbert, must be right. Domestic oil production seemed to spike in 1970 at about 3.5 billion barrels a year (about 10 million barrels/day), but declined, more or less steadily, for almost 40 years thereafter. It only bottomed out in 2009, when oil captured from tight formations began to be recovered.[6] Because U.S. oil demand was pretty steady during the nearly four decades that domestic oil production was falling, foreign oil increasingly made up the difference.[7] The widespread pessimism throughout this period, up to its very end—that this trend would only continue—was thus readily understandable, and drove politicians in both political parties to call repeatedly for comprehensive energy independence policies (though the parties differed on how this was to be achieved). Indeed, the fear that Iraq could play a destabilizing role in the Organization of the Petroleum Exporting Countries (OPEC) was one (albeit not publicly stated) factor that drove the United States to fight in both Gulf Wars (true, there were other factors, such as Iraq's invasion of Kuwait in 1991 and the belief that Iraq had weapons of mass destruction in 2003, that drove these decisions, but one wonders if the United States would have led the attack in each case if Iraq were not a major oil producer).

The problem with the peak-oil thesis that the fracking revolution has so clearly revealed is that it takes little or no account of the *economics* of the oil and gas industry, which if one consults any basic introductory economics textbook, are really no different from the economics of any other industry. Peak oil didn't take account of economics of the supply curve, which posits that as prices increase, firms find new, more expensive ways of bringing things to market, or in energy's case, more expensive energy technologies. Prices and profits were the powerful market-based motivators for oil and gas companies and drillers to perfect the combination of horizontal drilling and hydraulic fracturing that led to the new oil and gas energy boom. In hoping that he or I would hold on to his wells waiting for the secondary oil recovery revolution to happen (which not only enhanced recoveries from existing wells but encouraged drilling for new, more difficult-to-find oil and gas), Dad was unwittingly thinking like an economist. I wish I could have told him that.

The Energy Revolution as a Platform Technology

While most commentators have focused on the major impacts of the fracking revolution on the oil and gas industry, the effects on other sectors may be even more important. Oil and gas are inputs, directly or indirectly (for example, as fuel for electricity), in virtually every other sector of the economy. So it stands to reason that the benefits of any major technological change in oil and gas discovery, like innovations elsewhere in the economy, are going to be captured to a significant degree by the consumers of the products and services that depend on the innovation. Indeed, one well-known study by Yale University economist Bill Nordhaus (who is profiled in Chapter 14) documented that just 4 percent of the benefits of the invention of the lightbulb were captured by the inventor, and the other 96 percent by purchasers of lightbulbs.[8] Nordhaus argued that this was likely to be a general phenomenon, because in competitive industries, as most industries are, any reductions in cost get passed through entirely or nearly so to consumers.[9]

I will not be surprised if many readers are shocked, or even in a state of disbelief, over this result. After all, isn't the reason for our patent, copyright, and trademark system to give strong incentives to inventors and innovative entrepreneurs to come up with and commercialize innovations by granting them some of the monopoly rights to their inventions? What about the fabulous riches earned by the founders of Microsoft, Apple, Google, Intel, and so on? Doesn't that prove that most of the benefits of innovation accrue to inventors and entrepreneurs?

Actually, the answers are no. Even for firms that have temporary or moderately long-lasting monopolies in the industries defined by their inventions, they only get rich by selling massive quantities of their inventions to the consuming public. Think about Microsoft for a moment, which has sold billions of copies of its operating system and key applications software programs to consumers throughout the world. While these consumers fork over $100 to $500 or more for copies of this software, the benefits to purchasers and society as a whole surely exceed these costs.

Individuals use the software on their PCs, and more recently tablet computers, to organize their daily lives, and in many cases, to work at home, either for the companies that employ them or for their own startups, in ways that simply would not have been possible before the PC revolution (for which companies like Microsoft, the PC manufacturers, Intel, and others are responsible). For business users, or those who buy PCs, tablets, and related software in bulk, the information technology (IT) revolution has fundamentally transformed the way businesses operate. Organizations are flatter, which speeds up decision making, while supply-chain management, customer service, human resource departments, and virtually any other cross-cutting function of the modern corporation operate in ways that corporations in the pre-PC wouldn't even recognize.

To be sure, the IT industry has some large firms that in their niches have had either large market shares or market power (the ability to influence price as firms in competitive industries cannot), but even the firms in these industries cannot capture all of the gains from their innovations. In the IT sector, this is probably an understatement, since there are intangible ease-of-use benefits that individuals or companies realize from the use of Microsoft or Apple software, or the mobile apps enabled by Apple or Google, that are not necessarily captured in the productivity statistics.

In any event, the discovery of oil and gas, as a distinct activity or industry, is certainly a more competitive activity than the niche IT sectors where some firms still have dominant positions. Many oil companies either have the ability in-house, or can hire it from drillers, to deploy directional drilling and fracking technology to find oil and gas in tight formations, which makes the production end of the oil and gas industry highly competitive. One widely cited study, by IHS Global Insight, a leading economic and energy consulting firm led by, among others, the energy expert Daniel Yergin, confirmed this by calculating in 2013 the total benefits of fracking shale oil and gas. The study's verdict: In 2012 alone the energy revolution had saved the average household $1,200 per year, which is equivalent to increasing take-home pay by the same amount, or about 2.5 percent.[10] For the whole economy, McKinsey has estimated that the oil/shale gas boom will have increased GDP economy-wide by $380 to $690 billion by 2020, representing a 2 to 3.7 percent increase in annual GDP by that year (an estimate in line with IHS estimate for 2012).[11]

These are enormous figures, since annual productivity growth has been in the neighborhood of 2 percent per year over the last decade, which makes the gains from the shale oil/gas boom alone as much as one to two years' worth of economy-wide productivity growth.

Industries and sectors of the economy vary considerably by how much energy they use. But clearly, those industries that are more energy intensive, and especially those using natural gas or petroleum products as feedstock for other products, such as the chemicals industry, have especially benefited from the energy revolution.

Lower costs are analogous to platform effects, since they reduce costs and encourage investment by users of innovations elsewhere in the economy. The shale and oil gas revolution also created important geographically based platform effects. North Dakota, one of the most sparsely populated states in the United States, has experienced rapid growth in both population and incomes because of the discovery of oil in tight shale formations. To attract men willing to work in the harsh climate, oil-drilling companies are paying high wages coupled with bare-bones residential quarters. The men use some of the money to buy gas, food, and other items locally, while sending much of the rest home to their families. This multiplier effect may be less innovative than the new apps that software developers create for new operating systems for computers and mobile devices, but the economic effects are similar. The initial innovation—in this case, new drilling technologies— becomes the equivalent of a platform on which other industries and firms either expand or are created.

In addition, eastern states in the Marcellus shale gas formation also have experienced benefits, or really revivals, in many areas that were headed on their way down: portions of Ohio, West Virginia, and Pennsylvania in particular. New York is also in this gas region, but its policy makers have limited drilling out of fear of the environmental impacts of fracking on underground water supplies and the release of methane that sometimes accompanies the fracking process. At this writing, the Environmental Protection Agency has also been looking at the water contamination issue, and there is the possibility that the federal government will issue minimum standards drillers must meet to ensure underground water quality in states where fracking is taking place. Research about the methane problem, at least at wells operated by larger companies, suggests that it has been overstated.[12] Few energy experts believe that any new environmental requirements the federal government may set will significantly slow the fracking boom.

The Bottom Line

In sum, free markets, encouraged by economists, have had much wider benefits than those limited to looking for oil and gas. We can thank a number of economists in the 1960s and 1970s for that, as well as those of recent vintage who stood ready to counsel against any attempts to impose the oil and gas controls of an earlier era in the 1990s and 2000s, when prices soared (but since have come down).

Accordingly, when you think about the U.S. oil and gas boom remember the economists. Of course, there were powerful political forces pulling with them, unlike airline and trucking deregulation. But the intellectual case helped.

Notes

1. For a more elaborate, quantitative history of oil prices and their regulation since the end of World War II, see "Crude Oil Price History and Analysis," *WTRG Economics*, www.wtrg.com/prices.html.

2. This brief history is based on a combination of sources, including Stephen G. Breyer, *Regulation and Its Reform* (Cambridge, MA: Harvard University Press, 1982) and "The History of Regulation," *NaturalGas.org*, www.naturalgas .org/regulation/history/.

3. See, e.g., Paul W. MacAvoy and Robert S. Pindyck, "Alternative Regulatory Policies for Dealing with the Natural Gas Shortage," *The Bell Journal of*

Economics and Management Science 4, no. 2 (1973): 454–498 and Stephen Breyer and Paul W. MacAvoy, "The Natural Gas Shortage and the Regulation of Natural Gas Producers," *Harvard Law Review* 86, no. 6 (1973): 941–987, www.jstor.org/discover/10.2307/1340084?uid=309668551.

4. Breyer, *Regulation and Its Reform.*

5. Jonathan Rauch, "The New Old Economy: Oil, Computers, and the Reinvention of the Earth," *The Atlantic Online,* www.theatlantic.com/past/docs/issues/2001/01/rauch.htm.

6. See "U.S. Field Production of Crude Oil," *U.S. Energy Information Administration,* www.eia.gov/dnav/pet/hist/LeafHandler.ashx?n=pet&s=mcrfpus1&f=a.

7. See "U.S. Imports of Crude Oil," *U.S. Energy Information Administration,* www.eia.gov/dnav/pet/hist/LeafHandler.ashx?n=PET&s=MCRIMUS1&f=A.

8. William D. Nordhaus, "Schumpeterian Profits and the Alchemist Fallacy," Discussion Paper Number 6, *Yale Working Papers on Economic Applications and Policy* (2005), www.econ.yale.edu/sites/default/files/Working-Papers/wp000/ddp0006.pdf. On a personal note, Bill is a close friend who has been a lifelong mentor and was the coauthor of my first book, *Reforming Federal Regulation* (New Haven, CT: Yale University Press, 1983).

9. Elsewhere I have used this 4 percent finding to extrapolate how many new scale firms (those reaching $1 billion in sales) must be founded each year to generate a permanent increase in the overall U.S. economic growth rate of one percentage point: roughly 30 to 60 such firms a year. See Robert Litan, "Baseball's Answer to Growth" in *The 4% Solution: Unleashing the Economic Growth America Needs,* ed. Brendan Minter (New York: Crown Business, 2012), 127–143.

10. The study itself is only available to the company's subscribers, but the bottom-line result has been quoted widely. Two examples are in editorials by the *Wall Street Journal,* September 10 and September 14–15, 2013.

11. Susan Lund, James Manyika, Scott Nyquist, Lenny Mendonca, and Sreenivas Ramaswamy, "Game Changers: Five Opportunities for US Growth and Renewal," McKinsey and Company, www.mckinsey.com/insights/americas/us_game_changers.

12. Russell Gold, "Fracking Leaks Overstated, Study Says," *Wall Street Journal,* September 16, 2013.

Chapter 11

Economists and the Telecommunications Revolution

Perhaps no sector in modern economies has been more transformed by technological change than telecommunications. Young readers of this book surely take this for granted because they have known no other world: the ability to talk, text, watch videos, listen to music, and access an almost unlimited amount of information via the Internet, anytime over mobile phones or on landline connections. There are so many television channels available it is hard to keep track of them.

But this state of affairs is all relatively new, and is nothing like what older readers of this book will remember. Before the Internet, communications in modern countries consisted of voice and data messages routed largely over wire-based telephone networks. Poor countries were hardly wired, while most countries had only one or a few television channels, owned by the state or a wealthy connected few.

In this chapter, I focus on the contributions of economists to the sea change in the telecommunications landscape over the past several decades. As I tried to avoid with the energy revolution, I am also not going to overreach here. Certainly, the lion's share of the credit for the changes goes to the inventors, engineers, and computer scientists, among others, who developed and commercialized the multiple technologies that characterize the modern telecommunications industry.

My more modest, though I believe still powerful, claim is that economists played an integral role in shaping the public policies that encouraged these advances. In addition, economists are used by some of the firms in this industry to enable them to compete more effectively. This chapter tells these stories.

Economists in a Quick History of Communications

It is useful for the exposition in this chapter to distinguish between two types of communication: person-to-person and one-to-many. For most of human history, people have communicated with each other by talking face to face, or with handwritten messages delivered by humans or birds. "One-to-many" communications were limited to just the audiences who could physically hear the speakers.

Several technologies have revolutionized both forms of communication. Apart from the development of language and writing, arguably the most important innovation of the modern era was Gutenberg's invention of the printing press in the fourteenth century. That is the consensus, anyway, of a panel of experts on innovation convened by *The Atlantic* magazine, one of whose members observed that once books and shorter manuscripts were easily copied and distributed, "knowledge began replicating and quickly assumed a life of its own."[1]

Printed material is an example of a "one-to-many" communication, but is asynchronous because of the time lag between the preparation of the content by the author and its distribution to readers. Synchronized mass communication—radio and television—came much later, in the late nineteenth and twentieth centuries, respectively. Both technologies harnessed the electromagnetic spectrum to transmit signals through the air. Later in the twentieth century, television signals would be sent through cable lines, which permitted a great expansion in the numbers of channels and the range of content that audiences could receive.

As for personal communications, big technological breakthroughs came earlier, initially in the middle of the nineteenth century, with the invention of the telegraph, and several decades later with the invention of the telephone. For roughly eight decades, telephonic communications could only be transmitted via copper wires or by radio devices. In the 1970s, satellites enabled data and voice signals to be transmitted through the air in combination with the existing landline network to deliver messages to their ultimate destinations. Even then, satellites were used primarily for transmitting television signals and data, not voice. Over-the-air personal communication began to expand greatly with the deployment of microwave communications that replaced copper wire for long distance (more about this later) and the invention of cellular telephone devices and networks in the latter portion of the twentieth century.

Two things about these different forms of communication have made them interesting to economists. The landline telephone industry was assumed by policy makers to be a natural monopoly, a circumstance calling for price regulation to protect consumers, a topic that has long been of interest to economists. Radio and television broadcasters, meanwhile, made use of a scarce resource—certain parts of the electromagnetic spectrum (see following box) that could handle their signals—another state of affairs about which economists have much to say.

The Electromagnetic Spectrum: A Quick Primer

If you slept through your high school physics class, or otherwise have forgotten much of what you once knew, it is useful to briefly recollect how it is that radio, television, and cellular phone signals can travel through the air or other matter and reach their destinations.[2]

The spectrum refers to the range of various frequencies and wavelengths (the two are opposites) of radiation or energy that travels through air and space. Radio consists of long waves and low frequencies (and thus low energy) at one end of the spectrum; ultraviolet light and x-rays are short wavelength,

(continued)

high frequency (and thus high energy) forms of radiation. Ordinary light is somewhere in the middle of the spectrum.

In the telecommunications industry it is most common to refer to frequencies in different parts of the spectrum. They are measured in hertz, with one hertz representing one wave per second, a kilohertz (KHz) as 1,000 waves per second, and a megahertz (MHz) as 1 million waves per second. A typical FM radio station transmits signals at about 100 MHz.

Broadcast television consists of very high frequency (VHF) or ultrahigh frequency (UHF) bands of spectrum. As discussed later in the chapter, the Federal Communications Commission (FCC) will be auctioning up to 120 MHz of the VHF spectrum for use in mobile broadband communications.

That does not mean that they have always been listened to, at least not right away. Perhaps the clearest example of the lag in implementing an economist's idea relates to the way spectrum licenses have been handed out by the government, which asserted ownership of the airwaves shortly after radio was invented and commercialized in the early twentieth century. The agency making that claim, the Federal Radio Commission (today's Federal Communications Commission), did what comes naturally to government agencies: It established an applications procedure and handed out the licenses, first for radio and later to television, to those stations whose owners could meet various financial and public interest requirements. As you will learn later in this chapter, if you are not already aware, this is not how most economists think about how to allocate a scarce resource like the electromagnetic spectrum.

As for the natural monopoly in landline telephony, it took some human hands to make it possible, and then later, when competitors started challenging that notion, it took other humans to ensure that they were allowed to do so in a meaningful way. The monopoly was arranged in the early part of the twentieth century through the settlement of an antitrust case against AT&T (founded as the Bell Telephone Company in 1877, it became American Telephone and Telegraph in

1885). The case was brought largely because of the company's refusal to interconnect its fledgling network with that of rivals. The settlement cemented AT&T's monopoly in both interstate and most local telephone transmissions, but prohibited the company from acquiring other telephone companies, while subjecting its rates to regulation. Congress overrode the merger restriction in 1921 by giving the Interstate Commerce Commission (ICC) authority to exempt AT&T's acquisition of other companies to fill out its nationwide network, a power which in fact the ICC exercised.[3]

Congress gave more clarity to the regulatory mission when it created the Federal Communications Commission, giving that agency authority to ensure that the rates telephone companies charged were "nondiscriminatory" and at such a level to ensure service would be universally available (an obligation that came to be called "universal service"). State regulators oversaw the rates charged by the individual "operating companies' within AT&T's network. In combination, the federal and state regulatory regime eventually helped meet the universal service objective by keeping the rates of interstate calls high in order to subsidize local telephone connections for urban and suburban customers. Independent telephone companies (of which there were as many 1,500 as late as the 1980s) served primarily rural areas.

In 1949, the Justice Department filed another antitrust case against AT&T and its equipment manufacturing company, Western Electric, for excluding competing equipment companies from selling to AT&T. The department wanted Western Electric spun off from AT&T, while obligating AT&T to buy its equipment on a competitive basis. The department sought this relief in order to give other equipment manufacturers a chance to compete.

AT&T responded that its vertical structure was necessary to protect the "integrity of the network," and also was essential for national defense, arguments the company would invoke when it was sued by the government again 25 years later. The 1949 case was settled in 1956 with another consent decree, which allowed AT&T to retain ownership of Western Electric, but limited the company to making only telephonic equipment. The decree also limited AT&T to providing "common carrier" services, which meant it had to stay out of the computer, radio, TV, and motion picture industries (sectors the company either already had gotten out of or never entered in the first place).[4] The case was not about AT&T's control over long distance and local telephony (except in a few geographic areas of the country, mostly on the west coast and in Florida, where General Telephone & Telegraph had a significant presence). Within the Justice Department, many staff attorneys for years viewed the settlement as a sellout.

Ultimately, AT&T's monopoly in both long distance and equipment manufacture was undone in the 1980s by the Justice Department, with prior help from other parts of the federal government that, beginning in the Johnson administration, had been looking at ways to introduce more competition into the telecommunications industry. Equally, if not more significant, continuing technological advances in voice and data communication—including mobile telephony and the Internet—have essentially eliminated the vestiges of AT&T's claim to natural monopoly, especially in local landline phone service.

Though lawyers were critical to the government's final antitrust case against the company, ultimately forcing its breakup in 1984, economists played an important, but too easily forgotten, role before the case was launched and as it was proceeding. You'll learn how in the next section.

Finally, economists were central to inventing and promoting the use of a different form of price regulation of monopolies—incentive regulation" or "price caps"—in both the telecommunications and electric utility industries in the 1970s and 1980s. This new system differs from the standard practice up to that time of allowing monopolies to charge prices sufficient to guarantee them a given rate of return on their invested capital. Although price regulation is much less common today than it was then, price caps generally accomplished their main objective—encouraging greater efficiencies by regulated monopolies—and we have economists to thank for that outcome.

When Natural Monopolies End: The Run-Up to the AT&T Antitrust Case

AT&T's "natural" monopoly became "unnatural" because of a series of technological advances—microwave, satellites, and cellular transmission—that first changed the economics of the market for voice and data transmissions across state lines, and then obliterated the monopolies of the regional remnants of AT&T in local telephone markets. But technology could not do its magic without facilitative public policies. It is in this realm that economists helped push competition along at critical junctures, although admittedly, technologists and lawyers played the leading roles.

The first part of the AT&T network to crack was its monopoly over all equipment required to deliver telephone service, beginning with the telephone itself in the customer's hand, where claims of natural monopoly were weaker on their face than in the transmission lines and switches that routed calls.[5] The triggering event was so trivial and even laughable—AT&T's refusal in the mid-1950s to allow a cup-like device called the "hush-a-phone" to be attached to the telephone on the grounds that it threatened the integrity of its network—that, looking back, it is difficult to take seriously. But AT&T was deadly serious about it, fearing that any crack in its equipment monopoly would lead to others. The company's main regulator, the FCC, amazingly agreed with AT&T's refusal to allow its customers to use this simple device, but the Commission's decision was eventually overturned in the courts.[6]

AT&T was right, though, to fear the slippery slope of competition that further innovation would unleash. A little more than a decade after the fight over the hush-a-phone, in 1968, another company wanted the FCC's approval for a "Carterfone," a device that connected a telephone to a two-way radio. This time the commission showed that it had learned its lesson and gave its green light.

The commission went further, on its own initiative. In 1975, it issued "Part 68" rules that detailed how other equipment manufacturers could sell telephone-related equipment to the public without having to install special "coupling devices" to protect the integrity of the network. These rules also required AT&T to cooperate to ensure the supplementary devices would work (the company's failure to cooperate on other matters, principally interconnecting with long-distance competitors, formed the heart of the government's antitrust case against AT&T, to be discussed shortly). Those rules were worked out with the cooperation of the Antitrust Division at Justice and telecommunications experts in the White House.

The commission also issued a series of orders in the 1970s and 1980s requiring AT&T to sell equipment through a separate subsidiary and to "unbundle" the offering of that equipment from telephone service. In theory, these requirements were designed to prevent the company from playing games with its cost allocation between telephone service and equipment sales, while allowing customers the ability to choose telephone and related equipment from other providers. In practice, the settlement of the antitrust case would replace these regulatory attempts to inhibit AT&T's ability to frustrate competition.

As important as it was, the competition to AT&T's manufacturing operations did not really threaten the core activity of the company, which was to provide end-to-end telephone service from anywhere in the country. When the company's leaders invoked the need for its monopoly to "protect the integrity of the network," this is what they were talking about.

Yet the network was not indivisible. While the company's local lines and switches arguably still constituted a natural monopoly because there really was no other way, yet, to complete local calls or to route long-distance calls to their local destinations, one pesky upstart, a small company called Microwave Communications Inc. ("MCI"), began in the 1960s to test the natural monopoly thesis in AT&T's long-distance or interstate calling market by rolling out its own microwave towers to compete with AT&T's. Ma Bell's pricing structure, with long-distance rates approved much above cost in order to subsidize local service, attracted such entry. So it was only a matter of time before companies like MCI sprang up to chip away at the most vulnerable part of AT&T's empire. Knowing this, and understanding that competitive entry into long-distance would be like pulling a thread in a sweater only to eventually see the whole garment unravel, AT&T fought MCI in the marketplace, before the FCC, and later in the courts.

MCI began seemingly innocently enough in the late 1960s by offering private lines to businesses that wanted to transmit voice and data between their different locations (television broadcasters had constructed private lines for themselves years before, but MCI was the first firm to sell private-line service to third parties). The FCC approved the company as a "specialized common carrier" to offer this service. MCI did not stop there, however. Through successive petitions in the 1970s, it gained the commission's approval first to connect to AT&T's network at the organization of a voice or data transmission, and later at the point of termination. Ultimately, MCI was selling its long-distance service not just to businesses for private-line service, but also to residential customers. To accomplish all this, MCI bought bulk service from AT&T at discounted rates because of its heavy call volume, and then resold the service at a higher price to MCI's customers. In essence, MCI was taking advantage of AT&T's volume discount, coupled with MCI's own growing microwave transmission network, to compete directly with AT&T in the long-distance market.

Not surprisingly, AT&T did not take this arrangement lying down, refusing to interconnect with MCI and even unplugging MCI's private lines.[7] AT&T defended itself by arguing that not only was MCI unfairly "cream skimming" AT&T's customers but, in doing so, it was undermining the ability of the AT&T system to ensure universal service through the subsidy of its long-distance. AT&T had made similar arguments in the early 1960s, when it wanted to counter the competitive threat posed by private line suppliers, by offering its own TELPAK service, but at prices at low incremental costs. The FCC rejected this attempt, largely on the grounds that such prices could drive private line competitors out of business, and once that happened, there was no way for the commission to guarantee that ATT's incremental cost-based prices would remain so low.[8]

Even before all these events played out, the Johnson administration began an inquiry into the need for competition in telecommunications markets generally. In 1967, it formed a Task Force on Communications Policy, chaired by Eugene Rostow, the former dean of the Yale Law School who was then serving as Undersecretary of State for Political Affairs. It also included representatives from other federal agencies and the president's Council of Economic Advisers (CEA). The general counsel of the task force was the young Richard Posner (yes, the same Posner I discussed in Chapter 5, who later became one of the nation's leading legal scholars and judges), whose recollections of its work I draw on here.[9] Of particular importance to the thesis of this book, the task force had three distinguished economists working on it; one full-time, Leland Johnson, and two representing the CEA, Merton "Joe" Peck, a member of the Council, and then senior staffer Roger Noll (the same Roger Noll I referred to in the introduction to this section).

In Posner's words, Leland Johnson (no relation to the president) had already achieved "a measure of academic celebrity" for what was called the Averch–Johnson effect—the incentive of price-regulated firms to over-invest because they can recover a rate of return on capital investment in their regulated rates.[10] I will have more to say about this well-known effect in the next section. Joe Peck was one of the nation's leading microeconomists, and Noll later would become one, too, as well as a widely recognized expert in telecommunications economics and policy, among many other topics (sports economics, for example).

Donald Baker, who would later head the Antitrust Division at the end of the Ford administration and in the early part of the Carter administration, was the Justice Department's representative. Though Baker is an outstanding lawyer, he worked closely with economists inside and outside of the department (see the discussion in the next chapter about fixed brokerage commissions) and appreciated the importance of their thoughts and contributions.

The task force had a broad mandate that went beyond the future of AT&T's monopoly, including developing policies for cable television, then a fledgling part of the television market, and satellite communications. Toward the very end of President Johnson's term, the task force issued its report, recommending more competition in satellites, but little more. According to Posner, although the task force was skeptical about the social value of maintaining AT&T's monopoly and wanted more competition in telecommunications,[11] its final report did not advocate a major shift in policy toward the company.

Nonetheless, just by suggesting that more competition was important—the predilection of the economists—the task force encouraged the FCC and the Justice Department to open the edges of the telephone network to competitors, and help worked out the rules to facilitate this. The intellectual groundwork plowed by the task force also helped Justice to eventually decide that rules alone weren't enough. AT&T simply had to be broken up so real competition in telecommunications markets could really take root.

However, no agency of the federal government, including Justice, can simply order a company's breakup. Under the antitrust laws, specifically Section 2 of the Sherman Act of 1890 that prohibits monopolization, the government must file suit in a court of law and convince a judge or a jury that a company has monopolized one or markets in an unlawful way and that these misdeeds are so egregious that a simple injunction against their repetition is not enough to prevent them from happening again. The government must convince the courts that only "structural relief" can ensure competition going forward.

That is exactly what Justice decided to do in November 1974 when it filed its landmark monopolization case against AT&T. Justice's core complaint: that AT&T was using its bottleneck monopoly in local telephone service to force customers to buy telephone equipment and long-distance service, thereby frustrating competition in both of these latter two markets. This was not a "big-is-bad" case, as some critics alleged at the time. Rather, the AT&T case was all about the abuse of monopoly power in one market (local telephone service) that prevented competition in adjacent markets (equipment and long distance).

The department did not come to its decision lightly; its lawyers, economists, and engineers spent several years reviewing mountains of internal material obtained from the company and other external evidence.[12] In launching the case, the department rejected AT&T's core defense: that maintenance of its monopoly was essential to protect the integrity of its network and to ensure universal service. AT&T also claimed that its monopoly was essential to the national defense, and even had the Defense Department convinced of this view.[13]

Economists inside and outside the Antitrust Division played an important role in the deliberations that led to the complaint. Within the division, chief economist George Hay was asked by then Assistant Attorney General Thomas Kauper to review materials relating to AT&T's activities, which he did with Bob Reynolds, an economist Hay had recruited to the division that year. They concluded, in a memo simply titled "Bell," written primarily by Reynolds, that from an economic perspective it was desirable and feasible to separate AT&T's local, equipment manufacturing, and long-distance operations. Separately, unbeknownst to the economists, the division's legal staff had opened two separate investigations into the company's conduct in the long-distance and equipment markets. Once the various parts of the division were aware of each other's efforts in early 1974 they began to interact. Hay recalls that one of the main contributions of the economists was to convince the division's leadership that only divestiture would prevent future anticompetitive conduct.[14]

Outside the division, Bruce Owen, currently a professor at Stanford, wrote an influential memo (which eventually found its way to the antitrust division) while serving as chief economist of the newly created Office of Technology Policy (OTP) and later as a consultant upon his return to Stanford, advocating what would become a main objective of the case: the divestiture of equipment manufacturing and long-distance operations from AT&T's local telephone monopolies. OTP was established inside the executive office of the president on the recommendation of the Johnson task force (the office was later abolished in the Ford administration and its duties were transferred to the Commerce Department).[15]

The government and AT&T spent eight years in discovery and litigation arguing the merits of their respective positions, before reaching an approved settlement in 1982. Once the complaint had been filed and the trial was under way, the division's lawyers and economists (who also were in frequent contact with their counterparts at the FCC) were largely separated, though the latter continued to have input into the case, primarily about relief. The settlement was reached toward the end of the trial, and was driven by the Assistant Attorney General for Antitrust in the Reagan administration, William Baxter, who was on leave from his law professorship at Stanford Law School. Although not a professional economist, Baxter, like many law professors who taught and wrote about antitrust law, clearly thought like most microeconomists who presumptively favor competition. He believed that firms subject to rate-of-return regulation should not be allowed into other unregulated businesses, and he frequently asked his top staffers as the case was proceeding and as relief was being considered, "What do the economists think?"[16]

Baxter convinced AT&T that it was likely to lose at trial, and that it would save time and money to settle the case essentially on the terms of the original complaint: by agreeing to a breakup of the company that separated its long-distance business, which remained as part of the old AT&T, from its local telephone and equipment businesses. Local telephony was split into seven "regional Bell operating companies" or "RBOCs" as they came to be known, while the equipment company became Lucent, which also took the research and development gem of the old AT&T, Bell Labs. Because the RBOCs each still had monopoly power in local landline service, they also were subjected to a nondiscrimination requirement: Each had to deal fairly and on the same terms with all long-distance and equipment competitors, including both the former constituent parts of AT&T and any existing and new rivals.

Baxter almost never got a chance to settle the case on its original terms. While the case was being tried, Secretary of Defense Weinberger and Secretary of Commerce Baldrige, along with Presidential Counselor (and later Attorney General) Ed Meese led an effort within the Reagan administration to persuade the president to end the case by supporting legislation that would require Bell's operating companies to provide equal access to all long-distance companies. Baxter was strongly opposed to this notion because it relied too much on regulation and, in any event, would never have made it through Congress. Baxter and his opponents had a showdown at a cabinet meeting with the president in 1981 (Baxter's boss, Attorney General William French Smith, was recused from the AT&T case because of his prior board membership at Pacific Telephone & Telegraph, a Bell operating company). For all its theatrics, the meeting ended inconclusively. In the end, the matter was delegated to then Chief of Staff James Baker who decided that the political benefits for the President to stop the case were not worth the cost.[17]

Baxter also never would have been in a position to settle the case on such far-reaching terms had the Carter administration reached a settlement earlier. Toward the end of the Carter term, the Assistant Attorney General for Antitrust, Sanford Litvack (who had replaced John Shenefield, who served in that post earlier in the administration), and his legal staff were considering a settlement that would have allowed AT&T to keep its long-distance operations, while divesting a few operating companies and a portion of Western Electric. Inside the Division, Bob Reynolds and Bruce Owen, who was then serving as chief economist, strongly objected that such a settlement did not go far enough by omitting the divestiture of all of AT&T's multiple local operating companies from AT&T's long-distance division. According to one popular account of the incredible twists and turns in the case, Litvack came very close to settling the case, even after Reagan was elected, and until Baxter was named as his replacement.[18] It is not clear whether it was Litvack or Baxter who called off the settlement negotiations in early 1981, but the outcome then and later was consistent with what the economists had been pushing all along—full breakup.[19] For reasons I discuss next, history will judge both the decision not to settle "on the cheap" in 1981 and Baxter's decision the following year to press for the larger divestiture that included the spinoff of AT&T's long-distance operations as two very fortunate outcomes.

In the end, it is difficult to apportion credit among the many public servants who made the breakup of AT&T possible, and thus the social and business benefits that breakup achieved. However, it is clear that various economists played important roles, especially at the beginning in framing the case and the desired relief so broadly, and in continuing at appropriate times to press that vision on the attorneys who were in charge of the case.

Competition in Telecommunications: The Benefits of AT&T's Breakup

In the two decades following the breakup or the "divestiture," mergers among the RBOCs eventually reduced their number to three, one of which, Southwestern Bell, eventually bought the "old AT&T" long-distance company (post-breakup) and thus became the "new AT&T." The other surviving RBOCs were Verizon and Qwest. While consolidating the local landline exchange industry, these mergers did not enhance the market power of the resulting companies in their local markets which were already monopolized. In theory, the mergers reduced the *potential* competition that each RBOC could have provided in the long-distance markets outside their territories (which the 1984 breakup consent decree allowed). But over time, technological advances coupled with entry of new firms turned all of telephony, long-distance and local, into far more competitive markets than many may have thought possible at the time of the breakup.

Take long-distance first, where a main objective of hiving off the local telephone monopolies from AT&T's long-distance business was to give other firms in long-distance a fair shot at competing. That is exactly what happened. MCI and Sprint, a follow-on upstart, not only made inroads into the long-distance market, but they each built out new fiber optic networks, compelling the "old AT&T" to do the same. Although these networks had high fixed costs, with their enormously increased capacity to carry voice and data signals at essentially zero marginal cost, they induced vigorous price competition in long-distance, which drove down calling rates.

Even more important, the new fiber optic networks in the United States and overseas ultimately became the backbone of the Internet, which has totally transformed telecommunications and indeed the way of life in modern and developing societies alike. I recall one meeting in which I participated sometime in 1994, while serving as a Deputy Assistant Attorney General in the Antitrust Division, with senior officers of Corning Glass, a major manufacturer of fiber optic cables. They told us that had it not been for AT&T's breakup, their company never would have been able to sell as much, or any, fiber optic cable to Sprint and MCI. Both these companies, in turn, built out fiber optic networks, which became part of the Internet's backbone.

We will never know, of course, if the Internet would have developed at the same pace had AT&T's long-distance monopoly never been opened up to competition, but the presumption has to be that the breakup accelerated the pace of change. The best evidence for this is that although the fiber optic cables that constitute the Internet's basic infrastructure had been invented in Bell Labs, the parent company did not really roll out the technology until competitive pressures forced the AT&T long-distance company to do so.[20] In addition, the earlier 1956 AT&T consent decree and later regulatory decisions by the FCC in its "Computer I" and "Computer II" decisions forcing that company and GT&E to offer packet switching services through separate subsidiaries meant that when the Internet and its packet switching technology came along, that technology was built out by companies that were separated from the dominant telecom providers. This buttressed competition in the packet switching market that also helped accelerate the commercial build out of the Internet.[21]

The competitive race to build fiber networks had profound implications for many, now iconic American businesses. Companies like eBay, Amazon, Facebook, and Google, let alone their counterparts abroad, especially in China, owe their existence to the Internet. Each was founded by one or more innovative entrepreneurs who implemented their ideas at the right time in their careers. As Bill Gates has said of Microsoft's success, "Our timing in setting up the first software company aimed at personal computers was essential to our success."[22] Had Gates been born even one or two years earlier or later, he might never have formed Microsoft, while Apple's closed operating system might have achieved much greater success than it did. Likewise, had the build out of the Internet come several years later it is entirely possible that one or more of the Net-based companies that are now household names never would have launched. In some respects, then, these businesses and their founders may have the breakup of AT&T to thank. Economists who played some role in the events and decisions that ultimately led to AT&T's dismantling also deserve some of the credit.

The other great post-breakup development was the introduction and explosive growth of mobile telephony, which, among other things, ultimately undermined the core monopoly of the old AT&T and its local landline telephone services. Of course, the lion's share of credit for the mobile telecommunications revolution goes to the technologists at Bell Labs who developed the system of cellular communications based on the transmission of microwave signals between cell towers in widespread use today. After trying out the system in the late 1970s, the old AT&T received the first license in 1982 from the FCC for widespread commercial use of a portion of the electromagnetic spectrum for cellular telephony. As part of AT&T's breakup these licenses were distributed to the seven RBOCs. In retrospect, it is somewhat amazing that the new AT&T long-distance company did not ask Justice for permission to keep the cellular licenses, which would have done more to promote landline versus wireless competition than vesting the licenses with the RBOCs. Justice probably would have granted such a request, but it was not forthcoming.[23]

The FCC also handed out one other cellular license in about 100 local markets by lottery so, for over a decade, cell phone service in each area was a duopoly. As long as this was the case, mobile phone service, which was much more expensive than landline service, provided only limited competition to the RBOCs' own local landline monopolies. Some of the winners of the lotteries, meanwhile, turned the licenses into fortunes. Craig McCaw, in particular, assembled a national network of licenses by buying other winners, ultimately selling his McCaw Communications to the "new AT&T" in 1994 for over $11 billion. McCaw later went on to rejuvenate and sell Nextel, and later to purchase Clearwire, subsequently bought out by Sprint Nextel, which has become a major wireless broadband provider.

Broadband Communications in the Internet Age

What has made the Internet so ubiquitous and useful is the increasing speed of the communications that broadband providers made possible. As a result, what constitutes "broadband" Internet service has been and continues to be a moving target.

Internet service speeds are measured by the number of *bits*, or digital zeroes and ones, of voice or data per second that are able to travel through the Internet. The constraining factor is not the long-distance fiber optic cables that can carry bits at the speed of light, but the "last-mile" connection to a customer's premises. In the early days of the Internet, customers were limited to the copper wires of the telephone network that ran into their homes, and thus could only communicate through dial-up modems that carried messages at speeds measured in the tens of thousands of bits. Over time, these speeds increased greatly, as coaxial cables, upgraded telephone (digital subscriber or DSL) lines, and even fiber-optic cables—each a form of broadband—have been connected to homes and businesses.

At this writing, minimum broadband speeds, as defined by the FCC, are 4 million bits per second (Mbps) for downloading information from the Internet, and 1 Mbps for uploading data. As of early 2013, more than 90 percent of U.S. households had access to landline broadband connections, and most of the rest were able to buy broadband services from wireless providers.[24]

Broadband speeds will continue increasing over time. Already, much of America has access to landline service with average download speeds of 15–20 Mbps, far faster than the FCC-defined minimum. Google has been rolling out in selected cities its "Google Fiber" connections with speeds of 1,000 Mbps, or 1 gigabit.

(continued)

As speeds increase, the number and variety of applications proliferate. As just one example, video streaming of television shows and movies, which only a few years ago was a pipedream, has made huge inroads into the entertainment market, posing a significant competitive threat to cable-based television. Real-time video transmission has made telemedicine and remote surgery possible, and online videos on demand have begun to revolutionize education at all levels. The possibilities for other broadband applications seem limitless.

Economists played an important, though largely unseen, role in the subsequent explosive growth of cellular telephony in the United States through many years of advocating the auction of licenses to the electromagnetic spectrum in lieu of more lotteries or administrative decisions (the way the FCC handled radio and television licenses). The details relating to the auctions will be discussed in the last section of this chapter.

At this point, however, I only want to highlight the importance of the auctions in expanding the number of competitors in mobile communications, which has brought down rates over time and improved quality of service. With a duopoly in cellular service in each service territory, neither one of the providers had strong incentives to compete on price or quality. This changed when the FCC launched its personal communications services, or PCS, broadband auctions in 1994, after Congress gave it broad authority to do so in 1993 (for a definition of *broadband*, see the preceding box in this chapter). When it began its auctions, which have continued intermittently in the succeeding two decades, the FCC accepted bids for 99 licenses, two each in 48 geographic regions in the United States, plus one for New York, Los Angeles, and Washington, D.C., where one such license had already been granted without an auction. The auctions added more wireless providers throughout the country, greatly increasing competition not only in mobile telephony but also in broadband access.[25]

Federal policy makers were (and continue to be) most interested in the auctions as a way of raising money, either to reduce the deficit or to contribute toward funding federal programs. Economists who have advocated auctioning off spectrum have long highlighted this advantage of auctions over alternative means of allocating spectrum licenses. But economists have also placed equal, if not more, importance on the efficiency benefits of auctions, which allocate licenses to the highest bidder rather than to the first in line, the one with the best lawyer, or the best political connections. Being the highest bidder concentrates the mind toward making the most profitable use of the spectrum as quickly as possible. Successful bidders who find they cannot do this on their own have the ability, under an auction system, to resell their licenses to those who can make better use of the license. In contrast, those who gain licenses through administrative means are not likely to be as eager, creative, or efficient as those who actually have to pay market value for their use of spectrum.

Mobile telephony, and later smartphones, really took off in the United States after the PCS auctions in the 1990s. With multiple wireless carriers serving customers throughout the country, competition drove down prices and encouraged greater use. This has continued to happen even though the wireless industry has experienced significant consolidation, with the major players buying out local and regional carriers to assemble nationwide networks that permit calls from and to any destination in the country without handing them off to multiple carriers in between. In the process, wireless telephony and broadband have obliterated the once stark distinction between local and long-distance calls and data transmissions, and in the process have undermined the once seemingly impregnable local landline monopolies. Today, cell phones outnumber landline connections; this is even truer abroad, especially in developing countries, where getting a landline connection can take months or years.

Again, technologists and engineers deserve most of the credit for the wireless communications revolution. But their creations would not have been commercialized as rapidly or as efficiently without the wisdom of economists who urged the auction of the electromagnetic spectrum that helped make this revolution possible.

Economists and Price Cap Regulation

While economists were important behind the scenes in facilitating the introduction of more competition in telephony, they were front and center in developing an important innovation in the way all monopoly utilities, including telephone service, are regulated.[26]

Mindful of the tendency of profit-maximizing monopolies to limit output, which artificially raises prices to consumers, regulators for many decades adopted "rate of return" or "cost of service" regulation to limit prices or rates. Under this approach, regulators assure utilities they can earn a "reasonable" profit on investments in the physical capital required to deliver such services as electricity, water, or telephony, but not monopoly-level profits. Regulators define a "rate base" of total allowed physical investment, multiply it by a rate of return they believe fair, and then add the total permitted profit to the total allowable costs for providing service in a given area to generate target revenue. This figure can be divided by a projection of the total units of service provided— kilowatts of electricity or total number of basic phone lines for local telephony—to arrive at an approved rate or price of service. Alternatively, if regulators don't want to project future service levels, they can simply limit this year's rates to the prior year's costs, including an allowance for reasonable profit.

As briefly noted in the previous section, Leland Johnson and Harvey Averch highlighted an important weakness of this traditional method of limiting prices: It gives utilities an incentive to overinvest or to "gold plate" because the larger the rate base, the greater their profits.[27] In addition, although regulatory agencies can second-guess the necessity of some operating costs, as a practical matter, regulated firms are in a better position than their overseers to make these judgments. As a result, regulators are likely to allow the firms they regulate to operate with some inefficiencies included in their allowable rates.

Another drawback to rate-of-return regulation arises if the utility is in another business than the one for which rates are set, such as the equipment manufacturing business of the old AT&T. In these situations, regulators must render some judgment on the allocation of overhead costs that the regulated entity (telephone service) shares with its unregulated affiliate (equipment manufacturing). There are no hard and

fast rules about how this should be done. Under rate-of-return regulation, the regulated enterprise has clear incentives to allocate as much
cost as it can get away with to the regulated enterprise, which can be
recovered through permitted rates. In this way, the regulated monopoly can effectively subsidize the operations of its unregulated affiliate,
potentially leveraging monopoly power from the regulated market to
the market where the unregulated entity competes.[28]

Regulators traditionally had several ways of countering these tendencies, none ideal. One approach, as noted, is to carefully scrutinize
operating and fixed costs, which has its limits. Another approach, which
Elizabeth Bailey (highlighted in Chapter 9) documented in her PhD
thesis, is the byproduct of the regulatory process itself known as "regulatory lag."[29] Because regulated firms must seek approval for the price
they plan to charge in the future based on the costs and investments they
have made in the past, lags are an inherent part of the regulatory process.
These lags can also work to the regulators' advantage, since any unanticipated costs that the firms experience in a current period cannot be partially or fully recovered until a future period, assuming regulators permit
this to happen. This introduces some uncertainty into the process, which
should encourage the regulated firms to exercise some caution in incur-
ring expenses, a tendency that may offset any laxness toward cost control
induced by cost of service rate regulation.[30]

Even regulatory lags are not ideal for encouraging efficiency, however, because regulated firms always have an informational advantage
relative to their regulators, who then tend to defer to the firms on the
legitimacy of their expenses. Couple this with the gold-plating incentives for excessive investment built into regulation and you can understand why economists and regulators began to look for better ways to
encourage regulated firms to be more efficient.

The answer, beginning in the 1980s, came in the form of "incentive
regulation," a broad term that covers a range of devices for incentivizing
regulated firms to control costs. Perhaps the best known of these alternatives is "price cap" regulation, in which regulators limit the price of the
firm's service at or close to last year's costs, generally with adjustments
upward for inflation and downward for an assumed level of productivity improvement, typically based on industry-wide experience. Stephen
Littlechild, a British academic economist who also was a regulator

(like Alfred Kahn in the United States), was instrumental in developing this formula.[31] Price caps can be and often are reset every several years to establish a new base level, in light of recent historical experience. Research has shown that price cap regulation in telecommunications has encouraged productivity improvements.[32]

Price caps are not perfect, however, since they entail two very different sorts of potential problems. On the one hand, if they are too binding, they may induce the regulated firm to cut corners in serving customers in order to reduce costs and keep profits up. There is evidence that this has occurred to some degree among telecommunication firms in the United States.[33] Regulators can offset some tendencies for service-quality deterioration by including service-performance measures (such as outages, customer complaints, and so on) in setting the caps, as electricity regulators have done in the United Kingdom and in Massachusetts in this country.[34] On the other hand, if the caps are not sufficiently tight, they allow the regulated firm to earn higher profits—at the expense of consumers—than it would under a system of rate of return regulation.

For these reasons, two leading microeconomists who pioneered some of the best thinking about incentive regulation (among other topics), Jean-Jacques Laffont and Jean Tirole, suggested in the mid-1980s that regulators are best served by giving regulated utilities a menu of options, including not only price caps but also profit-sharing schemes that enable consumers and even employees to share in the additional profits that efficient regulated firms might achieve, or conversely share in the shortfalls that those firms may experience if they are not as efficient or productive as a specific price cap might imply.[35] In fact, as various researchers have noted, a version of profit sharing was used in the United Kingdom in the late nineteenth and early twentieth centuries in the regulation of manufactured gas, but was essentially ignored by U.S. electricity and telephone regulators in the early twentieth century, who adopted cost of service methods instead.[36]

As it has turned out, although some form of incentive regulation of utility prices is now widely used in United States and elsewhere around the world, few regulators have adopted the menu idea. Instead, utility regulators, those overseeing telecommunications firms in particular, prefer either caps with productivity adjustments or some version of the profit- or earnings-sharing idea promoted by Laffont and Tirole and others.[37] These alternatives seem to be superior to rate-of-return methods in balancing the needs of regulated firms to raise capital to support continued investment, on the one hand, and the welfare of consumers purchasing their services, on the other.[38]

Economists and Spectrum Allocation

From the days of Adam Smith in the late eighteenth century, economists were writing about and singing the praises of markets and prices for efficiently allocating resources. So if anything, it was a surprise that it took a couple of decades after the federal government began handing out spectrum licenses for the first economist to suggest that there was a better way: auctioning them. That economist was Ronald Coase, who also wrote a number of other path-breaking articles, for which he was awarded the Nobel Prize in 1991 (see following box).

Ronald Coase: The "English" Economist

In a social science where mathematic agility is increasingly prized, Ronald Coase was an amazing exception. He eschewed math in his published work and spoke to his readers in crystal-clear English.

Coase was born in Great Britain, earned his doctorate in economics at the University of London, and came to the United States after World War II. He taught, successively, at the Universities of Buffalo, Virginia, and Chicago.

Coase was one of those individuals who wrote sparingly, but when he did, some of the products were blockbusters. As one biography of him put it, in his long career—he died in 2013 at the age of 102—he published only "about a dozen" papers using little or no mathematics, or what he called "blackboard economics."[39] But two of those articles earned him the Nobel Prize in 1991.

(continued)

In the first of those papers, written in the late 1930s when he was 27, he wondered how capitalists could decry state ownership of firms in such socialist countries as Russia, when the U.S. economy hosted such large industrial giants (then) as General Motors and Ford. His answer came in a now famous article "The Nature of the Firm," in which he analogized firms to centrally planned economies with one important difference: Firms in capitalist economies are formed out of choice, and specifically out of the inspiration and hard work of their founder-entrepreneurs.[40] What determines the scale of a firm, Coase posited, is the relative benefits and costs of conducting transactions with people and suppliers inside the firm and thus outside of a market, compared with doing the same thing in a market setting at arm's length with third parties. Firms exist, then, because at least for the activities conducted inside them, it is more cost effective to transact within the firm than using markets.

Coase's second great article, written 23 years later in 1960, addresses the "Problem of Social Cost." The article provides a novel market-based solution to the problem of externalities, such as pollution which, up to that time, economists thought could only be corrected with government intervention—taxation or regulation—to correct a "market failure." Not so, Coase argued. If it was costless, or at least very inexpensive, for parties to bargain, it wouldn't matter which party, the polluter or pollution victim, had a property right because the cheapest solution from a societal perspective would be reached through bargaining by the parties. If the victims had the right not to suffer pollution, the polluter could compensate them. Conversely, if the polluter had the right to pollute, the victims could pay to make it stop. Either transaction would take place only if it was in the best interest of society as a whole.[41]

Coase had a famous debate with free-market legend Milton Friedman—who initially contested what has since been called the "Coase theorem"—at the home of Chicago economist Aaron Director, at which he persuaded all those attending of the correctness of his insight. In the real world, however, where polluters or creators of externalities may be relatively few in number, those affected are much more numerous. So the costs of organizing all those involved to engage in a Coasian "negotiation" can be prohibitively high. In this likely typical situation, most economists believe that some kind of government involvement is appropriate, provided the cost of "government failure" is not greater than the cost of "market failure."[42]

Of immediate relevance to this chapter, Coase was the first economist to make the case for auctioning scarce public goods, such as licenses to portions of the electromagnetic spectrum. He did this in 1959.[43] As three economists (including Nobel laureate Vernon Smith) have put it, Coase's proposal at the time was "mocked by communications policy experts, opposed by industry experts, and ridiculed by policy makers." Today auctions are the standard way the commission allocates spectrum. Since Congress adopted the idea in 1993 and through 2010, the FCC had held 73 auctions, selling over 27,000 licenses, and generating over $50 billion for the U.S. Treasury.[44]

As noted in the box, Coase suggested spectrum auctions in 1959. It took Congress more than three decades to adopt the idea. Economists played significant roles both in designing the auctions, and also helping some of the companies bidding in them.

Auctioning licenses to transmit and carry wireless voice and data signals in each of almost 50 geographic markets, which policy makers ultimately wanted to link together in nationwide networks, is a lot more complicated than auctioning a single piece of art or other scarce collectible. It is more expensive and less helpful to consumers if ownership of the licenses is fragmented among many parties, each having to interconnect with the other. At the same time, policy makers did not want the mobile telephony market to be dominated by just one or two carriers; they wanted vigorous competition among several of them, not just to better serve consumers but also to maximize the revenue earned by the government in selling the licenses.

Various economists had ideas for how the commission could best achieve these apparently conflicting objectives, but none were as influential as Paul Milgrom (see following box), his colleague Robert Wilson, and longtime senior economic advisor at the FCC Evan Kwerel, who was put in charge of auction design by the commission.

The key mechanism these economists designed was the *simultaneous auction* that required bidders to remain active in every round of bidding in order to be eligible to receive *any* licenses at the end. The auction ends when no more new bids in any market are submitted.

Paul Milgrom: Auction Designer

While Ronald Coase deserves the credit for coming up with the idea for auctioning spectrum, Paul Milgrom deserves most of the credit for designing the auctions themselves, along with his thesis adviser Robert Wilson.[45]

The difference between the concept and implementation also is reflected in the very different kind of research that Coase and Milgrom published. Whereas Coase was a man of words, Milgrom's work is highly mathematical, but also highly useful.

After earning his undergraduate degree in mathematics from the University of Michigan, Milgrom spent several years applying his education as an actuary, before returning to the academy to earn his master's degree in statistics and Stanford, where he also gained his PhD in business.

Milgrom since has taught at three universities: Northwestern, Yale, and Stanford, where he has spent most of his professional career, combining his research and interest in auctions with game theory. His work in designing auctions has been applied in the United States and other countries not only in telecommunications, but also in electricity and natural gas. Milgrom has also advised various firms on auction strategy and various public bodies, in addition to the FCC, in the United States and other countries.

The procedure thus described differs from a market-by-market auction, which allows individual bidders to pick off certain markets with high bids, but gives no incentive to any of them to bid in other markets.

As of this writing, in 2014, the FCC is preparing to auction by mid-2015 additional low-frequency spectrum (below one gigahertz) for wireless purposes, especially for broadband communications. Designing these auctions has been an unusual challenge, but once this latest round of auctions is complete, it should significantly expand wireless broadband capacity and speeds.

Unlike earlier auctions where the FCC marked off a portion of the spectrum that was not previously being used or was easily reallocated away from other purposes, most of the spectrum being auctioned this time has been held by television broadcasters that must be induced to give it up (much of the rest is held by the Departments of Commerce and Defense, which have to release it for commercial purposes). As a result, the commission must approach the 2015 auctions in two steps: first, by holding a "reverse auction," where broadcasters bid the minimum price they are willing accept for their licensed spectrum, which determines how much revenue the FCC has to share with the broadcasters. Only with sufficient participation by the broadcasters will the FCC be in a position to proceed to the second stage of the auction, selling the spectrum given up to wireless broadband providers.

Another complication of the purely private sector incentive auction is whether, or to what extent, the commission is going to allow the two largest mobile providers, AT&T and Verizon, to participate in the second stage of the auction. Not surprisingly, smaller competitors do not want the commission to allow these two mobile giants into the auction, or at least to place tight limits on the fraction of the population they could serve with new licenses. The two large carriers, in contrast, argue that the scale economies of serving a nationwide market, coupled with the additional revenue that their active bidding will most likely generate for the federal government, are two strong reasons why they should be allowed to bid without restrictions. In addition, even if they won most or all of the auctioned low-frequency spectrum, existing licensees of low-frequency spectrum would still be able to compete without any significant impairment, so competition in mobile broadband would continue to be healthy.[46]

At this writing, it is not clear whether the FCC will restrict any firm from bidding. One factor in its decision will be the extent to which it wants to maximize auction revenue for the government. Depriving or limiting AT&T and Verizon from bidding would reduce federal revenue, both for deficit reduction and for funding the build out of a better first responder network that was authorized in the 2012 legislation that instructed the commission to proceed with the latest auctions.

Economists will play an important role in these auctions, as they have before. Within the FCC, economists helped design both stages of the auction. Outside the FCC, economists surely will assist various bidders to navigate their way through the auctions. It is difficult to think of a government activity where economists have been such an important part of the process, from conception to implementation.

The Bottom Line

It can be easy to forget or ignore the role of economists in a technology-intensive industry such as telecommunications, where engineers and technologists rule the roost. Nonetheless, all firms in any industry must abide by the rules of the road set by policy makers: legislators, regulators, and judges. Those actors, in turn, are often highly influenced by the ideas of economists. This could not be more evident than in the telecommunications industry.

For a long time, monopoly and scarcity were the watchwords in telecoms. AT&T dominated telephone service, locally and throughout the nation. The federal government, as steward for the electromagnetic spectrum, handled the spectrum's scarcity by overseeing an administrative system of licensing that also constrained competition. Economists, aided by technological advances, helped persuade policy makers to undo monopolies where possible, so when economies of scale still required monopoly firms, the government could regulate them more effectively and respond to the scarcity of spectrum in nontraditional ways.

Economists played a critical role in designing and implementing the legal action that ultimately unwound AT&T's control over not just telephone service, but also the equipment used to provide it. In doing so, economists helped pave the way for the investments in the physical infrastructure that later became the backbone of one of the great technologies and business platforms of the modern era, the Internet.

Local telephony and other utility services are still regulated at the state level and economists have had important impacts here, too, helping to shift price regulation away from reimbursing costs, guaranteeing a reasonable profit on investments in physical plants and equipment, and toward regulatory systems that provide incentives for cost control. Although not perfect (no system of price regulation can be), incentive-based approaches are generally regarded to serve the interests of consumers better than the prior rate-of-return systems they replaced.

Last but not least, economists have been prime movers behind the idea that spectrum for mobile communications should be auctioned, and how those auctions are structured. In addition, economists have been essential advisers to the firms participating in the auctions.

In short, it is no overstatement to claim that the modern Internet-based business landscape of today owes much of its shape, if not existence, to the behind-the-scenes thoughts and research of numerous economists. Keynes' aphorism about "practical men" being slaves to some defunct (and mostly still very much alive) economists could not be better validated than in the telecommunications industry and the many firms that have been built on its platforms.

Notes

1. Quotation attributed to George Dyson in James Fallows, "The 50 Greatest Breakthroughs since the Wheel," *The Atlantic*, September 2013, 56–68. This section also draws on a similar history of telecommunications in Robert E. Litan and Hal J. Singer, *The Need for Speed: A New Framework for Telecommunications Policy for the 21st Century* (Washington, DC: Brookings Institution Press, 2013).

2. This box draws on www.darvill.clara.net/emag/.

3. Peter Temin with Louis Galambos, *The Fall of the Bell System* (Cambridge, United Kingdom: Cambridge University Press, 1987), 11. For an excellent journalistic account of the breakup of AT&T, see Steve Coll, *The Deal of the Century* (New York: Atheneum, 1986).

4. Temin, *Fall of the Bell System*, 15.

5. Fred Kahn outlined a more nuanced and uncertain view of whether Western Electric's equipment manufacturing activities had the characteristics of natural monopoly. Alfred E. Kahn, *The Economics of Regulation: Principles and Institutions, Volume II* (Cambridge, MA: MIT Press, 1995), 297–305.

6. A more detailed treatment of the history briefly summarized here can be found in Jonathan Nuechterlein and Philip J. Weiser, *Digital Crossroads: American Telecommunications Policy in the Internet Age* (Cambridge, MA: MIT Press, 2007), 57–64.

7. Ibid., 62.

8. Temin, *Fall of the Bell System*, 34–40.

9. Richard A. Posner, "The Decline and Fall of AT&T: A Personal Recollection," *Federal Communications Law Journal* 61, no. 1 (2008): 11–19.

10. Ibid., 12.

11. Ibid.

12. Interview of Donald Baker, December 3, 2013, and Remarks of Donald I. Baker, Deputy Assistant Attorney General, Antitrust Division, Department of Justice, before the Federal Communications Bar Association, at the Army–Navy Town Club, Washington, DC, January 17, 1975.

13. Posner, "The Decline and Fall of AT&T," 14–15.

14. Correspondence with George Hay, December 4, 2013, and interview of Bob Reynolds, December 6, 2013.

15. Communication with Bruce Owen, December 8, 2013.

16. Based on interview of Richard Levine (director of Policy and Planning at the Division during Baxter's tenure), December 6, 2013.

17. Coll, *Deal of the Century*, 211–229.

18. Ibid., 172–199.

19. This accounting of economists during the trial, leading up to settlement, is based on communications with Owen during November 2013 and through my interview with Bob Reynolds, December 6, 2013.

20. The story about AT&T delaying its fiber optic rollout in the absence of competition was also confirmed in communications with Richard Levine, December 9, 2013.

21. Ibid.

22. Quoted in Michael J. Maubossin, *The Success Equation: Untangling Skill and Luck in Business, Sports, and Investing* (Cambridge, MA: Harvard Business School Press, 2012). See also www.fastcompany.com/3002729/facts-luck.

23. Based on communication with Richard Levine, December 6, 2013.

24. See generally, Litan and Singer, *Need for Speed*, 2–3.

25. Robert J. Weber, "Making More from Less: Strategic Demand Reduction in the FCC Spectrum Auctions," www.kellogg.northwestern.edu/faculty/weber/papers/pcs_auc.htm.

26. I am especially indebted to Roger Noll, who provided invaluable assistance to me in developing this section on incentive regulation.

27. Harvey Averch and Leland Johnson, "Behavior of the Firm Under Regulatory Constraint," *American Economic Review* (December 1962): 1052–1069.

28. Nuechterlein and Weiser, *Digital Crossroads*, 51.

29. A version of Bailey's argument was published in Elizabeth E. Bailey and Roger D. Coleman, "The Effect of Lagged Regulation in an Averch-Johnson Model," *Bell Journal of Economics and Management* 2, no. 1 (Spring 1971): 278–292.

30. This notion was explored by Paul Joskow, one of the leading experts on regulatory economics for decades while at MIT, and currently president of the Alfred P. Sloan Foundation. See Paul L. Joskow, "Inflation and Environmental Concern: Change in the Process of Public Utility Price Regulation," *Journal of Law and Economics* 17 (1974): 291–327.

31. M. E. Beesley and S. C. Littlechild, "The Regulation of Privatized Monopolies in the United Kingdom," *The RAND Journal of Economics* 20, no. 3 (Autumn 1989): 454–472.

32. Daigyo Seo and Jonghyup Shin, "The Impact of Incentive Regulation on Productivity in the US Telecommunications Industry: A Stochastic Frontier Approach," *Information Economics and Policy* 23, no. 1 (March 2011): 3–11.

33. Ai Chunrung and Salvador Martinez, "Incentive Regulation and Telecommunications Service Quality," *Journal of Regulatory Economics* 26, no. 3 (2004): 263–285.

34. See Paul L. Joskow, "Incentive Regulation in Theory and Practice: Electricity Distribution and Transmission Networks," January 21, 2006, unpublished manuscript, 26–31, http://economics.mit.edu/files/1181. See also Paul L. Joskow, "Incentive Regulation and its Application to Electricity Networks," *Review of Network Economics* 7, no. 4 (December 2008): 547–560. These essays provide an extensive guide to the academic literature on incentive regulation.

35. Jean Jacques Laffont and Jean Tirole, "Using Cost Observations to Regulate Firms," *Journal of Political Economy* 94, no. 3 (1986): 614–641.

36. Joskow, "Incentive Regulation in Theory and Practice," 18–19.

37. Ibid., 16. See also Donald J. Kridel, "The Effects of Incentive Regulation in the Telecommunications Industry: A Survey," *Journal of Regulatory Economics* 9 (1996): 269–306.

38. Nuechterlein and Weiser, *Digital Crossroads*, 51–52.

39. "Ronald Coase" in *The Concise Encyclopedia of Economics*, at www.econlib.org/library/Enc/bios/Coase.html. This profile draws heavily on this essay.

40. Ronald Coase, "The Nature of the Firm," *Economica* 4 (November 1937): 386–405.

41. Ronald Coase, "The Problem of Social Cost," *Journal of Law and Economics* 3 (October 1960): 1–44.

42. Recounted by another Nobel laureate, George Stigler, *Memoirs of an Unregulated Economist* (New York: Basic Books, 1988), 76.

43. Ronald Coase, "The Federal Communications Commission," *Journal of Law and Economics* 2 (October 1959): 1–40.

44. Thomas W. Hazlett, David Porter, and Vernon L. Smith, "Markets, Firms and Property Rights: A Celebration of the Research of Ronald Coase," *George Mason Law & Economics Research Paper No. 10–18*, April 1, 2010 (quote in the abstract).

45. This profile draws on www.gsb.stanford.edu/users/milgrom.

46. David Balto and Hal Singer, *The FCC's Incentive Auction: Getting Spectrum Policy Right* (Washington, DC: Progressive Policy Institute, 2013).

Chapter 12

Economists, Financial Policy, and Mostly Good Finance

I now come to what is likely to be one of the more controversial chapters in the book, the one dealing with economists and financial policy. Given the many errors in policy in this realm that led to the financial crisis, it is only natural to ask whether economists have had any useful impact on financial policy and, in turn, in promoting business activity in finance that has contributed to the social good, or whether the verdict is all negative.

I take a generally positive view in this chapter, focusing on some key financial policy decisions where I believe economists have been influential and where the business implications have been significant. Where policy mistakes have occurred, mainly in connection with the financial crisis, I do not believe it is fair to blame the economists (except for generally failing to see the crisis coming).

This chapter differs from Chapter 8, which focused on business applications in finance stemming directly from economists' ideas. Here we concentrate on financial policy as an intermediate condition, or platform, to use the metaphor of the earlier chapters in this section, and examine how those policy decisions affected the business landscape.

There are two broad themes to the policies that most economists advocate for financial firms. Economists generally support more competition, and thus the removal of artificial barriers to entry (such as the Glass–Steagall Act, which once separated investment from commercial banking) or constraints on price competition. More competition benefits efficient firms and encourages innovative firms to enter markets that were previously closed to them.

At the same time, however, most economists have not opposed, but rather have strongly supported, regulation aimed at ensuring that financial firms have sufficient capital, or shareholders' money at risk, to discourage excessive risk-taking. Capital is also important for absorbing losses from loans or investments that turn sour, or losses due to other factors, such as movements of interest rates. Regulators set and enforce capital "standards"—essentially ratios of capital to assets—to help ensure both the stability of financial firms and the economy. As I discuss later in this chapter, regulators' failure to carry out this essential function both contributed to the financial crisis of 2007–2008 and goes a long way toward explaining why it was so severe.

Finally, one bit of disclosure at the outset: I have spent much of my professional life researching and writing about financial policy and, as you will see, in some cases I was directly involved in policy decisions or in group efforts to affect the outcomes of those decisions. Accordingly, I have a substantial record on these matters that anyone can discover through any Internet search engine, so it should not surprise you that I took a special interest in writing this chapter. If I have any bias toward the subject it is reflected in the economists' consensus just described: to favor competition, but also to endorse effective regulation of capital supporting the assets of financial institutions, banks especially.

Economists and Competition in Brokerage Commissions

Economists and antitrust lawyers agree on at least one thing: that competitors should not be allowed to fix prices. Yet until 1975, the federal government, specifically the Securities and Exchange Commission (SEC), sanctioned the fixing of commissions that stock brokers charged their investor clients. The securities industry had argued up to that point that fixed brokerage commissions—a system dating from the founding of the once broker-owned New York Stock Exchange (NYSE)—were necessary to enable brokers to earn a reasonable profit. That argument is hardly surprising; it's the motivation behind all price fixing.

In retrospect, what is surprising is that it took almost two centuries for this practice to be seriously questioned by federal policy makers.[1] In 1971, the SEC ended fixed commissions on large institutional trades, those over $500,000, and lowered that threshold to $300,000 the following year. It took the Commission three more years (on May 1, 1975) to scrap the fixed-commission system altogether. The SEC hurried to beat Congress to the punch, as legislation ending fixed commissions was then being seriously considered.

Ironically, the NYSE itself unwittingly got the ball rolling that ended fixed commissions by asking the SEC in 1968 for permission to raise its minimum commission schedule.[2] That petition came to the attention of the Antitrust Division of the Justice Department, and to Donald Baker, in particular. Baker, who I mentioned in the last chapter, then was the head of the division's regulatory unit, and like any good antitrust enforcement official, he was offended by not only the brokers' long-standing practice of setting minimum commissions, but by the SEC's approval of the practice. Baker was the point person at the division in asking the SEC for hearings not only on the NYSE's specific request, but on the underlying issue of why a fixed commission system was necessary or appropriate at all.

Baker and the Division went farther. They asked an all-star line-up of leading economists at the time—Paul Samuelson of MIT, William Baumol (then of Princeton), Henry Wallich (then of Yale and later a governor of the Federal Reserve Board), and Harold Demsetz of UCLA—to testify before the SEC. All agreed to do so, and not surprisingly, all predictably said there was no justification for the fixed commission system. The division subsequently submitted a brief to the SEC citing their testimony and urging the commission to reject the NYSE's request and simply abandon fixed commissions.[3]

It is difficult to know how much influence the economists' testimony had on the SEC's decisions to unwind fixed commissions, but the urgings of such a distinguished group of economists certainly didn't hurt. It is likely that the commission was also influenced by the behavior of large institutional investors, who were increasingly deserting the NYSE to execute their trades off exchanges, or over-the-counter (through telephone calls between brokers), to avoid paying the fixed commissions.

When the commission finally moved on May Day in 1975 to end the system, the easily predictable good things followed. Charles Schwab was the first of many discount brokers to enter the securities brokerage business, offering to execute trades at much lower rates than full-service brokers. With unrestricted competition and new entry, commissions have dropped like a stone, by roughly 80 percent since 1978.[4]

In sum, the elimination of fixed commissions was a boon for innovative brokerages and for investors. Well-established, full-service brokers lost revenue and profits in the process, but this is money they never should have had if the basic principles of market economics had been applied to the securities brokerage business from the outset.

Economists as Detectives: Accelerating Automated Trading

There are fundamentally two types of markets for securities (I'll restrict my attention for convenience to stocks): broker markets and dealer markets. In broker markets, exemplified by the old New York Stock Exchange or the Big Board (which merged with Euronext in 2007 and then was bought out by the Intercontinental Exchange, or ICE, in 2013), a stockbroker acts as the investor's agent and is obligated to get the best price for buying or selling stock on behalf of the investor. In the days before trading was automated—where offers to buy and sell are matched and executed by computers—floor brokers (acting for the brokers who received the original customer order) would offer to sell or bid to buy stocks on the floor of exchanges. A specialist broker-member would act as the auctioneer and in normal conditions would make markets, using his (rarely were there women) capital to buy and sell (if others wouldn't) the limited number of stocks for which he was responsible.

Some readers may be old enough to remember the chaotic scenes of this open-outcry system from the NYSE on the nightly news. Today, futures contracts for commodities are sold in such a fashion, but the floor of the old NYSE now handles only a small minority of the overall trading volume on that exchange since most trading is now completely electronic. It turns out that economists had something to do with how things got to be this way. That story is best understood if I continue reviewing some of the basics of stock trading first.

In dealer markets, such as NASDAQ, brokers channel orders to buy and sell stocks to market makers or dealers who hold positions in the stocks that investors are interested in. The dealers buy and sell from each other, earning profits on the spread, or the difference between the prices that dealers are willing to pay for a stock (the bid) and what they are willing to sell it for (the ask). Investors really bear the cost of the spread, in addition to any commissions they pay to their brokers (who either may be dealers themselves or who route customer orders to dealers).

NASDAQ is actually quite young relative to the Big Board, having been formed in 1971 to automate orders and to provide a computer-based method for disseminating stock quotes. NASDAQ (since merged with OMX) was a dealer market at the outset and remains that way.

The NASDAQ market was also the subject of major private and public antitrust investigations and litigations in the mid-1990s; they were launched on the basis of a single economic study published in an academic journal. I played a small role in the public litigation when, as deputy assistant attorney general in the Antitrust Division, I briefly oversaw the division's investigation of the matter (before moving on to another job in government). Nonetheless, what happened in this investigation during and after the time I was at the division remains nothing short of amazing, at least to me, and I want to try to share that excitement with you because it powerfully demonstrates how economists can influence policy and business, especially in unexpected ways.

It all started with the publication of a study, in March 1994, by two young assistant finance professors, William Christie of Vanderbilt and Paul Schultz of Ohio State. The article reported the spreads on the 100 most frequently traded stocks in 1991 on the NASDAQ system, such as Apple, Dell, Intel, and Microsoft.[5] What they found was a surprise to say the least: The bid to ask spreads on these stocks were almost universally quoted in even eighths, or a difference of 25 cents per share. This contrasted with the same-sized sample of stocks of similar prices and market capitalizations on the NYSE and American Stock Exchange, in which the spreads were frequently quoted using the full spectrum of eighths, with spreads as small as 12.5 cents. The authors concluded that this "surprising result"—the even-eighth quote pattern on NASDAQ—reflected "an implicit agreement among market makers to avoid using odd-eighths . . ."[6]

Those words *implicit agreement* were like a bomb going off in a room of plaintiffs' antitrust lawyers, and shortly after the article became known, a class action private antitrust lawsuit alleging price fixing was filed against multiple market makers on NASDAQ. Shortly thereafter, the attorneys then came to the Antitrust Division with the article, specifically to see me and the career staff, urging us to mount a government investigation. (This frequently happens when private lawsuits are filed; the attorneys want the division to do a lot of their homework for them.)

I must admit that when I was told that the consistency of the even-eighths quotes on many stocks that had more than a dozen market makers was evidence of price collusion, I was a bit skeptical. How could so many individuals actually fix the spreads? There were no smoking-gun meetings in hotel rooms where price fixing ordinarily takes place. But the circumstantial evidence of the Christie–Schultz paper was extremely powerful. The two economists showed that as a statistical matter it was extremely unlikely the even-eighths spread pattern happened by chance. The division decided to look into the matter more formally and thus opened an official investigation.

What the lawyers found was nothing short of astonishing. Exchanges like NASDAQ were required by law to maintain tape recordings of the conversations of market makers, which the division's lawyers obtained through the discovery process that is part of any public or private litigation. The NASDAQ dealers' conversations revealed a clear and consistent pattern of intimidation of and threatened retribution against market makers who dared to quote a price on any of the 100 stocks that differed from the even-eighths spread (the conversations also were laced with profanity, which was a bit shocking, but then we realized that's just the way traders talk). Those transcripts helped lead to a consent decree in 1976 between the Justice Department and 24 securities firms that were subject to the investigation. The decree banned the intimidation and set up strict compliance mechanisms to prevent reoccurrences. Two years later a broader set of 37 securities firms settled the private class action lawsuit for $1 billion.[7] In addition to the settlement, investors immediately began saving money as soon as the Christie and Schultz study was announced in 1994: Average spreads on highly traded stocks fell in half, from an average of 30 cents per trade to 15 cents.[8]

As important as these legal and immediate marketplace outcomes were, the results of a parallel investigation by the Securities and Exchange Commission (in cooperation with the Justice Department) had a much greater long-term impact on the structure of securities markets. In addition to levying fines against the dealers, the SEC proposed and then implemented major changes in its order handling rules for stocks traded on NASDAQ. Of special importance, the SEC required NASDAQ dealers to publicly display investor limit orders (buy orders specifying a price limit above which a purchase would not be made, or sell orders below which a sale would not be completed) between 100 and 10,000 shares (or most shares traded on NASDAQ). In addition, dealers had to notify the public of the best available prices at which they could buy and sell stocks.

The impact of these directives was revolutionary. Opening the order book to public scrutiny gave investors, for the first time, the array of bids and asks for various stocks—simply by clicking on the web pages of NASDAQ and various electronic communications networks (ECNs), which enable investors to complete trades through the network's computer rather than through an exchange. The new openness not only helped investors decide how to frame their offers, but it accelerated the completion of trades on ECNs, which found it easier to match crossing orders (bids and asks at identical prices). With trading migrating to ECNs, the importance of dealers and even brokers began to decline, while new completely automated exchanges that executed trades through computers, such as BATS and Direct Edge, arose to take market share away from the Big Board and even from NASDAQ. In late 2005, the once unthinkable happened: The trader-members of the NYSE voted to enable the Big Board to become a publicly held corporation, which it did in 2006. This step eventually paved the way for the NYSE to be taken over by ICE, another relative upstart.

The automation of trading also led to its fragmentation, which was encouraged by the decimalization of stock prices—the quotation of prices in pennies rather than in fractions—that the SEC mandated in late 2000 and early 2001 as a way of reducing spreads. At smaller tick sizes, there is less volume at each price, which encourages institutional investors with large volume orders to look to multiple alternative trading venues to complete trades as a way of minimizing the impact of their orders on prices.[9]

With the NYSE no longer dominant, trading now takes place in many public exchanges, as well as in *dark pools*—private venues owned and operated by large securities firms or other entities where offers are not publicly displayed.[10] Some critics believe the fragmentation of trading reduces liquidity at any single venue and thus raises trading costs for investors. Others maintain that more competition among trading venues has led to more innovation in trading technologies, despite a number of highly publicized glitches in the public exchanges (for example, the halting of trading when Facebook went public or the ironic breakdown of BATS, one of the leading electronic exchanges, when it tried to go public itself, both in 2012).

The automation of trading, in turn, led to two other phenomena: algorithmic and high-frequency trading. Algorithmic trading occurs when preprogrammed computers, using various market-based signals, automatically enter orders without human assistance. A special, controversial type of algo trading is high-frequency trading, the use of computers to enter rapid-fire buy and sell orders, communicated in milliseconds, thereby enabling the operators of these computers to get in the front of the line before other orders. To make this happen, high-frequency traders (HFTs) have persuaded exchanges, which have been eager for the volume and fees such rapid trading generates, to permit computers owned by high-frequency traders to be co-located with the exchange's own computers. Some HFTs also have invested hundreds of millions of dollars to lay fiber optic cables that can communicate trade orders from distant locations essentially at the speed of light to assure trade priority. In recent years, HFTs have accounted for over half of all trading volume in U.S. equities.[11]

The growth of HFTs has become a hot debate topic. Critics assert that HFTs amplify fluctuations in the market and, like runaway trains, can sometimes trigger violent, especially downward, movements in stock prices. The flash crash of May 2010—when some stock prices dropped to pennies because of massive sell orders with no one to buy—has been blamed on HFTs. In addition, some critics attack the co-location of HFT facilities with those of the exchanges as unfair to less well-heeled investors. The publication in early 2014 of Michael Lewis's latest best-seller, *Flash Boys*, amplifies these arguments for a wide audience.[12]

Defenders of HFTs counter with several arguments. One is that the high volumes of rapid-fire trades add liquidity to the market under normal market conditions and thus reduce spreads, which benefits individual and institutional investors alike. Unusual episodes like a flash crash can be addressed by short-term circuit breakers in which no trading is allowed—so that orders can fill up the order book like water in a sink—or even slowing it down with proposals like a securities transaction tax. As for the unfairness of colocation, HFT defenders note that NYSE members in the old days and current commodities floor traders who trade for their account had or have informational advantages by virtue of their locations. In an electronic world, locational advantages have simply moved to different players.

The debates over HFT, algo trading, and the implications of auto-mated trading for market structure will surely continue, and I doubt whether their resolution (if that ever happens) will be driven by a con-sensus among economists on these subjects, which I do not believe yet exists. The major point I would like readers to take away from this section is to realize how a seemingly obscure academic economic study led to powerful, unintended, and I believe largely desirable outcomes. Stock trading surely was going to be automated, but the decision to make orders public was clearly accelerated as a result of the govern-ment's investigation of collusion among NASDAQ's market makers. The resolution of the investigation armed investors with information they didn't have before, while making it far easier for the upstart ECNs to challenge the established exchanges. In addition, the mere announce-ment of the investigation, followed by the Justice Department's consent decree, saved investors billions of dollars in trading costs over the years. Economists had much to do with all these outcomes.

As for the SEC, it has been studying what, if anything, to do about the change in structure in trading markets since at least 2010.[13] In early

June 2014, the SEC unveiled a sweeping set of regulatory proposals and initiatives to regulate HFT. Among the various proposals, HFTs would have to register with the Commission as broker-dealers, which would subject them to reporting requirements and potentially much greater regulatory scrutiny. The initiatives also instructed the SEC staff to develop proposals for preventing HFTs from contributing to market instability. (Good luck.)

Economists and the Financial Crisis

Bank-related financial crises are not a new phenomenon, in either the United States or in other countries.[14] Roughly one-third of this country's banks failed during the Great Depression.[15] In the 1980s, virtually all the nation's largest banks would have probably been insolvent if the banks' loans to the governments of less-developed countries (LDCs) been recorded at depressed but realistic market values, rather than at their face values. During the same decade, well over 1,000 of the country's savings and loan institutions collapsed, initially because of high funding costs at the beginning of the decade (when interest rates were well into double digits) and later because of disastrous lending and, in some cases, fraud. Later in the 1980s and into early 1990s, banks also failed at their highest rates up to that time since the Depression, largely because of excessive commercial real estate lending, especially in the Northeast.

The financial crisis of 2007–2008 was as bad for the banking system as the Great Depression, far worse than the banking and S&L crises of the late 1980s and early 1990s. This was not because of the numbers of banks that toppled—roughly 500 over the five years from 2008 to 2012—but because of the size of some of the banks that collapsed or came close to failure, and the fact that lending between banks essentially ground to a halt in September 2008.[16] If banks wouldn't lend to each other, how could they be expected to lend to anyone else? That question drove Treasury Secretary Henry "Hank" Paulson and Federal Reserve Chairman Ben Bernanke to do what before that crisis would have been unthinkable, especially by a Republican administration committed to free markets: Go to Congress and ask for the unprecedented sum of $700 billion to rescue the banking system. Paulson and Bernanke took this huge step because they believed without it the economy faced a real prospect of experiencing another Great Depression.

I am not writing to defend the wisdom of what those two public servants did, along with Congress, and both Presidents Bush and Obama (although I believe that Paulson, Bernanke, and later Treasury Secretary Geithner will be praised by historians for their courage). I focus instead on what, if anything, economists had to do with the crisis. Beyond not seeing it coming (with a few notable exceptions), are they to blame in any way? And did they contribute anything good on the financial policy front in the years before the crisis for which they deserve some credit?

I ask these questions because they are relevant to the main objective of this book, which focuses on the impact of economic ideas on business. While financial policy, whether recommended by economists or not, certainly has a clear impact on the firms or markets directly affected by it, such as banks, securities markets, and nonbank financial institutions, the policies affecting finance also indirectly have a major impact on the entire economy. Pick your metaphor: The banking system either represents the plumbing of the economy, or its circulatory system; but each one underscores the importance of a sound banking and financial system. Without confidence in finance, firms don't invest, consumers don't buy, and the economy collapses. So issues relating to banking crises, and how policy has reacted to and tried to prevent them, could not be more important to every business, large or small.

How Did the Crisis Happen?
A Quick and Easy Guide

To answer the questions I just posed, it is first important to realize what got us into the financial mess. I'm not going to write a tome on this matter, since there are so many excellent analyses and accounts already published (and surely more to come). I have several favorites, as of this writing, in case you're looking for thoughtful, interesting accounts: Alan Blinder's *After the Music Stopped*, Sheila Bair's *Bull by the Horns*, Gillian Tett's *Fool's Gold*, and Michael Lewis's very popular classic,

The Big Short.[17] The most serious and comprehensive economic treatment of the crisis is Blinder's (see following box). If you want to read the official version of why the crisis happened, then pick up the report of the national commission created by Congress to study the causes of the crisis.[18]

Alan Blinder: A Gifted Economist Who Can Really Write

Many of the economists I feature in this book write well, in addition to having first-rate technical chops. Alan Blinder, widely recognized as one of the world's leading economists, is at the top of the list on both these scores.

Blinder is a Brooklyn native, sounds like one, and is proud of it. He went to Princeton, followed with a master's in economics at the London School of Economics, then earned his PhD at MIT. From there, he has spent most of his academic life at Princeton, writing about a broad range of subjects—monetary and fiscal policy, income distribution, the theory of price-setting, the art and science of central banking, and, most recently, financial regulation since the crisis. He is coauthor (with William Baumol) of a leading text on introductory economics, and has coauthored papers with former Federal Reserve Chairman Ben Bernanke (who also spent most of his academic life at Princeton and, at this writing, is a Distinguished Scholar at the Brookings Institution). Blinder's recent book on the financial crisis, the highly readable *After the Music Stopped*, was named by the *New York Times* as one of the 10 best books of 2013 (over all subjects, fiction and nonfiction).

Blinder's talents have been put to good use in numerous influential policy positions. He was one of the first staff members that Alice Rivlin hired to work at the Congressional Budget Office. Upon President Clinton's election he was appointed a member of the Council of Economic Advisers, and went from there to be vice-chairman of the Federal Reserve Board.

> Blinder's great ability to explain complicated economics concepts in plain English—sometimes through the eyes of his Uncle Harry—has been recognized by the *Wall Street Journal*, where he has for years been the regular Democratic economist op-ed writer. He also appears frequently on television.
>
> Blinder has a practical business side to him, too. He cofounded both the Promontory Financial Group (a consulting company) and the Promontory Interfinancial Network (a financial services company) with former Comptroller of the Currency Eugene Ludwig. He remains active in the latter, as the firm's vice chairman. Blinder is the highly unusual economist who has blended academic life, government service, and entrepreneurship into a remarkably successful career. Oh, and one more thing: Alan is one of the nicest, humblest individuals you will meet (not always a trait of some superstar economists, I unfortunately must admit), and always available to provide advice and counsel to others.

If you read all these and other books on the subject, you deserve a medal; but you're also likely to come away with your head swimming about all of the causes. In fact, Congress already had that mind-set, not only in creating the national commission but also in enacting the Dodd–Frank financial reform act to prevent future financial crises, or at least mitigate their severity. The commission was directed to study and report on almost 20 causes of the crisis. Meanwhile, Dodd–Frank became long (by some measures over 1,000 pages) and complex because multiple provisions were necessary to address the multiple causes (later identified in the commission's report but well understood at the time Dodd–Frank was enacted). I won't discuss the merits or drawbacks of the Act itself, a subject which also has a large and growing literature, although readers deserve to know where I stand on it: I think the Act was and remains necessary and that its detriments have been overstated, but the rules implementing the Act have turned out to be excessively complex.[19]

Good economic theorists, like other social and physical scientists, are taught to apply "Occam's Razor" (named after William of

Ockham of the fourteenth century) when developing their theories: Simpler explanations of phenomena are better than those that are more complicated. In that spirit, I believe the underlying causes of the financial crisis can be reduced to two: (1) far too much subprime mortgage lending (loans to borrowers posing well-above-average risks of default) by banks and nonbank lenders and (2) excessive leverage by banks and certain nonbanks (securities firms and one large insurer, AIG) that greatly magnified the losses to financial institutions and the economy when subprime mortgages turned sour.

Of course, it was more complicated than this, because various subfactors contributed to each of these two main causes. Subprime lending was facilitated by the packaging of such loans into securities, the massive failure of the ratings agencies to rate them properly, and excessive purchases of these securities by the two government-sponsored housing entities, Fannie Mae and Freddie Mac (which were created to buy or guarantee mortgages originated by primary lenders), and by excessive bank lending to nonbank lenders that handed out most of the subprime loans.

Excessive leverage, meanwhile, meant that too many banks and two of the largest securities firms—Goldman Sachs and Morgan Stanley— had very thin layers of shareholder money to absorb the losses of the subprime loans or securities backed by those loans when borrowers couldn't make their payments. By wiping out much or all of shareholders' stakes in too many of the largest banks and securities firms, the loss of $1 trillion or so in subprime loans thus almost brought down the entire financial system. Subprime losses were aggravated by the fact that the largest banks and securities firms were funded by very short-term liabilities that were not backed by federal deposit insurance—large, uninsured deposits in the case of the banks and overnight repurchase agreements or borrowing secured by Treasury bills, in the case of the securities firms—so when the financial institutions began to question each other's solvency (because their own was at risk), few or none were willing to lend to each other. That's how the financial system came close to crashing after Lehman, AIG, and Fannie Mae/Freddie Mac all failed in September 2008, and why even Republican leaders at the Treasury and the Fed, and Republican President George W. Bush, had to go hat in hand to Congress and ask for a massive government bailout to keep the financial system, and thus the entire economy, from crashing.

The books I recommended earlier, and others, tell this frightening story in gory detail, and so there is no need for me to repeat or embellish it. Instead, I want to address an issue these books do not take up, but which I know many readers and citizens who may never read these books have asked themselves at some point: To what extent were economists responsible for either of the two causes? The short answer is: perhaps a small bit but not much more.

Politicians promoted home ownership and so did many economists, who argued with some justification that those who owned their homes were more likely to take care of them, benefiting surrounding neighborhoods, and making them nicer, safer places to live. What the home-ownership advocates did not take fully into account—at least not until after the financial crisis and the crash in home prices—is that most Americans' wealth consists of the equity in their homes, and when that equity is slashed or disappears, so does their sense of wellbeing and their willingness to spend, which surely dampened the pace of the subsequent recovery. Moreover, with as many as one-quarter of home owners under water after the crisis—that is, their home values were less than their mortgages—even households that were able to keep their homes out of foreclosure were reluctant to move to other areas of the country where jobs were more plentiful. When the economic wheel of fortune turned, the large numbers of people who felt locked into their homes added to the normal frictions in the labor market and slowed the pace of hiring and economic growth after the economy began to recover.[20]

This is not to say that the financial crisis proved that home ownership is bad, only that any full accounting of the social benefits and costs of owning a home must take into account the very real macroeconomic costs associated with high levels of home ownership. With the benefit of hindsight, those economists who joined the politicians (either privately or publicly) in supporting the great expansion of home ownership before the crisis were mistaken. Knowing what we know now, there is a strong case that a home ownership rate of roughly 65 percent, which prevailed before the explosive rise in real estate prices and cheap mortgage money of the 2000s, is much closer to the social optimum than the 69 percent at which the ownership rate peaked in 2004, before the proverbial roof on the housing market caved in several years later.

But not all economists supported the great expansion of home ownership, and I doubt whether there were many who missed the two main reasons for the crisis: excessive subprime mortgage lending and securitization and excessive financial institution leverage. Nonetheless, were economists or the economics profession guilty of errors of *omission?* Did enough economists fail to warn policy makers of the dangers to the economy that were brewing because mortgage lending standards were too loose and the financial sector was too highly leveraged? And if more economists had issued warnings, would it have made any difference?

Subprime Lending

Certainly more economists should have expressed concern about the bubble in the housing market and the contribution made by subprime lending. There were a few exceptions, notably 2013 Nobel winner Robert Shiller of Yale, who warned of the housing price bubble well before it burst. In addition, the late Edward "Ned" Gramlich, warned his colleagues on the board of governors at the Federal Reserve, policy makers, and the public about the unsustainable growth in subprime lending. Gramlich's main villains were the lenders, many of whom Gramlich (and others) believed were misleading borrowers to take out mortgages they were not financially equipped to handle.[21] Gramlich urged the Fed to crack down on such lending, but he lost his battle with then Federal Reserve Chairman Alan Greenspan—a component of a broader failure to recognize that free markets do not always regulate themselves, which Greenspan later admitted was an error.[22]

Clearly, Greenspan, as Fed chairman, was in a position to have reined in subprime lending through the Fed's supervisory control over the largest banks (and through their holding companies), many of which were lenders to the nonbank originators of most subprime loans. It is also likely that had there been an earlier, publicly stated consensus among economists about doing this, Greenspan and his Fed colleagues, as well as other federal bank regulators, would have felt more comfortable about acting earlier to restrain subprime mortgage origination.

Regulators very likely still would have faced stiff political opposition in Congress, however, from advocates of more lending to low- and moderate-income households, especially minorities. Even if economists were more united earlier in warning about the egregious ways in which mortgage lenders relaxed their mortgage underwriting—by reducing borrowers' down payments, extending interest-only loans and loans with negative amortization (allowing borrowers to *add* to their mortgage balances rather than reduce them over time), and offering low initial teaser rates that then adjusted to much higher rates after some initial period— it is possible that this wouldn't have been enough to have significantly changed the trajectory of subprime lending. The same statement can be made had more economists known about and warned of the mistakes that the credit-rating agencies were making by assigning excessively optimistic ratings to securities backed by subprime loans.

My bottom line on economists and subprime lending is that we all should have been there earlier; it might have made a difference, but unfortunately, probably not.

Excessive Leverage: An Introduction

On the leverage front, the story is longer and more complicated, but in a different way. All financial economists I know have long supported strong, well-enforced capital standards for banks in particular, because more capital limits leverage and provides a thicker cushion against losses. Since the financial crisis, however, there has been no clear consensus among economists (and policy makers) about how those standards should be defined, and how high they should be.

First, some background: For much of American history, except for rules setting minimum capital amounts for new banks, the bank regulatory agencies haven't had formal ongoing rules for bank capital—the sum of shareholders' equity and the retained earnings of the bank—or what some economists call skin in the game. For decades before federal deposit insurance, banks maintained capital-to-asset ratios well above

10 percent, meaning that banks could suffer a loss equivalent to 10 percent of their assets before failing.

Capital-to-asset ratios are defined on a book value or historical cost basis, meaning that bank loans are counted at face value, less an amount projected for losses (typically only a few percentage points or less), and thus do not reflect current market values of bank loans (where there is a market, which often is not the case). Accordingly, even reported bank capital ratios at the 10 percent level or more did not prevent thousands of banks from failing when the Great Depression hit and real estate values plummeted. The huge drop in these prices, coupled with mass unemployment, meant that too many banks could not collect on their loans, both to businesses and mortgages on houses. In those days, mortgage maturities generally were no longer than five years, so borrowers had to refinance when the mortgages were due or pay the mortgage balances off, options that were unavailable to large numbers of borrowers during the Depression.

To make matters worse, after the 1929 stock market crash and subsequent decline in economic activity, depositors feared that their banks were truly insolvent, and ran to take their money back, actions which expedited bank failures, and caused President Roosevelt to declare a short-term bank holiday as one of his very first actions upon taking office in March 1933. The rash of bank failures during the Depression underscores the fact that it is not only banks' capital ratios that matter for survival (whether those ratios are computed by assuming loans are recorded at the face values but with a sizeable reserve for future loan losses, or measured at some estimate of their market values), but also their *liquidity*, or the ability to pay depositors on demand. Of course, solvency and liquidity can be interrelated, as both the Depression and financial crisis of 2008 demonstrated. If banks are forced into selling their loans or securities at fire-sale prices in order to raise cash to pay off depositors who suddenly want much of their money back, then banks that may be solvent in normal circumstances can become insolvent in a general crisis.

The banking panic in the Depression caused Roosevelt to embrace an idea he had rejected before and that has been a staple of financial policy ever since: Federal deposit insurance for banks was initially established for accounts up to $2,500, but over time has been raised to $250,000. The presence of deposit insurance has had conflicting impacts on bank capital: On the one hand, it strengthens the case for having regulatory minimum capital-to-asset ratios in order to protect the deposit insurance fund (which is financed by banks, though it has a line of credit from the U.S. Treasury), but on the other hand, by reducing the risk of bank deposit runs, deposit insurance has allowed banks to operate with lower capital ratios than in the era before that insurance. For the latter reason, some critics of deposit insurance have charged that it leads to "moral hazard"—an economic term that has nothing to do with morals but everything to do with hazard, or the taking of extra risks knowing that if things turn out badly shareholders will not bear the full loss because the deposit insurer will.

Of course, all insurance entails this problem. Some people, knowing they have insurance on homes or cars, may be less careful. Private insurers attempt to curtail risky behavior by adding deductibles to their insurance policies, so insured customers bear at least some loss in case of an insured event. Health insurers add co-insurance provisions to deductibles to address the moral hazard challenge.

In the case of banks, however, co-insurance or deductibles are likely to be self-defeating since the purpose of the insurance in the first place is to prevent depositors from running; they may still run even if they bore the first loss of a fixed amount or a percentage of their account balances. A good example of this was the run on the Northern Rock bank in the United Kingdom during the most recent financial crisis, which shook public confidence in that country's banking system at the time. Bank regulation and supervision, coupled with minimum ratios of capital-to-bank assets—effectively a deductible for shareholders—are the policy tools that act like deductibles and co-insurance that are typically found in other types of insurance.

Federal bank regulators began to give more formal guidance about minimum bank capital ratios in the late 1970s and early 1980s, but a number of financial economists were long uncomfortable with the less-than-formal way that bank regulators enforced their capital guidelines. This was especially true of the regulators overseeing savings and loan associations, which disappeared in massive numbers in the 1980s.[23] Federal regulators looked the other way—in supervisory jargon they engaged in "regulatory forbearance"—when the federal insurance fund for thrift depositors had very limited funds that could not possibly be stretched to cover the recognition of all of the thrift institution losses. Accordingly, regulators waited until they could find buyers of the troubled firms or, in rare cases, shut them down. Banking regulators did the same thing with the nation's largest banks during the 1980s, which were severely troubled if not insolvent by lending too much to governments of less developed countries (LDCs) that couldn't service their debts. Like the thrift insurance fund that couldn't come close to covering the rash of small thrift insolvencies, the bank insurance fund couldn't cover the potential losses if the large banks failed.

Two economists watching these events unfold, the late George Benston of Emory University and George Kaufman of Loyola University of Chicago, laid out a system during the 1980s for bringing much greater rigor to enforcing minimum capital requirements so that policy makers need never again be forced to engage in forbearance. Dubbed "structured early intervention and resolution" or SEIR, the Benston/Kaufman proposal spelled out specific sanctions that regulators should apply as bank ratios of capital-to-assets declined: the suspension of dividends to shareholders, limits on managerial salaries, and ultimately the takeover by regulators of weak institutions *before* they technically became insolvent. Having clear and progressively stiffer sanctions ideally would encourage the owners and managers of banks to steer clear of the risks that could get them punished, while sanctions, if they had to be applied, would force troubled institutions either to shrink or raise new shareholder money so they could stay afloat and not become a burden on the deposit insurance fund.

Benston and Kaufman presented their proposal to a conference at the American Enterprise Institute shortly after Kaufman and Robert Eisenbeis (then at the University of North Carolina) formed the Shadow Financial Regulatory Committee (SFRC),[24] a group of market-oriented experts in banking and finance (mainly but not always from academia) that was modeled on a similar shadow committee on monetary policy (the Shadow Open Market Committee) launched in the 1970s by economists Karl Brunner of Rochester University and Allan Meltzer of Carnegie Mellon University. Like its monetary policy counterpart, the SFRC meets regularly and issues statements, aimed at policy makers and the media, to both support and criticize legislative and regulatory policies that affect the financial sector. The U.S. SFRC now has replicas in five other regions of the world, and the committees from the various regions attempt to meet every other year to discuss and issue statements on financial regulatory issues that are now common among countries in these regions.

The American SFRC had plenty to comment on: The 1980s had the largest number of bank and thrift failures since the Great Depression. Benston and Kaufman had an easy time persuading the full SFRC to endorse their idea (SEIR), which the committee did in several statements. Individual members of the SFRC also endorsed the idea in their own writings. [Full disclosure: I was asked to join the SFRC in the mid-1980s and was privileged to serve as a member of the group, with a few years off for government service, until 2012.]

Despite its free-market orientation, the SFRC and its members saw a proper role for government regulation of financial institutions, primarily to protect the deposit insurance fund and to offset the moral hazard created by deposit insurance (an idea which the committee did not contest, but also never wanted to go too far; namely, to morph into protecting *all liabilities* of banks or their holding companies, which in fact regulators did during the financial crisis of 2008).

Looking back, what is remarkable is how quickly the idea of formalizing capital requirements and their enforcement for insured depositories was implemented by policy makers. Congress took a first, small step in 1989 when it enacted a minimum 3 percent of assets-to-capital ratio for thrift institutions. Two years later, Congress instructed bank regulators to set a higher capital ratio for banks, backed by an enforcement regime that was almost identical to the concept that Benston and Kaufman originally suggested and which the SFRC had then consistently championed. In less than a decade, SEIR went from an academic idea to policy—a truly remarkable success story and one which I suspect is little known outside the small circle of people who developed, embraced, and implemented the idea.

The Pre-crisis Demise of SEIR

SEIR appeared to work for over a decade after it was implemented, well into the mid-2000s, when bank regulators failed to miss the signs of trouble in the housing market and the loans and securities that were supporting it. Bank failures were uncommon during this period, harking back to the post-war decades before the 1980s when that was the case as well. But it wasn't just that regulators suddenly forgot about SEIR in the mid to late 2000s; two other important developments played central roles in the effective demise of SEIR, which contributed to the subsequent financial crisis.

The first reason why the SEIR system eroded is that regulators essentially failed to stick to it. They did not compel banks to provide sufficient reserves against mounting mortgage losses, which would have lowered reported capital (under either standard leverage ratios or the risk-based measures, which I discuss shortly), and thus would have triggered SEIR enforcement measures much earlier in the 2000s. The principal error came through the failure to recognize the potential threat to the solvency of some of the largest banks posed by their supposedly independent structured investment vehicles (SIVs), which the banks created to warehouse, theoretically only for a short time, mortgage-based securities fully or partially backed by subprime loans.

After reading the multiple books on the crisis, it is still not clear to me, at least, when bank regulators became aware that SIVs existed, but outsiders, including academics, congressional members, and the public did not become aware of them until sometime in 2007, when it was too late. By then, they were unraveling, and the largest bank sponsors of SIVs came to the Treasury asking for the government to bail them out, which Treasury was reluctant to do. When that happened, the banks took SIVs back on their balance sheets, shearing them of their illusory independence, but thereby importing their financial troubles back to the bank sponsors. These decisions played major roles in weakening the banks' own solvency.

Economists were not to blame for the SIV end-run around bank capital standards or the demise of SEIR, designed to enforce them. They were as much in the dark about what was happening as the rest of the public.

The second reason for the failure of SEIR to prevent or limit the crisis is far more complicated, and so in advance, I ask readers to bear with me. It's a story that has not been widely told and thus bears some explanation.

The short version, and I don't know how else to say this, is that bank regulators got too cute, or too complicated, depending on which description one prefers. The initial actors were central bank regulators in the United States and the United Kingdom in the mid-1980s, who took an obviously correct theoretical insight—not all bank assets posed equivalent risks of causing a bank's failure—but had the arrogance to believe that they could redefine minimum capital standards in a way that would accurately take account of these differential risks without also causing unintended harm. Events eventually would prove the dangers outweighed any potential benefits.

The central bankers from the two countries implemented the idea that the risks of bank assets varied by developing a new *risk-based* bank capital system. This system assigned risk weights to four buckets of assets; the weights were then multiplied by the total assets in each category. The risk-weighted amounts were summed into a single measure of risk-weighted assets, which were then divided into two different kinds of capital: Tier 1 (essentially common equity and retained earnings) and Tier 2 (Tier 1 capital plus preferred stock, subordinated debt, and a limited amount of loan-loss reserves).

The net result was a system requiring banks to have capital equal to or exceeding two risk-adjusted capital ratios, 4 percent for Tier I capital and 8 percent for Tier II capital. These two standards were subsequently adopted in the late 1980s by other advanced countries whose central banks belonged to the Basel Committee on Banking Supervision, an exclusive club of central bankers who regularly meet in Basel, Switzerland to discuss common bank supervisory problems and challenges.

The Basel standards, as they have come to be known, may have looked good in principle (how could one object to the notion that different bank assets carried different kinds of risks?), but on closer inspection in practice they proved highly problematic, to put it charitably. At bottom, the problem was that the risk weights not only were arbitrary but flawed.

Under the new system, including subsequent refinements, a bank's investments in the government bonds of each other's countries (later expanded to the debt of over 30 countries belonging to what some have called the rich countries club, the Organization for Economic

Cooperation and Development, or OECD) had no risk weight. This meant that not only did banks need no capital to support these investments, but that banks essentially were given the green light to load up on these securities, a consequence that would prove especially disastrous for European banks after the U.S. financial crisis spread across the Atlantic. When various European governments ran into severe financial troubles (Cyprus, Greece, Italy, Spain, Portugal, Iceland, and Ireland), so did their countries' leading banks which had been encouraged by the Basel risk weights to buy their debts (though surely the governments also applied some arm twisting to accomplish this goal as well).

The Basel system also assigned a 100 percent risk weight to most all loans, except for residential mortgages, which were assigned a 50 percent risk weight, a compromise to bring the German regulators on board (who, like their American counterparts, oversaw many financial institutions devoted largely to mortgage lending). In retrospect that decision gave another bad green light to banks on both sides of the Atlantic to load up on securities backed by mortgages, including the toxic subprime mortgages that later almost sank the world's financial system.

In the mid-1990s, the Basel rules were updated to take account of various critiques, and even then the central banks couldn't stop fiddling, and they initiated toward the end of the century a nearly decade-long process of further updating. That process was almost complete toward the end of the 2000s and then the financial crisis struck. In the post-crisis atmosphere, the central bankers got religion and substantially increased the minimum levels of capital required of banks, adding another 1 to 2.5 percentage points of additional risk-weighted capital for the largest, most complex banks deemed to be "systemically important." But worried about causing banks and their lenders too much disruption, the committee delayed the effective date for its higher standards for roughly another decade (nonetheless, at this writing, most large U.S. banks already comply with the higher requirements).

Throughout this evolution, the Basel standards grew increasingly complex, in part because banks complained that the rules were too rigid and did not take account of their own internal risk models and controls, an argument the Basel Committee appeared to accept until the financial crisis struck. The post–crisis rules leave less discretion for banks, but still run into the hundreds of pages, requiring an army of internal staff and outside lawyers and consultants to help banks comply (in their growing complexity, the Basel rules share much in common with the Volcker rule, adopted in the United States after the crisis, and discussed in detail in the next section).[25]

It didn't have to be this way. Early into the Basel regime, the SFRC, among others, began criticizing the rules, at first for their arbitrariness and for ignoring a fundamental proposition in financial economics: that risks should not be measured by individual asset classes, but on the basis of *entire asset portfolios*, since the ups and downs of the values of loans, securities, and other bank assets can offset each other (or amplify risk in certain cases). As the Basel rules grew more complex, the SFRC statements criticized the Basel Committee and its rules for complexity, too. In their place, the SFRC recommended that bank regulators return to simple minimum leverage ratios (the standard capital-to-asset ratios without any risk weights), supplemented by a minimum amount of subordinated debt (long-term uninsured debt that cannot be withdrawn on demand), expressed as a percent of assets. The Basel rules allowed subordinated debt to count on a *voluntary basis* as part of a bank's Tier 2 capital ratio, but the rules did not require it. The SFRC viewed subordinated debt as a way for bond investors who only had downside risk to monitor bank managers for excessive risk taking. An additional advantage is that the price on such debt, or conversely its interest rate, would serve as a market-based warning signal for regulators to help implement SEIR.

Except for the FDIC, which pressed for a minimum 6 percent leverage ratio to backstop the Basel standards for U.S banks, U.S. bank regulators never considered abandoning the Basel risk-weighting regime or mandating a minimum subordinated debt ratio, even after the financial crisis. However, since the crisis, there have been various calls for essentially replacing the capital ratios in Basel with a minimum leverage ratio, although some proposals have more than that as an objective: setting minimum capital thresholds so high, at least for the largest banks, that they will be forced to break up. This is the main objective of the Brown–Vitter bill introduced in the Congress in 2013 that, if passed, would establish a minimum capital ratio of 15 percent of assets for banks with assets over \$500 billion. One academic study proposes an even more ambitious target: a 30 percent capital-to-asset minimum.[26] The Basel committee, meanwhile, with a clear vested interest in maintaining its complicated risk-based system, concedes the role for a simple leverage ratio as a backup—but at a paltry 3 percent of assets.

The desire to break up the largest banks is understandable because in the midst of the financial crisis, the federal government, over two administrations (George W. Bush and Barack Obama), injected government funds as capital in the nine largest banks (and many other smaller ones) to keep them from failing. In addition, the government supported certain nonbanks, including direct capital injections into the nation's largest insurer, AIG, the two government-sponsored housing entities, Fannie Mae and Freddie Mac, and even in two of the big three domestic auto companies (General Motors and Chrysler). Putting aside the fact that the government since has been nearly paid back for the hundreds of billions in emergency funding,[27] the fact that the investments were made rankles political leaders and voters in both political parties, especially at a time when such largesse was not available to smaller Main Street businesses, and to millions of individual homeowners who lost their homes after the plunge in housing prices put them under water with mortgage balances greater than the values of the houses.

Aside from its unfairness, the rescue of the largest banks—especially all of the uninsured creditors—creates the moral hazard that vigilant enforcement of capital standards and supervision is designed to offset. The Dodd–Frank Act contains various provisions designed to prevent reoccurrences of this "too-big-to-fail" problem, but no one knows whether they will work or if regulators will faithfully carry out the law until the provisions are tested by the next financial crisis.

Meanwhile, there is no consensus among economists about the adequacy of the too-big-to-fail parts of Dodd–Frank or about the appropriate level of capital for banks going forward. But one thing financial economists agree on is that without sufficient capital, banks and securities firms will not have an adequate cushion against future losses nor proper incentives for avoiding the risks that can lead to such losses. The failure to pay heed to this simple insight caused misery for many businesses and individuals alike.

The Glass–Steagall Debate

Much of the legal and regulatory framework governing the financial industry—banks in particular—was established in the wake of the Depression: Federal deposit insurance, securities regulation, and strengthened bank regulation all occurred in 1933 and 1934; several years later, the creation of institutions to facilitate residential mortgage lending (which, among other things, led to the 30-year mortgage) and regulation of the mutual fund industry.

One of the signature pieces of legislation enacted in 1933 was the Glass–Steagall Act, which divorced commercial banking (mainly the business of taking deposits and lending them out to businesses and individuals) from underwriting securities (purchasing securities from firms wanting to go public or sell more shares, or from firms and governments wanting to issue debt, and then reselling those securities to the public).

The conventional wisdom is that Glass–Steagall—named after its two main sponsors, Senator Carter Glass and Representative Henry Steagall—responded to findings in a famous congressional investigation of the 1929 stock market crash (headed by Senate counsel Fernand Pecora) that banks had misled customers about the value of securities they sold. For their sins, the banks were punished by having securities underwriting taken away from them.

While it is certainly true that some banks engaged in deception, that sort of misdeed was addressed in the Securities Acts of 1933 and 1934, which enacted new disclosure requirements for companies seeking to go public and those that remained publicly held. This legislation applied to all securities firms, and would have applied to banks selling securities had they been permitted to continue doing so.

But much like the Volcker rule that was adopted in the wake of the 2007–2008 financial crisis, the Glass–Steagall Act was principally a way for Congress and the public (to the extent it followed such matters) to punish banks during a period when many of them had failed and when some had behaved improperly. But as subsequent economic research has shown, there was no evidence that banks' underwriting of securities contributed to the massive numbers of bank failures, nor any logical reason why Congress could not have applied their new securities protections to banks had they not been outlawed from underwriting securities (the prohibition was not complete, since it did not apply to bank underwriting of federal or municipal general obligation bonds, or to state-chartered banks that did not belong to the Federal Reserve system).[28]

In short, there was little economic evidence (some would say none) in support of Glass–Steagall, and I have been unable to find many economists who favored it, even at the time. Indeed, as time went on, those banking scholars (including me, in my PhD dissertation, later published as a book) who studied the Act noted that it began and continued as an artificial legal barrier to competition from banks to standalone investment banks in the underwriting of securities.[29] In this respect, the Act was little different from other forms of economic regulation that were later dismantled, although Glass–Steagall did not impose price controls of any sort; that job was left to other Depression-era legislation that put limits on the interest banks could pay their depositors, a restriction that was eventually lifted in the 1980s.

In any event, the Glass–Steagall Act stayed on the books for more than 60 years, despite many efforts to repeal it. Banks that began lobbying for financial reform legislation in the 1980s to repeal or scale back the Act consistently ran into a fierce wall of resistance from the securities industry, which obviously did not want additional competition from banks. The two sides of the debate, through their political contributions and lobbying activities, made for gridlock in the banking committees in the Congress, and so large-scale financial reform was not in the cards.

Bank regulators, specifically the Federal Reserve, were more receptive to the need for competition in securities underwriting. So, beginning in the late 1980s and extending well into the next decade, the Fed began to expand the percentage of overall activity that bank affiliates could devote to underwriting corporate securities. The Fed did this under another exception to Glass–Steagall's broad prohibitions: Bank affiliates that were not primarily engaged in underwriting could underwrite otherwise impermissible securities (mainly corporate debt and equity) to a limited degree.

Eventually, so much securities underwriting by banking affiliates was going on that by the end of the 1990s, Congress was ready to throw in the towel and to dismantle Glass–Steagall altogether through enactment of the Gramm–Leach–Bliley Act of 1999 (GLBA). As a result, Glass–Steagall essentially died not with a bang but a whimper, although the process was significantly accelerated by Citigroup's purchase of Travelers Insurance. Citigroup would have had to substantially reorganize, or even abandon the Travelers acquisition, had GLBA not passed Congress. Citigroup wanted to be the first to test the commercial viability of the financial supermarket model, in which a single financial services holding company would own subsidiaries in multiple lines of financial activity—banking, insurance, and securities—and seek to cross-sell customers the services provided by each of the subsidiaries, while realizing efficiencies (or economies of scope) in consolidating all these financial activities under one roof. I can't say that economists were decisive in convincing Congress to enact GLBA, but a steady stream of economic scholarship over the roughly two decades before supporting the repeal of Glass–Steagall certainly didn't hurt the effort.

In any event, the full-service financial supermarket model that Citigroup wanted to test was a flop. Several years after getting the green light to put the model together from Congress, Citigroup began unraveling it, principally by selling off Travelers. JP Morgan Chase (a large bank that was the product of a merger of two large banks before it) and others tried a less ambitious version of the supermarket idea—combining commercial and investment banking, the very combination prohibited by Glass–Steagall—and at this writing still seem committed to it.

However these experiments in financial market models turn out is a sideshow compared to the renewed debate since the financial crisis of 2007–2008 over the wisdom of sticking with GLBA or returning in some fashion to the Glass–Steagall world. Although the issue was little more than a footnote during the initial congressional deliberations of financial reform legislation after the financial crisis, the securities activities of banks began to attract much greater congressional attention in 2010, after Scott Brown was elected to fill the Massachusetts Senate seat long occupied by Senator Ted Kennedy, who died early in that year (Brown later was defeated in 2012 by Senator Elizabeth Warren, an advocate of Glass–Steagall, who developed the idea and campaigned, successfully, for the creation of a separate federal consumer financial products safety commission).

At that time, the financial reform law that was to become the Dodd–Frank Act of 2010 was still making its way through Congress. To jump-start that process and to regain some political momentum behind its passage, the Obama administration turned to the chairman of its

Economic Advisory Board, Paul Volcker (see following box), one of the most distinguished public servants in economic policy making of the previous half century, who up to then had more of a titular than an actual policy making function in the administration.

Volcker has long been a believer that banks should stick to their knitting, namely taking in deposits and lending them out, and should not branch out to engage in other activities, especially those related to underwriting securities, or even worse in his view, betting on asset price movements—what has come to be known as "proprietary trading. Apparently not believing there was sufficient support then for repealing GLBA in its entirety, Volcker urged Obama and, in turn, Congress to implement what on the surface seemed to be a simple, second-best solution: Simply ban banks from engaging in proprietary trading. The president embraced the idea, quickly naming the idea the Volcker rule and urged its inclusion in the financial reform legislation. By that time, public sentiment had turned on the large banks, and so the president's idea was an easy sell at least to the Democrats in Congress, who ultimately voted for Dodd–Frank (then newly elected Senator Brown was one of only three Republican Senators to vote for the bill).

Paul Volcker: A Giant Among Economists

When the economic history of the twentieth and early twenty-first centuries is written, no figure will stand taller, figuratively and literally, than Paul Volcker. Although he never gained the economists' union card, the PhD, his private sector and public experience, combined with his formal training in the subject at Princeton and Harvard, put him at the top ranks of the profession.[30]

Volcker is best known for leading the Federal Reserve from 1979 to 1987 during one of the most difficult economic times of the past century—with the exception of the Depression and the financial crisis of 2007–2008. Nominated for the Fed chairmanship by President Jimmy Carter when annual inflation was nearing double digits while the economy was suffering from recession—a deadly combination often referred to as stagflation—Volcker put his emphasis on fighting the former, which eventually laid the foundation for curing the latter.

It took guts, a man with giant convictions, and a giant personality to ward off the many attacks he got for wringing inflation out of the economy, which he and his Fed colleagues eventually did. Volcker was greatly aided along the way by President Reagan, whose administration never wavered in its support of the Fed's tight monetary policy as a way of slaying inflation, even as the unemployment rate climbed over 10 percent in 1982. Once hitting that peak, however, the unemployment rate declined rapidly as the fiscal stimulus of the 1980 tax cuts took hold and the economy came roaring back (though not without an unprecedented, at the time, increase in federal budget deficits).

Volcker became Fed chairman after an already highly successful financial career. He began initially as a staff economist at the Federal Reserve Bank of New York, moved to Chase Manhattan Bank, then went to the Treasury department to work under the famed Robert Roosa, who was the department's undersecretary for international and monetary affairs. After going back to a vice-presidency at Chase, Volcker returned to Treasury from 1969 to 1974 to assume the job that Roosa had, where he played a crucial role in decisions leading to the end of the Bretton Woods era of fixed exchange rates. He thereafter made another return, to his first employer, the Federal Reserve Bank of New York, but as its president.

After leading the Fed, Volcker came back to private life as chairman of Wolfensohn and Co., a private investment and corporate advisory firm. President Obama, shortly after assuming office, asked Volcker to chair the President's Economic Advisory Board, a body that lacked real power. It was widely reported that Volcker was frustrated as a result. The president's adoption of the idea that Volcker was then urging—a ban on proprietary trading by banks—put Volcker back squarely in

(*continued*)

the public eye. The Volcker rule, as it has since become known, took multiple regulators over three years to implement and remains highly controversial, but its author is not. Volcker will always be a giant among professional economists.

One small personal footnote: I have had the great privilege of interacting with Volcker on professional issues over the years. I can tell you that he is warm, funny, and generous with his time. We had firm, but polite disagreements (the virtues of financial innovation being one, the wisdom of the Volcker rule being another, although I never voiced my views on this directly to him). His graciousness I will never forget.

I haven't taken a scientific poll, nor have I seen one, but I suspect that most economists who are knowledgeable about finance do not support the Volcker rule (though there are notable exceptions, such as Simon Johnson of MIT and formerly chief economist at the International Monetary Fund). Just as the economic case for Glass–Steagall was weak or nonexistent, there was no evidence that the mixing of commercial and investment banking contributed in any significant way to the extension of subprime loans or their packaging into securities (which was accomplished by a number of standalone investment banks, having no formal connection with the banking industry). Most microeconomists also instinctively oppose artificial legal barriers to competition, which is what Glass–Steagall represented: a wall that put a protective moat around investment banks that were underwriting securities.

The implementation of the Volcker rule has not been smooth. It took over three years for five regulatory agencies to write the rules, in part because of stiff opposition from large banks that had major trading operations (which reinforced the conviction of Volcker's advocates that the rule was necessary), and also because the apparently simple rule was difficult to operationalize. Just two examples: Despite its prohibition on proprietary trading, the rule allowed trades for hedging purposes and to facilitate market making. After much consideration, the final rule achieved more clarity with the hedging exception (essentially requiring banks to tie any specific trade for hedging purposes to the risks posed by a specific customer transaction), but regulators almost certainly will find the market-making exception difficult to enforce.

In order to meet the needs of their clients, banks (like securities firms), buy certain securities to hold in their inventory from which they sell to or buy from clients. By definition, many of these transactions anticipate orders by clients, and thus expose banks to some risk for some short period of time (much shorter than the typical maturity of a business loan). It is not clear how, even on a case-by-case basis, regulators will be able to draw defensible lines between impermissible proprietary trading and permissible market making. While banks continue to wrestle with these uncertainties, and some may abandon trading altogether, depriving customers of services and thinning liquidity in the markets in which they were once active, two groups of firms clearly will benefit from the Volcker rule: the lawyers and consultants that banks have hired to help them comply with the rule and, if necessary, contest the regulators' ongoing interpretations of it.

To accomplish all this, the agencies took more than 70 pages of actual text (and many hundreds of pages of preamble) to explain the rule's deceptively simple proprietary trading prohibition. My guess is that either regulators or the courts eventually will draw the bright lines about market making, and to a lesser extent, hedging that are not in the initial Volcker rule. If this process is not satisfactory to Volcker's advocates, or if one or more large banks (or more precisely their uninsured creditors) require a bailout in a future financial crisis, the pressure for a full-scale return to Glass–Steagall (without some or all of *its* initial exceptions) will only grow. It is unlikely that this outcome will be supported by a majority of financial or even macroeconomists, but that is not likely to matter in the face of another political backlash against large banks. That same backlash may lead to a forced breakup of those institutions in an effort to mitigate the too-big-to-fail problem (another issue on which a consensus of economists has been difficult to assemble).

In the meantime, policy makers in the United States may be watching how European policy makers are approaching these issues. After initially flirting with something like the Volcker rule for its banks, the European Union backed off in early 2014, proposing instead that the divorce between bank lending and trading activities be handled on a case-by-case basis rather than imposed as a hard-and-fast rule (even with its blurry lines) as is now the case in the United States.[31]

The Bottom Line

The indirect influences of economists on the financial industry, on national economic policy, and on the businesses that make up the larger economy are a lot more beneficial than popularly believed.

- Economists provided the intellectual support for ending fixed commissions, or essentially legalized price fixing, which enabled a wave of discount brokers to enter the securities industry, conferring large benefits on investors.
- Two economists played an even larger role, though unexpected at the outset, in accelerating electronic exchanges for transactions in equities and other financial instruments, lowering trading costs.
- Two other economists, backed by many more, established the intellectual foundation for an enforceable system of bank-capital regulation that stood the financial system and the economy as a whole in good stead for roughly 15 years before policy makers within the regulatory agencies, the executive branch, and Congress undermined it.

There is no consensus on some fundamental bank and financial regulatory issues since the financial crisis of 2007–2008. The intellectual vacuum has been filled by highly complex systems of bank capital regulation (the Basel standards) and by new restrictions on bank activities (the Volcker rule). There is some irony in this: We are left with complexity instead of simplicity. It is far from clear that this system will serve the financial industry or the economy as a whole well going forward. Count me as one skeptical economist.

Notes

1. For this history, see www.thinkadvisor.com/2010/05/01/the-great-unfixing.
2. Jeffrey A. Esienach and James C. Miller III, "Price Competition on the NYSE," *Regulation* (January/February 1981): 16–19.

3. This history is based on an interview with Donald Baker, December 3, 2013.

4. Jason Zweig, "Even When Stocks Make You Nervous, Count Your Blessings," *Wall Street Journal*, November 30–December 1, 2013.

5. William G. Christie and Paul H. Schultz, "Why Do NASDAQ Market Makers Avoid Odd-Eighth Quotes?" *The Journal of Finance* 49, no. 5 (December 1994): 1813–1840.

6. Ibid., 1814.

7. For a description of the evidence supporting the consent decree, see U.S. Department of Justice, Antitrust Division, *United States v. Alex. Brown & Sons Inc., et al.—Competitive Impact Statement*. Washington, DC: U.S. Department of Justice, July 16, 1998, www.usdoj.gov/atr/cases/f0700/0739.htm.

8. Jeffrey Perloff, "Economists Prevent Collusion," wps.aw.com/aw_perloff_microcalc_2/149/38380/9825344.cw/content/index.html.

9. Nela Richardson and Jeffrey H. Harris, "Slowing Down High-Speed Trading," Bloomberg Government.com, August 12, 2013 [behind paywall].

10. For an excellent and entertaining guide to dark pools, see Scott Patterson, *Dark Pools: The Rise of the Machine Traders and the Rigging of the U.S. Stock Market* (New York: Crown Publishing, 2012).

11. Matthew Phillips, "How the Robots Lost: High-Frequency Trading's Rise and Fall," *Bloomberg Businessweek*, June 6, 2013, www.businessweek.com/articles/2013-06-06/how-the-robots-lost-high-frequency-tradings-rise-and-fall; and Financial Stability Oversight Council, *Annual Report 2012*, www.treasury.gov/initiatives/fsoc/Documents/annual-report.aspx.

12. Lewis, Michael, *Flash Boys* (New York: W.W. Norton & Co., 2014).

13. Securities and Exchange Commission, *Concept Release on Equity Market Structure*, 2010, www.sec.gov/rules/concept/2010/34-61358.pdf. See also Robert E. Litan and Harold Bradley, "Choking the Recovery: Why New Growth Companies Aren't Going Public and Unrecognized Risks of Future Market Disruptions," Ewing Marion Kauffman Foundation, http://papers.ssrn.com/sol3/papers.cfm?abstract_id=1706174.

14. Carmen M. Reinhardt and Kenneth Rogoff, *This Time Is Different: Eight Centuries of Financial Folly* (Princeton, NJ: Princeton University Press, 2011).

15. Robert E. Litan, *What Should Banks Do?* (Washington, DC: Brookings Institution, 1987).

16. Bank failure data are from the Federal Deposit Insurance Corporation, www2.fdic.gov/hsob/HSOBRpt.asp.

17. Alan Blinder, *After the Music Stopped: The Financial Crisis, the Response, and the Work Ahead* (New York: Penguin Press, 2013); Sheila Bair, *Bull by the Horns: Fighting to Save Main Street from Wall Street and Wall Street from Itself* (New

York: Free Press, 2012); Gillian Tett, *Fool's Gold: The Inside Story of J.P. Morgan and How Wall Street Greed Corrupted Its Bold Dream and Created a Financial Catastrophe* (New York: Free Press, 2010); and Michael Lewis, *The Big Short: Inside the Doomsday Machine* (New York: W.W. Norton & Co., 2011).

18. National Commission on the Causes of the Financial and Economic Crisis in the United States, *The Financial Crisis Inquiry Report*, January 2011, http:// fcic-static.law.stanford.edu/cdn_media/fcic-reports/fcic_final_report_full .pdf.

19. For a longer exposition of what I think about the financial crisis and the response to it, see Robert E. Litan, "The Political Economy of the Financial Crisis," in *Rethinking the Financial Crisis*, ed. Alan S. Blinder, Andrew W. Lo, and Robert M. Solow (New York: Russell Sage Foundation): 269–302.

20. For an excellent summary of changing views among economists about the benefits and costs of home ownership, especially since the onset of the financial crisis, see "Shelter or Burden?" *The Economist*, April 16, 2009, www .economist.com/node/13491933.

21. Edward M. Gramlich, *Subprime Mortgages: America's Latest Boom and Bust* (Washington, DC: Urban Institute Press, 2007).

22. See, e.g., Edmund L. Andrews, "Greenspan Concedes Error on Regulation," *New York Times*, www.nytimes.com/2008/10/24/business/ economy/24panel.html?_r=0.

23. There are many academic accounts of the S&L crisis in the 1980s. Two of the better ones are Edward J. Kane, *The S&L Insurance Mess; How Did It Happen?* (New York: University Press of America, 1989) and Lawrence J. White, *The S&L Debacle: Public Policy Lessons for Bank and Thrift Regulation* (New York: Oxford University Press, 1991). I had the privilege of serving on a congres- sionally authorized commission on the causes of the savings and loan crisis, which issued its report, *Origins and Causes of the S&L Debacle: A Blueprint for Reform*, in 1993.

24. For an excellent history of SEIR, see George G. Kaufman and George J. Benston, "The Intellectual History of the Federal Deposit Insurance Corporation Improvement Act of 1991," in *Assessing Bank Reform: FDICIA One Year Later*, ed. George G. Kaufman and Robert E. Litan (Washington, DC: The Brookings Institution, 1993).

25. For a thorough critique of the Basel standards, see Daniel Tarullo, *Banking on Basel: The Future of International Bank Regulation* (Washington, DC: The Petersen Institute of International Economics, 2008). Shortly after this book was pub- lished, Tarullo was nominated and then confirmed as a governor of the Federal Reserve Board, where his primary duties have been to oversee the Fed's super- vision of bank and financial holding companies, and the state-chartered banks belonging to the Federal Reserve System.

26. Anat Admati and Martin Hellwig, *The Bankers' New Clothes* (Washington, DC: Peterson Institute for International Economics, 2013).

27. Blinder (2013).

28. See, e.g., Mark Flannery, "Economic Evaluation of Bank Securities Activities," in Ingo Walter, ed., *Deregulating Wall Street: Commercial Bank Penetration of the Corporate Securities Market* (New York: John Wiley & Sons, 1985), 67–87; Thomas F. Huertas, "An Economic Brief Against Glass–Steagall," *Journal of Bank Research* 14 (Autumn, 1984): 148–159; and George J. Benson, *The Separation of Commercial and Investment Banking: The Glass–Steagall Act Revisited and Reconsidered* (New York: Oxford University Press, 1990).

29. Litan, *What Should Banks Do?*

30. For a thorough account of Volcker's life in public service, see William Silber, *Volcker: The Triumph of Persistence* (New York: Bloomsbury Press, 2012).

31. Alex Barker, "Europe Set to Soften Bank Split Reforms," *Financial Times*, January 6, 2014.

Part III

LOOKING AHEAD

I hope the chapters up to this point have convinced you that economists and their ideas have made important contributions to the world of business and to the general economy. I now want to engage in a bit of crystal ball gazing and look ahead to additional ways that already developed economic ideas (and thus on the shelf) are waiting to be commercially exploited, either directly by entrepreneurs or established firms, or by policy makers at multiple levels of government, in which case the ideas would help establish additional platforms for many new firms to get started or existing firms to branch into new lines of business.

I necessarily have to be selective so, given my own limitations, I will stick to those ideas with which I am most familiar.

The book concludes with some ruminations on the future of the economics profession itself. Economists will continue to be important, but their field will change and possibly meld with other disciplines. Economists will continue to theorize about, participate in, and be affected by what goes in the real world and the explosion of Big Data will help them do it.

Chapter 13

Economic Ideas in Waiting: Business Applications

Economic ideas can find their ways into business applications through multiple channels: because a founder or an executive is exposed to them in college or in reading the professional literature (or from mainstream articles that summarize that literature); because a company learns of or expands on an idea from an economist whom they have hired as a consultant; or because the originator of the idea, whether or not a formally trained economist, implements it by launching a new business.

As New York Yankee Yogi Berra famously once said, "It's tough to make predictions, especially about the future." This aphorism couldn't be more apt than when attempting to project which of the many possible economic ideas already out there will generate new business opportunities. But I'm going to try in this chapter by focusing on three areas where much thinking already has been done and related ideas are waiting to be commercialized. What I won't do is attempt to predict what economic ideas not yet thought up might also have important business implications. If I could do that, I would not have spent so much time writing this book.

Prediction Markets

One of the tenets that most economists strongly hold is that markets—where people or firms are actually spending their own money—are better than opinion polls or focus groups in gauging the level of interest in any particular product or idea. For example, one can ask a lot of people what they think gross domestic product (GDP) is going to be next year and then compute the average of the answer. If there were a market in GDP forecasts, where people could win or lose depending on the accuracy of their projections, the average of those forecasts is likely to be more on target than if people are asked to volunteer their estimates or guesses for free.

Actually, examples of such "prediction markets" are already in place. Perhaps the first example was the Iowa Electronic Market for presidential candidates, operated by the faculty at the business school at the University of Iowa since 1988.[1] Individuals could and still can place limited bets on the outcome of presidential elections, with the payoff being $1 in case the chosen candidate wins, and zero otherwise. The price at any one time for each candidate is expressed in fractions of a dollar, and thus represents the market's best estimate of the probability that the candidate will win. Iowa runs similar markets for congressional elections and for monetary policy decisions by the Federal Reserve.

Prediction markets harness the wisdom of the crowd, and often (but not always) the informed crowd, to project outcomes.[2] A spirited academic literature over additional uses, design, and performance of prediction markets, both in private market and public policy settings, is reflected in peer-reviewed academic articles in the *Journal of Prediction Markets*.[3]

The enthusiasm for prediction markets seemed to be exponentially rising until two events chilled interest. In the policy sphere, prediction markets were tarnished by the exposure of their potential use by government employees as a way of forecasting the timing, location, and likelihood of terrorist attacks. The objective surely seems worthwhile; in principle, making such predictions is one reason we have intelligence agencies. But when it came to light in 2003 that the Defense Department was considering allowing investors to bet on acts of terrorism, prompt political and media condemnation quickly forced the program to shut down, and even helped lead to the resignation of Admiral

John Poindexter, then head of DARPA, the Defense Department's highly regarded research arm.[4] Although a terrorism prediction market may well have done better at predicting terrorist acts than any human or satellite intelligence, there was revulsion at the notion that anyone could profit from a terrorist act. This negative attitude was reinforced in the Dodd–Frank financial reform law of 2010 that contained a little-noticed provision that also banned futures contracts related to terrorism, assassination, gaming, or anything "contrary to the public interest."

More recently, and more damaging, was the highly public failure of the leading prediction market, Intrade, in 2013. The Commodities Futures Trading Commission (CFTC) filed lawsuits against the company for facilitating gambling and violating the securities laws. There were also disclosures that Intrade's former, late CEO had taken customer funds for himself.[5] Before these events, Intrade had racked up some notable successes, such as out-predicting polling data in the 2004 presidential election and for many statewide political races in 2008. The prediction market also performed well despite some very large, and ultimately wrong, bets placed on the 2012 election that appeared to prop up the election prospects of former Governor Mitt Romney.[6]

With the closure of Intrade, economists who had supported prediction markets have become decidedly pessimistic about their use in the future. One leading prediction market expert, Koleman Strumpf of the University of Kansas, pretty much summed it up when he concluded that the "CFTC's intransigent interpretation of the law" (about what is a permissible futures contract and what is impermissible betting) made it unlikely that such markets would be used on a large scale again.[7]

Even if Strumpf's forecast about future regulatory hostility toward general-purpose prediction markets proves accurate, I believe it is premature to write off the use of prediction markets in other, business-related contexts. Already, a number of private companies have used internal prediction markets among their employees to predict future sales, or which projects in the research pipeline are most likely to be commercially successful. The failure of Intrade should not dampen the use of internal prediction markets by other companies in the future. The core insight of the wisdom of crowds, after all, is too irresistible to ignore.

In addition, although the financial crisis unleashed criticism of perhaps the most widely known example of a prediction market at work—the credit default swap or CDS market—that market continues to exist, and in my opinion will grow over the long run, thanks in part to regulatory reforms enacted in the wake of the crisis.

A CDS is like an insurance contract in which the underwriter of the swap, most typically a bank (but also a hedge fund or, most infamously, an affiliate of an insurance company, like AIG), guarantees to make good on a loan default. Initially, banks bought CDS protection as a way of hedging their loan portfolios. Structured mortgage securities that were not guaranteed by Fannie Mae and Freddie Mac became marketable once bankers (J.P. Morgan was the first) figured out that they could convince credit rating agencies of the securities' safety if they were protected by a CDS.[8]

The CDS market was heavily criticized in the wake of the financial crisis, mostly for two reasons. First, unlike conventional insurance, which protects things that people or firms *already own*, purchasers of CDS buy them without having an insurable interest in the underlying loans or securities they protect. In other words, buyers of CDSs can gamble or speculate on a loan or a security going into default, the kind of criticism that the CFTC leveled at Intrade (though the cash shortfall from the diversion of funds by its former CEO was the more immediate cause of the platform's demise). Second, because a CDS contract can be sold to any qualified buyer (virtually all of the buyers are institutions) without the purchaser needing the insurance, theoretically there is no limit to how many CDS contracts underwriters can sell and purchasers can buy. For this reason, an explosion of CDS contracts that *are not honored* can expose an entire financial system to collapse.

Both these criticisms were reflected in the behavior of AIG's structured products subsidiary, which sold over $400 billion in CDS contracts on securities backed by subprime mortgages, measured by the total face value of the securities.[9] Because the parent of this subsidiary, AIG, was so large and well capitalized, the ratings agencies gave the company their top rating, AAA. That was enough for the buyers of the CDS sold by AIG, who otherwise may have insisted that AIG post some margin or collateral both to protect the buyers in the event the seller couldn't pay, and to limit how many contracts AIG's affiliate could write.

Most readers know the end of this story: Despite its sterling credit rating, AIG did not have enough margin or reserves set aside to fully honor all of its CDS commitments when they came due in fall 2008. Because so many of AIG's counterparties (those who bought the CDS contracts from the AIG affiliate) could have been short of cash had AIG been unable to pay off, the Federal Reserve took the unprecedented step of rescuing the creditors of the entire company, putting in loans and capital infusions that eventually totaled nearly $200 billion in return for almost 80 percent of AIG's common stock. Eventually, AIG recovered, and the Fed got most of its money back, though the net cost of the bailout remains in dispute.[10] The rescue damaged both the Fed's credibility and the glamor status of the CDS contract.

The CDS market remains very much alive, however, since the crisis. Although the notional value of those contracts—the total face amount of the loans and securities underlying the contracts—peaked at nearly $60 trillion just before the crisis, there were still almost $25 trillion in over-the-counter CDS in notional value outstanding at mid-2013.[11]

A major reason the CDS exists is that it still performs two useful functions, only one of which is insurance. The other function is that the CDS market acts as the functional equivalent of a prediction market in loan or bond defaults. In principle, investors could look to the markets where these debt securities are traded—not only for mortgage-backed securities but for bonds issued by private companies and even sovereign governments—to see how investors assess the likelihood of default.[12] But bonds and individual loans are traded intermittently in the marketplace, so any market prices, if they exist, are likely to be infrequent and dated. A more liquid market for CDS thus provides a timely market-based indicator of credit quality, one that would not exist or be as effective as it is, without both hedgers and speculators participating in the market.[13]

The Dodd-Frank Act has led to fundamental reform and regulation of the CDS market, most importantly by requiring that standardized CDSs (well over half the market) that are readily traded must be "cleared" through centralized clearinghouses, analogous to those for banks. What this means in plain English is that instead of sellers and buyers of these standardized contracts dealing directly (or bilaterally) with each other, they are now required to contract with a clearinghouse. Thus, buyers pay the clearinghouse, while sellers receive funds from the clearinghouse, which requires its counterparties to post margin (or collateral). Margin provides the clearinghouse at least some financial protection in case any counterparty reneges on its deal. The clearinghouse also must have capital and liquid assets of its own (subject to regulation) to cover any shortfalls arising from the failure of margin to cover payments that may be required.

It is not clear yet whether the clearinghouse function is a natural monopoly or whether multiple clearinghouses can coexist and through their competition encourage innovation. The key fact, however, is that because the clearinghouse is the counterparty to the swaps rather than the seller, then in principle another AIG cannot threaten to bring down the financial system—as long as the clearinghouse itself is regulated, as Dodd–Frank requires (and because these clearinghouses are implicitly or explicitly backed by the Federal Reserve in another financial crisis).

The experiences in the CDS market underscore an essential element to the effective workings of any prediction market: Those running the market or the rules governing it must assure that those making predictions through their bets collect their winnings when their bets prove accurate (those losing will have already paid either by buying a ticket up front, as in the case of the Iowa presidential market or internal private sector markets, or buying a swaps contract in the case of CDS). The fact that regulators and policy makers do not appear willing to sanction some kinds of bets does not mean that prediction markets are dead. In fact, they are very much alive in some business contexts, and my prediction is that they will become more widely used over time.

Potentially Good Financial Innovations

The financial crisis demonstrated all too clearly that not all financial innovation is good. But as I hope to have convinced you in Chapters 8 and 12, many financial innovations are.

Just as in other sectors of the economy that will surely continue to experience innovation, finance is unlikely to be left out. One of the leading thinkers about future financial innovation, 2013 Nobel winner Robert Shiller who was profiled in Chapter 8, has already set out in his frequent writings an extensive menu of economic ideas to be taken up. The common theme among all of them is that each is designed to shelter individuals and institutions from uncertainty and change.[14] The following ideas are worth mention.

The first, and perhaps most obvious suggestion, made especially relevant by the financial crisis, is to enable homebuyers to buy financial protection against future declines in the value of their homes. These contracts, or long-term put options, would have greater attractiveness and marketability if they were based on city-wide price indices (Shiller, with his collaborator Karl Case, has created them for 20 of the nation's largest cities) rather than customized to the values of individual homes (which would make them like traditional insurance contracts which are not tradable). Despite the crisis, however, sufficient interest has not yet developed among either sellers or buyers of such instruments, so the market for them does not yet exist. But that doesn't mean the idea eventually won't take off at some point, either as an insurance product or a security, or both.

Second, wage insurance is another idea that would seem to be attractive given the large wage cuts that millions of Americans have been forced to accept in the wake of the Great Recession triggered by the financial crisis. Shiller views this as a product that insurance companies can sell to individuals in case they involuntarily take a new job that pays them less than their previous one, by compensating them for some portion of the wage difference for some limited period of time.

With various co-authors, I have long championed this idea, but have argued that it must instead be a government program funded by a small levy on earnings, analogous to unemployment insurance.[15] I highlight this policy idea in this chapter on economic ideas that may provide future business opportunities because government-provided wage insurance is a close intellectual cousin of Shiller's private sector proposal.

The reason for making wage insurance a government program is that otherwise the market for wage insurance will not develop, because of "adverse selection." Private insurers will be reluctant to sell such insurance because of the fear that only those most likely to be laid off will buy the insurance. Unemployment insurance, for example, was not provided by the private market until the government stepped in to do it for the same reason.

Nonetheless, there are potentially significant societal benefits to a program of wage insurance for individuals who are involuntarily displaced. Knowing the government will make up some portion of any wage loss and that the offer extends only for a set time once unemployment begins gives those who are forced into unemployment strong incentives to accept new jobs, even if they are lower-paying. For employers, the limited wage insurance paid to employees can be viewed as a kind of subsidy for training them. These outcomes should be especially appealing in the wake of the Great Recession, after which long-term unemployment as a share of total unemployment spiked to the 40 percent range, far higher than it has been for at least the past four decades.[16]

Shiller, and later with colleagues, has proposed a third financial innovation: a security whose payoffs are linked to national GDP. In principle, as many such securities could be designed and sold as there are countries, or roughly 200.[17] Shiller explains why many investors would want to own GDP-linked securities as means of diversifying their portfolios and also to hedge against risks posed by other financial instruments they may hold.

There are good reasons why these instruments do not yet exist, however. On the buy side, investors can already buy the market, as it were, by buying mutual funds or exchange-traded funds linked to the performance of broad market indices. It is not clear how much additional diversification benefits GDP-linked securities would provide.

On the sell side, the impediments seem even more insurmountable. Who would issue these securities? Shiller envisions institutions offering them, much as they now sell puts or calls on individual stocks or baskets of securities. In these latter instances, sellers can cover or hedge the risks of these contracts by holding the underlying security. But there is no underlying GDP-linked security that can hedge against the risk of selling it, except another GDP-linked instrument issued by another financial institution. But some institution must start the process, by taking an unhedged risk in selling a GDP-linked instrument. That has not happened. Perhaps this problem will be solved by clever entrepreneurs in the future, and perhaps there will be a ready market for these securities that existing index-linked instruments do not yet provide. At the very least, Shiller has planted the seed for the concept.

A fourth idea, one not developed by Shiller or his colleagues, that awaits implementation is the application of financial engineering to the financing of drug discoveries, cancer drugs initially, then drugs for all kinds of diseases.

Drug research costs a lot of money and outcomes are highly risky. Drugs must pass three progressively stiffer rounds of testing with the Food and Drug Administration before they can be sold to the public. Pharmaceutical companies are shying away from such risky endeavors. Venture capitalists, which once were quite interested in funding life science startups, have backed away in light of poor returns.

Andrew Lo, one of the world's leading financial economists, and his colleagues at MIT, have come up with a different financing model for drug research, modeled on the way that mortgage-backed securities are structured.[18] The notion is for securities firms to assemble and issue research-backed securities, in which the assets are drugs in testing trials. If the securities are backed by a sufficiently large number of trials—say 100 or more—then all it takes to compensate investors for the risk is for several of the trials to produce home-run drugs whose royalties more than make up for all the strikeouts in the fund. A computer simulation suggests that a $5 to 15 billion mega-fund would return equity investors 9 to 12 percent and bond investors 5 to 8 percent. These are attractive returns for institutional investors like pension funds.

At this writing, no such research-backed securities have been issued to my knowledge, perhaps because there are many details still to be worked out, and possibly because institutional investors are still traumatized by the financial crisis and the role that asset-backed securities in general played in it. But this risk aversion should fade, and eventually I believe the time will come when we will see a major market in these innovative securities, and even more importantly, new life-saving drugs that these securities will help make possible.

A final financial innovation—virtual currency—is already here, and though it was not thought up by economists, but rather by technologists, it has attracted much spirited commentary about its future from economists (and others).

The famous (or infamous depending on your point of view) example at this writing is Bitcoin, a virtual peer-to-peer currency developed by someone named Satoshi Nakamato, who may or may not be Japanese or the code name for more than one software developer. Whoever it is, he, she, or the group left the project in 2010, a year after the currency was launched in 2009. The Bitcoin system operates with publicly available software, which any developer can review.[19]

Since Bitcoin's launch, its popularity has had its ups and downs while its price in terms of dollars has fluctuated wildly. By the time you read this, it may not even be around, or it could be more popular than ever. But even if Bitcoin fails for any of the reasons discussed shortly, its short history (with the discussion below reworded to be in the past tense) is worth knowing because the notion of a virtual currency is not likely to die.

As recently as 2011, a Bitcoin could be purchased for less than one dollar. As 2014 opened, it was trading for over $1000, although the price fell back later in the year after disclosure that the vice-chairman of the Bitcoin Foundation was being prosecuted for money laundering, and a number of countries, including Russia and China were cracking down on its use. The closure of one of the most popular Bitcoin exchanges, Mt. Gox in Japan, in February 2014, also rocked confidence in the currency. In the future, Bitcoin's price could either collapse, as some notable economists have predicted (more about them soon), or continue to climb, although not without continued price fluctuations.

The huge increase and variability in Bitcoin's value conflict with the objectives of its founder and promoters, which is to make Bitcoin a new kind of money, used as a means of payment. If a commodity, even a virtual one, becomes more valuable to hold for speculative purposes than to use, then it's not really functioning as a means of payment. In March 2014 the Internal Revenue Service ruled that capital gains taxes were owed every time Bitcoin was sold, on the theory that Bitcoin was "property" and not money. This ruling should effectively rule out Bitcoin from replacing official currency, at least in the United States, although if Bitcoin's price settles down, some users may find it more attractive than conventional money for some transactions for two reasons.

First, the total volume of Bitcoins, by design, is limited, allowed to increase at a progressively slower rate until the total reaches 21 million units.[20] This contrasts with fiat monies whose supply is governed by human beings running central banks.

Second, Bitcoin users pay little or no fees, in contrast with transaction fees associated with credit cards, which can be as high as 3 percent of the total value of a purchase. Some vendors accepting Bitcoin pass the savings on to consumers in the form of a discount (analogous to some retailers giving discounts for cash payments instead of payment by credit card). In addition, Bitcoin claims it is more useful than conventional currencies for micropayments on the web.

One misconception about Bitcoin is that users leave no trail and thus are anonymous. For this reason, the currency initially was (and almost certainly still is) used in black markets for goods, drugs, and perhaps terrorism. In 2013, the Federal Bureau of Investigation shut down one of the largest black market websites, Silk Road, an action from which users of Bitcoin drew some comfort. The Bitcoin website (www.bitcoin.org) makes clear that if one wants true anonymity, then use cash, but this of course is impossible on the Internet. Nonetheless, the site indicates that various mechanisms associated with Bitcoin provide users some privacy and more are in the works.

Other than how it is treated for tax purposes, the other key question about Bitcoin or any other virtual currency is security. Bitcoin's official website claims it has an unprecedented level of cryptographic protections. Users have their own Bitcoin wallets from which they can either send or receive Bitcoins, with each transaction being authenticated by digital signatures and publicly available through open source software. Bitcoin balances are maintained in a protected, highly distributed network of computers.

Despite all this, however, in early 2014, hackers forced at least two Bitcoin exchanges to temporarily shut down, one of them permanently, as noted earlier. Only time will tell whether all the protections built into Bitcoin and presumably others to be added over time will be sufficient to resurrect confidence in Bitcoin while warding off an army of hackers, who also will have greater incentives to break Bitcoin's code if the currency becomes more popular and its price increases.

Various economists have downplayed Bitcoin for other reasons: that new entrants may be attracted into competition with it, or current holders of Bitcoins may begin selling them off, triggering more sales and thus a collapse in its price.[21] Bitcoin advocates respond that the currency should at least hold its value since its supply is limited. The steady accumulation of websites and real companies accepting Bitcoin for payment may even call into question the critique that the currency won't be used widely until its value stabilizes.

Ironically, if Bitcoin survives, and the more accepted it becomes for transactions (which may require further technological advances), the less demand will exist for speculative purposes. If this sequence of events occurs, the causation may be reversed: more transactions, less speculation. One thing is reasonably clear, however: Some kind of light-touch regulation of those who offer and transfer the currency, which even the Bitcoin foundation welcomes,[22] is likely to be integral to the success of Bitcoin or any virtual currency, since regulation would confer legitimacy and instill confidence among users, especially in the wake of the hacked exchanges.

Only time will tell, of course. That's the way it is with innovations, especially potentially disruptive ones like Bitcoin. But even if, for any number of reasons, Bitcoin fails to become a meaningful alternative currency, experimentation in payments, including other virtual means of payment, will surely continue. Economic history is littered with first movers that failed (think Netscape among web browsers), while second and later movers achieved success (Microsoft with Internet Explorer and more recently, Google with Chrome). Yale's Robert Shiller, a Bitcoin skeptic, nonetheless believes that an electronic currency tied to one or more price indices may be the way forward.[23] If his notion, or some other virtual currency, makes it and Bitcoin does not, Bitcoin's experience at least will have paved the way.

Congestion Pricing

The decaying state of much of America's infrastructure—especially its bridges—is well known and much commented on. Also, like the weather, the congested state of automobile traffic, especially in America's large urban areas, is a staple of everyday conversation and, more so than the weather, a source of constant irritation. The American Society of Civil Engineers reported in late 2013 that one in nine of America's bridges were structurally deficient and over 40 percent of the country's major urban highways were congested.[24] Admittedly, the organization's claims are self-interested, but I am reasonably confident that the average American would find these estimates not unreasonable, and perhaps even low.

The answer to infrastructure decay, like the depreciation of any building or piece of physical equipment, is repair and replacement. That requires money, which will be in short supply given austere budgets at all levels of government and the public's resistance to higher taxes. Very difficult tradeoffs will thus have to be made if America's broken infrastructure is to be fixed.

Congestion is a very different sort of problem, and one where many economists' first answer is not necessarily for the government to spend more money. As my longtime Brookings colleague Anthony Downs (one of the country's leading economists on the housing and real estate sectors) frequently said, "If you build more roads more cars will come to fill them" (which some refer to as Downs' law). In the end, more roads will not necessarily solve the congestion problem.

Ironically, it was the same William Vickrey (profiled in Chapter 3) who first noted in the 1950s that congestion, whether on the highway, or relating to the use of any other limited resource, entails an externality: Each user imposes costs on others in the form of delay. The first best solution to this problem, Vickrey suggested, and many economists have later agreed, is to charge drivers or users of any scarce resource more during peak times, such as rush hours. The congestion charges will encourage employers to adopt different work schedules and consumers in other contexts to shift their uses to other less busy times. The highly regarded urban economist Edward Glaeser of Harvard imagines that Vickrey, who died of a heart attack while driving late at night, was driving at that hour to avoid congestion.[25]

Vickery's heirs or relatives nonetheless can have the satisfaction that the congestion or peak-load pricing he suggested has since been widely adopted in the United States and other countries for telephone and electric utility use, and for urban transportation systems in a few countries. Its application to road pricing in the United States, so far, has been more controversial, for two reasons.

First, there are concerns that government agencies and/or litigants will have access to the time of day and location data encoded in the transponders mounted in vehicles necessary for congestion pricing to work. Indeed, the same concerns have been voiced about the widely discussed technological solution to road congestion, the driverless car, which I discuss in more detail shortly. Legislation could limit access to time of day and location data, but at the very least law enforcement agencies would want exemptions.

Second, congestion charges will take larger bites, on a percentage basis, out of the incomes of low- and middle-income workers, most of whom (at least for a while) will continue to work for employers that will not change their work schedules. In principle, low- and middle-income users could be compensated out of the additional revenues generated from congestion charges, either through general tax relief or more targeted, income-based rebates verified through the submission of annual state income tax returns. At this writing, no such systems have been adopted anywhere in the United States (although one rebate scheme was floated in the California legislature in early 2014).

Cities in other countries—notably, Singapore, London, and Stockholm—nonetheless have implemented some form of congestion pricing, mostly in inner city areas and largely based on driving location rather than time of day. In contrast, in the United States, rationing has been used instead so far to control congestion, through special high-occupancy vehicle (HOV) lanes devoted during peak driving hours to cars with more than occupant.

HOV lanes are only a stopgap solution to traffic congestion, which is more than an irritant to drivers. Traffic congestion, especially the uncertainty of when it is likely to be worst, complicates the business of manufacturers who increasingly rely on just-in-time delivery for both their inputs and their finished goods. To mitigate this problem, companies at all levels of the value chain can hold more inventory, but financing it costs money and thus introduces additional costs that ultimately consumers pay for.

It is possible, and maybe inevitable, that driverless vehicles will be the technological fix that substantially reduces congestion without requiring the construction of new roads, though such a system will require new investments in software and hardware, and further advances in the technology itself, including modifications to existing roads. Even if the technological impediments to a driverless world are overcome, some legal hurdles, in addition to concerns about privacy, stand in the way. High on the list is how liability for the inevitable accidents will be assigned or apportioned among companies producing the software and hardware for driverless vehicles, or even among the drivers themselves in cases where they have a chance to override the automatic features but fail to take action. The earlier such rules are established, preferably through legislation rather than years of litigation, the sooner this technology is likely to be deployed.

In the meantime, population and the number of conventional vehicles continue to grow, adding to congestion, especially in already highly populated urban areas. What is to be done?

Building more publicly financed roads will be difficult, given the pressures on public finances from growing costs of entitlement programs for aging baby boomers (like me) at the federal level and rising health-care and prison costs at the state and local levels. One suggested way around this problem that has been under discussion in Congress (and was supported by the Obama administration) is for the federal government and/or the states to establish infrastructure banks, which governments would capitalize but that would be largely funded by government-guaranteed bonds. These banks, in effect, would be government-sponsored enterprises (GSEs), like Fannie Mae and Freddie Mac, which could fund not only the construction of roads but also capital investment in rail and public transportation. But the GSE status of an infrastructure bank also could be one of its main political problems. Since Fannie and Freddie had to be bailed out by the federal government (even though in the end the payments were fully repaid), federally guaranteed infrastructure banks would run the same risk. That may not prevent their creation, but the prospect of future bailouts, however distant, would significantly complicate the politics of creating the banks, even though the credit subsidy for guaranteeing their bonds and even possible future bailouts might cost the government much less than the cumulative amount of direct federal spending for new roads.

Congestion pricing, thus, may turn out to be the only realistic alternative solution in the medium run for at least slowing the increase of, or ideally reducing, traffic congestion. But because of its drawbacks in a public context, we may see it penetrate most rapidly in private settings—that is, for privately financed toll roads where operators are not subject to the same degree of public scrutiny and concerns that so far have frustrated the implementation of the idea for public roads.

Yet even privatized road construction and operation has hurdles. For one thing, a number of privatized toll roads in the United States have run into financial difficulties, primarily because the projected amounts of traffic, and thus toll revenue required to pay off the bonds that financed the roads, have not lived up to expectations.[26] In addition, where reasonably substitutable public roads are not available, regulation may be required to prevent monopoly pricing by road owners. At the same time, however, the prospect of rate regulation limits the upside gains to these owners of private roads, which could discourage private investment in these projects.

Each of these problems is not insurmountable. The uncertainty in revenue projections caused by uncertain traffic flows, which are sensitive to both toll prices and local economic conditions, can be addressed by using more equity to finance future toll roads than has been true in the past. A higher mix of equity financing will require higher tolls than otherwise, since equity is more expensive than debt, but this should not be a barrier to getting the deals done. To keep tolls down, it may be necessary for governments to chip in some of the capital costs, perhaps 10 to 15 percent, but these efforts will be constrained by the limited availability of government funding.

Adverse public policies, whether in the form of lengthy construction permitting processes or excessively tight price controls, can inhibit or totally prevent more private roads. But these problems can be overcome. State and local governments committed to providing additional roads can move approval processes along if government officials know public funds will not be required for their construction and operation. As for monopoly power requiring some form of rate regulation, this is much more likely to exist for bottleneck structures like bridges than it is for roads, where there is typically more than one way for drivers to reach their destinations. Furthermore, the financial pressure and attractiveness of selling existing roads and other public assets may limit the desire of governments to put too heavy a hand on the regulatory scale.[27]

Indeed, some clever experimentation with privatization is going on in various states at this writing. Aware that investors have little appetite for funding greenfield road construction projects where predicting future traffic volumes is especially hazardous, Georgia and Texas allow private firms to own and build additional lanes next to *existing* roads that are already congested and thus where investors can have greater confidence in future tolled-traffic forecasts. Puerto Rico, a U.S. territory plagued with financial problems, privatized two existing roads in 2013. Each of these experiments is aided by technologies, such as E-Z

Passes that drivers can purchase, or video monitoring that can send regular bills to drivers who don't have passes.

My guess is that other states facing financial pressures, especially those with large unfunded pension funds, will look to privatized roads, either existing or new ones close to current ones, as a way of killing two birds with one stone: harnessing the financial power of private investors and owners to build and operate roads while taking some of the funds or the bonds issued to finance the projects and using them to shore up the state and local government pension funds.[28]

In the end, one of the nation's leading transportation economists, Clifford Winston, is probably right when he concludes that governments will have to inch their way toward privatized roads (and other traditionally public infrastructure) and congestion charges through a process of experimentation before embracing these ideas wholesale.[29] But at least the ideas are out there and have been widely recommended by many economists, who someday may see their visions for wider use of congestion pricing actually realized.

Which businesses will flourish from more extensive use of congestion charges? I suspect many more than most people imagine now, since the notion of charging for peak use has broad potential application in a wide range of retail and wholesale markets. Congestion pricing not only will enhance revenues and profits of the firms that adopt it, but also change consumer and business behavior.

With respect to congestion charges for transportation in particular, the firms that will benefit most will be the private firms that own roads and related facilities. Investment bankers will take their cut of the equity and debt used to finance such ventures. At the consumer end, applications software will be written to enable users to minimize the charges they have to pay. Residential patterns and work hours will change. I can't outline all of the implications, but one thing I know: Life would be different, and with an economist's faith, I believe, on balance, better.

The Bottom Line

There are many great ideas out there waiting to be exploited. Some ideas are tried out too early and fail. Others are copied, but in some cases, the first or second movers are difficult, if not impossible, to dislodge. Timing is thus not everything in business—execution and effort are also critical—but timing often really matters.

There is an old saying that good economists should never forecast a number and a date at the same time. I've implicitly followed that adage here, outlining ideas on the shelf relating to prediction markets, financial innovation, and congestion pricing that have been introduced into the marketplace to a limited degree, but are waiting for much more extensive commercialization possibilities, many beyond those imagined here. Such is the power and usefulness of economists and their ideas.

Notes

1. For more complete information about this market, see http://tippie.uiowa.edu/iem/.

2. The *New Yorker* columnist James Surowiecki invented and popularized the term in his now classic *The Wisdom of Crowds* (New York: Anchor, 2005).

3. See http://ubplj.org/index.php/jpm/index. For a wider application of prediction markets to public policy decisions, see Robin Hanson, "Decision Markets," in *Entrepreneurial Economics: Bright Ideas from the Dismal Science*, ed. Alexander Tabarrok (New York: Oxford University Press, 2002), 79–85.

4. See www.cnn.com/2003/ALLPOLITICS/07/29/terror.market/.

5. Andrew Rice, "The Fall of Intrade and the Business of Betting on Real Life," *Buzzfeed*, February 20, 2014, 13, www.buzzfeed.com/andrewrice/the-fall-of-intrade-and-the-business-of-betting-on-real-life.

6. Ibid. One of Intrade's co-founders, Ron Bernstein, has since reentered the prediction market business, with the website Tradesports.com, which lets people bet on the outcomes of sports events.

7. Ibid., 16.

8. Gillian Tett provides an excellent history of how these deals began in her highly recommended account of the precursors of the financial crisis, *Fools' Gold: The Inside Story of J.P. Morgan and How Wall Street Greed Corrupted Its Bold Dream and Created a Financial Catastrophe* (New York: Free Press, 2009).

9. Adam Davidson, "How AIG Fell Apart," Reuters, September 18, 2008, www.reuters.com/article/2008/09/18/us-how-aig-fell-apart-idUSMAR85972720080918.

10. James Kwak, "The Profitable Bailout? The Real Cost of Saving AIG and Wall St.," *The Atlantic*, September 12, 2012, www.theatlantic.com/business/

archive/2012/09/the-profitable-bailout-inside-the-real-costs-of-the-saving-aig-and-wall-st/262281/.

11. Data from the Bank for International Settlements.

12. The market interest rate on a bond is simply its annual promised interest payment, or its *coupon*, divided by the market price of the bond at any given time.

13. The charge that CDS markets offer a means for speculation and therefore should be condemned is thus fundamentally misplaced, just as it would be if applied to stocks or commodities where speculators are essential to add liquidity and to take the other sides of trades that no one else may be willing to take.

14. See Robert J. Shiller, *Finance and the Good Society* (Princeton: Princeton University Press, 2012), and *The New Financial Order: Risk in the 21st Century* (Princeton, NJ: Princeton University Press, 2004).

15. See, e.g., Robert Z. Lawrence and Robert E. Litan, *Saving Free Trade* (Washington, DC: Brookings Institution, 1986); Martin N. Baily, Gary Burtless, and Robert E. Litan, *Growth with Equity* (Washington, DC: Brookings Institution, 1993); Gary Burtless, et al., *Globaphobia* (Washington, DC: Brookings Institution, 2001); Lori Kletzer and Robert E. Litan, "A Prescription for Worker Anxiety: Wage and Health Insurance for Displaced Workers," Brookings Policy Brief 73, March 2001, www.brookings.edu/events/2001/03/06unemployment; and Lael Brainard, Robert E. Litan, and Nicholas Warren, "Insuring America's Workers in a New Age of Offshoring," Brookings Policy Brief 143, July 2005, www.brookings.edu/~/media/research/files/papers/2005/7/macroeconomics%20brainard/pb143.pdf.

16. *Economic Report of the President, 2013*, Table B-44, 376.

17. Robert J. Shiller, *Macro Markets: Creating Institutions for Managing Society's Largest Economic Risks* (New York: Clarendon Press, 1993) and Stefano Athanasoulis, Robert Shiller, and Eric von Wincoup, in Tabarrok, *Entrepreneurial Economics*, 23–46.

18. See Jessica Leber, "Economist Proposes a $30 Billion Megafund for New Cancer Drugs," *MIT Technology Review*, November 19, 2012, www.technologyreview.com/news/506916/economist-proposes-a-30-billion-megafund-for-new-cancer-drugs/. The idea is explained in a video by one of Lo's colleagues, Roger Stein, www.ted.com/talks/roger_stein_a_bold_new_way_to_fund_drug_research.html.

19. Detailed technical information about Bitcoin is available on its official website, where its Frequently Asked Questions are most useful: http://bitcoin.org/en/faq#who-created-bitcoin.

20. The way in which Bitcoins are created and the fascinating industry that has grown up trying to collect them is described in detail in Ashlee Vance and

Brad Stone, "Bitcoin Rush," *Bloomberg Businessweek*, January 13–19 (2014): 46–51.

21. See, e.g., Brad Delong, "Watching Bitcoin, Dogecoin, Etc.," Washington Center for Equitable Growth, December 28, 2013, http://equitablegrowth .org/2013/12/28/1466/watching-bitcoin-dogecoin-etc, and Paul Krugman, "Bitcoin Is Evil," *New York Times*, December 28, 2013, http://krugman.blogs .nytimes.com/2013/12/28/bitcoin-is-evil/?_r=0.

22. This is based on an on-the-record interview with the foundation's general counsel, Patrick Murck, January 29, 2014, with other Bloomberg analysts and reporters.

23. Robert J. Shiller, "In Search of a Stable Electronic Currency," *New York Times*, March 1, 2014.

24. Bob Tita, "Slow Road to Recovery," *Wall Street Journal*, October 14, 2013.

25. Edward Glaeser, *Triumph of the City: How Our Greatest Invention Makes Us Richer, Smarter, Greener, Healthier and Happier* (New York: Penguin Books, 2012): 105.

26. See Ryan Dezember and Emily Glazer, "Drop in Traffic Takes Toll on Investors in Private Roads," *Wall Street Journal*, November 21, 2013, and Nathan Koppel and Emily Glazer, "Fast Toll Road Struggles to Pick Up Drivers," *Wall Street Journal*, January 3, 2014.

27. *The Economist* had a cover story in early 2014 on the potentially huge revenue gains governments around the world could realize by selling off state-owned assets, and in the process improving the efficiency of the assets and functions after privatization. See "Selling Out the Store," *The Economist*, January 11–17, 2014.

28. Information for this paragraph provided by employees of Standard & Poor's.

29. Clifford Winston, "On the Performance of the U.S. Transportation System: Caution Ahead," *Journal of Economic Literature* 51, no. 3 (2013): 7773–7824. For an analysis of how technological advances will ultimately address at least the road congestion problem, see Clifford Winston and Fred Mannering, "Implementing Technology to Improve Public Highway Performance: A Leapfrog Technology from the Private Sector Is Going to Be Necessary," *Economics of Transportation* (2014), http://dx.doi.org/10.1016/j .ecotra.2013.12.004.

Chapter 14

Economic Ideas
and Challenges
on the Policy Shelf:
Business Implications

Economists who are in the profession because they want to influence policy makers, with some exceptions, typically have to wait some time for their ideas to be taken seriously, if at all, and perhaps even longer to be implemented. A prime example, discussed in Chapter 11, is the idea of auctioning off licenses to the electromagnetic spectrum, floated by Ronald Coase in 1959, but not put into effect until 1993. Coase, who lived to the age of 102, was lucky enough to be alive to see his idea become a reality. Most economists don't get that pleasure, either because the time was never right while they were alive for a crisis or action-forcing event that could bring their ideas to policy makers' attention, or because the ideas were impractical or even wrongheaded.

It is thus a bit hazardous for anyone to project which of the many possible economic policy ideas already out there on the proverbial policy shelf will be implemented by legislators, regulators, or possibly judges. Nonetheless, I believe three sound ideas long in the public domain have a reasonable chance of being adopted in some version at some point. I'm not going to predict when this might happen, like I didn't do with the direct business ideas outlined in Chapter 13. But any one or all of the ideas discussed in this chapter could be adopted in the context of a successful effort addressing the long-term federal deficit, whenever that happens (hopefully sooner than later). I also highlight some potential business impacts if these ideas are implemented.

Federal Budget Deficits as Drivers of Policy Change

For over a decade, the nation's official scorekeeper for federal budgets, the Congressional Budget Office, has projected that the federal deficit, at this writing in 2014 at about 3 percent of the nation's output (GDP), will grow, in the absence of offsetting policy measures, to unsustainable levels over the next 30 to 50 years. The main reason: soaring health-care spending, driven in part by more baby boomers drawing on Medicare, and also by rising health-care costs. To a lesser extent, rising costs for Medicaid, the federal and state health-care program for low-income households, also are projected to contribute to the growth in deficits. None of this is new, of course, since budget experts for years have been warning of these problems. One of the earliest was Charles Schultze, President Johnson's budget director, President Carter's chief economist, and a longtime scholar at the Brookings Institution (see following box).

Charles Schultze: The Quintessential Economic Policy Expert

He often gets confused with the author of *Peanuts*—the other Charles Schultz (without the *e*)—but no one who knows policy and how economics can be used to inform policy makers confuses the importance, humanity, and originality of Charles Schultze.

Schultze is a Washington, DC, native who went to Georgetown for college and to the University of Maryland for his PhD. He began his teaching career at the University of Indiana, moved to the University of Maryland, and then was tapped by the Kennedy administration to become an assistant director of the Bureau of the Budget (since renamed the Office of Management and Budget, or OMB). His quick mind and deep understanding of the mechanics of the budget were recognized by the budget bureau's director, Kermit Gordon, who upon leaving to assume the presidency of the Brookings Institution in 1966, recommended Schultze as his replacement to President Johnson, who readily agreed.

The Johnson years were an exciting time for public policy, and especially to be OMB director. Schultze had to manage the competing demands for federal resources devoted to Johnson's multiple Great Society programs (aimed at helping the disadvantaged), and to fund America's escalating involvement in the Vietnam War, a venture that eventually contributed to Johnson's decision not to run for reelection in 1968.

After the Johnson years, Schultze joined the Brookings Institution as a senior fellow where, off and on, he has spent the rest of his career, turning out a steady stream of books, professional papers, and popular articles on a wide range of public policy issues, including budget policy, economic growth, energy and environmental economics, and industrial policy (which he has vigorously opposed). His book *Public Use of the Private Interest* is essential reading for those who urge that regulators use market-like incentives rather than command-and-control detailed regulations to achieve social goals.[1] Later, Schultze wrote a popular guide to macroeconomics, *Memos to the President: A Guide through Macroeconomics for the Busy Policymaker*,[2] which in my view is the most readable and informed treatise on the subject ever written.

Charlie (as he was and is known to all his colleagues and the media) couldn't stay out of the policy fray entirely, however. He knew too much and Democratic political leaders

(continued)

wanted his experience and advice. So he returned to public service after President Carter was elected, chairing the Council of Economic Advisers for all four years of that presidency (two of which I had the privilege to work for him and with Bill Nordhaus, another giant in the profession, whom you will meet later in this chapter).

After CEA, Charlie returned to Brookings, where for a time he directed the economic studies program, after the passing of the longtime director and tax expert Joseph Pechman (who is discussed in the next section). Upon his return to Brookings, Schultze was an early advocate of long-term deficit reduction, warning that continued high and rising deficits were more like "termites in the woodwork" eating away at the long-run growth prospects for the country, and less likely (at least at the time) to be the spark for a sudden run on the dollar or a recession-inducing spike in interest rates. Schultze's concerns about the nation's fiscal health predate the concerns expressed by leaders in both political parties since the Great Recession about the corrosive effects of long-term federal deficits.

Schultze's economic prowess is also widely valued by many in the private sector. He served on a number of corporate advisory boards, and has given countless speeches and written numerous op-eds for newspaper and magazines, in addition to writing for his professional colleagues.

Charlie is and always will be Brookings personified. Brookings officers, directors, and staff constantly seek his counsel. To me, Charlie is a professional father figure (he even looks a bit like my own dad), whose advice and friendship I always will treasure.

During the Obama administration, a number of bipartisan panels issued reports and recommendations for a grand bargain to rein in long-run deficits—consisting of a combination of tax increases and cuts in the growth of spending of entitlement spending—but the president and the Congress (especially the Republican-controlled House) could not come to agreement. The failure to do so triggered across-the-board cuts in spending, known as the sequester, over 10 years in discretionary spending (that part of the budget that runs the government and does not transfer income, as do the three major entitlement programs, Medicare, Medicaid, and Social Security) in 2012, which was partially offset in 2014 to 2015 by a limited budget deal reached in January 2014. In addition, in January 2013, Congress enacted, at the president's urging, tax legislation that canceled the cut in the top marginal tax bracket for very high-income individuals and families under the 2001 tax bill designed by the George W. Bush administration and enacted by the Congress in that year.

The combination of the tax increases and spending reductions, coupled with a slowdown in the rate of increase in health-care spending, brought some stability to the projections of the ratio of federal debt to GDP, one widely watched measure of debt sustainability. By late 2013, the Congressional Budget Office (CBO) was projecting that this ratio would remain in the mid-70 percent range through the early years of the 2020's, much higher than the 35 to 40 percent range before the Great Recession, but at least not exploding.

Unfortunately, from the mid-2020s and beyond, the outlook is expected to darken. Rising health-care costs spread over an increasing beneficiary population (seniors and the indigent), coupled with rising interest costs on a mounting public debt, are eventually projected to drive both the deficit and the total federal debt burden as a share of national output to unprecedented peacetime levels. CBO's forecast in late 2013 is that by 2038, the ratio of publicly held federal debt to GDP will hit 100 percent. The debt-to-GDP ratio could be almost twice as high under some more pessimistic budget assumptions.[3]

Economists continue to debate at what level or rate of increase this key ratio becomes unsustainable, though one thing is clear: At some point investors can lose confidence in the willingness and ability of policy makers to get the debt burden under control. When confidence goes, and it can do so suddenly, it can trigger a sharp rise in interest rates, perhaps even a seizure in financial markets. This is precisely what happened (for different reasons) during the financial crisis of September 2008. At the very least, high and rising federal deficits keep interest rates higher than they otherwise would be, discouraging private investment, which is one key to long-run economic growth—Schultze's termites in the woodwork scenario played out over decades.

Each of the policy measures discussed in the balance of this chapter could directly, or indirectly, reduce deficits and debt and thus reduce the likelihood of their unwelcome effects. Each would also have private sector impacts, hurting some firms while helping others. In this sense, each of the measures described next represents a policy platform for business analogous to the deregulation platforms highlighted in Chapters 9 through 12.

But don't expect any of these ideas to become reality anytime soon. If the federal deficit as a share of GDP remains in the 3 to 5 percent range for the next decade, as CBO has projected, then federal policy makers are likely to be complacent, and at least ten years away from making the kind of bold policy decisions described next and that have been in public circulation for some time.

Premium Support for Medicare and Medicaid

The main driver of increased federal deficits and debt over the long run, apart from rising interest costs on the mounting debt (combined with rising rates themselves as the economy gets back to normal), is the projected increase in federal costs for Medicare and Medicaid. Rising subsidy costs under the Affordable Care Act of 2010 will make things worse. CBO's 2013 long-term budget outlook projects that total federal health-care spending, which was just short of 5 percent of GDP in 2010, should hit 9 percent in 2040, and 13 percent by 2080.[4] In early 2014, CBO revised slightly downward the near-term Medicare cost growth projections,[5] but this revision doesn't fundamentally alter the organization's prior pessimistic long-term outlook.

Some health-care cost optimists point to the decade-long slowdown (2002 to 2012) in the annual rate of U.S. health-care spending growth as a potential game-changer. But even if annual U.S. health-care spending increases keep chugging along at 4 percent, down from about 10 percent a decade earlier—which is unlikely as the population ages and the millions enrolled under the ACA use health care more intensively—the CBO has calculated that aging alone will drive federal spending on health care as a percent of GDP steadily upward.

At any pace, the rise in federal costs for all federal health-care pro-grams, including the ACA, will crowd out other federal spending or lead to steadily larger and unsustainable deficits. While this fact may not be appreciated widely until the 2020s, when it is, there will be a search for solutions, and my guess is that interest eventually will center on an idea that two liberal economists—Henry Aaron and Robert Reischauer—hatched in the 1990s called premium support.[6]

Carefully avoiding the politically sensitive word *voucher* (the pub-lic school education arena has not made it popular), Aaron and Reischauer suggested that each Medicare beneficiary be given a fixed amount, adjusted for medical-care inflation, to purchase private insur-ance. These premium supports also would be adjusted for preexist-ing physical conditions of beneficiaries and where they live, to take account of differential risks and medical costs across the country. The authors acknowledged that making these adjustments would be diffi-cult (though one of them has become easier given one of the reforms in the Affordable Care Act, discussed shortly).

By effectively putting a cap on the growth in total Medicare expenditures, and letting individuals determine how best to live within their personal government-provided, health-care budgets (which could be supplemented with additional private insurance), Aaron and Reischauer argued that a premium-support program would har-ness market forces to slow the rate of increase of Medicare spending per beneficiary (the part that theoretically can be controlled, not the growth in the number of beneficiaries). The premium support idea theoretically also could be applied to Medicaid, the government sup-port program for health care for low-income individuals of all ages, and also nursing care for seniors without any resources, but the authors did not go that far. (One interesting historical fact: Aaron and Reischauer note that Medicaid was a Republican idea, which Democrats who favored Medicare accepted in a kind of trade. The combination com-prehensive law incorporating both ideas passed Congress and was signed into law by President Johnson in 1965.)

The premium-support proposal lay dormant for over a decade, until after President Obama was elected and interest ran high—though in retrospect only briefly—for developing a grand bargain to make a significant dent in the long-term federal deficit projections.

This led to a number of bipartisan proposals containing some element of premium support plus an annual cap on the growth in support payments. Some versions of the idea would have eventually replaced the entire fee-for-service Medicare payment system (allowing the smaller managed-care option that mostly healthy seniors choose as a voluntary option), while others would have allowed seniors to choose between a presumably more cost-effective, fee-for-service plan or premium support. One of the most widely publicized of these premium-support proposals was an idea floated and seemingly endorsed by Representative Paul Ryan (also chairman of the House Budget Committee and vice–presidential candidate in 2012) and one of the most experienced budget professionals in Washington, Alice Rivlin, of the Brookings Institution (see following box). The two eventually parted ways, largely over the generosity of the premium support payments, but it is significant that two prominent experts on both sides of the political aisle were able to agree at least on the general architecture of the idea.

Alice Rivlin: Policy Pioneer

Before there was Janet Yellen, there was Alice Rivlin (and it should not be a surprise that the two are good friends). Rivlin is the most experienced Washington policy expert of the past five decades, and she is still going strong.

In a day when few women became economists, Rivlin was a pioneer. She graduated from Bryn Mawr College and then obtained her PhD from Radcliffe (which hadn't yet been merged into Harvard). She established herself out of the box as one of the clearest thinkers and writers in the profession—her book *Systematic Thinking for Social Action* remains a must read for anyone wanting a public policy career. She was elected to the highest office in the profession's association, the presidency of the American Economic Association.

Rivlin cut her teeth in the policy world at the Brookings Institution and then as an assistant secretary for policy at the old Department of Health and Welfare (since renamed

the Department of Health and Human Services). After returning to Brookings and becoming director of the economic program, the public part of her public policy career began to soar.

Rivlin was the founding director of the Congressional
Budget Office, which Congress established in 1974. She later was
deputy director and then director of the Office of Management
in the Clinton administration, serving thereafter as vice-chair
of the Federal Reserve Board. Unlike most high-level federal
officials, who either lived in Washington before their appoint-
ment or moved there afterward, Rivlin has taken a longtime
interest in the public policies of the city. While she was still at
the Fed, Rivlin was named chair of the District of Columbia
Control Board and was instrumental in helping the city's finances
get back on solid ground after years of disrepair.

After she left government service, Rivlin continued her
public work on the long-term deficit as co-chair (with former senator Pete Domenici) of the Debt Reduction Task Force
sponsored by the Bipartisan Policy Center. Simultaneously,
President Obama appointed her to the Simpson–Bowles
Commission, to seek bipartisan solutions to the rising national
debt. In the course of that work, Rivlin worked with Rep. Paul
Ryan on a premium-support plan for controlling Medicare costs,
a policy stance for which she received some criticism from the
left in the Democratic Party. She has stood her ground as one
of the leading public intellectuals making the case for a grand
bargain to put the federal government on a more sustainable
long-run fiscal path.

Rivlin has received numerous awards for her published
work (which is extensive) and public service. She has also taught
at numerous universities, including Harvard, George Mason, the
New School, and Georgetown.

On a personal note, Alice has been a long-time mentor
and counselor to me throughout my career and a close friend.
I also worked with her during a portion of her tenure at OMB.
My thanks and admiration for her will live on as long as I do.

Things took a step backwards in the 2012 presidential campaign. After having endorsed premium support before his pick of Paul Ryan as his running mate, Mitt Romney downplayed the idea during the campaign itself. This didn't stop President Obama and other Democrats from attacking the idea as turning Medicare into a dreaded voucher program. Since Obama's reelection in 2012 premium support hasn't yet recovered from that distancing of both candidates.

In my view this recent history doesn't mean the idea is dead. At some point in the future, the inexorable rise in health-care costs, especially those paid by the federal government not just for the traditional entitlements Medicare and Medicaid, but eventually the costs of subsidizing insurance purchases by those in the workforce under the ACA, will compel policy makers to dust off ideas currently on the shelf, like premium support, in an effort to slow rising federal costs for health care.

Ironically, one of the features of the ACA itself that is most popular—prohibiting insurance companies from discriminating on the basis of a patient's preexisting medical conditions—should make a future premium-support plan for Medicare and possibly Medicaid easier to implement. The ban on discrimination reduces the need for complicated risk adjustments in the amount of the support required by individuals (risk adjustment may still be necessary for insurers, which have different mixes of insured populations, but this should be easier to accomplish than on a per-person basis). There still would be a need for some geographical variation in the amounts of the supports; otherwise beneficiaries in areas with high medical costs could be put at a serious disadvantage relative to those living in low-cost areas.

Admittedly, other ideas for controlling federal spending on health care will be tried before policy makers, or the public, will be ready to embrace premium support. Three of them are embodied in the ACA, and are meant to apply to both the non-senior and senior populations.

One idea is to encourage more providers to join together in integrated networks, in the hope of achieving the cost savings that one-stop-shop medical organizations like the Mayo Clinic, Intermountain Health Care in Utah, or the Geisinger health system in Pennsylvania appear to have achieved. These new networks, called Accountable Care Organizations, are not totally integrated in that the constituent parts are still nominally independent, but the ACOs attempt to achieve virtually, if not physically, the kind of integration that exists in the fully integrated systems. So far, preliminary results for the cost savings achieved by the ACOs are encouraging, though the jury is still out on the magnitude of those savings that are achievable.[7]

A second, much more controversial part of the ACA is its creation of an Independent Payment Advisory Board (IPAB) charged with identifying ways of reducing spending growth in the Medicare program, but only if spending exceeds a target rate. Although at this writing the president hadn't yet nominated any of the 15 health-care experts who are supposed to serve on the IPAB, the health-care law allows the board to function, and in its place the Secretary of Health and Human Services (HHS) to make the decisions that were vested in the Board. The IPAB's recommendations (or those of HHS) go into effect unless Congress stops them. Hospitals, however, are exempt from the IPAB recommendations until 2020, so any recommendations the board (or HHS) may make before then will be concentrated among physicians, skilled-nursing facilities, and pharmaceutical companies.

The IPAB has attracted strong criticism; some even labeled the body a death panel. Without debating the pejorative, the IPAB represents a top-down governmental approach as to which procedures will be reimbursed and what will not. Of course, Medicare already does this; IPAB would only sharpen the focus on cost control. Will it be successful without sacrificing quality of care? No one really knows, and it is far too early to tell.

Third, Medicare and Medicaid have been experimenting for several years with alternatives to fee-for-service payments systems for health-care providers. Like lawyers who get paid by the hour, doctors or hospitals that get paid by the services they provide, or by medical inputs, have incentives to maximize them whether they lead to improved health outcomes for patients or not. As alternatives, the government has experimented with various forms of bundled payments, or lump-sum payments for a single medical episode—say a particular surgical procedure and follow-up monitoring—or even care for a chronic disease over a given period. The payments are directed to a single general contractor-like provider, say a hospital, which then is able to subcontract specialized care, such as physical therapy or counseling, to other providers that may be more cost effective in providing these services. A variation of the bundled payment is payment by medical outcomes, more if the outcomes are successful, less if the opposite is true. In early 2014, Congress was considering writing such outcomes-based bonus systems into law.

In principle, these alternatives could save money and even lead to better outcomes through improved coordination of patient care. But like all fixed-fee arrangements for professionals, they shift the financial risks to providers, who try to compensate by charging higher upfront fees for assuming the risks. Competition among providers tends to hold down these added costs, but then competition may also lead to some providers delivering suboptimal care, outcomes that may not be known for some time.

None of this is to say that government payers should not continue to experiment with various alternatives to fee-for-service payments. It is just to raise a red flag of caution that these alternatives are unlikely to be silver-bullet solutions to cost control, especially in single-payer systems, such as Medicare and Medicaid. At the same time, single-payer systems also have no marketing costs, which are built into the cost structures of the competitive health-care insurance industry. The tradeoffs between the different kinds of savings under single payer versus a system of competitive insurers cannot be resolved in theory, but only in the everyday experiences of the real world, which is why health-care economics is one of the most interesting and challenging subfields in the economics profession.

In the end, my intuition is that the various measures currently aimed at controlling Medicare costs probably will not be sufficient, individually or collectively, to truly bend the cost curve over the long run to prevent either major increases in taxes or the deficit. That is why I believe some form of premium support one day will get its turn in the policy spotlight, but only for younger workers, or those below a certain cutoff age (the rest being grandfathered under the existing, but evolving, system dominated by fee-for-service but with different payment arrangements at the edges).

Unlike the other methods at cost control, which for the most part are top–down and controlled by government, premium support relies primarily on market forces, mediated primarily by competition among insurers and health-care networks that take on an insurance function (like the Kaiser system). The virtue of a decentralized system is that as long as there is sufficient choice among insurers/networks—a condition the authorities must assure—consumer decisions will ultimately drive the behavior of providers. Consumers will also demand more information about prices and quality of care in a choice-driven system. If and when premium support is adopted, the public and policy makers will then have economists to thank or to blame, probably some of both.

I do not have the space here or the expertise to flesh out all of the details of even a streamlined premium-support plan. One especially knotty issue is whether and to what extent to means test the amount of the premium-support payments. Critics of the idea express the legitimate worry that if the system does not succeed in constraining the growth of medical costs, then low- and even middle-income seniors will get shortchanged over time, and find that their government-assisted insurance covers less and less of their medical expenses. My inclination is to build in an income-based adjustment for the support payments, though I realize that also would introduce more complexity into the administration of the program.

What impact on health-care providers and insurers would a premium-support system have? Put another way, what is likely to be the *business* impact of such a major change in the Medicare and possibly Medicaid programs?

The short answer is that a premium-support system would accelerate the changes in health-care markets that are already underway. There would be greater pressure on health-care providers to become more efficient, and thus more pressure among small physician practices to sell out to larger providers or affiliate with ACOs. This is analogous to what has been happening to grocery stores, retailers, and banks for decades. Insurers, like the government, will continue to experiment with alternatives to fee-for-service, but most economists would probably say that the market would do a better job deciding the best outcomes than a potentially politicized government agency.

At the same time, because insurers and health-care networks will be looking to cut costs, there will be room for innovative new companies to offer solutions: more wireless medicine (wearable monitors and the technology to support them); more Minute Clinics staffed by nurse practitioners (as states face growing consumer pressure to allow them to widen the scope of their practices); and new organizational forms of health-care delivery. In principle, in their search for lower costs and better care, health-care providers will have stronger incentives to prescribe new pharmaceuticals, but as discussed in the previous chapter, new financing techniques will be necessary to encourage truly innovative drug discoveries.

Taxing Consumption

All governments must raise taxes to fund their spending. Economists generally support borrowing to fill any gap between revenues and expenses when the economy is not generating sufficient revenue to balance the budget, and ideally running surpluses when times are good. The ideal is sometimes met by local and state governments that must meet a balance requirement constitutionally, or because they can't print money to cover any deficits. National governments, or more precisely their monetary authorities, can print money to finance deficits, but there are limits to this: Too much money eventually means excessive inflation, which undermines people's trust in one of the things they count on their governments to manage well, the purchasing power of their currency. The rise of Nazism after Germany's experience with post-World War I hyperinflation is history's starkest proof that losing that trust can lead to revolutionary and sometimes horrible consequences.

But back to taxes: If you ask most economists, they'll tell you the best tax system is one that most efficiently raises revenue, least distorts private sector behavior, doesn't dampen economic growth, and is widely perceived as fair. Since 1913, the federal government has relied overwhelmingly on income taxes—on individuals and on corporations—to achieve these goals, with mixed results. Today, it is widely conceded that the income tax code is a mess, horribly long and complex, inefficient, and depending on your political party preference (as a declining share of Americans seem to have), unfair and punishing.

With the current state of affairs in mind, many tax experts and ordinary citizens old enough to remember look back fondly to the landmark 1986 tax reform legislation that significantly cut personal income tax rates while scaling back some tax preferences. History credits the several leading elected officials who brokered the deal: President Ronald Reagan, Senator Bill Bradley, Senator Robert Packwood, and then Representatives Dan Rostenkowski and Jack Kemp, who despite their many differences on other issues, were able to come together and push through the Congress perhaps the most important and constructive tax reform package of all time.

What many do not know, however, is the identity of the individual who did more than perhaps anyone to build the intellectual foundation for this broader base–lower rate reform. This idea continues to have strong appeal today, despite the fact that the 1986 reform was gradually undone in the decades that followed by a series of special tax breaks aimed at inducing changes in private behavior that could not otherwise be accomplished politically by direct federal spending. That individual is Joseph Pechman, the longtime director of economic studies at the Brookings Institution, and for decades one of the leading tax economists in the United States (see following box).

Joseph Pechman: An Original Tax Reformer[8]

Like a number of famous economists, Joseph (Joe) Pechman grew up in New York City and attended City College there, before going to Wisconsin for his PhD. Pechman got that degree shortly after the United States entered World War II, and was lucky enough to be able to use his quantitative skills as a meteorologist for the Army during the war. After the war, he began his professional career as an economist at the Treasury department, and later served on the staff of the Council of Economic Advisers and the Committee for Economic Development.

It wasn't until Pechman came to Brookings, however, that his professional economics career really began to blossom. Through numerous articles, he analyzed the economic impact

(*continued*)

of the income tax code, with special emphasis on its distributional impact. He eventually became one of the nation's leading economic authorities on taxation. His landmark book, *Federal Tax Policy*, went through five editions.

Joe was more than a scholar. He was one of Brookings' great administrators, serving as director of the Institution's economic studies program for 21 years (1962 to 1983). He had a remarkable ability to focus his energies: He followed a routine from which he rarely departed, of working on his scholarly papers in the morning, typically at home, and then coming to the Institution for lunch—as lunch was and is perhaps the most important component of the glue that holds Brookings scholars (or those at many organizations for that matter) together—after which he handled his administrative chores.

In addition to being one of the most important fathers of tax reform—lower rates, broader base—Joe was instrumental in designing a plan for revenue sharing by the federal government with states and localities. Although he worked with Kennedy's CEA Chairman Walter Heller on the idea, it was not implemented until the Nixon administration.

On a personal note, I was one of many research assistants (then working primarily for Arthur Okun) who had the privilege of working at Brookings during Joe's tenure as economic studies chairman. After I finished my own two-year stint at CEA, Joe offered me a job as a junior scholar at Brookings, but at the time I wanted to get some legal experience under my belt, and I think I disappointed him by not accepting the offer. I did return to Brookings in 1984, however, and so any disappointment on Joe's part hopefully was erased. When a dozen years later I was fortunate to be chosen director of economic studies myself, I would often go into the conference room across from the director's office and look at Joe's picture (along with Okun's and George Perry's) and pinch myself with my good fortune, and wonder whether Joe would have approved of the decisions I made.

One final thought and belated thank you to Joe: Even when I was a lowly research assistant at Brookings, he invited me to eat at lunch with the more senior stars in the department, a privilege I never forgot. One of the subjects that repeatedly came up at these lunches, often raised by Joe, would be the performance of the stock market, and thus the performance of the scholars' defined contribution pension plans. I early on was thus sensitized to the need to save a portion of my salary, a lesson for which I am forever grateful (if only everyone in the country could eat lunch at Brookings with the economists they would learn this lesson, too, and be much better off for doing so for this reason alone!).

As I write this, in the first half of 2014, Washington policy and tax wonks have been focused on the possibility—growing more remote by the day—that Congress and the president may eventually agree on some kind of comprehensive tax reform, aimed primarily at cleaning up the business tax code, eliminating or narrowing many of the tax preferences built into the code, and using the money thus generated to lower the top corporate tax rate. At 35 percent, this notional rate is among the highest in the developed world. But the reason I say notional is that many, if not most, C corporations (those whose income is taxed twice, once at the corporate level, and then at the shareholder level through the dividends that corporations distribute) pay effective tax rates far lower than 35 percent. They can do this by taking advantage of various deductions and credits built into the tax code. In addition, many multinational companies are able to move their income and expenses around to different countries, with lower tax rates than the United States, in ways that reduce their overall tax burdens.

Maybe corporate tax reform that broadens the base and lowers the rate will happen sometime over the next several years, in the same way that the 1986 tax reform initiative did for individuals. It will be an uphill effort because any such reform will create both winners and losers, and the latter will do everything in their power to stop reform dead in its tracks.

However important business tax reform may be, the larger issue for the country over the long run is to what extent federal taxes will *increase* in order to sustain an even reformed system of entitlement spending, which as I noted at the outset of this chapter, will inexorably grow as baby boomers continue to retire and age, and medical costs continue to go up. In principle, one way to increase revenues is to cut back on tax preferences (for individuals and businesses) *without* lowering tax rates, or at least not lowering them so much, so that any base broadening effort actually generates more revenue and thus is not merely revenue neutral. Apart from the political difficulty of pulling off such a feat, it is unlikely that such an effort will come anywhere close to raising sufficient revenue to support growing entitlement spending while keeping the deficit at sustainable levels. Raising marginal tax rates across the board, in principle, would solve this problem, but it is even more politically intractable, in my view. It was not an accident that when the income tax cuts enacted by Congress in 2001 during the first term of President George W. Bush were set to expire at the end of 2012, President Obama asked Congress to renew them on all taxpayers except the tiny group of those earning more than $450,000, if married, or $400,000, if filing as an individual. The president judged that a middle class that had taken it hard on the chin during the Great Recession and its aftermath was clearly in no mood to return to the pre-Bush era of higher marginal tax income rates. I do not see any reason why this political calculus will change anytime soon.

There are some optimists out there who believe that if the U.S. economy somehow grew much faster the federal government would have sufficient revenues to sustain rising entitlement costs. Of course, all of us (or at least most of us) would welcome faster growth, and I discuss earlier in the book how a pickup in entrepreneurship is essential to achieve that outcome. But while faster growth would generate more revenues, it would also have the effect of raising federal spending as well, for a number of reasons. Social security benefit payments, for example, are tied to general wage growth. A substantial portion of health-care spending—under Medicare and Medicaid, and through the subsidies under the ACA—goes directly toward payments to physicians and other medical workers, or indirectly to workers who make medical equipment and supplies. Then there are the salaries of federal workers, which are tied in the long run to private sector wages, since government must compete with private employers for talent (whatever your attitude toward government workers may be).

On net, therefore, even a sustained faster rate of economic growth of, say, one percentage point—above the anemic 2 percent long-term rate projected by the CBO—may reduce the federal budget deficit by several percentage points of GDP by, say, 2040, but not by anywhere near the more than 6 percent of GDP deficit projected for that year. The failure of any growth dividend to close the long-term budget gap would become even more apparent in future years, since the projected gap itself is projected to rise over time in the absence of major entitlement reform, more revenues, or both. This is why none of the major bipartisan deficit-reduction reports takes the easy way out by saying that the United States can simply grow its way out of the long-term deficit problem.

There is one revenue alternative to the income tax that many economists have long favored, some in lieu of a portion of the income tax, and others as a supplement to it. That alternative is a federal tax on consumption, and specifically on value added. In contrast to a sales tax, which is levied on only the final sales of goods, a value-added tax, or VAT, is assessed on the value added at each stage of production of goods, and in principle, services as well. Over 130 countries assess a VAT, including all developed economies except the United States.[9]

Up to now, a VAT has been opposed by many Republicans who fear that once it is in place, it will be too easy for Congress over time to simply raise the rate (though why Congress should be any more willing to raise the VAT than marginal income tax rates I have never understood). For a totally different reason, many Democrats have opposed the VAT on the grounds that it would have a disproportionate negative impact on the poor and even on those earning middle-class incomes, since these individuals and households save less and spend more out of their incomes than high-earning taxpayers. To meet this latter objection, many VAT proponents have been willing to exempt from the tax various necessities purchased by low- and middle-income individuals, such as food, clothing, and medicines. But the more exemptions that are created, the less money the VAT will raise, unless the tax rate is increased, which would encourage black market activity in an effort to avoid it.

Nonetheless, many economists through the years have proposed variations of a consumption tax. By taxing consumption, the government would encourage more saving and thus help finance more investment leading to higher economic growth. Next I briefly summarize three leading VAT proposals in particular, apologizing to any economists who have outlined other consumption-based tax plans.

One of the earliest VAT-like tax proposals was the flat tax proposal developed in 1981 by Stanford economist Robert Hall and Hoover Institution economist Alvin Rabushka.[10] Businesses would pay a flat rate based on their cash flow (revenues minus all nonwage expenses), while individuals would pay the same rate on their earnings above some exemption level. Syracuse economist Len Burman, who is also affiliated with the Urban Institute–Brookings Institution Tax Policy Center, has explained how this proposal is economically equivalent to a VAT, although not named as such, because wages are included in the value added subject to tax.[11] Like each of the first three VAT proposals discussed here, Hall–Rabushka was designed to *replace* the current income tax and therefore, in principle if not in fact, to be revenue neutral.

Another widely publicized VAT-like proposal was developed by the late Princeton economist David Bradford, who served as a member of the CEA under President George H. W. Bush. His proposal modified Hall–Rabushka by introducing a progressive marginal tax rate structure. Tax economists Robert Carroll and Alan Viard later elaborated Bradford's X tax, relabeling it explicitly as a progressive consumption tax.[12]

Most recently, Columbia law professor Michael Graetz, who served as an assistant secretary of the Treasury for tax policy under President George H. W. Bush, has outlined a very explicit revenue-neutral VAT plan. The Graetz proposal would impose a 12.9 percent tax on virtually all consumption (about 70 percent of GDP), while achieving the progressivity goal by eliminating the income tax for all those with incomes below $100,000, or about 80 percent of all taxpayers.[13]

As noted, each of these plans is designed to replace most or all of the current income tax and therefore by definition is revenue neutral. The revenue neutrality aspect makes each more politically palatable than any consumption tax levied *on top* of the existing income tax system, or even one designed to replace only a portion of the income tax in order to raise additional revenue overall. But since I have taken the view in this chapter that ultimately the federal government will need more revenues to sustain even a reformed benefit structure for the major entitlement programs, then I am most interested in consumption tax proposals as *supplements* to the income tax, ideally reformed to have a broader base and lower rate.

In principle, a consumption tax could simply be added in whatever amount is necessary to close the deficit to a certain level, but I do not believe that is politically achievable or sustainable. Any "fill the gap" consumption tax is too easily opposed by those who fear that once in place Congress would raise the tax rate to limit or eliminate the deficit, without imposing a significant constraint on federal spending.

When Congress, the president, and the public are ready for it, I think a more politically attractive approach is to tie the revenues of any consumption tax to a very specific, important part of the federal budget, and ideally one that is highly popular. The perfect candidate is Medicare, which has a strong and growing constituency, but also is a program whose costs require some constraint. Levying a VAT, for example, specifically to fund all or a portion of Medicare would make the tax easier to swallow, while also exerting some downward pressure on costs, especially if Medicare were converted to a premium support system. By dividing the estimated tax revenue from the VAT in a given year by the estimated number of beneficiaries, it would be possible to generate the average premium support payment for that year. Provisions can be made for having the general tax fund reimburse Medicare if tax revenues fell short of the premium support payments; or in the case of the reverse, if there were excess tax payments they could be applied toward deficit reduction in that year. Economists Henry Aaron, Len Burman, John Shoven, and Victor Fuchs of Stanford have proposed similar ideas.[14]

Furthermore, if the day comes when federal policy makers accept the need for a consumption tax, it is more likely to take the form of a VAT than a sales tax because many states already have their own sales taxes and would object to an additional federal tax of the same type. A VAT is at least different enough in character to minimize state opposition, although if the VAT were to take the form of a progressive wage tax, such as one like the Bradford plan (or its updated version outlined by Carroll and Viard), it would be extremely difficult, if not impossible, to impose it on top of the existing income tax. The stated objective of both the Bradford plan and the Hall–Rabushka flat tax is to *replace* the income tax, not to supplement it. Any of the VAT plans can easily be modified to generate additional revenue beyond that raised by the existing income tax: The tax rate could be increased and the number of taxpayers freed from paying income tax reduced from the initial proposals.

As with the premium support idea for Medicare, many detailed design issues must be resolved if and when federal elected officials and the public embrace a supplemental VAT. The central one is the trade-off between the breadth of the tax base and the tax rate. Clearly, the more consumption is taxed—Graetz essentially would tax it all while others would exempt different kinds of consumption, such as financial services and some necessities—then the lower the rate that is required to achieve any revenue objective. But with a narrower base and a higher rate, the incentives increase for black market activity aimed at avoiding the tax. By design, the VAT is more difficult to evade than a straight sales tax because each economic actor in the supply chain has an incentive to report all of its expenses, in order to lower the value added which is subject to tax. With these reporting incentives, federal tax authorities are thus in a position to check on the reported value added of the producers further behind in the supply chain, which proponents of a VAT argue help make the tax effectively self-enforcing. Still, higher tax rates can encourage entirely parallel economic activity aimed at evading the VAT at all stages, which is why policy makers must be sensitive to the level of the tax rate even under a VAT.

The business impact of any consumption tax is clear: If the goods or services are in the tax base, then any tax on them will reduce demand. The magnitude of this demand-depressing effect depends on the size of the tax (measured as a percentage of the final product or service price) and what economists call the *elasticity of demand*. If the product or service is price-elastic, then demand will fall by a greater percentage than the tax percentage; if the converse is true, then the percentage drop in volume will be less than the tax percentage.

These demand-related effects, which any undergraduate student in economics should learn in the first few weeks of class, are only the first round or direct impacts of a consumption tax. To the extent that the tax helps reduce the deficit, and especially if the tax is of sufficient magnitude to keep the deficit at a sustainable level, then the tax will reduce interest rates, and thus interest costs for all those who borrow funds. For consumers, this extra money enables them to spend more on goods and services generally than they otherwise would be able to spend. On net, demand for some goods and services therefore may increase once this indirect income effect is taken into account, while for other goods and services the income effect at least would partially offset the direct demand-depressing impact of the tax. As for firms, lower interest rates mean a lower cost of capital, and thus an inducement to increase investment in equipment and buildings. Firms providing these goods, and the services related to them, as well as their workers will benefit.

All of this is to say that the immediate or direct impacts of any tax will overstate, perhaps by a considerable margin, the negative impact on the goods and services subject to the tax, and will ignore the sectors that benefit from an economy less burdened by debt and interest costs than would otherwise be the case. Keep this thought in mind when considering an even more controversial tax, a tax on carbon emissions.

Taxing Carbon

Up to this point in the book, I have tried to stay away from highly controversial issues—even more controversial than premium support and consumption taxes—but now that ends. I simply can't write a book about economists and their ideas and their potential impact on business without discussing how economists approach the issue of climate change. At one point in the writing of the book, I hesitated even to broach the subject because I didn't want any readers to dismiss the rest of what I have to say—which I believe is important and at least widely accepted by most economists—simply because they may not accept what I have to say about climate change. I have ducked discussing another highly controversial policy issue, the Affordable Care Act, in any significant detail because, at least at this writing, there is no consensus among economists about the virtue of that law or what to replace it with.

That is not the case with climate change, since economists belonging to both political parties at least have been willing to entertain the need for a public policy response. So I ask any readers who have made it to this point in the book to have an open mind and bear with me during this discussion because I am simply bringing up the subject as an illustration of how economic ideas already on the policy shelf could one day be implemented and have an important effect on business and the economy. By that test, it is impossible to ignore the subject of climate change.

I have been careful to phrase the issue in terms of climate change rather global warming because the impact of climate change, to the extent it is caused by man-made carbon emissions, may not always be manifested as warmer weather everywhere all the time, although there is strong evidence of a long trend in global warming that cannot be explained by natural causes alone.[15] In addition, I want to focus on the *net* impact of man-induced climate change. Some parts of the world may benefit from warmer climates induced by CO_2 emissions. At the same time, many other parts of the world are likely to be worse off from higher ocean levels (coastal areas), more severe storms, and other weather-related changes in climate. The world's leading modeler of the economic effects of climate change, William Nordhaus of Yale University (see following box), has calculated that the costs suffered by areas damaged by climate change outweigh the benefits to parts of the world from a man-made change in temperatures and weather patterns. To be more precise, he has calculated the net cost to the world economy, in 2008 prices, from waiting for 50 years to reduce CO_2 emissions to a sustainable level is $4.1 trillion. As Nordhaus puts it, "Wars have been started over smaller sums."[16] More recent studies have suggested a disturbing negative link between higher global temperatures and productivity, which if true, would add to the costs of waiting to address climate change that Nordhaus has calculated.[17]

In any event, here is the way most economists think about how we could reduce CO_2 emissions. There are far too many emitters of CO_2, and even more who may suffer from the effects of climate change, both residing in many different countries, to allow a negotiated Coasian solution to reduce CO_2 emissions. Accordingly, private markets and prices will not fully reflect the net social costs of CO_2 emissions in the prices of goods (and conceivably some services) that either directly or indirectly generate CO_2. To solve that problem, the sources of those emissions should be taxed at that social cost. Alternatively, one could put a cap on total emissions, and distribute or sell tradable permits for CO_2 emissions. The price of the permits represents an implicit tax on CO_2.

Notice, however, the two important ifs that are required to justify a carbon tax or a cap-and-trade system: *if* man-made emissions are altering the climate, and *if* those alterations on balance are net negative. Both those propositions are in dispute, although I think it is safe to say that the weight of scientific opinion is that both propositions are true.

William Nordhaus: An Economic Polymath

Though I know many of the economists I have featured in this book, only a few I have known personally for a long time. William Nordhaus is on that list and I owe much of my career to his influence. Some would tell me that because of this bias I shouldn't feature him here, but why should my friendship and admiration prevent others from knowing about one of the great economists of the latter portion of the twentieth and early twenty-first centuries?

Bill and his very talented brother Bob (who became one of the nation's leading energy lawyers and as a Senate staffer in the 1970s wrote a broad provision in the Clean Air Act that is cited as the legal authority for regulating carbon dioxide emissions) grew up in New Mexico. Upon high school graduation, Bill went to Yale, quickly found his calling in economics and earned his BA, then went to MIT to gain his PhD, studying under some of the greats in that department, including Paul Samuelson and Robert Solow.

I have no doubt that Bill's teachers recognized early on that he was an economics prodigy, gifted in math, highly creative, and yet able to write in clear and accessible English in

(continued)

an engaging way—a rare combination of skills among econ-omists that took Nordhaus far in the profession. Bill is "true blue" and so it was no surprise that he accepted his first post-graduate teaching job at Yale, where he has taught his entire career, except for a brief two year interlude as a young mem-ber of President Carter's Council of Economic Advisers (where I worked with him, following our work together during my graduate school years with Tjalling Koopmans on a major National Academy of Sciences study of the economic future of the nuclear breeder reactor—which as informed readers know, never fulfilled its early promise). Nordhaus also has served Yale as provost and vice president for finance and administration.

I call Bill an economic polymath because he has authored pioneering empirical and theoretical research across a broad range of topics, including the economics and measurement of growth, energy economics (he was one of the first to use linear programming techniques, described in Chapter 4, to model energy cost curves), inflation, unemployment, regula-tion generally (a subject on which I was lucky to write my first book, with him), and environmental economics, with a special emphasis on the costs of living with or introducing policies to control greenhouse gases. In the latter arena, Nordhaus has built sophisticated models to calculate the benefits and costs of different insurance policies to mitigate climate change, which he takes to be a serious and potentially catastrophic problem. The idea of a carbon tax as the most efficient and effective pol-icy to combat climate change grew naturally from his model-ing of the economics of this phenomenon.

It was surely because of the breadth of his work that the leg-endary Paul Samuelson chose Bill to be his coauthor in the later editions of Samuelson's landmark introductory economics text-book. In 2014, Bill became president-elect of the American Economic Association, one of the profession's highest hon-ors (and long overdue in my opinion). He will surely garner many more.

I am not a scientist or a climatologist, and thus cannot personally assess the truth of this scientific consensus or whether the minority of scientists who deny one or both of these propositions are right. My inclination, to put all my cards on the table, is to side with the scientific consensus on both propositions, but I will be the first to admit that I do not hold this view with 100 percent certainty. Likewise, except for perhaps some diehard climate-change deniers, I'll bet many of those who privately or publicly express skepticism about the fact or extent of man-made climate change also—deep down, privately—would admit they, too, are not 100 percent certain of the correctness of their positions.

The uncertainty about the existence and extent of climate change is like any other uncertainty in life—whether you will be hit by a car, or suffer damage to your house from fire, storms, or earthquakes. These events have some probability of occurring and can be costly or even catastrophic if they happen. Beginning with maritime risks, human beings have found a way to live with these uncertainties by reducing their economic impact by buying insurance that covers their losses if the events happen. The firms selling insurance are able to do so profitably by diversifying their customer bases, and thus their risks, across broad populations, while investing the insurance premiums they collect in interest or dividend-paying assets until they are needed to pay claims.

A carbon tax or a cap-and-trade system can be thought of as social insurance against potentially catastrophic costs associated with greenhouse gases. Purchasing insurance against uncertain outcomes should not be a political issue; it is really a matter of prudence. Even Judge Richard Posner, a noted conservative intellectual, endorses the broad concept of purchasing some kind of climate change insurance in one of his many books.[18]

Of course, global climate change presents a special problem because it is *global*, meaning that any steps taken to reduce CO_2 emissions even by one of the largest emitting countries, such as the United States, will benefit the world. Or, in the language of economists, unilateral carbon taxes of cap-and-trade systems benefit free riders that reap the benefits without paying the costs. That is why the United States and other countries have sought to bind all countries to commitments to reduce greenhouse gases; this has proved problematic because poorer countries believe they should not have to pay, or even must be compensated by richer ones, since they believe that any country-specific limits on CO_2 emissions will disproportionately inhibit their economic growth. Put another way, poorer countries see a global climate change regime as a way for rich countries to pull up the economic ladder before others can really climb on. For this reason, I (and many others) are dubious that any meaningful and enforceable global or even multilateral climate change agreement—one requiring either a carbon tax or a hard limit on CO_2 emissions—will ever be reached (virtually all of the world's countries signed on to the Kyoto Protocol in the late 1990s and many have imposed binding CO_2 emissions limits in their own countries, but the U.S. Congress did not ratify Kyoto, and it is unclear at this point whether Congress would accept any international agreement).

There are also numerous technical issues that must be resolved in designing any carbon tax or a cap-and-trade system. With respect to the tax, one central issue is the tax base: Does the tax apply both to energy producers and consumers, or should a subset of energy users be exempt for strategic or political reasons, such as automobile manufacturers? In addition, it is generally understood that the tax should extend to imported products, but as a matter of fairness and most likely legality under international trade rules that bar discrimination, the tax on imports should vary depending on the amount of the carbon tax or its equivalent assessed in exporting countries. Another issue is the level of the tax, which in principle should be set at the social cost of carbon, a figure on which there is no consensus, and understandably so, since even those who worry about climate change admit that all of its harmful consequences are not yet known. And then there is the issue of how to handle the regressive nature of the tax: Who should get rebates and in what form? There is an extensive literature on all these issues that I cannot summarize here, but I mention these questions just to illustrate that implementing even a relatively simple economic idea can be quite difficult.

Cap and trade is potentially even more complicated. In addition to deciding who must have permits and how many—analogous to determining the tax base under any carbon tax—the central issue in any cap-and-trade system is whether the government should hand out the initial permits for free, which would make the system more politically palatable, or whether it should charge for the permits initially with the objective of raising revenue (analogous to both the carbon tax and to auctioning off electromagnetic spectrum). How should imported products be treated? Does the cap (or the tax) start immediately, or is it phased in, presumably at more stringent levels over time?

Despite the free-rider problem and putting aside the myriad technical details of how a carbon tax or tradable permit system would be designed, there is one large potential benefit from the United States unilaterally imposing the tax or, equivalently, by selling permits: The money raised can make a substantial contribution toward deficit reduction. My former Bloomberg Government colleague Rob Barnett has estimated, for example, that a tax of \$20/ton on carbon content would raise \$1 trillion over a 10-year period, without any rebates to low and possibly middle-income residents to offset any distributional affects. Others who have not accepted the idea of a carbon tax as a net revenue raiser nonetheless have expressed support for a revenue-neutral trade of the tax for a reduction in other federal taxes, such as the social security tax, which is a tax on labor.

However it may come about, a carbon tax or a cap-and-trade system could have significant business impacts, though they would be uneven. Firms engaged in producing carbon-free energy (such as nuclear or wind) or low in carbon content (natural gas) would benefit; oil producers and coal mining firms would be penalized, which of course is precisely the point of such a tax (to ensure that their prices reflect the full social costs of these energy sources). It is conceivable that a carbon tax or tradable permit system could be even more effective in promoting research and development and innovation in alternative energy than direct federal spending. A cap-and-trade system also would resuscitate one or more exchanges like the Chicago Climate Exchange, which was founded by an economist, Richard Sandor, in 2010, but later was purchased by the Intercontinental Exchange, which also now owns the New York Stock Exchange. Intercontinental has since closed the Climate Exchange because of inactivity in carbon credit markets.

Apart from the effects on particular kinds of business, the net impact of a carbon tax or cap-and-trade system on GDP and job growth is unlikely to be large (and has been overstated by its critics).[19] There are two reasons for this. If the tax is indeed part of a revenue-neutral arrangement, then there is no net fiscal drag from the tax, and thus no net dampening effect on the economy. But even if the tax is part of a larger deficit-reduction package, meaning that in the short run it may depress overall demand somewhat, over the long term deficit reduction will reduce interest rates below what they otherwise would be, stimulating investment spending. In addition, a reduction in the deficit toward a sustainable level substantially reduces, if not eliminates, the possibility of a sudden spike in interest rates caused by a collapse of investor confidence in the fiscal health of the United States, a low probability but high consequence event that is worth paying to avoid.

There are no easy solutions for addressing threats from climate change. Any policy will produce winners and losers, but nearly all economists would prefer a tax or cap-and-trade system over a top-down command-and-control system of emissions limits.

The Bottom Line

This chapter has surveyed three broad policy ideas developed by economists that have been in the public domain for some time. Each either directly or indirectly can be deployed as part of a medium to grand long-term deficit reduction package and, in fact, none is likely to be implemented outside that context. I cannot predict when a president and Congress will seriously consider such a package, but I hope for the sake of my children's generation and those who follow that this will happen sooner rather than later.

Each one of the ideas surveyed here would have major impacts on business, with winners and losers. The impacts on the overall economy, however, are likely to be modest to highly positive, to the extent that each idea or all of them in combination make a major contribution toward changing the upward trajectory of the federal budget deficit.

Notes

1. Charles L Schultze, *Public Use of the Private Interest* (Washington, DC: The Brookings Institution, 1977).
2. Charles L. Schultze, *Memos to the President: A Guide to Macroeconomics for the Busy Policymaker* (Washington, DC: Brookings Institution Press, 1993).

3. Congressional Budget Office, *The 2013 Long-Term Budget Outlook*, originally posted September 19, 2013, revised October 31, 2013, at www.cbo.gov.

4. Calculated from charts compiled by the Peter G. Peterson Foundation, www.pgpf.org.

5. Congressional Budget Office, *The Budget and Economic Outlook: 2014 to 2024*, www.cbo.gov/publication/45010.

6. H.J. Aaron and R.D. Reischauer, "The Medicare Reform Debate: What Is the Next Step?" *Health Affairs* 14, no. 4 (1995): 8–30.

7. Melinda Beck, "Coordinated Health-Care Program Saves Millions," *Wall Street Journal*, January 30, 2104, http://online.wsj.com/news/articles/SB1000142405 270230374360457935313381140031 4?KEYWORDS=Health+Savings.

8. This summary is based on both the author's recollections and on a biography and tribute to Pechman's life written by another longtime Brookings giant, George Perry. See www.brookings.edu/~/media/Projects/BPEA/1989%20 2/1989b_bpea_perry.PDF.

9. Eric Toder, et al., "Using a VAT for Deficit Reduction," Tax Policy Center and the Pew Charitable Trusts, www.pewtrusts.org/uploadedFiles/ wwwpewtrustsorg/Reports/Fiscal_and_Budget_Policy/Using%20a%20 VAT%20for%20Deficit%20Reduction.pdf.

10. The best reference for this proposal is the updated version published on the twenty-five year anniversary of their idea, Robert E. Hall and Alvin Rabushka, *The Flat Tax* (Stanford, CA: Hoover Institution and Stanford University, 2007).

11. Len Burman, "What Is a Flat Tax? (Surprise! It Is a VAT)," *Forbes*, www.forbes .com/sites/leonardburman/2011/10/24/what-is-a-flat-tax-surprise-it-is-a-vat/.

12. The two proposals are summarized in Len Burman, "A Progressive Consumption Tax?" *Forbes*, www.forbes.com/sites/leonardburman/2012/ 06/04/a-progressive-consumption-tax/. For the original Bradford tax proposal, see David F. Bradford, *Untangling the Income Tax* (Cambridge, MA: Harvard University Press, 1986); for the Carroll and Viard proposal, see Alan D. Viard and Robert Carroll, *Progressive Consumption Taxation: The X-Tax Revisited* (Washington, DC: AEI Press, 2012).

13. For a summary of the plan see Howard Gleckman, "A Value-Added Tax that Won't Raise Revenues or Boost Taxes on the Poor," *Forbes*, November 26, 2013.

14. See Henry J. Aaron, *Serious and Unstable Condition: Financing America's Health Care* (Washington, DC: Brookings Institution Press, 1991); Leonard E. Burman, "Pathways to Tax Reform Revisited," *Public Finance Review* 41 (2013): 755; Leonard E. Burman, "The Value Added Tax: Gateway to the Elusive Grand Bargain?" *Milken Institute Review*, 2014; and John Shoven and

Victor R. Fuchs, "The Dedicated VAT Solution," SIEPR Policy Brief, http://fsi.stanford.edu/publications/the_dedicated_vat_solution/.

15. William D. Nordhaus, "Why the Global Warming Skeptics Are Wrong," *New York Review of Books*, March 22, 2012. Nordhaus displays a graph in this piece, which is one of the most cogently argued responses to critics of global climate change that I have seen, showing that despite year-to-year variations, the mean global temperature has risen about 0.8 degrees Celsius since the late 1800s.

16. William D. Nordhaus, *A Question of Balance: Weighing the Options on Global Warming Policies* (New Haven, CT: Yale University Press, 2008), 82.

17. See "Free Exchange: The Weather Report," *The Economist*, January 18, 2014, 76.

18. Richard A. Posner, *Catastrophe: Risk and Response* (New York: Oxford University Press, 2004). For a shorter version of his thesis, see this interview: www.foreignpolicy.com/articles/2007/12/10/seven_questions_planning_for_a_climate_catastrophe.

19. Nordhaus, "Why the Global Warming Skeptics Are Wrong."

Chapter 15

The Future of Economics: What It Means for Business and Economists

It may seem odd to end a book about the huge, often unseen, benefits of economists and their ideas, primarily for business but also for society at large, by speculating about the future of economics itself. Will economics continue to deliver these benefits, or will the field suffer diminishing returns, one of the economic propositions that has given economics its unwanted name: the dismal science?

In this concluding chapter, I explore how the economics profession is changing, where it is likely to go from here, and what the future of economics means for innovation, business, and economists themselves. I begin by describing the current and continuing revolution in economics, focusing on how it is merging with other disciplines and how the data revolution, in particular, has affected economic analysis. I then discuss how these changes in the profession will likely affect businesses and society in the coming years and decades.

As I explain below, the future of economics looks far from dismal. In fact, as the field becomes more practical, it will become ever more valuable to society. The tools and methodology of economics will influence other disciplines and enhance our understanding of how the world works. As the field becomes more empirical and evidence-based, economics will become increasingly intertwined with other technical disciplines and will play a critical role in harnessing the power of information technology and Big Data analytics to help businesses exploit new markets, cut costs, and earn more revenues.

The Revolution in Economics

Whether economists realize it or not, the economics profession is in the midst of a revolution, driven by two factors. The first one is accidental and is the topic I discussed at the outset of this book: the financial crisis of 2008 and the Great Recession that followed it, here and in other developed economies. These crises have resurrected many of the age-old theoretical debates in the profession about how recessions begin and what policies can best end them quickly. As I write this, economists continue to debate the merits of the fiscal stimulus in 2009 and the unorthodox and unprecedented monetary easing of 2009 to 2103. At the same time, macroeconomics has become a hot subject in economics again, with theorists attempting to incorporate models of the financial sector into larger macroeconomic frameworks. I wish them luck because modeling abrupt turns in the economy has been the Achilles heel of macroeconomics in the past, and getting this right in the future will be no easy undertaking.

The other driver of change is technology, specifically the continually increasing power of information technology to analyze ever-larger bodies of data that allows economists and other social scientists to ask and answer new questions. As we saw in Chapter 5, many of the innovative tools and methods that economists use today depend on the use of advanced network services and software to store and analyze large quantities of data. Indeed, analyses that used to be virtually impossible to do a quarter century ago can now be performed in a matter of seconds and with much greater precision than ever before.

Because of these IT advances, economists who have computer and statistical skills, and have used their formal training in economic theory to conduct empirical research, have been in the vanguard of the profession. This trend should continue. It is noteworthy, for example, that two of the recent winners of the Clark Medal are superstars with a strong empirical bent: Esther Duflo of MIT and Raj Chetty of Harvard.

If empirical economics is largely the future of the profession, which I believe it is, what topics will economists study and how will their toolkit evolve over time? I don't have the foresight to be able to answer this question with sufficient specificity to make you happy. But I have two relevant quasi-answers.

First, if the past is any guide to the future, then economists will continue to apply their skills to subjects not traditionally thought to be within the economic domain. The best examples come from the University of Chicago. The late Gary Becker was a pioneer in this respect, applying economic insights to crime, marriage, and education. The Chicago tradition of expanding the scope of economics continued with Richard Posner's pioneering insights into how law and economics can and should be fused. Steven Leavitt, the author of the highly popular *Freakonomics* books, is the most recent example of this genre, with his studies of education, drug markets, and naming conventions followed by parents. The experimental economics of Duflo and Harvard's Abhijit Banerjee, discussed in Chapter 6, show how out-of-the-box thinking is taking place outside of Chicago.

Second, as Tyler Cowen has persuasively argued,[1] and I too believe, economics will merge with other professions in the coming decades, in which researchers from related academic disciplines who are trained to analyze large data sets (sociologists, political scientists, psychologists, anthropologists, and perhaps others) work together to ask new questions, solve new problems, and uncover new business opportunities. Some specialists in other disciplines have even won Nobel Prizes in economics, including Daniel Kahneman (psychology), Elinor Ostrom (political science), and John Nash (mathematics).

The notion that the economics of the future will continue to blend with other disciplines is nothing new.[2] After all, as a social science, economics has been embedded with philosophy, political science, and mathematics for centuries. The relatively recent field of agent-based modeling, which describes and predicts the course of contagious events such as financial panics or diseases, is pioneered by my good friend Joshua Epstein of Johns Hopkins Medical School (and others).

Josh was originally trained as a political scientist, but he also brings a deep knowledge of advanced mathematics, computer science, genetics, and biology to this work.[3]

To be sure, because it attempts to describe and predict human behavior rather than natural laws, economics and other social sciences have a tougher task than their counterparts in the physical sciences.[4] Nonetheless, I agree with Harvard's Ray Chetty who argues that, notwithstanding its difficulties, economics should be considered a science because of its sophisticated methodology, which is characterized by formulating and testing precise hypotheses.[5] Understandably, economists themselves widely share this view, though they also accept the challenges the discipline faces, such as the limited ability to run experiments. As the discipline becomes more empirical, however, there is reason to believe that, as Nobel laureate Robert Shiller has noted, "it will broaden its repertory of methods and sources of evidence."[6]

But as the profession becomes more evidence-based and data-driven, what will happen to the theoretical economists who create mathematical models to explain economic phenomena? The short answer is that the profession will always have a place for theorists. Theories guide the construction of empirical work, just as theoretical scientists form hypotheses for their more practical colleagues to test. Often, theorists and empiricists are one and the same, but this is not always the case.

At the same time, theorists can also become too abstract, distant from the realities of the actual economy. I think many agree that this is what happened to economics prior to the financial crisis. Nobel Prize winner and *New York Times* columnist Paul Krugman hit the nail on the head when he asserted that in the run-up to the financial crisis, economists "mistook beauty, clad in impressive-looking mathematics, for truth."[7] The challenge facing theorists in the future who are busy incorporating finance into their macroeconomic models will be to avoid this danger.

How Economics Will Continue to Affect Business

The future of economics is here. Economics has begun merging with other disciplines, and the traditional domain of what economists study has dramatically expanded over a relatively short period of time. In addition, the Big Data revolution has vastly improved economists' toolkit, enabling economists to perform more powerful empirical research.

To paraphrase a popular political phrase, what dog does business have in this hunt? Well, if you buy the thesis of the preceding chapters that economists and their ideas have had powerful direct and indirect effects on business, many and perhaps most of them not immediately evident at the time, then there is no reason for believing that this won't be true in the future. And if the economics of the future (and present) is increasingly about formulating hypotheses to test with large data sets, then some of those hypotheses and their results cannot help but be useful in business: in identifying new markets, better targeting of customers, and customizing products and services for customers. Indeed, many firms already in the vanguard of the Big Data revolution are engaged in these activities.

But firms tend not to be as persnickety as economists about hatching a theory first and then testing it. In business, the temptation is to take whatever Big Data set exists and then hunt for any and all correlations, without identifying or structuring any theory. That approach is fine if the correlations remain valid in the future, but as any economist will tell you, *correlation is not causation*. Just because sunspots may be correlated with sales of a particular item (you choose it) does not mean that sunspots *cause* the variation in sales. Ideally, firms should want to know the underlying causes before trusting their correlations too blindly. Want proof? Then look no further than the housing and later the financial crisis of the last decade. Lenders kept lending, and the ratings agencies kept handing out AAA ratings, on the basis of statistical relationships that the sudden decline in housing prices destroyed. In all fairness, as I said at the outset of this book, not many economists foresaw this problem in advance either. But that is not a reason to abandon the quest for underlying structures in relationships between economic variables, and that is what economists are trained to do. Business ignores this quest at its peril.

Implications for Economists

For a long time, economists outside of academia have found lucrative jobs in industries as diverse as banking, public policy, and litigation consulting. In recent years, however, the Big Data revolution has opened the doors to a much broader set of career opportunities. Indeed, as a recent McKinsey Global Institute report on the Big Data revolution found, in the next several years, "the United States alone could face a shortage of 140,000 to 190,000 people with deep analytical skills as well as 1.5 million managers and analysts with the know-how to use the analysis of Big Data to make effective decisions."[8]

As sophisticated data analysts, economists stand to benefit from the Big Data revolution, and companies in turn stand to gain immensely from application of economic ideas and tools to solve new business challenges. As an example, let's consider the health-care industry, where Big Data is already generating enormous value and will continue to do so in the coming decades. Three of the biggest challenges in the health IT space today—detecting fraud, delivering the best care, and keeping costs low—have economic components. The work of the best software engineers and computer scientists mining large bodies of data would benefit from the insights of the best empirical health-care economists in addressing these challenges.

Since the Big Data revolution is only in its infancy, there is tremendous scope for innovation and cross-disciplinary work between empirical economists, computer scientists, statisticians, and perhaps trained specialists in other academic disciplines in the years ahead. To be most in demand, however, economists will need to improve their empirical techniques, and to acquire other technical skills. As economists Lirav Einav and Jonathan Levin of Stanford University recently noted, "our expectation is that future economists who want to work with large datasets will have to acquire at least some of the new tools of the computer scientists, so they can combine the conceptual framework with the ability to actually implement ideas quickly and efficiently on large-scale data."[9]

If this sounds vaguely familiar, it's because in a way it is. Some of the best economists of tomorrow, armed with the conceptual framework and technical aptitude to conduct sophisticated analyses of large-scale datasets, will resemble some of the great empirical economists of the past: Lawrence Klein, Otto Eckstein, and others who had the ability to translate economic theory into the construction of large-scale econometric models. Those models may no longer be in use, at least in the form in which they were constructed then, but the skills it took to build them were analogous to the skills that economists working with Big Data will need in the future. In the process, the economists of tomorrow may have a greater impact on innovation and business than those macroeconomic forecasters.

There is some irony in all this. As discussed in Chapter 5, the IT revolution of the past thirty years and the transition from mainframe computers to PCs greatly diminished the demand for large macroeconomic modeling. Although economics certainly remained an empirical discipline, the arrival of the PC meant that economists could now run their own models, and the days of large-scale macroeconomic forecasting gave way to an era of individual empirical research on a smaller and more focused scale. Now, the Big Data revolution has called for more computing power, greater technical skills, and more cross-disciplinary work in order to tackle the most difficult problems facing businesses and society. Empirical economics is back with a vengeance, but with much more powerful personal computers that made one major economic endeavor obsolete.

Concluding Thoughts

There is another irony. The same innovations in IT and automation that are reducing the need for low- and mid-skilled labor in many occupations throughout all economies, but especially advanced ones, are also likely to do the same to economics.[10] There will be less demand for economics teachers, for example, as the kinks in online education get ironed out. The melding of economics with other disciplines in the age of Big Data also will reduce the demand for pure economists.

Yet if the discipline becomes more empirical and evidence-based, it will adapt to the needs of the business world and continue to foster innovation, and thereby become even more practical and thus more valuable to society. The trillion-dollar economists of today may be superseded by the more well-rounded and skilled economists of tomorrow, whose social and economic worth may have even more zeroes at the end than the trillion dollar economists of recent vintage.

Notes

1. Tyler Cowen, *Average Is Over: Powering America Beyond the Age of the Great Stagnation* (New York: Dutton, 2013): 221–224.

2. See David Collander, "The Future of Economics: The Appropriately Educated in Pursuit of the Knowable," *Cambridge Journal of Economics* 29 (2005): 927–941.

3. One early example of this work, which is now much more advanced, can be found in Robert Axtell and Joshua Epstein, *Growing Artificial Societies from the Bottom Up* (Cambridge, MA: MIT Press, 1996).

4. Robert J. Shiller, "Is Economics a Science?" Project Syndicate, November 6, 2013, www.project-syndicate.org/commentary/robert-j-shilleron-whether-he-is-a-scientist.

5. Raj Chetty, "Yes, Economics Is a Science," *New York Times*, October 20, 2013, www.nytimes.com/2013/10/21/opinion/yes-economics-is-a-science.html.

6. Shiller, "Is Economics a Science?"

7. Paul Krugman, "How Did Economics Get It So Wrong?" *New York Times*, September 6, 2009, www.nytimes.com/2009/09/06/magazine/06Economic-t.html.

8. James Manyika, Michael Chui, Brad Brown, Jacques Bughin, Richard Dobbs, Charles Roxburgh, and Angela Hung Byers, "Big Data: The Next Frontier for Innovation, Competition, and Productivity," McKinsey Global Institute, May 2011, www.mckinsey.com/insights/business_technology/big_data_the_next_frontier_for_innovation.

9. Liran Einav and Jonathan Levin, "The Data Revolution and Economic Analysis," NBER, April 2013, www.stanford.edu/~jdlevin/Papers/BigData.pdf.

10. *The Economist*, "The Onrushing Wave," January 18, 2014, www.economist.com/news/briefing/21594264-previous-technological-innovation-has-always-delivered-more-long-run-employment-not-less.

Appendix

Prizes in Economics

L ike other academic disciplines, economics has its share of prizes for outstanding research work. Three are briefly described here; readers may know two well, the third less so (but it is one I am proud to say I had a hand in creating and I believe its importance will grow over time).

For its winners, the Nobel Prize is probably the most prestigious accolade they receive in their lives. The money that comes with the prize, currently about $1.2 million, which must be split when multiple winners in the same year are announced, is surely a welcome surprise for those who get that unforgettable phone call on an October morning (when the prize is announced each year). But for most winners, the prize's money is not its main virtue. At least for a time, the winners become famous, while giving them satisfaction that the years they may have been working in relative obscurity have finally been validated and given worldwide recognition beyond the technical fields in which they have labored.

The prize has other advantages. If they wish to take advantage of it, the Nobel gives the winners a platform they may not have had before to speak out not only about subjects in their field but often outside it. Op-ed editorial chiefs solicit or will more readily accept their pieces. Journalists will seek out Nobel winners for their opinions and quotes. All of the attention can lead to speaking engagements, with honoraria that can handsomely supplement the money from the prize itself. And some Nobel winners may find themselves heavily recruited by other academic institutions (if they are still teaching), at higher salaries and with even more prestige than those they had before winning the prize.

The Nobel Prizes in general were established in 1895 with an endowment from Alfred Nobel, a Swedish entrepreneur who made his fortune primarily in the armaments industry. Nobel is most famous for his invention of dynamite—ironic, since one of the prizes in his name is awarded for promoting peace. The other fields initially eligible for the prize have been in the hard sciences, medicine, and literature.

Economists were not added to the list of recipients until 1969, and even then, as an appendage. Whereas the winners in the other fields received their monetary awards from the Nobel Foundation, the Swedish central bank gave the Foundation funds in 1968 to establish a separate Nobel Memorial Prize in Economic Sciences. The winners of this particular prize are selected by the Royal Swedish Academy of Sciences rather than by the Nobel Committees organized for the other fields. The economics award is thus technically not a Nobel Prize, though it is announced in the fall of each year when the other Nobel awards also are named, and the economics winners are commonly referred to in the media as Nobel recipients.

Because the economics Nobel came much later than the prize for the other fields, there was a long pipeline of potential winners waiting to be anointed when Sweden's central bank established the prize. In the intervening 45-plus years, that pipeline has been mostly exhausted, and along the way, most of the profession's leading lights who were still living at the time the award was announced have been honored. You learned about a number of the winners in different chapters of this book.[1]

Two other prizes are given to a particular age-group of economists, those under the age of 40. Of the two, the Clark Medal carries the most prestige and is the oldest. Established in 1947 in memory and honor of John Bates Clark, one of the founders of the American Economic Association, the medal (which carries no money with it, like the next prize to be described) is given to an American economist (one either born here or working here at the time) who is judged to have made a "significant contribution to economic thought and knowledge." Until 2009, the medal was awarded by the AEA every other year, but since then a Clark winner has been named every year.

The Clark Medal is not only highly sought for its own sake, but because economists often make their research or theoretical breakthroughs when they are younger, winning the Clark is a good predictor of later winning the Nobel.

The Kauffman Medal is also given every year to an economist under the age of 40. The Ewing Marion Kauffman Foundation established it in 2004 to recognize research breakthroughs specifically related to entrepreneurship and its importance to economies. I had a little something to do with the creation of the Medal, since it happened during the time I was vice president of the Kauffman Foundation, the world's largest foundation devoted to advancing the understanding and promotion of entrepreneurship. Full credit for the idea goes to the Foundation's president at the time, Carl Schramm, and to one of foundation's directors who worked with me, Robert Strom, who both thought it up as a way to give economists greater incentives to study entrepreneurship. Like the Nobel, when it was created, there was a backlog of prominent researchers who have since been awarded the prize.

Note

1. For more details about the lives of the Nobel winners in economics, see William Breit and Barry T. Hirsch, eds., *Lives of the Laureates*, 5th ed. (Boston: MIT Press, 2009). I draw on this source in this book where I discuss some of the Nobel winners and their ideas.

About the Author

As an economist and attorney, Robert Litan has nearly four decades of experience in the worlds of the law, economic research and policy, economic consulting, and as an executive in the private, public, and government sectors. Through his extensive publications and many speeches and testimony, he is a widely recognized national expert in regulation, antitrust, and finance, among other economic policy subjects.

Litan has directed economic research at nationally prominent organizations: The Brookings Institution (where he also was a resident research scholar for nearly two decades); the Kauffman Foundation (the world's leading foundation supporting entrepreneurship); and Bloomberg Government (the subsidiary of Bloomberg LP that provides analysis of federal government decisions that affect business).

Litan has served in several high-level federal government positions: as principal deputy assistant attorney general in the Antitrust Division of the Justice Department, as associate director of the Office of Management and Budget, and as a consultant to the Department of Treasury on financial modernization and the effectiveness of the Community Reinvestment Act (coauthoring several reports on these subjects). In the early 1990s he served as a member of the

Presidential–Congressional Commission on the Causes of the Savings and Loan Crisis. He began his career as a staff economist at the President's Council of Economic Advisers.

Litan currently is a nonresident senior fellow at the Brookings Institution and of counsel to Korein Tillery, a law firm specializing in complex commercial litigation based in St. Louis and Chicago. He also blogs regularly for the *Wall Street Journal's* "Think Tank" page.

During his research career, Litan has authored or coauthored 27 books and edited another 14, and authored or coauthored more than 200 articles in professional and popular publications. His latest books include *Better Capitalism*, coauthored with Carl Schramm, published by Yale University Press in 2012, and *Good Capitalism, Bad Capitalism* (coauthored with William Baumol and Carl Schramm), also published by Yale in 2007, which is used widely in college courses and has been translated into 10 languages.

Litan earned his BS in Economics at the Wharton School of Finance at the University of Pennsylvania; his JD at Yale Law School; and his M. Phil. and PhD in Economics at Yale University.

Index